R. Gupta's®

NORTH-EAST
General Knowledge

• North-East India • Arunachal Pradesh
• Assam • Manipur • Meghalaya • Mizoram
• Nagaland • Sikkim • Tripura

A Complete Description of History, Geography, Flora & Fauna, Economy, Polity, Culture and more...

by
RPH Editorial Board

Ramesh Publishing House, New Delhi

Published by
O.P. Gupta *for* Ramesh Publishing House
Admin. Office
12-H, New Daryaganj Road, Opp. Officers' Mess,
New Delhi-110002 ✆ 23261567, 23275224, 23275124
E-mail: info@rameshpublishinghouse.com
Website: www.rameshpublishinghouse.com
Showroom
- Balaji Market, Nai Sarak, Delhi-6 ✆ 23253720, 23282525
- 4457, Nai Sarak, Delhi-6, ✆ 23918938

Book Code: R-1019

8th Edition : 1810

ISBN: 978-81-7812-565-7

HSN Code: 49011010

Contents

ASSAM 60-117

MANIPUR 118-155

TRIPURA 288-320

North-East General Knowledge

• • • • • • • • • • • •

• North-East India • Arunachal Pradesh
• Assam • Manipur • Meghalaya
• Mizoram • Nagaland
• Sikkim • Tripura

1

NORTH-EAST INDIA

Location of North-east India within India

North-east India is the eastern-most region of India connected to East India via a narrow corridor squeezed between Nepal and Bangladesh. It comprises the contiguous Seven Sister States (Arunachal Pradesh, Assam,

Manipur, Meghalaya, Mizoram, Nagaland, and Tripura), plus the Himalayan state of Sikkim. These states are grouped under the MDONER ministry of the Government of India.

The Ministry of Development of North Eastern Region	
Agency overview	
Formed	September, 2001
Jurisdiction	Republic of India
Headquarter	Vigyan Bhavan Annexe, Maulana Azad Road, New Delhi-110011
Website	www.mdoner.gov.in

The current, Minister of Development of North Eastern Region is Jitendra Singh (Minister of State, Independent Charge).

The **Ministry of Development of North Eastern Region (MDONER)** is a Government of India ministry, established in September 2001, which functions as the nodal Department of the Central Government to deal with matters related to the socio-economic development of the eight States of Northeast India, Arunachal Pradesh, Assam, Manipur, Meghalaya, Mizoram, Nagaland, Tripura and Sikkim. It acts as a facilitator between the Central Ministries/Departments and the State Governments of the North Eastern Region including Sikkim in the economic development including removal of infrastructural bottlenecks, provision of basic minimum services, creating an environment for private investment and to remove impediments to lasting peace and security in the North Eastern Region including, Sikkim.

Except for the Goalpara region of Assam, the rest were late entrants to the British India, the Brahmaputra valley area of Assam became a part of British India in 1824, and the hill regions were incorporated even later. Sikkim was annexed to the Indian union through a referendum in 1975 and was recognized as part of Northeast India in the 1990s.

In terms of geographical size, Northeast India constitute about 8% of the total India's size, and is roughly 3/4th the size of the state of Maharashtra. Northeast India's population (all 8 states combined) is approximately 40 million (2011 census), which represents 3.1% of the total Indian population (1,210 million). Northeast India's population size is roughly equal to the state of Odisha.

The Siliguri Corridor in West Bengal, with a width of 21 to 40 kilometres (13 to 25 miles), connects the North Eastern region with the main part of India. The region shares more than 4,500 kilometres (2,800 miles) of international border (about 90 per cent of its entire border area) with China (southern Tibet) in the north, Myanmar in the east, Bangladesh in the southwest, and Bhutan to the northwest.

The states are officially recognised under the North Eastern Council (NEC), constituted in 1971 as the acting agency for the development of the eight states. The North Eastern Development Finance Corporation Ltd (NEDFCL) was incorporated on 9 August 1995 and the Ministry of Development of North Eastern Region (DoNER) was set up in September 2001.

HISTORY

Madan Kamdev

The earliest settlers were Austro-Asiatic speakers, followed by Tibet-Burmese and then by Indo-Aryans. Due to the bio- and crop diversity of the region the focus of current archaeological research has been on domestication of several important plants by early settlers. Writers have suspected an early trade route via Northeast India in the references of Chinese explorer, Zhang Qian made in 100 BC. The *Periplus of the Erythraean Sea* mention a people called Sêsatai in the region, who were the source of malabathron, so prized in the old world.

In the early historical period (most of first millennium), Kamarupa straddled most of present-day Northeast India, besides Bhutan and Sylhet in Bangladesh. Xuanzang, the travelling Chinese monk, visited Kamarupa in the 7th century, and described the people as "short in stature and black-looking", whose speech differed a little from mid-India and who were of simple but violent disposition; and that the people in Kamarupa knew of Sichuan that lay to the kingdom's east beyond a treacherous mountain. Established during the British Raj, the northeastern states were isolated from their traditional trading partners such as Bhutan and Myanmar.

FORMATION OF NORTH EASTERN STATES

In the early 19th century, both the Ahom and the Manipur kingdoms fell to a Burmese invasion. The ensuing First Anglo-Burmese War resulted in the entire region coming under British control. In the colonial period (1826-1947), North East India was a part of Bengal Province from 1839 to 1873, when Assam became its own province. After the Indian Independence from British Rule in 1947, the Northeastern region of British India consisted of Assam and the princely states of Manipur and Tripura. Subsequently,

Nagaland in 1963, Meghalaya in 1972, Arunachal Pradesh in 1975 (Capital changed to Itanagar) (actually formed on 20 Feb, 1987) and Mizoram in 1987 were formed out of Assam. Manipur and Tripura remained as Union Territories of India between 1956 until 1972 when they attained fully-fledged statehood. Sikkim was integrated as the eighth North Eastern Council state in 2002.

The city of Shillong acted as the capital of the Assam province created during the British Rule. It remained as the capital of undivided Assam until formation of the state of Meghalaya in 1972. The capital of Assam was then shifted to Dispur, a part of Guwahati, and Shillong became the capital of Meghalaya.

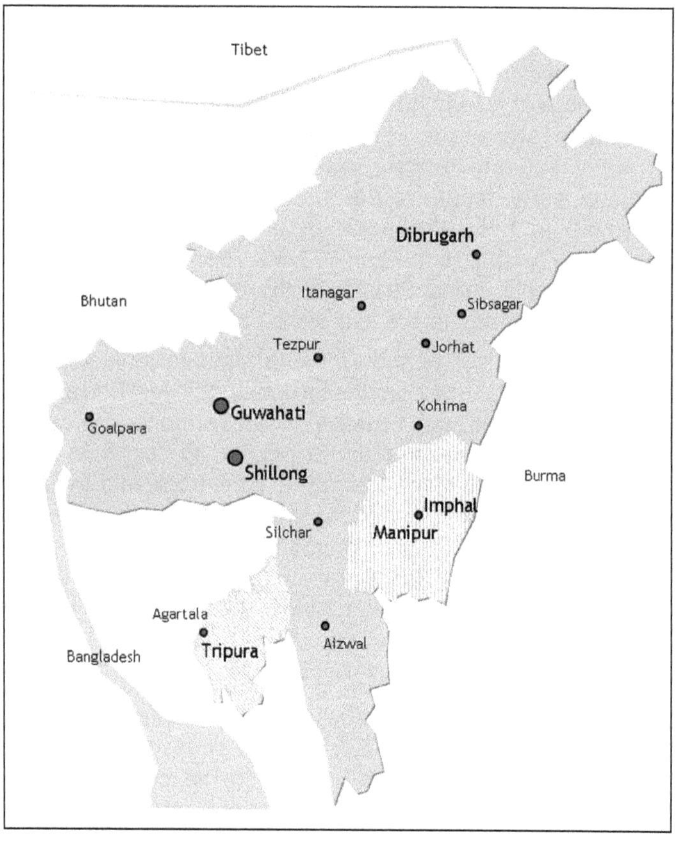

Map of Assam in the 1950s, along with the princely states of Manipur and Tripura

WORLD WAR II

In 1944, the Japanese planned a daring attack on India. Travelling through Burma, it was stopped at Kohima and Imphal by British and Indian troops. This marked the furthest western expansion of the Japanese Empire and presaged Allied victory.

Sino-Indian War (1962)

Arunachal Pradesh, a state in the North-eastern tip of India, is claimed by China as South Tibet. Sino-Indian relations degraded during the Sino-Indian War of 1962. The cause of the escalation into war is still disputed by both Chinese and Indian sources. During the war in 1962, the PRC (China) captured much of the NEFA (North-East Frontier Agency) created by India in 1954. However on November 21, 1962, China declared a unilateral ceasefire, withdrew its troops 20 kilometres (12 miles) behind the McMahon Line and returned Indian prisoners of war in 1963.

21st Century Unrest

In 1947 Indian independence and partition resulted in a landlocked region, exacerbating the isolation that has been recognized, but not studied. Muslim Bangladesh controlled access to the Indian Ocean. The mountainous terrain has hampered the road and railways connection in the region.

On 2 November 2000, in Malom, a town in the Imphal Valley of Manipur, ten civilians were shot and killed while waiting at a bus stop. The incident, known as the "Malom Massacre", was allegedly committed by the Assam Rifles, one of the Indian Paramilitary forces operating in the state. This incident resulted in continuing unrest in the area.

The militant groups have formed an alliance to fight against the Governments of India, Bhutan and Myanmar and now use the term "Western Southeast Asia" (WESEA) to refer to the region. The groups include the Kangleipak Communist Party (KCP), Kanglei Yawol Kanna Lup (KYKL), People's Revolutionary Party of Kangleipak (PREPAK), People's Revolutionary Party of Kangleipak-Pro (PREPAK-Pro), Revolutionary People's Front (RPF) and United National Liberation Front (UNLF) of Manipur, Hynniewtrep National Liberation Council (HNLC) of Meghalaya, Kamatapur Liberation Organization (KLO), which operates in Assam and North Bengal, National Democratic Front of Bodoland and ULFA of Assam and the National Liberation Front of Tripura (NLFT).

GEOGRAPHY

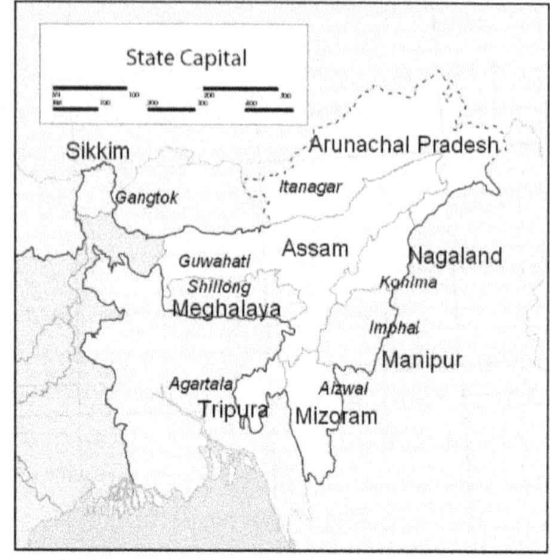

States and Capitals in Northeast India

The Northeast region can be physiographically categorised into the Eastern Himalayas, Northeast Hills (Patkai-Naga Hills and Lushai Hills) and the Brahmaputra and the Barak Valley Plains. Northeast India (at the confluence of Indo-Malayan, Indo-Chinese, and Indian bio-geographical realms) has a predominantly humid sub-tropical climate with hot, humid summers, severe monsoons and mild winters. Along with the west coast of India, this region has some of the Indian sub-continent's last remaining rain forests which supports diverse flora and fauna and several crop species. Similarly, reserves of petroleum and natural gas in the region constitute a fifth of India's total potential. The region is covered by the mighty Brahmaputra-Barak river systems and their tributaries. Geographically, apart from the Brahmaputra, Barak and Imphal valleys and some flat lands in between the hills of Meghalaya and Tripura, the remaining two-thirds of the area is hilly terrain interspersed with valleys and plains; the altitude varies from almost sea-level to over 7,000 metres (23,000 ft) above mean sea leavel (MSL). The region's high rainfall averaging around 10,000 millimetres (390 inches) and above creates problems of ecosystem, high seismic activity and floods. The states of Arunachal Pradesh and Sikkim have a montane climate with cold, snowy winters and mild summers.

Flora

Snowy peak at Sikkim

World Wide Fund (WWF) has identified the entire Eastern Himalayas as a priority Global 200 Ecoregion while Conservation International has up scaled the Eastern Himalaya Hotspot which initially covered the states of Arunachal Pradesh, Sikkim, Darjeeling Hills, Bhutan, and Southern China to the Indo Burma (Hotspot) which now includes all the eight states of North-East India, along with the neighbouring countries of Bhutan, southern China and Myanmar. The population and diversity of the region's birds largely reflects the diversity of habitats associated with a wide altitudinal range. North-East India supports some of the highest bird diversities in the orient with about 850 bird species. The Eastern Himalaya and the Assam plains have been identified as an Endemic Bird Area by the Royal Society for Protection of Birds, (ICBP 1992). The global distribution of 24 restricted-range species is limited to the region. The region's lowland and montane moist-to-wet tropical evergreen forests are considered to be the northern-most limit of true tropical rainforests in the world.

Sela Pass

The region has been identified by the Indian Council of Agricultural Research as a centre of rice germ plasm while the National Bureau of Plant Genetic Resources (NBPGR), India, has highlighted the region as being rich in wild relatives of crop plants. It is the centre of origin of citrus fruits. Two primitive variety of maize, Sikkim Primitive 1 and 2 have been reported from Sikkim (Dhawan, 1964). Although jhum cultivation, a traditional system of agriculture, is often cited as a reason for the loss of forest cover of the region, this primary agricultural economic activity practiced by local tribes reflects the usage of 35 varieties of crops. The region is rich in medicinal plants and many other rare and endangered taxa. Its high endemism in both higher plants, vertebrates and avian diversity has qualified it to be a biodiversity 'hotspot' and this aspect has been elaborated in details in the subsequent sections. In 1995, International Union for Conservation of Nature identified Namdapha in Arunachal Pradesh as a centre of plant diversity.

The following figures highlight the biodiversity significance of the region:

- 51 forest types are found in the region broadly classified into six major types—tropical moist deciduous forests, tropical semi evergreen forests, tropical wet evergreen forests, subtropical forests, temperate forests and alpine forests.
- Out of the nine important vegetation types of India, six are found in the North Eastern region.

- These forests harbour 8,000 out of 15,000 species of flowering plants. In floral species richness, the highest diversity is reported from the states of Arunachal Pradesh (5000 species) and Sikkim (4500 species) amongst the North Eastern States.
- According to the Indian Red data book published by the Botanical Survey of India, 10 per cent of the flowering plants in the country are endangered. Of the 1500 endangered floral species, 800 are reported from North East India.
- Most of the North Eastern states have more than 60% of their area under forest cover, a minimum suggested coverage for the hill states in the country.
- North East India is a part of Indo-Burma 'hotspot'. The hotspot is the world's second largest, next only to the Mediterranean basin with an area 2,206,000 square kilometres (852,000 sq mi) among the 25 identified.

Fauna

The International Council for Bird Preservation, UK identified the Assam plains and the Eastern Himalaya as an Endemic Bird Area (EBA). The EBA has an area of 220,000 square kms following the Himalayan range in the countries of Bangladesh, Bhutan, China, Nepal, Myanmar and the Indian states of Sikkim, northern West Bengal, Arunachal Pradesh, southern Assam, Nagaland, Manipur, Meghalaya and Mizoram. Because of a southward occurrence of this mountain range in comparison to other Himalayan ranges, this region has a distinctly different climate with warmer mean temperatures and fewer days with frost and have much higher rainfall. This has resulted in the occurrence of a rich array of restricted range bird species. More than two critically endangered species, three endangered species and 14 vulnerable species of birds are in this EBA. Stattersfield et al. (1998) identified 22 restricted range species out of which 19 are confined to this region and the remaining three are present in other endemic and secondary areas. Eleven out of the 22 restricted range species found in this region are considered as threatened (Birdlife International 2001), a number greater than in any other EBA of India.

WWF has identified the following priority ecoregions in North-East India:

- Brahmaputra Valley Semi Evergreen Forests
- The Eastern Himalayan Broadleaved Forests
- The Eastern Himalayan Sub-alpine Coniferous Forests
- India–Myanmar Pine Forests

Forest Reserves

Namdapha National Park: Spread over an area of 1,985 square kilometres (766 sq miles) in Arunachal Pradesh, Namdapha National Park is the largest national park of the northeast region. Situated 150 kilometres (93 miles) from Miao (district headquarters on the Indo-Burma border), Namdapha National Park is one of the largest wildlife protected areas in India. The altitude rises from 200 to 4,500 metres (660 to 14,760 feet) in the snow-capped mountains. The ecosystem abounds in more than 150 species of timber. Important rare fauna species include *Pinus merkusii, Abies delavayi*, blue vanda and Mishimi teeta. The Namdapha tiger reserve in Changlang district of Arunachal Pradesh, in an area of 1,850 square kilometres (710 sq miles) rugged terrain, is home to feline species such as tiger, clouded leopard, snow leopard and lesser cats. Primates such as Assamese macaque, pig-tailed macaque, stump-tailed macaque, hoolock gibbon, besides other mammals (elephant, Asian black bear, Indian bison, deer), birds (white-winged wood duck, great Indian hornbill, jungle fowl, pheasant) and reptiles add to the rich fauna diversity.

Manas National Park: Wildlife sanctuary and a World Heritage Site (declared by UNESCO), in the Barpeta district of Assam and partly along Bhutan foothills, the Manas National Park is shelter to rare species of as many as 55 mammals, 50 reptiles, 380 birds and three amphibians. Besides tiger, elephant, rhinoceros and wild water buffalo, leopard, pigmy hog, red panda, swamp deer, capped langur, sambar, hispid hare, golden langur, fowl, bulbul, brahminy duck, Indian grey hornbill and roofed turtle are protected in the Manas National Park. It is also an elephant reserve and biosphere reserve.

Manas National Park

Kaziranga National Park: Spread over an area of approximately 430 square kilometres (170 sq miles), 217 kilometres (135 miles) from Guwahati, with annual rainfall of 2300 mm, Kaziranga National Park is on the bank of Brahmaputra river with its swamps and tall thickets of elephant-grass. It is home to the world's largest population of great Indian one-horned rhinoceros, largest of the three Asian rhinos. The grasslands of semi-evergreen forest are inhabited by leopard, elephant, barasingha or swamp deer, barking deer, wild boar, hog deer, bison, otter, hoolock gibbon, golden langur, wild water buffalo, capped langur, pygmy hog, bear, grey-headed fish eagle, Pallas's fish eagle, crested serpent eagle, swamp partridge, red jungle fowl, Bengal florican, whistling teal, pelican, red-breasted parakeet, black-necked stork, adjutant stork, open-bill stork, egret, heron, white-winged wood duck, rock python, monitor lizard, turtle and other commonly found species.

Orang National Park: Also known as 'Mini Kaziranga', the Orang National Park is on the northern bank of the river Brahmaputra, in the state of Assam, covering 78.81 square kilometres (30.43 sq miles). Established as a sanctuary in 1985 and declared a national park in 1999, it is 32 kilometres (20 miles) from Tezpur and 120 kilometres (75 miles) from Guwahati. The terrain slopes gently from north to south covered with natural forest vegetation like *Bombax ceiba, Dalbergia sissoo, Sterculia villosa, Trewia nudiflora, Ziziphus jujuba, Litsaea polyantha* and other non-aquatic grassland species. One-horned rhinoceros, royal Bengal tiger, Asiatic elephant, hog deer, wild boar, civet, leopard, hare, porcupines and commonly found birds and reptiles in the region. Orang National Park is an important habitat of the Bengal florican.

Pobitora Wildlife Sanctuary: Situated in the Morigaon district of Assam, about 50 kilometres (31 miles) from Guwahati, Pobitora Wildlife Sanctuary covers 38.8 square kilometres (15.0 sq miles) and is famous for great Indian one-horned rhinoceros. The sanctuary also protects Asian buffalo, leopard, wild bear, civet, reptiles and some 2000 migratory birds.

Sepahijola Wildlife Sanctuary: Sepahijola Wildlife Sanctuary is a wildlife sanctuary in Tripura, India. It covers an area of about 18.53 square kilometres (7.15 sq miles) and is located about 25 kilometres (16 miles) from the city centre. It is the woodland with an artificial lake and natural botanical and zoological gardens. The sanctuary boasts of abounding congregation of wildlife, especially birds and primates, the terrain is absolutely green throughout the year and so is the beautiful weather except for the two humid summer months of March and April. It gives shelter to about 150 species of birds and the unique bespectacled monkey (Phayre's langur).

Clouded Leopard National Park Sanctuary, Sepahijala

Keibul Lamjao National Park: Keibul Lamjao National Park is about 53 kilometres (33 miles) from Imphal in Manipur. Temperatures range from a maximum of 34.4°C (93.9°F) to a minimum of the only Floating Park in the world. 1.7°C (35.1°F). Established as a wildlife sanctuary in 1966, it became a national park in 1977. The area of the park, about 40 square kilometres (15 sq miles), mostly comprises wetlands overgrown with 1.5 metres (4 feet 11 inches) deep floating vegetation called *Phumdi.* Loktak lake, the largest fresh water lake in India, falls primarily within the park. Brow-antlered deer (*sangai* in Meitei dialect) is particularly popular among the species of deer that abounds here. Extremely rare lesser cats like the marbled cat and Temminck's golden cat, Himalayan black bear, Malayan bear, black eagle, shaheen falcon, great white pelican, bamboo-partridge and green peafowl, hooded crane, brown hornbill, wreathed hornbill, great pied hornbill (great Indian hornbill) constitute the diverse fauna in the park.

DEMOGRAPHICS

According to 2011 census, the total literacy rate of the population in the region at 78.87 per cent, with female literacy rate at 74.12 per cent, is higher than the country's average of 73.0 per cent and 64.6 per cent respectively. There are variations in the literacy rates among different states with Assam, Arunachal Pradesh and Meghalaya below the national average while Mizoram and Tripura tops the list not only in the following region but in the entire nation.

Largest cities according to population of census 2011 are Guwahati, Agartala, Shillong, Aizawl, Imphal, Silchar, Dibrugarh, Nagaon, Jorhat, Dimapur, Darjeeling, Gangtok and Kohima.

Languages

Northeast India constitutes a single linguistic region with about 220 languages in multiple language families (Indo-European, Sino-Tibetan, Tai–Kadai, Austro-Asiatic) that share common structural features. Assamese, an Indo-Aryan language spoken mostly in the Brahmaputra Valley, developed as a *lingua franca* for many speech communities. Assamese-based pidgin/creoles have developed in Nagaland (Nagamese) and Arunachal (Nefamese), though their use has been on a decline in recent times. The Austro-Asiatic family is represented by the Khasi, Jaintia and War languages of Meghalaya. A small number of Tai–Kadai languages (Ahom, Tai Phake, Khamti, etc.) are also spoken. Sino-Tibetan is represented by a number of languages that differ significantly from each other, some of which are: Bodo, Rabha, Karbi, Mising, Tiwa, Deuri etc. (Assam); Garo, (Meghalaya) Ao, Tangkhul, Angami, Sema, Lotha, Konyak etc. (Nagaland); Mizo, Hmar, Chakma (Mizoram); Hrusso, Tanee, Nisi, Adi, Abor, Nocte, Apatani, Misimi etc. (Arunachal). Manipuri is the official language in Manipur, the dominant language of the Imphal Valley; while Naga languages such as Mao, Maram and Tangkul, and Kuki languages such as Hmar and Paite predominate in individual hill areas of the state.

Among other Indo-Aryan languages, Sylheti is spoken in South Assam in the Barak Valley. Besides the Sino-Tibetan Tripuri language, Bengali is a majority language in Tripura. Nepali, an Indo-Aryan language, is dominant in Sikkim, besides the Sino-Tibetan languages Limbu, Bhutia and Lepcha. Bengali was the official language of Colonial Assam for about forty years from the 1830s.

Communities

Northeast India has over 220 ethnic groups and equal number of dialects. The hills states in the region like Arunachal Pradesh, Meghalaya, Mizoram and Nagaland are predominantly inhabited by tribal people with a degree of diversity even within the tribal groups. Besides the indigenous inhabitants people from Tibet, Burma, Thailand, West Bengal and Bangladesh have migrated into the region at various periods of history.

Adivasi, Assamese, Bhutia, Bishnupriya Manipuri, Biate, Bodo , Chakma, Chhetri, Dimasa, Garo, Gurung, Hajong, Hmar, Hrankhwl, Jamatia, Karbi, Khasi, Khampti, Koch, Kom, Kuki, Paite, Vaiphei, Zou, Teddim, Simte, Gangte Lepcha, Lushai, Meitei, Mishing, Mizo, Naga, Nepali, Noatia, Paite, Pnar, Purvottar maithili, Rabha, Reang, Singpho, Sylheti, various Tibetan tribes, Tamang, Tiwa, Tripuri, Zeme Naga, Chorei and Limbu are different ethnic groups inhabiting the region.

GOVERNMENT

The northeastern states, having 3.8% of India's total population, are allotted 25 out of a total of 543 seats in the Lok Sabha. This is 4.6% of the total number of seats.

ECONOMY

The economy is agrarian. Little land is available for settled agriculture. Along with settled agriculture, *jhum* (slash-and-burn) cultivation is still practised by a few indigenous groups of people. The inaccessible terrain and internal disturbances has made rapid industrialisation difficult in the region.

Jhum Cultivation

In the 21st century, there has been recognition among policy makers and economists of the region that the main stumbling block for economic development of the Northeastern region is the disadvantageous geographical location. It was argued that globalization propagates deterritorialization and a borderless world which is often associated with economic integration.

With 98 per cent of its borders with China, Myanmar, Bhutan, Bangladesh and Nepal, Northeast India appears to have a better scope for development in the era of globalization.

As a result, a new policy developed among intellectuals and politicians that one direction the Northeastern region must be looking to as a new way of development lies with political integration with the rest of India and economic integration with the rest of Asia, with East and Southeast Asia in particular, as the policy of economic integration with the rest of India did not yield much dividends. With the development of this new policy the Government of India directed its Look East policy towards developing the Northeastern region.

This policy is reflected in the Year End Review 2004 of the Ministry of External Affairs, which stated that: "India's Look East Policy has now been given a new dimension by the Government. India is now looking towards a partnership with the ASEAN countries, both within BIMSTEC and the India-ASEAN Summit dialogue as integrally linked to economic and security interests, particularly for India's East and North-East region."

NORTH-EAST INDIA AT A GLANCE

- Population : 4,57,72,188
- Area : 2,62,179 km^2
- Population Density : 160.25/km^2
- Time Zone : IST (UTC +5:30)
- States and Territories : Arunachal Pradesh, Assam, Manipur, Meghalaya, Mizoram, Nagaland, Sikkim, Tripura
- Largest Cities (2017) : Guwahati, Jorhat, Agartala, Dimapur, Shillong, Aizawl, Imphal
- Official Languages : Assamese, Bengali, Bodo, English, Garo, Khasi, Kokborok, Manipuri, Mishing, Mizo, Nepali, Sikkimese
- Religion : Hinduism, Islam, Buddhism, Christianity, Animism (Sanamahism, Seng Khasi, Donyi-Polo, etc.)

OBJECTIVE QUESTIONS

1. Northeast India is the eastern-most region of India connected to East India via a narrow corridor squeezed between
   A. Nepal and Bhutan
   B. Nepal and China
   C. Nepal and Bangladesh
   D. Nepal and Mayanmar
2. Northeast India comprises the contiguous of how many states?
   A. 7
   B. 8
   C. 9
   D. 6
3. Northeast India states are grouped under the which ministry of the Government of India.
   A. Minister of Development of North Eastern Region
   B. Minister of Planning
   C. Minister of Energy
   D. Minister of Health
4. Who is the current, Minister of Development of North Eastern Region?
   A. Jitendra Singh
   B. Amrinder Singh
   C. V.K. Singh
   D. Daulat Singh
5. When Ministry of Development of North Eastern Region was established?
   A. 1998
   B. 1999
   C. 2000
   D. 2001
6. When the Brahmaputra valley area of Assam became a part of British?
   A. 1768
   B. 1824
   C. 1901
   D. 1956
7. When Sikkim was annexed to the Indian union through a referendum?
   A. 1975
   B. 1987
   C. 1990
   D. 1994
8. In terms of geographical size, Northeast India constitutes how many % of the total India's size?
   A. 5%
   B. 6%
   C. 7%
   D. 8%
9. According to 2011 census Northeast India's population (all 8 states combined) is approximately.......... Million.
   A. 45
   B. 35
   C. 30
   D. 25
10. Which corridor in West Bengal, with a width of 21 to 40 kilometres (13 to 25 miles), connects the North Eastern region with the main part of India.

A. New Jalpaigudi B. Siliguri
C. Guwahati D. Darjeeling

11. The region shares how many kilometres of international border (about 90 per cent of its entire border area) with China (South Tibet) in the north, Myanmar in the east, Bangladesh in the southwest, and Bhutan to the northwest.
A. more than 4,300 kilometres
B. more than 4,400 kilometres
C. more than 4,500 kilometres
D. more than 4,550 kilometres

12. The states are officially recognized under the North Eastern Council (NEC), constituted in ....as the acting agency for the development of the eight states.
A. 1971 B. 1972
C. 1978 D. 1989

13. When the North Eastern Development Finance Corporation Ltd (NEDFCL) was incorporated?
A. 29 August 1995 B. 19 August 1995
C. 9 August 1995 D. 9 September 1995

14. Who were the earliest settlers, followed by Tibet-Burmese and then by Indo-Aryans in the northeast region?
A. Austro-Arabic speakers B. Austro-Chinese speakers
C. Austro-Tibbato speakers D. Austro-Asiatic speakers

15. By which reason the focus of current archaeological research has been on domestication of several important plants by early settlers.
A. Due to the archi and crop diversity
B. Due to the medico and crop diversity
C. Due to the bio and crop diversity
D. Due to the geo and crop diversity

16. Who have suspected an early trade route via Northeast India in the references of Chinese explorer, Zhang Qian made in 100 BC?
A. Academician B. Writers
C. Barber D. Cobler

17. The *Periplus of the Erythraean Sea* mention a people called .... in the region.
A. Qêsatai B. Rêsatai
C. Sêsatai D. Têsatai

18. When did Xuanzang, the travelling Chinese monk, visited in the Kamarupa and described the people as "short in stature and black-looking", whose speech differed a little from mid-India and who were of simple but violent disposition; and that the people in Kamarupa knew of Sichuan that lay to the kingdom's east beyond a treacherous mountain?

A. 4th century
B. 5th century
C. 6th century
D. 7th century

19. Established during the British Raj, the northeastern states were isolated from their traditional trading partners such as.....................

A. Bhutan and Nepal
B. Bhutan and Myanmar
C. Bhutan and Bangladesh
D. Bhutan and Thailand

20. In the early 19th century, which kingdoms fell to a Burmese invasion?

A. Ahom and the Manipur
B. Ahom and the Nagaland
C. Ahom and the Tripura
D. Ahom and the Meghalaya

21. In the colonial period (1826-1947), North East India was a part of which Province from 1839 to 1873, when Assam became its own province?

A. Bengal
B. Bihar
C. Odisha
D. Sikkim

22. After the Indian Independence from British Rule in 1947, the Northeastern region of British India consisted of Assam and the princely states of Manipur and ....

A. Nagaland
B. Tripura
C. Meghalaya
D. Arunachal Pradesh

23. Subsequently, Nagaland in 1963, Meghalaya in 1972, Arunachal Pradesh in 1975 (Capital changed to Itanagar) (actually formed on 20 Feb, 1987) and Mizoram in 1987 were formed out of ....

A. Sikkim
B. Bihar
C. West Bengal
D. Assam

24. Sikkim was integrated as the eighth North Eastern Council state ....

A. in 2000
B. in 2001
C. in 2002
D. in 2003

25. The city of .... acted as the capital of the Assam province created during the British Rule.

A. Dispur
B. Shillong
C. Guwahati
D. Itanagar

26. Shillong remained as the capital of undivided Assam until formation of the state of ....in 1972.

A. Meghalaya
B. Nagaland
C. Tripura
D. Manipur

27. The capital of Assam was then shifted to ...., a part of Guwahati, and Shillong became the capital of Meghalaya.

A. Aizawl B. Dispur
C. Agartala D. Gangtok

28. When did the Japanese plan a daring attack on India, travelling through Burma, it was stopped at Kohima and Imphal by British and Indian troops?

A. In 1943 B. In 1944
C. In 1945 D. In 1946

29. When was the furthest western expansion of the Japanese Empire and presaged Allied victory held?

A. 1944 B. 1967
C. 1930 D. 1940

30. Arunachal Pradesh, a state in the North-eastern tip of India, is claimed by China as South Tibet, Sino-Indian relations degraded during the Sino-Indian War of ....

A. 1971 B. 1945
C. 1961 D. 1962

31. The cause of the escalation into war is still disputed by both Chinese and Indian sources. During the war in 1962, the PRC (China) captured much of the NEFA (North-East Frontier Agency) created by India in 1954. However on November 21, 1962, China declared a unilateral ceasefire, withdrew its troops 20 kilometres (12 miles) behind the .... and returned Indian prisoners of war in 1963.

A. McMahon Line B. Durand line
C. Silk line D. Rohtang line

32. The incident, known as the "..................", was allegedly committed by the Assam Rifles, one of the Indian Paramilitary forces operating in the state. This incident resulted in continuing unrest in the area.

A. Kalom Massacre B. Malom Massacre
C. Nalom Massacre D. Salom Massacre

33. The militant groups have formed an alliance to fight against the Governments of India, Bhutan and Myanmar and now use the term .... to refer to the region.

A. "Eastern Southeast Asia" (ESEA)
B. "Western Southeast Asia" (WSEA)
C. "Nothern Southeast Asia" (NSEA)
D. "Southern Southeast Asia" (SSEA)

34. The group HNLC stands for

A. Hynniewtrep National Liberation Centre

B. Hynniewtrep National Liberation Council
C. Hynniewtrep National Loyal Council (HNLC)
D. Hynniewtrep Nylon Liberation Council (HNLC)

35. The Northeast region can be physiographically categorised into the Eastern Himalayas, Northeast Hills (Patkai-Naga Hills and Lushai Hills) and the Brahmaputra and the ....Valley Plains.
A. Oarak B. Earak
C. Darak D. Barak

36. Northeast India (at the confluence of Indo-Malayan, Indo-Chinese, and Indian biogeographical realms) has a predominantly .... with hot, humid summers, severe monsoons and mild winters.
A. non-humid tropical climate
B. humid sub-tropical climate
C. humid non-tropical climate
D. non-humid sub-tropical climate

37. Along with .... coast of India, this region has some of the Indian sub-continent's last remaining rain forests which support diverse flora and fauna and several crop species.
A. the east B. the west
C. the north D. the south

38. Reserves of petroleum and natural gas in the region constitute a .... of India's total potential.
A. fifth B. sixth
C. seventh D. eight

39. Northeast region is covered by the mighty Brahmaputra-Barak river systems and their tributaries. Geographically, apart from the Brahmaputra, Barak and Imphal valleys and some flat lands in between the hills of Meghalaya and Tripura, the remaining two-thirds of the area is hilly terrain interspersed with valleys and plains; the altitude varies from almost sea-level to over ....
A. 7,000 metres above mean sea level (MSL)
B. 6,000 metres above mean sea level (MSL)
C. 5,000 metres above mean sea level (MSL)
D. 4,000 metres above mean sea level (MSL)

40. The region's high .... averaging around 10,000 millimetres (390 inches) and above creates problems of ecosystem, high seismic activity and floods. The states of Arunachal Pradesh and Sikkim have a montane climate with cold, snowy winters and mild summers.
A. skyfall B. fogfall
C. rainfall D. snowfall

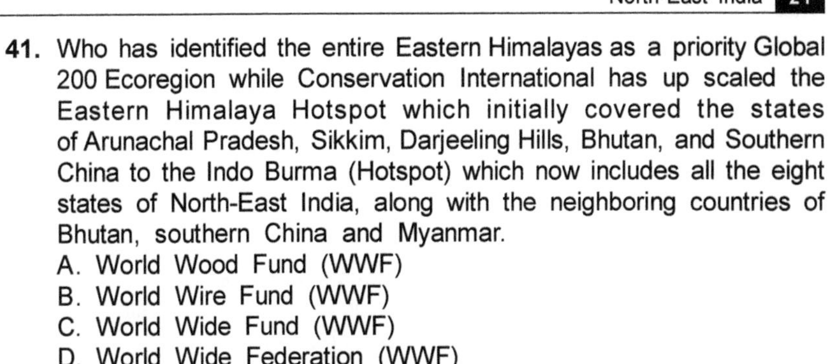

41. Who has identified the entire Eastern Himalayas as a priority Global 200 Ecoregion while Conservation International has up scaled the Eastern Himalaya Hotspot which initially covered the states of Arunachal Pradesh, Sikkim, Darjeeling Hills, Bhutan, and Southern China to the Indo Burma (Hotspot) which now includes all the eight states of North-East India, along with the neighboring countries of Bhutan, southern China and Myanmar.

A. World Wood Fund (WWF)
B. World Wire Fund (WWF)
C. World Wide Fund (WWF)
D. World Wide Federation (WWF)

42. The population and diversity of the region's .... largely reflects the diversity of habitats associated with a wide altitudinal range.

A. animals B. birds
C. humans D. minerals

43. North East India supports some of the highest bird diversities in the orient with about .... bird species.

A. 768 B. 750
C. 850 D. 876

44. The Eastern Himalaya and the Assam plains have been identified as an .... by the Royal Society for Protection of Birds, (ICBP 1992).

A. Endemic Bird Area B. Anemic Bird Area
C. Fndemic Bird Area D. Ondemic Bird Area

45. The global distribution of .... restricted-range species is limited to the region. The region's lowland and montane moist-to-wet tropical evergreen forests are considered to be the northern-most limit of true tropical rainforests in the world.

A. 20 B. 22
C. 24 D. 34

46. Northeast region has been identified by the Indian Council of Agricultural Research as a centre of .... while the National Bureau of Plant Genetic Resources (NBPGR), India, has highlighted the region as being rich in wild relatives of crop plants.

A. rice germ plasm B. gram germ plasm
C. mica germ plasm D. wheat germ plasm

47. Northeast is the centre of origin of .... Two primitive variety of maize, Sikkim Primitive 1 and 2 have been reported from Sikkim (Dhawan, 1964).

A. warm fruits B. cold fruits
C. sweet fruits D. citrus fruits

48. Although jhum cultivation, a traditional system of agriculture, is often cited as a reason for the loss of forest cover of Northeast the region, this primary agricultural economic activity practiced by local tribes reflects the usage of .... varieties of crops.

A. 35 B. 40
C. 45 D. 47

49. Northeast region is rich in ....and many other rare and endangered taxa. Its high endemism in higher plants, vertebrates and avian diversity has qualified it to be a biodiversity 'hotspot'.

A. medicinal plants B. chemical plants
C. artificial plants D. decorative plants

50. When was International Union for Conservation of Nature identified Namdapha in Arunachal Pradesh as a centre of plant diversity?

A. In 1995 B. In 1996
C. In 1997 D. In 1998

51. How many types of forest are found in the region broadly classified into six major types—tropical moist deciduous forests, tropical semi-evergreen forests, tropical wet evergreen forests, subtropical forests, temperate forests and alpine forests.

A. 40 B. 45
C. 49 D. 51

52. Out of the nine important vegetation types of India, ... are found in the North Eastern region.

A. six B. seven
C. eight D. nine

53. Northeast region forests harbour .... out of 15,000 species of flowering plants. In floral species richness, the highest diversity is reported from the states of Arunachal Pradesh (5000 species) and Sikkim (4500 species) amongst the North Eastern States.

A. 8,500 B. 8,000
C. 8,050 D. 8,550

54. According to the Indian Red data book published by the Botanical Survey of India, 10 per cent of the flowering plants in the country are endangered. Of the 1500 endangered floral species, ... are reported from North East India.

A. 800 B. 850
C. 875 D. 890

55. Most of the North Eastern states have more than .... of their area under forest cover, a minimum suggested coverage for the hill states in the country.

A. 60% B. 70%
C. 75% D. 76%

56. North East India is a part of Indo-Burma 'hotspot'. The hotspot is the world's second largest, next only to the Mediterranean basin with an area 2,206,000 square kilometres (852,000 sq mi) among the .... identified.

A. 20 B. 25
C. 28 D. 29

57. The International Council for Bird Preservation, UK, identified the Assam plains and the Eastern Himalaya as an .... Bird Area (EBA).

A. Pandemic B. Cadmic
C. Dndemic D. Endemic

58. The Endemic Bird Area has an area of .... following the Himalayan range in the countries of Bangladesh, Bhutan, China, Nepal, Myanmar and the Indian states of Sikkim, northern West Bengal, Arunachal Pradesh, southern Assam, Nagaland, Manipur, Meghalaya and Mizoram.

A. 220,800 square kms
B. 219,900 square kms
C. 220,000 square kms
D. 220,100 square kms

59. Because of a .... occurrence of this mountain range in comparison to other Himalayan ranges, this region has a distinctly different climate with warmer mean temperatures and fewer days with frost and have much higher rainfall.

A. northward
B. southward
C. eastward
D. westward

60. More than two critically endangered species, three endangered species and .... vulnerable species of birds are in Endemic Bird Area.

A. 14 B. 16
C. 18 D. 20

61. Satterfield et al. (1998) identified .... restricted range species out of which 19 are confined to this region and the remaining three are present in other endemic and secondary areas.

A. 21 B. 22
C. 28 D. 30

ANSWERS

1	2	3	4	5	6	7	8	9	10
C	B	A	A	D	B	A	D	A	B
11	**12**	**13**	**14**	**15**	**16**	**17**	**18**	**19**	**20**
C	A	C	D	C	B	C	D	B	A
21	**22**	**23**	**24**	**25**	**26**	**27**	**28**	**29**	**30**
A	B	D	C	B	A	B	B	A	D
31	**32**	**33**	**34**	**35**	**36**	**37**	**38**	**39**	**40**
A	B	B	B	D	B	B	A	A	C
41	**42**	**43**	**44**	**45**	**46**	**47**	**48**	**49**	**50**
C	B	C	A	C	A	D	A	A	A
51	**52**	**53**	**54**	**55**	**56**	**57**	**58**	**59**	**60**
D	A	B	A	A	B	D	C	B	A
61									
B									

2

ARUNACHAL PRADESH

INTRODUCTION

Arunachal Pradesh, one of the most sparsely populated states of India, covers an area of 83743 sq. Kms. "Arunachal Pradesh" means "land of the dawn-lit mountains" or "land of the rising sun". It is a part of what are called the **Seven Sister States** of the Northeast of India. McMahon Line separates it from the zone of control of the People's Republic of China to the north. Itanagar is the capital of the state. Arunachal Pradesh is the largest state (area-wise) in the north-east region. The entire region had remained isolated since 1873 when the British stopped free movement. After 1947, Arunachal became part of the North East Frontier Agency (NEFA). This region acquired an independent political status in January 20, 1972, when it was declared as Union Territory under the name of Arunachal Pradesh. The state of Arunachal Pradesh Bill was passed by the Parliament in 1986 and with effect from February 20, 1987 Arunachal Pradesh became the 24th state of Indian Union.

Arunachal Pradesh finds mention in the literature such as the Kalki Puran and in the epics of Mahabharata and Ramayana. It is believed that sage Vyasa meditated there and also that the remains of the brick structure, scattered around two villages in the hills north of Roing was the palace of Rukmini, the consort of Lord Krishna. The sixth Dalai Lama was also born on the soil of Arunachal Pradesh.

Arunachal Pradesh is endowed with thick evergreen forests with numerous streams, rivers and gorges and hundreds and thousands of species of flora and fauna covering more than 60% of the total area. Its rivers are ideal for angling, boating and rafting and its terrain is suitable for trekking, hiking and holidaying in a serene atmosphere. Out of about a thousand species of orchids in India, over 500 are to be found in Arunachal alone. Some of the orchids are rare and classified as endangered. The land is mostly mountainous with the Himalayan range along the northern borders criss-crossed with ranges running north-south. These divide the state into **five river valleys**: the **Kameng**, the **Subansiri**, the **Siang**, the **Lohit** and the **Tirap**. The mightiest of these rivers is the **Siang**, called the **Tsangpo** in Tibet, which becomes the **Brahmaputra** after the **Dibang** and the **Lohit** in the plains of Assam joins it. Nature has provided the people with a deep sense of beauty that finds delightful expression in their songs, dances and crafts.

HISTORY

The history of pre-modern Arunachal Pradesh remains shrouded in mystery. Oral histories possessed to this day by many Arunachali tribes of Tibeto-Burman stock are much richer and point unambiguously to a northern origin in modern-day Tibet. Again corroboration remains difficult. From the point of view of material culture it is clear that most indigenous Arunachali groups align with Burma-area hill tribals, a fact that could either be explainable in terms of a northern Burmese origin or from westward cultural diffusion.

From the same perspective the most unusual Arunachali group by far is the Puroik/Sulung, whose traditional staple food is called "tasey" or "taase" made from sago palm and whose primary traditional productive strategy is foraging. While speculatively considered a Tibeto-Burman population, the uniqueness of Puroik culture and language may well represent a tenuous reflection of a distant and all but unknown pre-Tibeto-Burman, Tai and Indo-Aryan past.

According to the Arunachal Pradesh government, the Hindu texts Kalki Purana and Mahabharata mention the region as the Prabhu Mountains of the Puranas, and where sage Parashuram washed away sins, the sage Vyasa meditated, King Bhishmaka founded his kingdom, and Lord Krishna married his consort Rukmini.

Recorded history from an outside perspective only became available in the Ahom and Sutiya chronicles. The Monpa and Sherdukpen do keep historical records of the existence of local chiefdoms in the northwest as well. Northwestern parts of this area came under the control of the Monpa kingdom of Monyul, which flourished between 500 B.C. and 600 A.D. This region then came under the loose control of Tibet and Bhutan, especially in the Northern areas. The remaining parts of the state, especially those bordering Myanmar, were under the control of the Sutiya Kings until the Ahom-Sutiya battle in the 16th century. The Ahoms held the areas until the annexation of India by the British in 1858. However, most Arunachali tribes remained in practice largely autonomous up until Indian independence and the formalisation of indigenous administration in 1947.

Recent excavations of ruins of Hindu temples such as the 14th century Malinithan at the foot of the Siang hills in West Siang were built during the Sutiya reign. Another notable heritage site, Bhismaknagar, has led to suggestions that the Idu (Mishmi) had an advanced culture and administration in pre-historical times. Again, however, no evidence directly associates Bhismaknagar with this or any other known culture but the Sutiya rulers held the areas around Bhismaknagar from the 12th to 16th century. The third heritage site, the 400-year-old Tawang Monastery in the extreme north-west of the state, provides some historical evidence of the Buddhist tribal people. The sixth Dalai Lama Tsangyang Gyatso was born in Tawang. Major tribe of Arunachal Pradesh Nyishi, Apatani, Galo, Adi, Monpa, Mishmi, Shingpo, Khamti, Serdukpen.

Drawing of McMahon Line

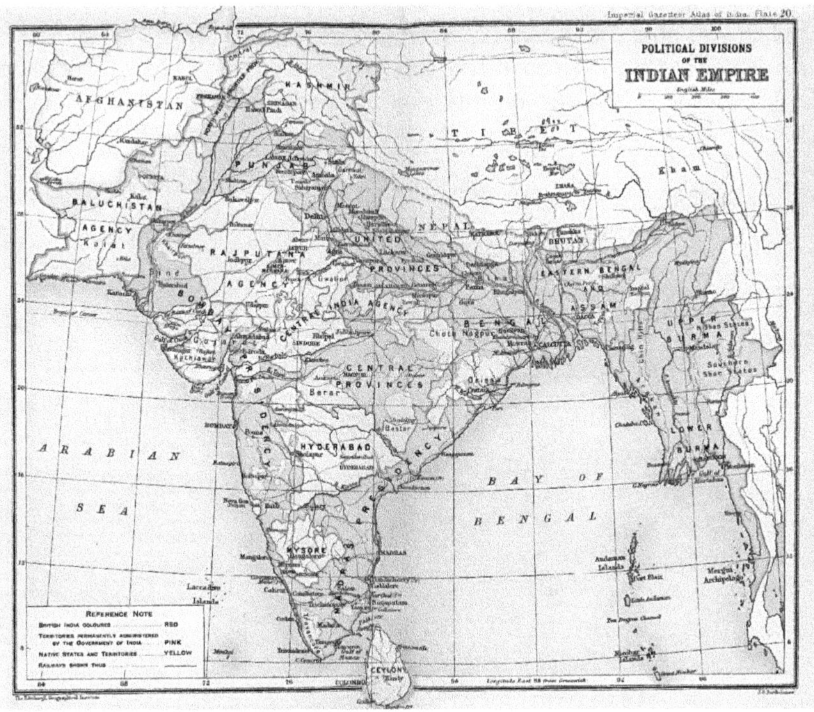

British map published in 1909 showing the Indo-Tibetan traditional border (eastern section on the top right)

In 1913-1914 representatives of China, Tibet and Britain met in India ending with the Simla Accord. However, the Chinese representatives refused the territory negotiation. This treaty's objective was to define the borders between Inner and Outer Tibet as well as between Outer Tibet and British India. British administrator, Sir Henry McMahon, drew up the 550 miles (890 km) McMahon Line as the border between British India and Outer Tibet during the Simla Conference. The Tibetan and British representatives at the conference agreed to the line and Tibet ceded Tawang and other Tibetan areas to the British Empire.

The Chinese representative had no problems with the border between British India and Outer Tibet; however on the issue of the border between Outer Tibet and Inner Tibet the talks broke down. Thus, the Chinese representative refused to accept the agreement and walked out. The Tibetan Government and British Government went ahead with the Simla Agreement and declared that the benefits of other articles of this treaty would not be bestowed on China as long as it stays out of the purview. The Chinese position was that Tibet was not independent from China, so Tibet cannot have independently signed treaty and per the Anglo-Chinese (1906) and Anglo-Russian (1907) conventions, any such agreement was invalid without Chinese assent.

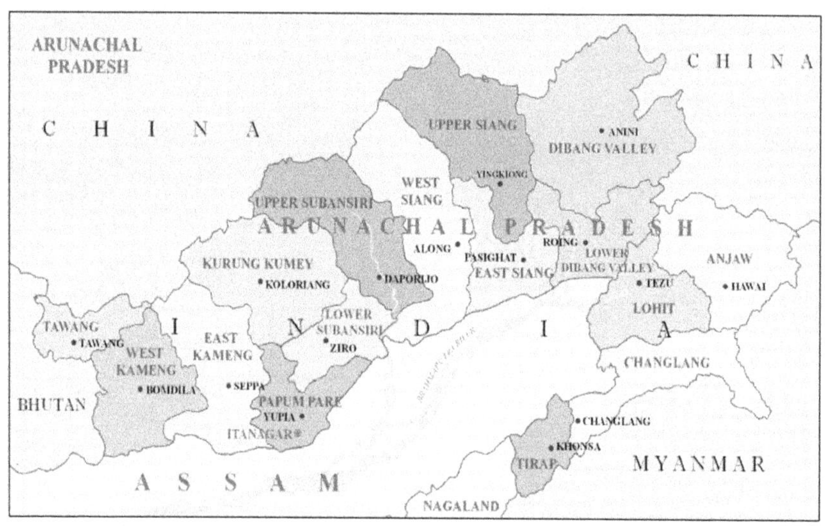

Arunachal Pradesh Map

Simla was initially rejected by the Government of India as incompatible with the 1907 Anglo-Russian Convention. However, this agreement (Anglo-Russian Convention) was renounced by Russia and Britain jointly in 1921. However, with the collapse of Chinese power in Tibet, the line had no serious challenges as Tibet had signed the convention; therefore it was forgotten to the extent that no new maps were published until 1935, when civil service officer Olaf Carole called attention to this issue. The Survey of India published a map showing the McMahon Line as the official boundary in 1937. In 1938, the British finally published the Simla Convention as a bilateral accord two decades after the Simla Conference; in 1938 the Survey of India published a detailed map showing Tawang as part of North-East Frontier Agency. In 1944 Britain established administrations in the area from Dirang Dzong in the west to Walong in the east. Tibet, however, altered its position on the McMahon Line in late 1947 when the Tibetan government wrote a note presented to the newly independent Indian Ministry of External Affairs laying claims to (Tawang) south of the McMahon Line. The situation developed further as India became independent and the People's Republic of China was established in 1949. In November 1950, with the PRC poised to take over Tibet, India unilaterally declared that the McMahon Line is the boundary—and, in 1951, forced the last remnants of Tibetan administration out of the Tawang area. The PRC has never recognised the McMahon Line, and claims Tawang on behalf of Tibetans. The 14th Dalai Lama, who led the Tibetan government from 1950 to 1959, was quoted in 2003 as saying that Tawang was "actually part of the Tibetan administration" before the Simla Accord. He clarified his position in 2008, saying that as far as Tibet was concerned "Tawang is part of India". According to the Dalai Lama, "In 1962 during the India-China war, the People's Liberation Army (PLA) already occupied all these areas (Arunachal Pradesh) but they announced a unilateral ceasefire and withdrew, accepting the current international boundary.

Sino-Indian War

The NEFA (North-East Frontier Agency) was created in 1955. The issue was quiet for nearly a decade, a period of cordial Sino-Indian relations, but the re-emergence of the issue was a major cause of the Sino-Indian War of 1962. The cause of the escalation into war is still disputed by both Chinese and Indian sources. During the war in 1962, the People Republic of China captured most area of Arunachal Pradesh. However, China soon declared victory, voluntarily withdrew back to the McMahon Line and returned Indian prisoners of war in 1963. The war resulted in the termination of barter trade with Tibet, although in 2007 the state government has shown signs to resume barter trade with Tibet.

Tawang

In recent years, People Republic of China has occasionally made statements in conjunction with its 'claims' on Tawang. India has rebutted these claims by the Chinese government and the Indian Prime Minister has informed the Chinese government that Tawang is an integral part of India. India reiterated this to the Chinese prime minister when the two prime ministers met in Thailand in October 2009.

China objected to the visit of the Dalai Lama to Tawang in November 2009. Though the Dalai Lama had previously visited Tawang several times since he left Tibet in 1959. India rejected the Chinese objection and said that the Dalai Lama is an honoured guest in India and could visit any place in India. The Dalai Lama visited Tawang on 8 November 2009. About 30,000 people including those from neighbouring countries, Nepal and Bhutan, attended his religious discourse.

He was received and welcomed by the Chief Minister of Arunachal Pradesh and the people of Arunachal Pradesh. The residents of Tawang painted their houses and decorated the town.

Current Name

NEFA was renamed as Arunachal Pradesh by Late Sri Bibhabasu Das Shastri, the then Director of Research, on 20 January 1972 and it became a Union Territory. Arunachal Pradesh became a state on 20 February 1987.

More recently, Arunachal Pradesh has come to face threats from certain insurgent groups. There are occasional reports of these groups harassing local people and extorting protection money.

Especially along the Tibetan border, the Indian army has a considerable presence due to concerns about Chinese intentions in the region. Special permits called Inner Line Permits (ILP) are required to enter Arunachal Pradesh through any of its check gates on the border with Assam.

Evolution of Arunachal Pradesh

The tri-junction of the Eastern Himalayan foothills, the Patkai Hills and the plains, may be identified with Sadiya and Matak sub-divisions of Lakhimpur district of British Assam in the 1840. This was where tea plantation made a beginning in 1838. At the time, the Adis (Abors), Miris, Khamtis, Singphos, Mishmis and some Nagas inhabited the adjoining hill areas. Some of them were considered as the slaves of others, who paid token tributes in kind to the Abors or Singphos. Many of the claimed slaves ran away from the hills and got settled in plains in the British district for protection. These settlers worked for the British and paid taxes as per existing rules. But the hill tribes continued to raid the new settlements and imposed traditional tributes on the plea that they were their run away slaves. On the pattern of the old Ahom system of **posa** (blackmail money or tribute), the British contracted to pay a 100 iron hoes, 30 maunds of salt, 80 bottles of rum, and two maunds of tobacco annually to the Abors as tribute (posa) in 1862 and a treaty of peace was signed with the chiefs. But this arrangement did not deter the Abors, who used to descend on Miri settlements (their "former" slaves) in the plains during the winter, stayed in their houses as free board forced tributes and retired to their hills with the booty.

With a view to securing the plains and foothills from raids and reprisals of the hill tribes, a number of armed outposts were established by the British at Dirijeme, Poba, Sessiri, Nizamghat, Bomjor and Rukong by 1882. That was the year, Joseph R. Needham was appointed as the Assistant Political Officer at Sadiya, who laid the foundation of a personalized administration of this Frontier Tract in his more than two decades old posting. The Chief Commissioner passed the Rules for the administration of Lakhimpur Frontier Tract in 1886. Needham undertook a number of expeditions in tribal areas to befriend them. By large, there were no major confrontations between the British administration and the tribes. However, by the turn of the century, runaway slaves of the tribesmen, inter-tribal feuds, personal jealousies and suspicion led to troubles on the frontiers. So much so that, in May 1900, restrictions were imposed on official tours beyond "the areas of political control through out the Assam frontiers". This was also the beginning of the change in the British Himalayan policy by adopting a more active and vigorous attitude towards the frontier region as a whole.

The Deputy Commissioner of Lakhimpur, **A.H.W. Bentick**, in his 'Political Report on the Expedition', furnished the proposals as to the future of this frontier tract on April 23, 1912. Accordingly, the North East Frontier Tract was divided into three sections: the central and eastern sections to control the Ponpong Nagas, Singphos, Mijus, Chulikata and Babejia Mishmis and the various tribes of Abors as far as the Siang-Subansiri divide, and the western section (which came to be known as the Balipara Frontier Tract) to deal with the tribes from this divide westwards to Bhutan. The two eastern sections were placed in the charge of one Political Officer with head quarters at Sadiya, which came to be known as 'Sadiya Frontier Tract'. Under this dispensation, two Assistant Political Officers, one, for Abor subdivision at Pasighat and another, at Wallong for the Lohit Valley subdivision, were proposed. The Government of India Act, 1919 vested with the Governor of Assam with the administration of the three Frontier tracts and declared them as "Backward Tracts". Similarly, the Government of

India Act, 1935 termed these tracts as the "Excluded Areas" in 1936, by which it was meant that the State Assembly of Assam was not empowered to frame rules for these 'Excluded Frontier Tracts' and the Governor of the State was to govern them directly. Between 1943 to 1948, these frontier tracts were re-organized into five Agencies: Sela, Subansiri, Abor, Mishmi, and Tirap.

Arunachal Pradesh in the Indian Union

In 1954 North East Frontier Agency (NEFA) Administration Regulation was passed, by which, for the first time, the region was given a nomenclature—NEFA. The former Agencies were renamed after the rivers within their areas: Kameng, Subansiri, Siang, Lohit, and Tirap and they were termed as the frontier divisions. It was also decided to shift the headquarters of the divisions from the foothills to the interior of the hills. And for that Bomdila, Ziro, Along, Tezu and Khela were selected as the sites for the five divisions respectively. After the Chinese aggression on India in 1962, another NEFA Regulation was enacted, by which divisions were changed to the districts like anywhere in the country and the Political Officers were termed as the Deputy Commissioners. Further more, NEFA administration was transferred from Ministry of Foreign Affairs to the Ministry of Home Affairs and its State capital was to be shifted to a new site in NEFA. With the Indian parliament enacting North Eastern Areas (Re-organisation) Act, 1971, NEFA became Arunachal Pradesh with the status of a Union Territory and a Pradesh (provincial) Council of 26 members, and five-member Interim Council of Ministers. Two seats in the Indian lower house of Parliament (Lok Sabha: Arunachal East and West) and one seat in the upper house (Rajya Sabha) of the Parliament were allotted to Arunachal. And finally, on 20th February 1987, Statehood was conferred on Arunachal Pradesh when Rajiv Gandhi was the Prime Minister and it became the 24th State of the Union of India.

GEOGRAPHY

Arunachal Pradesh is situated in the North-Eastern part of India with 83,743 sq. kms area and has a long international border with Bhutan to the west (160 km), China to the north and north-east (1,080 km) and Myanmar to the east (440 km). It stretches from snow-capped mountains in the north to the plains of Brahmaputra valley in the south. Arunachal is the largest state area-wise in the north-east region, even larger than Assam which is the most populous. It is situated between latitude 26°30′N and 29°30′N and longitude 91°30′E and 97°30′E. Its main river are Siang, Kameng, Subansiri, Kamla, Siyum, Dibang, Lohit, Noa-Dihing, Kamlang, Tirap. Much of Arunachal Pradesh is covered by the Himalayas, although parts of Lohit,

Changlang and Tirap are covered by the Patkai. Kangto (7090 m), Nyegi Kangsang (7050 m), the main Gorichen peak (6488 m) and the Eastern Gorichen peak (6222 m) are some of the highest peaks in the Himalayas.

Mountainous Zones

Kangto Massif

Kangto Massif is one zone of mountaineering interest that is the least known of all Himalayan areas. It is the first great mountain range in the Arunachal Himalayas that will come into view as one moves from east to west. Visible from the distant plains of Assam and the Meghalaya state hills, the high range of the Kangto Massif lies in a gigantic S-curve running roughly west-southwest and east-northeast between the passes of Tulung La and Keshong La in the region.

The **McMahon line**—the border between India and China — runs more or less along the top. To the south lies a high rain-sodden, thickly forested ridge of the lesser Himalayas, which makes a difficult and dangerous access from Assam. The access from Tibet is considerably easy.

Peaks of Kangto Region

Major peaks in the Kangto Section are **Gori Chen** (6,538 m), **Kangto** (7,090 m), **Nyegyi Kangsang** (7,047 m) and **Takpa Siri** (6,655 m). Takpa Siri is a holy mountain just north of the Indian border, near the Tibetan village of Migyitun. Walking around to this mountain is said to have religious merit, much like that of the famous Kailash Parbat. However, its height is not higher than 6,655 m.

The Rain Bearer

It is because of the existence the Kangto Massif in this region that the rain bearing monsoon clouds are trapped and the resulting water, forms Kameng—a major river and one of the main tributaries of the Dihang, which is the name by which the Brahmaputra River is known in the region.The riverside areas from where these mighty rivers flow through, have extremely dense vegetation.

Namcha Barwa Massif

Situated on the easternmost frontiers of the Himalayas is another mountaineering paradise—the Namcha Barwa Massif. The mountain ranges that lie beyond the Tsangpo-Dihang are not considered a part of the Himalayas. Standing at an elevation of 7,756 m above sea level Namcha Barwa is the highest point of this range. Known as the 'Mysterious Giant' the actual exploration expedition of this range was done in 1912, although the Pandit explorers had reported its existence first. It's from these mountain masses of Namcha Barwa that the mighty Brahmaputra River enters India. Flowing through the Trans Himalayas, where it is known as the "Yarlung Tsangpo", river Brahmaputra enters India forming a gorge around the Namcha Barwa. The gorge of the Yarlung Tsangpo is known to be one of the wildest and least explored areas in the world. The gorge is three times as deep as the Grand Canyon of Colorado.

MINERALS

Geologically, Arunachal Pradesh is the least explored State and most of the mineral resources lie hidden underground. Arunachal Pradesh Mineral Development and Trading Corporation Limited was set up in 1991 and Namchik-Namphuk coal fields are under APMDTCL. Occurrences of oil have been reported from Ningru, Kumchai, Kharsang, Manabhum and across the Noa Dithing river in Arunachal Pradesh. Nevertheless, preliminary studies of geological formations promise important economic mineral deposit in considerable quantity. On the basis of the explorations so far carried out by GSI, CIL, OIL, MECL, CMPDIL & APMDTCL, mineral reserves reported in Arunachal Pradesh are as detailed below:

Sl. No.	Name of Mineral	Location	District	Estimated Reserves (in million tones)
1.	Coal	Namchik-Namphuk	Changlang	84.23
2.	Dolomite	Rupa	West Kameng	143.0
		Kapsi (Jameri)	West Kameng	11.13
3.	Limestone	Tidding	Lohit	140.0
		Pangin	East Siang	225.0
		Hunli	Dibang Valley	13.35
		Menga	Upper Subansiri	0.75
4.	Graphite	Bopi	Upper Subansiri	2.46
		Khetabari	Lower Subansiri	0.50
		Taliha	Upper Subansiri	0.30
5.	Marble	Tezu	Lohit	30.30
		Dora	Lohit	43.30
		Hunli	Dibang Valley	2.34
		Pyuli	Dibang Valley	0.18
6.	Ferro-Silicon Quartzite	Kalaktang	West Kameng	1.25
7.	Oil & Natural Gas	Kharsang & Diyun (Khumchai)	Changlang	Yet to be estimated
		Kanubari	Tirap	
8.	Lead & Zinc	Shergaon	West Kameng	

CLIMATE

The weather and the climate of Arunachal Pradesh are quite distinct from the rest of the country. The climate of the State is dominated by the Himalayan system and the altitudinal variations. The climate is highly hot and humid at the lower altitudes and in the valleys covered by swampy dense forest particularly in the eastern section, while it becomes exceedingly cold in the higher altitudes. Average temperature during the winter months range from 15 to 21 degree celsius and 22 to 30 degree celsius during monsoon. Between June and August the temperature may go up to 40-42 degree celsius. The annual average rainfall in Arunachal Pradesh is more than 350 cm.

AGRICULTURE

Agriculture is the mainstay of the people of Arunachal Pradesh and had mainly depended on **jhum cultivation.** The principal crop of this area is rice, and other important crops include maize, millets, wheat, pulses, potato, sugarcane and oilseeds. The ecological conditions are suitable for horticulture and fruits like pineapple, orange, lemon, papaya, plum, pear, guava, cherries, walnut and peach thrive here. 65.6% of the working population of the State is engaged in agriculture. Thus, agriculture is the main stay of the economy of the State. However, agriculture continues to be dependent on rains. So far the State has not been able to achieve the desired growth rate to attain self-sufficiency in foodgrain production though there have been remarkable achievements on overall context in the field of agriculture to boost up the rural economy and income of the farmers.

Stretching over an area of 83,743 Sq. km. with a population of about 13.84 lakh, the State has around 2.11 lakh hect. of net cultivable area and 2.755 lakh hect. of gross cultivable area. The net irrigation area under utilization is around 51,700 hect. with cropping intensity in the level of 130.56%.

The shifting cultivation which has come to be known as Jhuming which means collective farming occupies the central position in Arunachal Pradesh in the field of agriculture. This is the form of cultivation that sustains majority of the people in the area which has been practiced from earlier days.

1. **Major crops :** Rice, Maize, Millet, Wheat, Pulses, Sugarcane.
2. **Major plantations :** Rubber, Coffee, Tea.

3. **Fruits, vegetables & spices :** Banana, Apple, Pineapple, Plum, Orange, Walnut, Guava, Grapes, Potato, Ginger, Chilli, Turmeric.

FLORA AND FAUNA

The forest area is about 79.96% of the total geographical area of 83,743 Sq.km in Arunachal Pradesh. The socio-economic life of the tribal population of the State centre round the forests and have also pervaded the life and culture of the tribal people of the State. The local people are directly depending upon the forest for timber, fuel wood and a variety of minor forest produces. Arunachal Pradesh is the richest bio-geographical region in eastern Himalayan zone. The State has 20% species of country's fauna, 4500 species of flowering plants, 400 species of pteridophytes, 23 species of conifers, 35 species of bamboos, 20 species of canes, 52 rhododendron species and more than 500 species of orchids and is considered as one of the 12 mega diversity "Hot Spots" in the world.

Fauna

There are two national parks and eleven wildlife sanctuaries in the State managed by the state forest department.

National Parks

S.No.	Name	District	Area in Sq. Kms.	Major animals
1.	Namdhapa National Park (Tiger Project)	Tirap	1985.23	Elephant, Tiger, Gaur, Sambar Barking Deer, Binturong, Leopard, four Hornbill species, Pea-cock-Pheasant, Kalij pheasant.
2.	Mouling National Park	East Siang	483.00	Elephant, Barking Deer, Tiger, Leopard, Serow, Birds, Orchids.

Wildlife/Orchid Sanctuaries

S.No.	Name	District	Area in Sq. Kms.	Major animals
1.	Itanagar Wild life Sanctuary	Papum-Pare	140.30	Elephant, Barking Deer, Tiger, Leopard, Serow, Birds, Orchids.
2.	Dr. D. Ering Memorial Wild-life Sanctuary	Upper Siang	190.00	Honger, Hispid Hore, Bengal florican, Raptors, and migratory water birds.

3.	Mehao Wildlife Sanctuary	Dibang Valley	281.50	Hoolock Gibbon, Tiger, Leopard, Red Panda, Elephant, etc.
4.	Kamlang Wildlife Sanctuary	Lohit	783.00	Hoolock, Gibbon, Tiger, Leopard, Capped Langur, Red Panda, Takin.
5.	Eagle Nest Wildlife Sanctuary	West Kameng	217.00	Elephant, Tiger, Leopard, Sambar, Serow, Goral, Red Panda, Himalayan, Black Bear.
6.	Kane Wildlife Sanctuary	West Siang	31.00	Elephant, Small Cats, Deer.
7.	Pakhui Wildlife Sanctuary	East Kameng	861.95	Elephant, Tiger, Gaur, Sambar Barking Deer, Binturong, Leopard, four Hornbill species, Peacock-Pheasant, Kalij Pheasant.
8.	Sessa Orchid Sanctuary	West Kameng	100.00	Varieties of orchids, Red Panda, Pheasants, Serow, Goral, etc.
9.	Dibang Wildlife Sanctuary	Dibang Valley	190.00	—
10.	Tale Wildlife Sanctuary	Lower Subansiri	337.00	—
11.	Yordi Rabe Supse Wildlife Sanctuary	West Siang	397.00	—

POPULATION

The population of Arunachal Pradesh is 13,83,727 according to 2011 census and is scattered over 30 notified towns and 5258 census villages. The State has the lowest density of 17 persons per sq. km. As against decadal growth rate of 17.7% at the national level, the population of the State has grown by 26% over the period 2001-2011. The sex ratio of Arunachal Pradesh at 938 females to 1000 males is lower than the national average of 943. Total literacy of the State rose to 65.4% from 54.30% in 2001. There are 20 major tribes and a number of sub-tribes inhabiting the area.

Population : At a Glance

	Head	Unit	2011 Census
1.	Population	Lakh	13,83,727
2.	Decadal Growth	Per cent	26.00
3.	Density	Per Sq. Km.	17
4.	Sex-Ratio	Females per 1000 males	938
5.	Literacy	Per cent	65.4

Area, Population and Headquarters of Districts-2011 Census

District	Population	Density	Sex ratio	Literacy
Tawang	49,977	23	714	59
West Kameng	83,947	11	819	67.1
East Kameng	78,690	19	1029	60
Papum Pare	1,76,573	51	980	80
Upper Subansiri	83,448	12	998	63.8
West Siang	1,12,274	13	930	66.5
East Siang	99,214	28	980	72.5
Upper Siang	35,320	5	889	60
Changlang	1,48,226	32	926	59.8
Tirap	1,11,975	47	944	52.2
Lower Subansiri	83,030	24	984	74.3
Kurung Kumey	92,076	15	1032	48.8
Dibang Valley	8,004	1	813	64.1
Lower Dibang Valley	54,080	14	928	69.1
Lohit	1,45,726	28	912	68.2
Anjaw	21,167	3	839	56.5
Longdiang	—	—	—	—
Namsai	—	—	—	—
Kradadi	—	—	—	—
Siang	—	—	—	—
Lower Siang	—	—	—	—
Kamle	—	—	—	—
Pakke-Kessang	—	—	—	—
Lepa Rada	—	—	—	—
Shi-Yomi	—	—	—	—
Total	**13,83,727**	**17**	**938**	**65.4**

Population by religious communities-2011 census

According to the 2011 census the religions of Arunachal Pradesh break down as follows:

S.No	Religious Communities	Persons	Percentage
1.	Hindu	401,876	29.04%
2.	Christian	418,732	30.26%
3.	Buddhist	162,815	11.75%
4.	Muslim	27,045	1.9%
5.	Sikh	1,865	0.1%
6.	Jain	216	<0.1%
7.	Other (Mostly Donyi-Polo)	362,553	26.2%

SCHEDULED TRIBES

Districtwise, Lower Subansiri, Upper Subansiri, East Kameng, Tirap, and West Siang are predominantly ST districts with the proportion of ST population 80 per cent and above. These districts together share half of the total ST population of the state.

SCHEDULED CASTES

Namasudra (21.6 per cent), Kaibartta (21.4 per cent), and Dhupi (11.1 per cent) are the major SCs in the state of Arunachal Pradesh. They together constitute about 55 per cent of the total SC population of the state. Six SCs namely Mahara, Patni, Jhalo, Hira, Dugla, and Lalbegi are small in numbers and have less than hundred population each. Of the three main SCs, Dhupi has recorded the highest 61 per cent urban population, followed by Namasudra and Kaibartta.

SOCIAL GROUPS

The entire Arunachal Pradesh can be divided into six different social groups: Mahayana Bhotia society, Nishi society, Adi society, Mishmi society, Hinayana Khampti-Singpho society and Naga society.

The **Mahayana Bhotia society** comprises of the tribes of Sherdukpens, Monpas, Membas, Khambas and Nagas. Its main region is the western portion of the Kameng river in West Kameng district and Tawang district including the outer higher Himalayan regions, Valleys of Mipi, Matu and Yigrang and upper reaches of rivers Dri, Andra and Yongyap in Dibang Valley district. The common characteristics of this social groups are—

1. They belong to Tibeto-Mongoloid stock.
2. They resemble more with western Mongoloid group.
3. The skin colour is fair with reddish tint.
4. The language between tribes differs with slight variations only.
5. They follow an advanced terrace pattern of cultivation.
6. The rice beer called **Chang** is a common beverage in all places.
7. The rice-spirit, Ara, is a luxury drink.

The **Adi society** is represented by the Adi tribe itself which is divided into various sub-tribes. This social group extends itself in the vast areas between Siang and Subansiri occupying the central portion of Arunachal Pradesh. The striking feature of the Adi society is that it is a homogeneous society. It can be termed as the Siang valley society as the majority of the Adis inhabit both sides of this big river. The bachelors' dormitories are established both for young boys and girls. This unique social custom is prevalent in all sub-tribes uniformly. The central religious character prevalent in society is their belief in **Donyi-Polo**, which is form of animistic religion.

The **Mishmi society** comprises of the Idu-Mishmis, Digaru-Mishmis and Miju-Mishmis. This social group spread over the Mishmi Hills between the Dibang and the Kamlang rivers. They are Palaeo-Mongoloid with flat and broad faces, wide and round nostrils. All the Mishmis areas follow the animistic belief of polytheism. They believe in having spirit in trees, rivers, mountains, hills, jungles etc. The concept of malevolent and benevolent spirit is followed universally. They believed that spirits are the cause of all good and bad acts in human life.

The **Hinayana Khampti-Singphos** society is mainly composed of Khamptis and Singphos, but the Tangsas can also be included in this group. The Khampti-Singpho social group occupies the areas of south east of Lohit district and north east of Tirap district of the area between Kamlang and Tirap rivers. The Khampti-Singpho society is particularly influenced by the Hinayana Buddhist culture. The Tangsas have, however, not been able to come into the Buddhist-fold. Tangasa religion is, thus, animism of Shamanist type.

The Naga society is represented by the Noctes and Wanchos of Tirap district. This social group represents typical Naga society. The language is of the Naga group of Tibeto-Burman class. They practice the jhum type cultivation. The Chieftains system in form of autocracy is widely prevalent as socio-political institution. The Chieftainship is hereditary. The bachelors' dormitories for the young boys and young girls are well established institutions of their society. The **Morungs**, the boys' dormitories play a major role in the social activities. Head-hunting was prevalent in this social group. In the Morungs all collection of human skulls were exhibited as war trophies. Tattoo was a social custom. A bride before marriage gets her slender calves and thighs designed with tattoos. The tattoos are also applied on the navel, chin, and forehead of the ladies. There was a tradition to apply special tattoo on the body of the head-hunter after a successful expeditions.

EDUCATION

Till independence, educational scenario in Arunachal Pradesh was extremely pitiable with only four primary schools with literacy rate below one per cent. Nevertheless, a humble start was made right from the first five year plan despite, formidable constrictions like inaccessibility of territory, widespread ignorance among people and customary dependence on children for domestic and fieldwork etc. Amazingly, census record reveals epoch-making growth of literacy rate of the state with 7.23 per cent in 1961, 11.29 per cent in 1971, 20.79 per cent in 1981, 41.59 per cent in 1991, 54.74 per cent in 2001 and 65.38 per cent in 2011 respectively. The year 1996, has special reason to be committed to memory in the educational history of Arunachal Pradesh. As before it, Education Department under State Ministry of Education took the total responsibilities related to all affairs and levels of education running from Pre-Primary to Higher Education. Consequent upon bifurcation of Education Department of Arunachal Pradesh in January 1996, two important and separate wings under aegis of State Ministry of Education had taken birth in forms of Directorate of Higher & Technical Education and Directorate of Secondary Education respectively. The Directorate of Higher & Technical Education of Arunachal Pradesh is the Nodal Agency sponsored and activated by Ministry of Education, Govt. of Arunachal Pradesh to administer Higher Education of the state.

Occupying the apex of educational position, Arunachal Pradesh has lone but, central University namely, Rajiv Gandhi University (RGU). RGU came into existence in 1984 as State University which was then called as 'Arunachal University'. However, it got status of central University and subsequently renamed as 'Rajiv Gandhi University' in 2007. It has only one deemed University called as North Eastern Regional Institute of Science and Technology (NERIST) established in 1984. Unfortunately, it has still no State University in her account.

State Govt., has many degree colleges. These degree colleges are namely—Jawaharlal Nehru College (JNC), Dera Natung Government College (DNGC), Indira Gandhi Government College (IGGC), Bomdila Government College (BGC), Rang-Frah Government College (RFGC), Donyi Polo Government College (DPGC), Wangcha Rajkumar Government College (WRGC), Government College Yachuli (GCY), Government College Nyapin (GCN) and Government College Seppa (GCS) offering under graduate courses in B.A, B.Com and B.Sc respectively. Jawahar Lal Nehru College is the oldest Govt. degree college which had established dates back to 1964.

ECONOMY

The economy of Arunachal Pradesh is predominantly agrarian. Agriculture and allied activities have overriding importance as a source of livelihood to the people of Arunachal Pradesh. About 77.1% of the people of the State live in rural areas and their farming system is basically at subsistence level. Agricultural yields are low, while traditional farming, with a shrinking jhum cycle, has become ecologically unsustainable. The land is mostly owned by the community. Subsistence nature of farming coupled with modern consumption structure is the driving force behind the changing economic institutions in Arunachal Pradesh. The rural-urban migration, due to pull factors in the state, has resulted in substantial increase in employment in service sector. Thus, the process of modernization has led to the transformation of the traditional economic institutions in the State. There is no agricultural surplus and limited capital formation and entrepreneurial skills. Despite varied programmes by the State and Central Governments, self sufficiency in foodgrains remains unattainable in the foreseeable future. Heavy imports of food grains and basic primary products have drained away the financial resources of the State. In terms of per capita State Domestic Product and other development indices such as power, road length, Arunachal Pradesh ranks below national average. The State is confronting unique economic problems arising out of remoteness and poor connectivity, hilly and inhospitable terrain, a weak financial resource base, poor infrastructure, sparse population density and poor and limited marketing network and credit institutions.

Although Arunachal Pradesh started with an initial advantage of having high per capita income during 1990s, the State is now lagging behind steadily compared to all India average. Arunachal Pradesh has been growing at very slow pace and requires huge public and private investments to accelerate the development process. The poverty level is much higher than the national average. The low per capita income, lower growth rate of income and higher poverty ratio is a cause of concern. The Primary and Secondary Sectors continue to be overwhelmed by the Tertiary Sector.

Arunachal Pradesh is one of the Special Category States and is largely dependent on Central Assistance for Plan investment as the scope of internal mobilization of resources is limited in Arunachal Pradesh in view of low tax base. Therefore, the prime mover of the growth of the economy has been the flow of funds from the Centre. The State's economy is characterized by persistent stringent financial situation marked by a very low level of State's own resources co-existing with high level of borrowing. The growing fiscal gap has put severe strains on the economic system. Starting with a poor base and getting further heated in the process of growth; the economy of Arunachal Pradesh is beset with scarcities of resources. The regulatory measures have failed to save the economy from extreme difficulties like debt-servicing liability and debt trap. The fiscal vulnerability of the economy of the State is a consequence of low economic activity, absence of private sector and the disproportionate fiscal burden on the public sector of generating and maintaining economic activity. The low population density and poor infrastructural facility in the State is the primary bottleneck to enhance the scope of taxation and hence very limited. The most part of the State population lives in scattered villages away from the mainstream and their integration and involvement into the market economy is still a far cry. The economy being mainly agrarian in character, the scope for taxation in rural areas is basically nil.

Vast natural resources, particularly enormous hydropower potential, oil and natural gas, tourism and tourism sector offer a strong advantage to transform this strategically located State into one of the richest States of the country. And yet, on analysis of present economy of the State, following paradoxical and striking features emerge:

- Vast natural resources and potential for growth in agro-forestry and horticultural sectors, exotic flora etc.
- A bio-diversity hot spot.
- Tremendous hydropower and tourism potential.
- Rich heritage of traditional handlooms and handicrafts
- The reserves of mineral resources are capable of supporting industries like Fertilizer plants, refractory units based on dolomite, Calcium carbide manufacturing units and cement plants, Gasification and coking plants based on coal deposits.

Despite above added advantages, Arunachal Pradesh continues to remain poorest of the poor State with poor and inadequate basic infrastructure, low economic growth and poor resource base. However, it is expected that the economy of the State will flourish once hydropower projects being executed both by Public Sector Undertakings and Private Power Developers, commissioned by 2015.

POWER

Arunachal Pradesh is bestowed with hilly terrain and there is abundant rainfall and thus has vast potential for harnessing power from the rivers and their tributaries for developing hydroelectric power by constructing large, small, mini and micro power projects. The Department of Hydropower Development, Arunachal Pradesh is wholly entrusted with the design, construction, operation and maintenance of the Power Projects in the State. The Hydro power potential estimated in the State from the mega hydro electric projects is around 58676.40 MW and an additional 2000 MW hydropower potential is assessed from micro/mini/small hydro electric projects. However, the present domestic power scenario in the State is far from bright. The State is largely dependent on the power from the micro/mini/small hydels stations now besides supplements from the DG sets and Central sector power. The present installed capacity is only about 56.54 MW under State Sector due to slow pace of development of Micro/Mini/Small hydro projects mainly attributable to resource constraints with the State. The State is still having shortfall in power supply of 53.31 MW and the present average energy consumption per capita in the State is only 300 units which is far below the National Average of about 704 units.

Arunachal Pradesh Energy Development Agency (APEDA)

The Arunachal Pradesh Energy Development Agency is the nodal agency for all the programmes and schemes which are connected with Renewable and Non-conventional Energy Sources sponsored by the Ministry of New and Renewable Energy (MNRE). APEDA is provided with grants-in-aid by the Govt. of Arunachal Pradesh to meet its expenditure on Direction and Administration, Maintenance of Assets and also to meet the State share of Centrally Sponsored Schemes of IREP and NRSE.

TRANSPORTATION

Air

Switchbacks in the Himalayas

Itanagar Airport, a Greenfield project serving Itanagar is being planned at Holongi at a cost of ₹ 6.50 billion. The existing state owned Daporijo Airport, Ziro Airport, Along Airport, Tezu Airport and Pasighat Airport are small and are not in operation. The government has proposed to operationalise these airports. Before the state was connected by roads, these airstrips were originally used for the transportation of food.

Roads

Arunachal Pradesh has two highways: the 310 km National Highway 52, completed in 1998, which connects Jonai with Dirak, and another highway, which connects Tezpur in Assam with Tawang. As of 2007, every village has been connected by road thanks to funding provided by the central government. Every small town has its own bus station and daily bus services are available. All places are connected to Assam, which has increased trading activity. An additional National Highway is being constructed following the Stillwell Ledo Road, which connects Ledo in Assam to Jairampur in Arunachal. Work on the ambitious 2,400 km two-lane Trans-Arunachal Highway Project announced by the then Prime Minister Manmohan Singh on 31 January 2008 on his maiden visit to the state, was scheduled to be completed by 2015-16 but now due to political and social reasons it may take another decade.

In 2014, two major highways were proposed to be built in the state: East-West Industrial Corridor Highway, Arunachal Pradesh in the lower foot hills of the state and 2,000 kilometre (1,200 miles) long Mago-Thingbu to

Vijaynagar Arunachal Pradesh Frontier Highway along the McMahon Line, alignment map of which can be seen.

Railway

Arunachal Pradesh got its first railway line in late 2013 with the opening of the new link line from Harmuti on the main Rangpara North-Murkongselak railway line to Naharlagun in Arunachal Pradesh. The construction of the 33 kilometre 1,676 mm (5 ft 6 in) broad gauge railway line was completed in 2012, and the link became operational after the gauge conversion of the main line under Project Unigauge. The state capital Itanagar was added to the Indian railway map on 12 April 2014 via the newly-built 20 kilometre Harmuti-Naharlagun railway line, when a train from Dekargaon in Assam reached Naharlagun railway station, 10 kilometres from the centre of Itanagar, a total distance of 181 kilometres.

On 20 February 2015 the first through train was run from New Delhi to Naharlagun, flagged off from the capital by the Indian Prime Minister, Narendra Modi. India plans to eventually extend the railway to Tawang, near the border with China.

ADMINISTRATION

Arunachal Pradesh attained its statehood on 20th February 1987. Arunachal Pradesh is divided into **Twenty Five districts**, each administered by a district collector, who sees to the needs of the local people. Especially along the Tibetan border, the Indian army has considerable presence due to the concern about Chinese intentions. Special permits called **Inner Line Permits** (ILP) are required to enter Arunachal Pradesh through any of it checkgates on its border with Assam. The districts of Arunachal Pradesh are: **Tawang**, **West Kameng**, **East Kameng**, **Papum-Pare**,

Districts and their Headquarters

S. No.	District	Head-quarters	S. No.	District	Head-quarters
1.	Tawang	Tawang	14.	Papum-Pare	Itanagar
2.	West Kameng	Bomdila	15.	Upper Siang	Yingkiong
3.	East Kameng	Seppa	16.	Anjaw	Hawai
4.	Lower Subansiri	Ziro	17.	Longding	Longding
5.	Upper Subansiri	Daporijo	18.	Namsai	Namsai
6.	West Siang	Along	19.	Kra Daadi	Jamin
7.	East Siang	Pasighat	20.	Siang	Pangin
8.	Lohit	Tezu	21.	Lower Siang	Likabali
9.	Lower Dibang Valley	Roing	22.	Kamle	Raga
10.	Upper Dibang Valley	Anini	23.	Pakke-Kessang	Lemmi
11.	Kurung Kummey	Laying Yangte	24.	Lepa Rada	Basar
12.	Tirap	Khonsa	25.	Shi-Yomi	Tato
13.	Changlang	Changlang			

Lower Subansiri, **Upper Subansiri**, **East Siang**, **West Siang**, **Upper Siang**, **Dibang Valley**, **Lower Dibang Valley**, **Lohit, Changlang**, **Tirap**, **Kurung Kumey, Anjaw, Namsai, Kra Daadi, Siang, Lower Siang, Kamle, Pakke-Kessang, Lepa Rada and Shi-Yomi.** It also has 45 sub divisions, 99 blocks and 188 circles. Under the unicameral legislature system, it has 60 seats of legislative assembly. The state is represented in the Lok Sabha by two members and one member in the Rajya Sabha.

ARTS & CRAFTS

Sl.No.	Name of District	Items
1.	Tawang/West Kameng	Carpet, Tangka Painting Painted Musk, Wooden Statue, Driff wood
2.	East Kameng/Kurung/Kumey/ Lower/Subansiri/PapumPare/ Upper Subansiri/West Siang/ East Siang/Upper Siang/ Lower Dibang Valley	Cane & Bamboo articles like—Egin (Ladies Backsack), Tali (Gents Backsack), Murah, Cane furniture, decorative Items and domestic used Items
3.	Lohit/Dibang Valley	Silversmithy Like – Ladies traditionally decorated headgear, Earring etc. Cane & Bamboo items
4.	Changlang/Tirap	Wooden Statue, Carpet, and Cane & Bamboo Items – furniture, domestic used Items and decorative item etc.

FAIRS & FESTIVALS

Sr. No.	District	Headquarter	Festivals	Date & Month (Approx.)
1.	Tawang	Tawang	Losar (Monpas)	11 February
2.	West Kameng	Bomdila	Losar (Monpas) Khan (Mijis)	11 February February/March
3.	East Kameng	Seppa	Nyokum (Nishi) Gomkum Gompa (Sulungs)	26 February 15 April
4.	Lower Subansiri	Ziro	Boori Boot (Hill Miris) Nyokum (Nishi) Dree (Apatanis)	6 February 26 February 5 July
5.	Upper Subansiri	Daporijo	Si-Donyi (Tagins) Boori Boot (Hills Miris) Mopin (Adis)	6 January 6 February 5 April
6.	West Siang	Along	Si-Donyi (Tagins) Solung (Adis)	6 January 1 September

7.	East Siang	Pasighat	Aran (Adis)	7 March
			Mopin (Adis)	5 April
			Solung (Adis)	1 September
8.	Lohit	Tezu	Tamladu (Taraon &	15 February
			Kamman Mishmis)	15 April
			Sangken (Khampti)	14 February
			Shapawng Yawng	
			Mannu Poi (Singpho)	
9.	Dibang Valley	Anini	Reh (Idu Mishmis)	1 February
			Solung (Adis)	1 September
10.	Tirap	Khonsa	Oriah (Wanchos)	16 February
			Chalo-Loku (Noctes)	25 November
11.	Changlang	Changlang	Mol (Tangsas)	April
12.	Papum Pare	Itanagar	Nokum (Nishing)	26 February
13.	Upper Siang	Yingkiong	Mopin	5 April
			Solung	1 September

DANCES

Tribal dances expressing the various elements of nature and human emotions is a classic example of cultural efflorescence of this state.

Apart from the monastic dance performed by the lamas during the Torgya festival, the Monpas have extremely attractive traditional dances. The dancers wear masks, which have a human, an animal or a bird face and through their rhythmic movements and gestures they depict some mythical stories. They use musical instruments like trumpets, drums, cymbals, clarion and conch shell.

Aji Lhamu Dance

One of the most prominent of the traditional dances, this dance drama is performed during `Losai' festival. The five people who perform it represent Gueli, the Chief protagonist, Nyapa and Nyaro the autogonists and Lhamu and Lhum the female characters.

Yak Dance

This dance celebrates the joy of the discovery of yak many hundreds of years ago. It is quite interesting to note that the importance of yak in the life of the people is completely realized. The yak has a major role in the prosperity and economy of people with its multi-purpose use.

Lion and Peacock Dance

This dance displays the story of saint Tenteling who performed an extremely difficult fast and meditation of the mythical mount Gangikarpo in the Himalayas for three years. The two snow lions that lined in the ridges of the mountain and witnessed this severe and pions life of the saint befriended him and offered him milk and their company. Overjoyed by this strange relationship between man and animals the people danced. And till today the people perform this dance on every important occasion for they know peace and prosperity comes when there is a harmony between all living neatness of the world.

The Ponung Dance

This dance of the Minyong group of Adis is performed especially on the occasion of the solung festival. The priest called Miri rattles an ancient sword and sings legends.

The Popi Dance

Similar to Ponung but is performed on the occasion of Mopin, festival of the Galos. The dancers wear white dresses and elaborate headgear of straw.

The Dishang Dance

It is performed by the men folk. It is a community dance using sticks.

The Tapu Dance

It is an interesting martial dance, performed with long swords, vigorous cries and rapid movements.

PLACES OF RELIGIOUS AND HISTORICAL IMPORTANCE

Malinithan

Malinithan a Pilgrimage center for Hindu located at Likabali, headquarters of sub-division of West Siang District. Ruins of a big temple belonging to 14th–15th century include sculptures of Indra, Airavanta, Surya, Nandi Bull, Akashi-Ganga waterfalls etc. 5 km away from Malinithan a bathing Ghat is located where people take a holy bath.

Tawang

The district headquarters of Tawang District is situated at a distance of 180 km from Bomadila. The place is easily approachable by road from Bomadila. The place is famous for the 300-year-old Budhist monastery.

Parshuram Kund

Parshuram Kund is a Hindu pilgrimage centre situated on the Brahmaputra plateau in the lower reaches of the Lohit River and 21 km north of Tezu in Lohit district of Arunachal Pradesh. Dedicated to sage Parshuram, the popular site attracts pilgrims from Nepal, from across India, and from nearby states of Manipur and Assam. Over 70,000 devotees and sadhus take holy dip its water each year on the occasion of Makar Sankranti, in the month of January.

Religious Importance: It is a shrine of all-India importance located in the lower reaches of the Lohit River. Thousands of pilgrims visit the place in winter every year, especially on the Makar Sankranti day for a holy dip in the sacred kund which is believed to wash away one's sins. The legend behind the belief recorded in the Kalki Purana, is that the great sage Parshuram washed away the sins of killing kshatriyas (cause the latter killed Parshuram's father and waged a war against brahmins) as he was a brahmin (cause it is not correct of a brahmin fighting a war or taking up sword), in the waters of Brahma kund.

History: The site of the Parshuram Kund as established by the sadhu was in existence till 1950 when the old site was completely changed by the earthquake that shook the whole of the North-East and the kund was completely covered. A very strong current is now flowing over the original site of the kund but massive boulders have in a mysterious way embedded themselves in a circular formation in the river bed thus forming another kund in place of the old.

Tourism: Annual fair is held during Makara Sankranti, to which wild cows, rare fur-rugs and other curios are brought down by the mountain tribes. There are also facilities for trekking from Tezu to glow lake which takes one day, hiking and river rafting and angling on the river Lohit.

Connectivity: The nearest railway station is Tinsukia (120 km) from where buses are available via Namsai. There are also buses available from Sadia. The nearest airports are Tezu and Dibrugarh (Assam).

There are no railway available to Parshuram Kund as of now. A survey of 122 km Rupai-Parshuram Kund broad gauge railway line was complete at the initiative of Arunachal Chamber of Commerce and Industries, while preliminary engineering-traffic survey for the Pasighat-Tezu-Parshuram Kund was conducted by northeast frontier railways at the request of the state government.

Archeological Sites and Monuments in Arunachal Pradesh

Sr. No.	Name	District	Date	Remarks
1.	Vijaynagar	Changlang	18th Cen, A.D.	Khampti Buddhist Stupa excavated
2.	Ahom relics near Phansau Pass	Changlang		
3.	Miao-Bum	Changlang		
4.	Bhismaknagar	Dibang Valley	8th to 17th Cen, A.D.	Ancient Fortress excavated and maintained
5.	Tamreshwari Temple	Lohit	14th to 15th Cen, A.D	Lost under river bed
6.	Shivaling Temple	Lohit	14th to 15th Cen, A.D.	Excavated and Shivalinga re-installed
7.	Mud Fort	Lohit		Explored and Mapped
8.	Padam Pukhuri near Jia & some other parts	Dibang Valley		Partially explored
9.	Agom Pukhuri	Dibang Valley		Reported
10.	Chidu-Chimiri	Dibang Valley		Under Excavation
11.	Rajgor Ali	East Siang		Under Survey
12.	Brick Structures near Rani Village	East Siang		Partially Explored
14.	Malinithan	West Siang	9th to 10th Cen. A.D	Temple, site in A.P.
15.	Itanagar	Papum Pare		Brick Structures
16.	Borgong	Kameng		Stone sculptures reported
17.	Dikkalmukh	Kameng		Brick Structures reported
18.	Bhalukpong West	Kameng		Brick structures, destroyed in road building
19.	Dirang Dzong	West Kameng		Largest Monastery in India and Fort
20.	Tawang Monastery	Tawang		Archive of historical importance
21.	Zimithang Chorten		17th to 18th Cen, A.D.	Largest Chorten (Stupa in AP)

There are 11 wild life sanctuaries and also two national parks where a variety of wildlife animals and birds could be sighted. Prominent among them include elephants, tiger, gaur, musk deer, clouded leopard, red panda, Himalayan black bear, crapped langur, hillock, gibbon, hornbills, peacock, pheasants, florican, and host of other migratory birds. The State is famed for 50 species of orchids.

The wild life sanctuaries are:

1. Pakhuri
2. Eagles' nest
3. Itanagar
4. Dr Daying Ering Memorial
5. Mehao
6. Tale
7. Kamalang Memorial
8. Kane
9. Dibang
10. Sesa Orchid Memorial
11. Yordi Rabe Supse

The National Parks are:

1. Namdapha
2. Mouling

ADVENTURE TOURISM

Arunachal Pradesh is endowed with thick evergreen forests with numerous streams, rivers and gorges and hundreds of thousands of species of flora and fauna covering more than 60% of the total area. The five rivers of the state namely Kameng, Subansiri, Lohit, Siang and Tirap wind their way through the syluen green of the hills. Its rivers are ideal for angling, boating and rafting and its terrain is suitable for trekking, hiking and holidaying in a serene atmosphere. The upper reaches offer an ideal landscape for promoting adventure tourism of all kinds and is the best suited for tourist, looking for such opportunities.

Four major trekking routes have been identified by the Government namely:

1. Pasighat–Jengging–Yinkiong,
2. Bhalukpung–Bomdila–Tawang
3. Roing–Mayudia–Anini
4. Tezu–Hayuliang

Pasighat-Jengging-Yinkiong

This trek starts from the plains of Siang and leads through the thick forest area. The route is a photographer's delight and also a promising tract for catch and release mahaseer angling.

Bhalukpung-Bomdila-Tawang

This route passes through the Tipi orchidarium to Bomdila. It crosses the crest of the Sela pass at 14,000 ft. above sea level which runs through a small ridge and along a placid lake called the Paradise lake. All through the way, the Kameng river roaring down the hill provides excellent scope for angling, trekking and hiking.

Roing-Mayudia-Anini

This trekking route located in the Dibang valley district with its highest peak at Mayudia (2443 mts) on the way to Anini, has a picturesque beauty with a unique photography, floral and faunal diversity and a favourable natural setting. The main tourist trekking spots are Mehao lake sanctuary and boating in Salley lake.

Tezu-Hayuliang

The hills in the Tezu-Hayuliang route are rich in flora and fauna. A large number of migratory species of birds visit this region from the Sino-Himalayan area during the winter. The route is ideal for hiking, trekking and bird watching.

NATURAL TOURISM

Gekar Sinyi (Ganga lake) : Ganga lake situated in the foothills of the Himalayas is a unique part of the capital, Itanagar. The lake locally known as Geuar Sinyi (confined water) abounds in natural beauty with an Unpolluted healthy environment. The lake is surrounded by land mass and hard rock with slopes varying from 100 to 600. These hill slopes support a dense semi-evergreen type of forest consisting many interesting plant species which are academically and economically important.

Talley Valley : Tale in Apatani dialect is the name of a plant and to many other tribes the work means paradise. Talley valley is 30 km from Hapoli (Ziro) the densely populated township in the Apatani Plateau and the headquarters of Lower Subansiri district. It is a picturesque little township with the local population growing paddy, which is the main agricultural produce in terraces. The concept of paddy-cum-pisci-culture has attracted people and the practice is flourishing. The water management system for the paddy fields is remarkable. The lush green paddy fields in terraces makes it more attractive and a very soothing sight which gives the essence of Eco-tourism.

Pangang-Tang-Tso Lake : 17 km away from Tawang, the Pangang-Tang-Tso lake looks straight out of a picture postcard or perhaps straight out of the master painter's canvas. For God changes its hue with the seasons. It is blue on a clear day, Coyly hidden under the mists on the rainy days, surrounded by flowers of all colours in October and Stark white with snow in the winter.

Sangetsar Lake : It is located at 42 km. from Tawang. The lake was formed during the earthquake of 1950. It has bare trees standing like guards in vigil. A reflection of the azure sky, the lake is beautiful like a samaritan's soul and captivating like a gypey's eye.

Bagga-Tang Lake : At the distance of 10 km away from Sela Top diversion is the Bagga-Tang lake. The stories of mystical sights like candle burning in the nights, apparitions of gompa, gold coins and jewels makes the place more alluring.

Gorichen Lake : The highest in the region, the towering Gorichen Park has fascinated the minds of many mountaineers to scale its height of 22500 feet. At a distance of 164 km from Tawang, it is ideal for mountaineering expeditions.

Sela Pass and Peak : At a height of 13714 feet the pass meets the traveller on his way to Tawang and marks the beginning of the district. With its two lakes and tiny flowers of enchanting shades the Sela Pass fills one with escatsy.

Nuraneng Waterfalls : About 42 kms. from Tawang and 2 km. from Tang, the administrative circle, is enticing beauty of milky white water, which is thunderous and enthralling like an oration.

Babteng-Kang (BTK) Waterfalls : People say that watching its beauty even the sun lingers wistfully here, creating rainbows across the waterfalls. And the sound of water revels melodic song.

TRAVEL CIRCUITS

This circuit takes the visitors to the seventeenth century Tawang Monastery built on a jutting spur over looking the wide Tawang Valley at a height of 10,000 ft. The monastery is a vast complex of 65 building housing Lamas and antique scriptures written in gold letters. The route traverses through Nuranang, which offers snow and rainbow trout fishing.

There are seven Travel Circuit approved by the Government of Arunachal Pradesh:

1. **Pasighat-Jengging-Yenkiang :** The circuit starts from Pasighat the district Head quarter of East Siang District, the oldest administrative center of erstwhile North Eastern Frontier Area (NEFA). The circuit comprises with numerous beautiful destinations, lofty mountain with snow clad peaks and rivers. The circuit offers natural tourism, adventure tourism and cultural tourism. The Namdapha National Park also comes within the circuits. The Circuit is also famous for its Arts & Crafts; woolen carpets of various design are produced by Tibetan Refugees, they are well known.

2. **Roing-Mayudia-Anini :** The Circuit starts at Roing, the District Headqaurter of Dibang Valley. Mayudia, is located approximate 56 km from Pasighat. Places of Interest in and around are Bhismarknagar, Salley Lake, Mehao Lake. The nearest railhead is Tinsukia which links the circuits with other parts of the country.
3. **Tezpur–Bomdila-Tawang :** The circuit is very famous for its Buddhist monasteries. The route transverse through Naurang which offers snow clad and rainbow trout fishing. Sela Pass runs through high altitude lake viewing crystal blue colour. Another important destination along the route is Tipi, which is famous for orchidarium, and Botanical Garden. The circuit also offers several waterfalls on the bank of River Kameng. The circuit encompasses through Bhalukpong, Tipi, Chessa, Bomdila, Dirang, Sela Pass, and Jaswant Garh,
4. **Tinsukia-Tezu-Hayuliang :** This circuit starts at Tinsukia, a railhead in Assam and also a major urban center in Upper Assam, leading to Tezu, Parshuram Kund, and Hayuliang in the Lohit Districts. The circuit is very important from the religious point of view. Parshuram Kund is famous for its pious believe and organize a mela every year on the day of Makar Sankaranti.
5. **Tezpur-Seijo (Pakhui)-Bhalukpong-Tipi-Tezpur :** This circuit is considered as inter-state travel circuit, which connects entry point at Tezpur (Assam) to Seijosa and Bhalukpong of Assam. The circuit takes to Pakhui Wildlife Sanctuary, which is one of the largest Wild Life Sanctuary of Arunachal Pradesh.
6. **Margerita-Miao-Namdapha :** This circuit is also an inter-state tourist travel circuit. Margerita, located in Assam, is railhead and also linked with National Highway connects to Namdapha National Wildlife Sanctuary through Miao.
7. **Itanagar-Ziro-Daporijo-Along-Pasighat :** This travel circuit links all major tourist destinations located in central Arunachal Pradesh. Itanagar, the State capital has several places of interest within its vicinity such are; Itafort, Ganga Lake, Jawahar Lal Nehru Museum, Baba Vishwanath Temple, Kali Mandir, Legi Shopping Complex.

ARUNACHAL PRADESH AT A GLANCE

- Population of State (2011 Census)
  Approximate Population : 13.84 Lakhs
- Actual Population : 1,383,727
- Males : 713,912

- Females : 669,815
- Literate Persons : 766,005
- Literacy Rate : 65.4%
- Male Literacy : 72.6%
- Female Literacy : 57.7%
- Sex Ratio : 938 females to 1000 males
- Population Growth : 26%
- Percentage of total Population : 0.11%
- Density/km^2 : 17
- Density/mi^2 : 43
- Area km^2 : 83,743
- Area mi^2 : 32,333
- Total Child Population (0-6 Age) : 212,188
- National Parks : Namdapha, Mouling
- Main Rivers : Siang, Kameng, Subansiri, Kamla, Siyum, Dibang, Lohit, Noa-Dihing, Kamlang, Tirap
- No. of Districts : 25
- No. of Sub-Divisions : 45
- No. of Blocks : 99
- No. of Circles : 188
- Names of the Districts :
  - Tawang
  - West Kameng
  - East Kameng
  - Papum Pare
  - Lower Subansiri
  - Upper Subansiri
  - East Siang
  - West Siang
  - Upper Siang
  - Dibang Valley
  - Lower Dibang Valley
  - Lohit
  - Changlang
  - Tirap
  - Kurung Kumey
  - Anjaw.
  - Longding
  - Namsai
  - Kra Daadi
  - Siang
  - Lower Siang
  - Kamle
  - Pakke-Kessang
  - Lepa Rada
  - Shi-Yomi
- Major Towns :
  - Itanagar
  - Naharlagun
  - Tawang
  - Bomdila
  - Rupa
  - Bhalukpong
  - Seppa
  - Ziro
  - Daporijo
  - Along
  - Pasighat
  - Yingkiong
  - Roing
  - Tezu
  - Namsai
  - Khonsa

OBJECTIVE QUESTIONS

1. Area of the Arunachal Pradesh is
   A. 80,000 sq. km. B. 83,743 sq. km.
   C. 75,875 sq. km. D. None of these
2. How many districts are in Arunachal Pradesh?
   A. 25 B. 25
   C. 30 D. None of these
3. In Lok Sabha, total number of seats reserved for Arunachal Pradesh are
   A. 5 B. 6
   C. 4 D. None of these
4. In Rajya Sabha, Arunachal Pradesh has ....
   A. 2 seats B. 1 seat
   C. 3 seats D. None of these
5. Arunachal Pradesh Legislative Assembly consists of
   A. 60 members B. 40 members
   C. 50 members D. 120 members
6. Capital of Arunachal Pradesh is
   A. Itanagar B. Bomdila
   C. Ziro D. None of these
7. Headquarter of the Tirap district is
   A. Changlang B. Khonsa
   C. Hawai D. None of these
8. What is the name of the headquarter of Lohit district ?
   A. Along B. Anini
   C. Tezu D. None of these
9. Headquarter of the Papumpare district is
   A. Itanagar B. Roing
   C. Daporijo D. None of these
10. Name of the National Highways which passes through the Arunachal Pradesh are
    A. NH-52 and NH-153 B. NH-50 and NH-75
    C. NH-25 and NH-60 D. None of these
11. According to 2011 census, total population of Arunachal Pradesh is
    A. 13,83,727 B. 11,90,300
    C. 16,90,190 D. None of these
12. According to 2011 census, decadal growth (2001-2011) of population of Arunachal Pradesh is

A. 26.03%
B. 20.15%
C. 30.63%
D. None of these

13. Percentage of Urban Population (2011 census) in Arunachal Pradesh is

A. 25.35%
B. 35.25%
C. 22.9%
D. None of these

14. According to 2011 census, percentage of scheduled tribe's population in Arunachal Pradesh is

A. 74.2%
B. 68.8%
C. 54.2%
D. None of these

15. According to 2011 census, percentage of scheduled caste's population in Arunachal Pradesh is

A. 20%
B. 10%
C. 40%
D. None of these

16. According to 2011 census, total literacy rate in Arunachal Pradesh is

A. 65.4%
B. 50.30%
C. 75.30%
D. None of these

17. Female literacy rate in Arunachal Pradesh is

A. 57.7%
B. 73.30%
C. 33.30%
D. None of these

18. Male literacy rate in Arunachal Pradesh is

A. 72.6%
B. 64.2%
C. 78.8%
D. None of these

19. According to 2011 census, density of population in Arunachal Pradesh is

A. 217 square km
B. 113 square km
C. 17 square km
D. None of these

20. According to 2011 census, sex ratio in Arunachal Pradesh is

A. 938
B. 900
C. 1122
D. None of these

21. State Bird of Arunachal Pradesh is

A. Hornbill
B. Mithun
C. Parrot
D. None of these

22. Arunachal Pradesh is situated on latitude between

A. 26°30′N and 29°30′N
B. 36°30′N and 39°30′N
C. 19°30′N and 29°30′N
D. None of these

23. Arunachal Pradesh is situated on longitude between

A. 81°31′E and 91°31′E
B. 91°37′E and 97°30′E
C. 71°30′E and 81°30′E
D. None of these

24. In which district Namdhapa National Park is situated?
A. Tirap
B. East Siang
C. Lohit
D. None of these

25. In which district Mouling National Park is situated?
A. Lohit
B. West Siang
C. East Siang
D. None of these

26. Rajiv Gandhi University was established in
A. 1980
B. 1984
C. 1990
D. None of these

27. Solung Festival is associated with
A. Galos
B. Adis
C. Tagins
D. None of these

28. Headquarter of West Siang district is
A. Tezu
B. Along
C. Seppa
D. None of these

29. Arunachal Pradesh Mineral Development and Trading Corporation Limited was setup in
A. 1991
B. 1995
C. 1996
D. None of these

30. Recorded forest area of Arunachal Pradesh is
A. 10,178 km^2
B. 31,826 km^2
C. 66,964 km^2
D. None of these

31. In which year Arunachal Pradesh became the 24th State of Indian Union?
A. 1987
B. 1997
C. 1980
D. None of these

32. Former name of Arunachal Pradesh was
A. North West Frontier Agency (NWFA)
B. North East Frontier Agency (NEFA)
C. North Frontier Agency (NFA)
D. None of these

33. Kane wildlife sanctuary is situated in
A. West Siang District
B. East Kameng District
C. Lohit District
D. None of these

34. Longest National Highway of Arunachal Pradesh is
A. NH-52
B. NH-153
C. NH-150
D. None of these

35. State Animal of Arunachal Pradesh is
A. Mithun
B. Elephant
C. Horse
D. None of these

36. Highest peak in Arunachal Pradesh is
A. Kangte Peak
B. Eastern Gorichen Peak
C. Nyegi Kangsang Peak
D. None of these

37. Which of the following is not a bordering country of Arunachal Pradesh?
A. Myanmar
B. Bhutan
C. China
D. Bangladesh

38. Name of the first governor of Arunachal Pradesh is
A. R.D. Pradhan
B. Bhisma Narain Singh
C. D.D. Thakur
D. None of these

39. In Arunachal Pradesh, first general election to the assembly was held in
A. February, 1978
B. February, 1980
C. March, 1990
D. None of these

40. 'Ponung' is a
A. dance of Adis
B. bird
C. animal
D. None of these

ANSWERS

1	2	3	4	5	6	7	8	9	10
B	A	D	B	A	A	B	C	A	A
11	**12**	**13**	**14**	**15**	**16**	**17**	**18**	**19**	**20**
A	A	C	B	D	A	A	A	C	A
21	**22**	**23**	**24**	**25**	**26**	**27**	**28**	**29**	**30**
A	A	B	A	C	B	B	B	A	C
31	**32**	**33**	**34**	**35**	**36**	**37**	**38**	**39**	**40**
A	B	A	B	A	A	D	B	A	A

●●●●●●

3

ASSAM

INTRODUCTION

Assam is the gateway to the north-east, a state known for its breath taking scenic beauty, rarest flora and fauna, lofty green hills, vast rolling plain, mighty waterways and a land of fairs and festivals. It originally included in addition to modern Assam, parts of modern Bengal and modern Bangladesh. The name Assam is of recent origin. In ancient times Assam constituted a part of the land known successively as **Pragjyotisha** or **Pragjyotishpura**, and **Kamarupa**. **Assam** (Axom) or its anglisized version Assam is a comparatively modern name. Opinions on the root of the name vary with one view ascribing its origin to the Bodo word **Ha-Cham** which means "low or level country" and a second view ascribing it to the word **Asama**, meaning "unequalled" or "peerless", and used to denote the Ahoms, a Shan tribe which ruled the land for six centuries from the 13th Century A.D.

Assam is almost separated from central India by Bangladesh. Nagaland, Manipur and Myanmar bound it in the east, west by West Bengal, north by Bhutan and Arunachal Pradesh and south by Meghalaya, Bangladesh, Tripura and Mizoram. It is dominated by the mighty Brahmaputra, one of the great rivers of the world, which not only has a fertile alluvial plain for growing rice, but also is famous for tea.

Assam is known for **Assam tea**, **petroleum resources**, **Assam silk** and for its rich biodiversity. It has successfully conserved the one-horned Indian rhinoceros from near extinction in Kaziranga, the tiger in Manas and provides one of the last wild habitats for the Asian elephant. It is increasingly becoming a popular destination for wild-life tourism and notably Kaziranga and Manas are both World Heritage Sites. Assam was also known for its Sal tree forests and forest products, much depleted now. A land of high rainfall, Assam is endowed with lush greenery and the mighty river Brahmaputra, whose tributaries and oxbow lakes provide the region with a unique hydro-geomorphic and aesthetic environment.

HISTORY

Pre-History and Myths

First reference of Assam (Asom) is found in the epics and the religious legends. The Aryans belonging to the priestly (Brahmin) and warrior classes found their way into Assam in very early times. Numerous places referred in the epics, like Mahabharata, etc. are now identified with sites in this state. Known as '**Kamarupa**' or '**Pragjyotish**' in the period of the Epics, Assam is inhabited by human civilisation since about 2000 BC. The people of Assam consists of the migrants from Burma and China. They settled in Assam after the mongoloid migration. Mongoloids came from Punjab through Bihar and North Bengal. Henceforth, Assam presents a blend of Mongol-Aryan culture. The first known ruler of Assam was **Mahiranga Danava** of Danava dynasty, who was succeeded in turn, in the direct line by Hatakasur, Sambasur and Ratnasur. After them there was a chief named Ghatakasur, the ruler of the Kiratas. He made Pragjyotishpur (the modern Guwahati) his capital, and settled numerous Brahmans at Kamakhya. Narakasur was killed by Lord Krishna of Dwaraka. Narakasur's successor, Bhagadatta, figured in the Mahabharata war leading a vast army against the Pandavas.

Ancient and Modern Assam

Ancient Assam was known as Kamrupa and was ruled by many powerful dynasties. The **Varman dynasty** (350-650 AD) and the **Xalostombho dynasty** led Kamrupa as a strong ancient kingdom. During the rule of the greatest of the Varman kings, **Bhaskarvarman** (600-650 AD), a contemporary of Harshavardhana of Kannauj, the Chinese traveller **Hiuen Tsang** visited the region and recorded his travels. Other dynasties that ruled the region belonged to the Indo-Tibetan groups, such as the Kacharis and Chutias.

Varman dynasty

The first king who ruled over Kamrupa was Pushya Varman (350-380 AD), who was a contemporary of Samudragupta (350-375 AD). He took on the title of Maharajadhiraj and ensured steps to establish Kamrupa as a frontier state. Mahendra Varman, a descendent of Pushya Varman, was the first king of Kamrupa who waged a successful war against the Gupta army and also the first Varman king who performed the Ashwamedha Yagya. The rule of the Varman dynasty found apex in the rule of Bhaskar Varman (594-650 AD), because it is with the rule of Bhaskar Varman, that a new epoch of Assam history opened. Harshavardhan (606-648 AD) was a contemporary of Bhaskar Varman. Harshavardan honoured Bhaskar Varman at a conference held at Kannauj. The dynasty of the Varman kings ended with Bhaskar Varman (650 AD).

Salasthambha dynasty was the next in the line which began with the reign of a chieftain called Salastambha. Among all the kings of the Salastambha dynasty, it was Shri Harshadeva (725-750 AD) who acquitted himself as a good king. After the last king of this dynasty, Tyaga Singh (970-990), it was Brahmapala (990-1010 AD), who opened the door to a new dynasty—the Pala dynasty. Jayapala (1120-1138 AD) was the last ruler of this (Pala) dynasty.

Chutia Kingdom

Chutia king Birpal established the Chutia rule at Sadia in 1189 AD. He was succeeded by ten kings of whom the eighth king Dhirnarayan or Dharmadhwajpal, in his old age, handed over his kingdom to his son-in-law Nitai or Nityapal. Later on Nityapal's incompetent rule gave a wonderful chance to the Ahom king Suhungmung or Dihingia Raja, who annexed it to the Ahom kingdom.

Koch Kingdom

Bishwa Singh (1515-1540 AD) laid the foundation of the Koch dominion in the early part of the 16th century and established his capital in Cooch-Bihar. He was succeeded by his son Malladeva who took the name Naranarayana. His brother Sukladhvaj became his commander-in-chief. He was also called 'Chilarai' or 'Kite King' because of his ability to attack the enemy like a Chila (hawk or Kite). Naranarayan's rule was the most glorious epoch of Koch kingdom. It was during his reign that the Ahoms suffered defeat in 1562 AD. Chilarai also annexed the Kachari kingdom, Manipur, Tripura, Jayantia and Srihatta and extended its boundaries. Naranarayan died in 1584 after a reign of nearly fifty years (1540-1584 AD). During his rule, the power of the Koch kings reached its zenith. Naranarayan's rule is remarkable, for it was during his reign that the Assamese literature and culture flourished, which was inaugurated by Srimanta Sankardeva. After the death of Naranarayan, the Koch kingdom was not able to retain its glory.

Kachari Kingdom

The early part of the 13th century saw the rise of the Kachari kingdom, one of the ancient races of Assam. The powerful kings of the Kachari Kingdom were Jashanarayan, Pratapnarayan, Jamradwaj and Govindchandra. The Kacharis claim descent from Ghatotkacha, the son of Bhima. Towards the end of the 15th century the Kacharis had to surrender their capital Hidimbapur (now Dimapur) and the areas adjoining it to the Ahoms. The third and the final invasion of the Kachari kingdom took place in 1803 AD, when their king Krishna Chandra refused to send back the Moamarias to the Ahom king. The last king of the Kachari kingdom was Gobind Chandra (1813-1830 AD).

Ahom Rule

The 13th century witnessed the advent of the Ahoms, led by their first king Sukafa who was the prince of Monlung of Upper Burma (now Myanmar). In the early 13th century he together with a band of followers settled in the Patkai mountains. In 1228 AD he entered the boundaries of Assam through the Naga Kingdom. He formed his capital at Charaideo in 1253 AD. The base for 600 years of Ahom rule was set up by Sukafa. Sukafa died in 1268 AD. It was Suhungmung's reign (1497-1539 AD) which is counted as one of the most memorable in 600 years of Ahom rule. He assumed the Hindu name Swarganarayan. He was popularly known as Dihingia Raja, because he shifted the Ahom capital to Bokota near Dihing river. He annexed the Chutia and the Kachari territories to the Ahom domains. He created a third class of Ministers: Borgohain, Buragohain and Borpatra Gohain. It was during his reign that the first ever census took place.

The economic scenario of the State was also comprehensively surveyed. During his reign, the Mughals invaded thrice but they could not taste victory. This invasion taught Ahoms the use of gunpower, which was a deviation from the traditional system of warfare which comprised of bows, arrows and swords. The Mughal invasion had another positive effect; the Mughals who were taken as prisoner of war were settled in different areas of Assam. Later on, they came to be popularly known as "Morias". Srimanta Sankardev got full impetus to preach his Vaishnava Dharma during the rule of Swarganarayan. In 1539 AD he died at the hands of a Kachari servant as a result of a conspiracy hatched by his son Suklengmung (1539-1552 AD), who after becoming king, shifted the capital to Gargoan from Bokota which is why he is called 'Gargainya Raja'.

Susengpha, a descendant of Suklengmung, ascended the throne in 1603 AD. He took on the name of Pratap Singh. It was during his time that war between Ahoms and Mughals reached its peak and needless to say that Pratap Singh acquitted himself with full honours and was able to extend the boundaries of the state. He created a new post of **Barphukan** to look after the administration of the areas beyond Kaliabor. The three classes of ministers Buragohain, Borgohain and Borpatra Gohain had their well defined areas to rule and those part of the kingdom which did not fall under their jurisdiction were brought under the control of Barbaruah, a new post created during the rule of Pratap Singh. Momai Tamuli Barbaruah was the first official to hold this post. Pratap Singh tried his level best to upgrade the life of citizens. He also introduced Pyke (common rayat) system. Under this system, people were divided into groups of 1000, 100 and 20, and over groups—officials Hazarika, Saikia and Bora were elected. Creation of other posts like Rohiyal Barua, Jagiyal Gohain, Kajalimukhiya Gohain is also credited to him. For his organizational capability, political acumen and his great wisdom, he is also known as Buddhi Swarganarayan.

Supungmung or Chakradhvaj Singh (1663-1669 AD) was an independent minded king who prepared himself for another fight against the Mughals. He enlisted the help of Lachit Barphukan, who was the son of Momai Tamuli Barbaruah. In August 1667 AD, under the excellent leadership of Lachit Barphukan, the Ahoms were able to get back Guwahati and Pandu. Hearing the news of this defeat Aurangzeb sent a huge force with Ramsingh to attack the Ahom kingdom once again. A fierce battle took place between the Ahoms and the Mughals in 1671 AD at Saraighat. As expected, the Mughals suffered an ignominious defeat. Consequently in the west the Manas river became the demarcation line between the Ahom and Mughal territories and remained so until the British occupation in 1826 AD.

Supatpha or Gadapani who assumed the Hindu name Gadadhar Singh (1681-1696 AD), waged a war against the Mughals which is also famously known as Itakhulir Rann (war of Itakhuli) and captured back Guwahati from the Mughals. He was a Shaivite and to help propagate this form of Hindu worship he built 'Umananda Devaloi' at Guwahati. Gadadhar Singh's eldest son Lai succeeded him. He took on the Hindu name of Rudra Singh (1696-1714 AD) and the Ahom name Sukrumpha. In the honour of the memory of his mother Joymoti, he dug the Joysagar tank. Other architectural monuments and structures accredited to him are Kareng Ghar, stone bridge built over the Namdang river, Kharikatia Ali, Metaka Ali. Rudra Singh gave royal patronage to 'Bihu'. He also created Khels or positions like Khaund, Kotoki, Bairagi, Doloi, Kakoti.

In (1714-1744 AD) Sutanpha, son of Rudra Singh took on the Hindu name of Siva Singh. He became a Shakti worshipper, as he was initiated in the tenets of the Shakti cult by Krishnaram Bhattacharya, who was later on installed as head priest of Kamakhya temple which is situated atop the Nilachal Hills. Siva Singh was a weak person who relied heavily on astrologers which explains the fact that when an astrologer told him that he was in danger of being dethroned, he installed his Queen Phuleswari, who assumed the name Pramateswari (one of the name Durga), as Bor Raj, or chief king, thus engineering the beginning of the end of the Ahom Dynasty. Phuleswari was an orthodox Shakti worshipper who persecuted the Moamoria Mahantas by forcibly making them to take prasad of Durga worship and anointing their foreheads with sacrificial blood. This resulted in the famous Moamoria rebellion. After Phuleswari died in 1731 AD, Siva Singh married her sister Drupadi or Deopadi and made her the next Bor Raja, with the name Ambika. She was the one who constructed the Shiva Dol (temple) at Sivasagar, which is the highest Shiva temple in Assam. It was during her reign that 'Dhai Ali' was constructed at Sivasagar. Gauri Sagar tank and Sivasagar tank were dug at the instruction of 'Bor Raja' Phuleswari and Ambika respectively.

Modern Period

The Assamese had suffered more than enough on account of the Burmese invasion, Moamoria rebellion, downfall of the Ahom kingdom. With the Burmese having reached the doorsteps of the East India Company's borders, the First Anglo-Burmese War ensued, in which Assam was one of the sectors. The war ended with the Treaty of Yandaboo in 1826, which saw the East India Company take control of the Lower Assam and install Purander Singh as king of an independent Upper Assam in 1833. This arrangement only lasted until 1838 when the British annexed most of independent Assam, annexing the remainder the following year.

Under British administration, Assam was made a part of the British Indian province called the Bengal Presidency with its capital at Calcutta. In 1874, Assam was separated from Bengal, and was constituted into a separate province by itself, with its capital in Shillong. In 1905, on the initiative of the British Viceroy of India, Lord Curzon, the province was amalgamated with East Bengal following the partition of Bengal into the west and the east. In 1912, the partition was nullified, and Assam was made a separate province once more. The year 1912 is a memorable year in the annals of Assam history because of three things, which were: (1) Gandhiji's visit to Assam, (2) Strikes by Assam Bengal train service and steamer companies, which were the cause of widespread unrest and (3) After a period of 63 years *i.e.*, in 1912, Assam passed into the hands of a Governor, thus paving the way for a dual administration, which lasted till 1936.

In the post Independence period of India, Assam witnessed several separation of territories. In 1948, NEFA (Arunachal Pradesh) was separated. In 1963 Nagaland was separated. In 1972 Meghalaya and in 1987 Mizoram. The capital of Assam, which was in Shillong in present Meghalaya, had to be moved to Dispur, now a part of an expanding Guwahati.

GEOGRAPHY

Assam (Asom) is one of the seven states of Northeast India. It is situated between 24 to 28 degree North latitudes and 90 to 96 degree East longitudes.

Assam is bounded by Bhutan and Arunachal Pradesh on the north, Meghalaya and Tripura on the south, Manipur, Nagaland and Arunachal Pradesh on the east and Meghalaya and West Bengal and Bangladesh on the west. Assam covers a territory of 78,438 sq km, roughly a fourth of it comprising rugged hills and the rest verdant alluvial plains out of which 78,088 sq km is occupied by rural and 485 sq km is occupied by urban areas. The alluvial Brahmaputra valley commands the lion's share of the territory.

Assam is blended with hills and plains.Topographically it can be divided into three distinct zones:

1. Brahmaputra valley or the Brahmaputra plains in the north
2. Karbi Anglong and the North Cachar Hills in the middle, and
3. Barak valley or the Barak plain in the south.

The Brahmaputra valley which is about 500 km in length and 60 km in breadth is the most expansive plain area of the three zones. The Brahmaputra itself is highly braided due to low gradient and tends to form river islands. The largest of them, Majuli (929 sq kms) is said to be the world's largest. The hills of Karbi Anglong and North Cachar and those in and around Guwahati and North Guwahati (along with the Khasi and Garo Hills) are originally parts of the South Indian Plateau system. These are eroded and dissected by the numerous rivers in the region. Average height of these hills in Assam varies from 300 to 400 m. The southern Barak Valley is separated by the Karbi Anglong and North Cachar Hills from the Brahmaputra Valley in Assam. The Barak originates from the Barail Range in the border areas of Assam, Nagaland and Manipur and flowing through the district of Cachar, it confluences with the Brahmaputra in Bangladesh. Barak Valley in Assam is a small valley with an average width and length of approximately 40 to 50 km.

In the valleys of the Brahmaputra and the Barak, the soils are mostly alluvial. In the hill areas the soils are red in colour and they are also acidic. The climatic condition of the plains is quite suitable for the cultivation of the variety of crops, and the climatic condition of the soils in the hill areas are quite suitable for cultivation of certain crops like coffee and rubber.

Majuli Island

Majuli, the largest river island in the world, is a declared a new District. It is located 20 km off Jorhat town. Its length from east to west is about 90 km and width from north to south is average 16 km. Majuli is a natural and cultural heritage site. With water bodies covering most of the areas, Majuli attracts plenty of birds both local & migratory.

Soils

The major soils of Assam belong to **Inceptisols** (49.3%), **Entisols** (32.3%), **Alfisols** (12.3%) and **Ultisols** (6.1%). The most typical characteristics of Assam soil is acidity, where pH of the soils generally ranges between 4.2 to 5.8. Inorganic matter content of majority soils are medium to high. The available N, P_2O_5 and K_2O content of the soils of Assam varies between medium and low. The major soil groups are:

1. new alluvial soil
2. old alluvial soil
3. old mountain valley alluvial soil
4. non-laterised red soil and
5. laterised red soil

MINERALS

Coal, petroleum and natural gas, limestone and minor minerals are produced in Assam. Tertiary coal occurs in North Cachar Hills, Sivasagar and Lakhimpur districts. Assam coal is friable in nature and has a high sulphur content. Local railways, steamers, and hydro power stations mainly utilize it. Low moisture, low volatile cooking coal has been discovered in Hallidayganj Singrimari area. Deposits of banded magnetic quartzite occurs in Kamrup and Goalpara districts, Limestone occurs in Lakhimpur, North Cachar Hills, Karbi Anglong, Nagaon and Sivasagar districts. Kaolin is found in Karbi Anglong and Lakhimpur district. The Digboi oil fields in Lakhimpur district and Moran and Rudrasagar oil fields in Sivasagar district are the major source of oil and gas. Hydrocarbons are struck in Borsilla, Changmaigaon, Kurgaon and Rajgarh in the past. Sillimanite bearing rocks occur in Karbi Anglong district. Assam continued to be the 3rd largest producer of Petroleum (crude) and natural gas in the country amounting to 16% and 8% respectively of the total production of mineral in the country.

Major Minerals of Assam

Oil

Assam is the second place in the world (after Titusville in the United States of America) where petroleum was discovered. Assam is the first state in the country where in 1889 oil was struck at **Digboi**. Assam can boast of having the oldest oil refinery in the country. This refinery set up at Digboi, in Tinsukia district, started commercial production in 1901. The refinery, now belonging to the Assam Division of the Indian Oil Corporation, has a refining capacity of 3 lakh tonnes of petrol, kerosene, diesel and other petroleum products. Most of the oilfields of Assam are located in the Upper Assam region of the Brahmaputra Valley.

The second refinery in Assam was set up at **Noonmati** in Guwahati under the public sector. It started production in 1962. It produces liquified petroleum gas (LPG), petrol, kerosene, diesel, furnace oil, coke, etc.

The third refinery in the region was established at Dhaligaon near **Bongaigaon** in 1962. It is known as Bongaigaon Refinery and Petro-Chemicals Limited (BRPL).

The fourth refinery in the state was established at **Numaligarh** of Golaghat district in 1999, with a refining capacity of 3 million tonnes of oil and other products.

Natural Gas

In Assam, almost all the petroleum producing areas of the Brahmaputra Valley, especially **Naharkatia**, **Moran**, **Lakuwa** and **Rudrasagar**, contains 'associated natural gas'. The important industries so far built up on the basis of the natural gas of Assam are **Namrup Fertilizer Factory**, Namrup Thermal Power Project, Production of Carbon Black, Assam Petrochemicals and Assam Gas Company, which provides liquified petroleum gas for domestic use.

Coal

Assam has large reserves of coal, too. The State is said to contain about 1200 million tonnes of coal reserves. The first coal mining in the region was started in 1865 at the **Makum coal-fields** by the erstwhile Assam Railway and Trading Company and now it is mined by the North-Eastern Coal-Fields. The coal belt extends from **Dilli-Joypur** in the west to **Tipok** in the east. The entire coal in this region is unique in the sense that it is highly volatile (36%-42%), has low ash content (3%-15%) and possesses high crackling index (10%-29%).

Coal is found in **Koilajan**, **Umrangshu**, **Khota-Arda** in the Hills District of Assam and is mined by the Assam Mineral Development Corporation.

Granite

Assam is endowed with granites of variegated colours, ranging from off-white to grey and pink. It is found in central and lower parts of Assam. The grey granite is extensively used in road making and as a railway ballast. So far, it has hardly been exploited for decorative purposes and has great potential.

Limestone and Cement

Limestone is an important mineral which is used in the manufacture of cement, as flux in iron and steel production, and as raw materials for chemical industries. The **Kailajan** and **Dilai** area of Bokajan sub-division have high quality limestone, which is used in the Bokajan Cement Factory. Assam has only one large cement factory in Bokajan, in Karbi Anglong district. It now produces about 1.8 lakh metric tonnes of cement annually. Besides this there are a few mini cement plants in the North Cachar Hills based on limestone produced in the Umrangsho area of Assam.

CLIMATE

With the **'Tropical Monsoon Rainforest Climate'**, Assam is a temperate region and experiences heavy rainfall and high humidity. Pleasant sub-alpine climate prevails in the hills. The plains, however experience tropical climate making them uncomfortably humid especially during the rainy seasons. Winter sets in from around the end of the month of October and lasts till the end of February. The temperature drops to a minimum of 6 to 8 degree celsius, the nights and early mornings are foggy, and rain is scanty. Summer arrives in the middle of May accompanied by high humidity and rainfall. The temperature reaches a maximum of 35 to 38 degree celsius. The frequent rains, however, serve to push the mercury down. The Monsoons blow full blast during the month of June. Thunderstorms known as **Bordoichilla** is a frequent occurrence during the afternoons. Spring and autumn with moderate temperatures and modest rainfall are the best seasons.

The region is also prone to natural disasters. High rainfall, deforestation, and other factors have resulted in annual floods that cause widespread loss of life, livelihood and property. Assam falls in a zone prone to earthquakes. Though mild tremors are familiar to the region, high-intensity earthquakes are rather infrequent. However, they do occur as in 1869 when the bank of the Barak sank by 15 ft, in 1897, and again in 1950 when an earthquake of unprecedented intensity ravaged a large part of the State.

RIVERS

Important rivers of Assam are:

- The Brahmaputra River
- The Disang River
- The Dhansiri River
- The Barak River
- The Buridihing River
- The Jhanji River
- The Subansiri River

Information regarding the sources, the districts through which the rivers flow and name of the major industries on their banks are given in the following Table.

Major River Systems, their Origin and Flow Pattern of Various Rivers of Assam (Asom) State

S. No.	River	Source of the river	Confluence Point	Major Districts on the course of the river	Major industries on the course
1.	The Brahmaputra River	The river flows through Tibet and enter India at Arunachal Pradesh United with several rivers like Dibang, Lohit, Siang, Kundil etc. and flows through the Assam Valley to fall in the Bay of Bengal	Bay of Bengal	Tinsukia, Dibrugarh, Dhemaji, North Lakhimpur, Sivasagar, Jorhat, Golaghat, Sonitpur, Darrang, Nagaon, Kamrup, Barpeta, Goalpara, Bongaigaon, Dhubri	No major industries are situated at the river bank. Guwahati Refinery at Guwahati, Kamrup discharges their treated effluent directly into the river.
2.	The Buridihing River	Arunachal Pradesh	Brahmaputra at Dihingmukh	Tinsukia, Dibrugarh	Coal India Ltd., Margherita; Oil India Ltd., Duliajan; Assam Oil Division, Digboi
3.	The Disang River	Arunachal Pradesh	Brahmaputra at Disangmukh	Dibrugarh, Sivasagar	Brahmaputra Valley Fertilizer, Namrup, Assam Petrochemicals Ltd., Namrup; ONGCL drilling site are located at the site of the river bank.
4.	The Jhanji River	Nagaland	Brahmaputra at Jhanjimukh	Sivasagar, Jorhat	—
5.	The Dhansiri River	Nagaland	Brahmaputra at Dhansirimukh	Golaghat	Numaligarh Refinery (NRL)
6.	The Subansiri River	Arunachal Pradesh	Brahmaputra at Alichiga	Dhemaji, North Lakhimpur	Construction of 2000 MW Natioal Hydroelectric Power Corporation is going on
7.	The Barak River	Manipur	Meghna	Silchar, Karimganj, Badarpur	HPC, Cachar Paper Mill at Panchgram

IRRIGATION

Assam agriculture is primarily rain-fed. However, because of adverse & unpredictable weather condition experienced by the State time-to-time as well as to pursue multiple cropping and modernization of agricultural practices in the state agricultural sector to cope with the growing problem of food shortage due to formidable increase of population, natural calamities etc., irrigation is highly essential in Assam. Over and above, for a sustained development in the agricultural sector availability of assured irrigation facility is undoubtedly the most important pre-requisite. Thus, the importance of irrigation development bears special significance in the context of efforts towards economic development of the State, too.

Land use pattern in Assam indicates that out of the total geographical area of 78.44 lakh hectares, the Gross Cropped Area of Assam is 40.83 lakh hectares (2014-15). Against this, the ultimate irrigation potential *i.e.* the ultimate Gross Irrigation Potential (Annually Irrigable Area) has been estimated at about 27 lakh hectares, which constitutes 64.9 per cent of the Gross Cropped Area. It is planned to irrigate 17 lakh hectares through Minor Irrigation Schemes and 10 lakh hectares through Major and Medium Irrigation Projects out of the Ultimate Irrigation Potential. It is further planned to irrigate 10 lakh hectares through Minor Irrigation Schemes taken up by ground water sources and 7 lakh by surface water sources out of the 17 lakh under Minor Irrigation.

The development programmes for improvement of irrigation facility in Assam taken up under two broad heads, viz., Minor Irrigation and Major & Medium Irrigation. While the Irrigation Schemes are classified as Major, Medium and Minor, they are categorized as Surface Flow, Surface Lift (for Major/Medium and Minor) and Ground Water Lift (for Minor only). Three Departments, viz. Irrigation, Agriculture and Panchayat and Rural Development are associated with development of irrigation facilities in the State. While the State Irrigation Department, being the Nodal Department for development of irrigation in the State, executes and maintains Major, Medium and Minor Irrigation Schemes, the irrigation works of the other two departments are confined to minor irrigation schemes like Shallow Tube Wells, Low Lift Points and Temporary Minor Irrigation Schemes only.

Creation of Irrigated Area and Utilisation of Potential

It is worth mentioning that no works of Irrigation Schemes could be successfully completed under normal State Plan due to low allocation of fund during VIIIth to IXth Plan period. However, since 1996-97 Central Assistance was obtained under Accelerated Irrigation Benefit Programme (AIBP) in respect of Major and Medium Irrigation Sector and subsequently in respect of Minor Irrigation Sector also since 2000-01. Such assistance was also received from other programmes like Non Lapsable Central Pool of Resources (NLCPR), Assam Rural Infrastructure for Agricultural Services Programme (ARIASP) funded by World Bank and subsequently under RIDF-X and RIDF-XI from National Bank for Agriculture and Rural Development (NABARD). With the above sources of funding the position of creation of irrigation potential could be achieved to some extent.

Major and Medium Irrigation Sector

At present, there are 4(four) AIBP funded ongoing Major/Medium Irrigation Projects (Dhansiri I/P, Champamati I/P, Borolia I/P and Buridehing I/P) and all are in different stages of progress.

Name of Major/Medium Irrigation Project

1. Jamuna Irrigation Project
2. Sukla Irrigation Project
3. Dekadong Irrigation Project
4. Kaldiya Irrigation Project
5. Kulsik Irrigation Project
6. Bhumki Irrigation Project
7. Horguti Irrigation Project
8. Kaliabar Lift Irrigation Project
9. Longa Irrigation Project
10. Rupahi Irrigation Project
11. Bordikrai Irrigation Project
12. Hawaipur Irrigation Project
13. Dikhari Irrigation Project

AGRICULTURE

Agriculture and its allied activities played an important role in the socio-economic development of the State of Assam as this sector is the major contributor to the State economy as well as providing livelihood to a significant proportion of the population of the State. About 99 per cent area of total land mass of the State is rural. The net cultivated area of the State is 28.11 lakh hectares which is about 88 per cent of the total land available for agricultural cultivation in the State. The average operational holding is 1.10 hectare only and more than 85 per cent of the farmer family is small and marginal farmers [Provisional figure of 2010-11, Agricultural Census]. It has been observed that the contribution of Agriculture Sector to the State economy [GSDP at constant (2004-05) prices] has been recording gradual fall during the period 2005-06 to 2011-12. The year on year (YOY) analysis also shows that the trend of growth of the Agriculture Sector [GSDP (at constant 2004-05 prices)] was erratic during the same period and finally pegged at 2.4 per cent 2011-12 (Quick estimate). However, Agriculture sector continues to support more than 75 per cent population of the State directly or indirectly providing employment of more than 53 per cent of the total workforce.

The state has six Agro-climatic zones:

1. **Barak Valley Zone:** Cachar, Karimganj, Hailakandi
2. **Hill Zone:** Karbi Anglong, North Cachar Hills
3. **Central Brahmaputra Valley Zone:** Nagaon, Morigaon
4. **Upper Brahmaputra Valley Zone:** Jorhat, Golaghat, Sivasagar, Dibrugarh, Tinsukia
5. **North-bank Plain Zone:** Lakhimpur, Dhemajil, Sonitpur, Darrang
6. **Lower Brahmaputra Valley Zone:** Kokrajhar, Bongaigaon, Barpeta, Goalpara, Dhubri, Kamrup, Nalbari

The agriculture is mainly dependent on rainfall. The State belongs to rainfall belt where rainfall varies from 80 to 1580 mm during different periods of the year. Sufficient rainfall occurs mainly during the Kharif season which is beneficial for growing paddy, the principal crop of the State. Similarly, Jute cultivation also gets sufficient rainfall in pre-monsoon period.

Land Utilization Statistics

The Gross Cropped Area in the State was 40.83 lakh hectare in 2014-15 compared to 41.00 lakh hectare in 2013-14 showing and decline of 0.17 lakh hectare in 2014-15. The, area sown more than once has decreased from 12.80 lakh hectare in 2013-14 to 12.55 lakh hectare in 2014-15 while net cropped area increased from 28.20 lakh hectare in 2013-14 to 28.27 lakh hectare in 2014-15. Thus the ratio of area sown more than once to the net area sown was 44 per cent during 2014-15 compared to 45 per cent during 2013-14. The ratio of net sown area to gross cropped area, on the other hand, was calculated at 39 per cent during the year 2014-15 compared to 68 per cent during the year 2013-14.

Agricultural Holding

From the available data of the Agricultural Census, 2010-11 it reveals that, there were 27.2 lakh operational holdings in Assam covering an operated area of 29.99 lakh hectares as against 27.5 lakh operational holdings covering an operated area of 30.49 lakh hectares in 2005-06 and 27.1 lakh operational holdings covering an operated area of 31.1 lakh hectares in

2000-01. The decreasing of operated area was caused due to soil erosion of ever widening Brahmaputra River, increasing urbanization, industrialization, expansion of roadways and other infrastructural development activities, conversion of agricultural land to homestead land to accommodate ever increasing population, etc.

HORTICULTURE

Assam is traditionally rich in horticultural production due to its diverse and unique agro-climatic condition which is conducive for growing wide range of horticultural crops like various fruits, vegetables, flowers, spices, nuts, tuber crops and medicinal and aromatic plants. The World citrus belt encompasses Assam within it.

Horticultural crops occupy about 15 per cent of the gross cultivated area of Assam and annually produce more than 67 lakh MT of various horticultural produces besides nut crops, flowers and medicinal & aromatic plants thus contributing significantly towards food and nutritional security of the State. Statistically, according to the Directorate of Horticulture and Food Processing, Assam, the growth rate of production of fruits, spices and vegetables was 19.18 per cent, 6.40 per cent and 72.20 per cent respectively in last ten years. Having enormous inherent potentiality for employment and income generation as well as to sustain this growth, the Directorate targeted to strengthen production of various horticultural crops through area expansion and raising their productivity with the primary objective to transform the horticulture sector in Assam commercially viable. Of let, the efforts of the Directorate of Horticulture and FP helping the horticulture sector of the State limping towards commercialization.

Technology Mission for Integrated Development of Horticulture (TMIDH) in Assam

In spite of diverse and varied soil types and climatic situations ideally suited for growing vast numbers of Horticulture crops, this sector remained unexploited commercially. Keeping this point in view, a centrally sponsored scheme on Technology Mission for Integrated Development of Horticulture now named as "Horticulture Mission for North-East and Himalayan States (HMNEH)" was sponsored by Govt. of India for the N.E. States including Sikkim in 2001-02 considering the potential of Horticulture for socio-economic development of the N.E. States including Assam. Later, scheme was extended to J&K, Himachal Pradesh and Uttarakhand in 2003-04.

The objective of the Scheme is to augment the productivity of horticulture crops through bringing new area under cultivation to have the way for rapid commercialization of this vital sector with precise strategies in the form of

Mini Missions. The specialty of the scheme is comprehensive which encompasses all the issues associated with development of horticulture right from generation of technologies (Mini Mission-I), increasing production and productivity (MM-II), storage and marketing (MM-III) and processing (MM-IV). The impact of implementation of this scheme in the State is gradually emerging in various fronts including products, productivity, infrastructure development, per capita income, commercialization, etc.

Assam Small Farmers Agri-Business Consortium (ASFAC) receives fund from the Government of India who in turn releases fund to the State Horticulture Directorate for MM-II and also MM-III. The Assam State Agriculture Marketing Board (ASAMB) received fund to perform the activities under MM-III.

Consumption of Fertilizer

The trend of fertilizer consumption in the state in terms of nutrient (NPK) per hectare is much lower than the National average consumption. According to the State Agriculture Department consumption of fertilizer in the State was 68.6 kg per hectare during the year 2014-15 compared to 67.09 kg per hectare during the year 2010-11. The reason behind the lesser consumption is that the farmers are reluctant to use fertilizers during Kharif season fearing monetary loss due to heavy rainfall and flood. Moreover, disruption of transport movement fertilizers cannot reach destination in time for delivery to farmers. However, the level of consumption of fertilizer can be increased substantially by making timely availability of fertilizer in this season of the State.

Seed Certification

Assam State Seed Certification Agency (ASSCA) is the Nodal Agency for seed testing & seed certification in the State. ASSCA is entrusted for Seeds Certification of Paddy, Mustard and Pulses as per feasibility in the State. The planting crops like Coconuts, Litchi, Guava, etc. are under consideration for certification. There are 3 nos. of notified Seed Testing Laboratories under ASSCA located at Guwahati, Jorhat and Silchar. Total annual testing capacity of these three notified laboratories is 20,000 seed samples. Seed testing & certification guidelines are strictly followed for proper quality control and certification.

LIVESTOCK, ANIMAL HUSBANDRY AND DAIRY DEVELOPMENT

Assam economy continues to be an agrarian economy as more than 85 per cent of the population is living in the rural areas and about 52 per cent of the total labour force is found to be engaged in agriculture and allied activities. Animal Husbandry sector has significant impact on employment generation in the State and plays a vital role in income generation of both the rural and semi-urban economy. The Animal Husbandry and Veterinary Department of the State has been implementing various developmental programmes to create gainful employment/income opportunities in the rural areas with the objectives to boost up the socio-economic condition of the rural economy and act to enhance the volume of livestock and poultry products in the State to reduce the gap between demand and supply of these products. The Department has laid down the following objectives for improving the status of rural economy:

- To provide health coverage to all the livestock and poultry of any breed/species in respect of contagious and non-contagious diseases.
- To improve livestock generating production viz—milk, egg and meat as well as to improve socio-economic status of the farmers and enhance its contribution to the Gross Domestic Product of the State.

To achieve the goal, the Animal Husbandry and Veterinary Department of the State has been providing animal health care service and breed improvement facilities by setting up different type of veterinary infrastructures which are spread around the State. According to the Animal Husbandry and Veterinary department there are 22 nos. of Veterinary Hospitals, 337 nos. of Dispensaries, 684 nos. of Sub centres/ First Aid centres/ SMC and 30 nos. of Key Village Centres as on 2015.

Trend of Livestock Products in Assam

Item	2011-12	2012-13	2013-14	2014-15	2015-16
Milk (million litres)	838	845	857	873	888
Egg (million nos)	471	471	472	473	474
Meat ('000 tonnes)	34.19	36.63	38.34	42.0	44.81

Source : *Directorate of Animal Husbandry & Veterinary Department, Assam.*

Milk Production

It reveals from the report that the total milk production of the State for the year 2015-16 has been estimated at 888.18 million litres as against estimated production of 829.86 million liters during the year 2009-10. The cattle milk contributes more than 84 per cent of the total milk production during the year. The production of buffalo and goat milk shared, on the other hand, more than 15.0 per cent of the total milk production. While the milk production of Crossbreed Cattle registered a positive growth, the milk production of Indigenous cattle and Buffalo recorded a negative growth over the previous year. The quantity of goat milk production remained more or less at the same level during the year with that of previous year. The per capita/per day milk availability in the State during (2015-16) was estimated at 74 ml, which was remained at the same level compared to per capita/ per day availability of milk during the previous year. The availability of milk per capita/per day in the State during the year was far below the ICMR recommended milk requirement norms of 208 ml per head per day. During the year 2015-16 per capita national availability of milk was 337 grams.

Frozen Semen & Assam livestock Development (ALDA)

The semen station at Khanapara, Guwahati was initiated during 1968-69 under Intensive Cattle Development Project (ICDP). Later the station has been updated in the year 1975-76 under the Indo-Australian Cattle Breeding Project (IACBP) for production of chilled semen till the beginning of 1995-96. In the year 1995-96 under the ARIASP, Khanapara semen station was strengthened with new bulls and equipments for production of Frozen Semen. Of let the process of A.I. by using Frozen Semen to upgrade the local indigenous cattle with the objective to increase milk productivity has been gaining its popularity in the State. ALDA was constituted under the society Act as per guidelines of National Project on Cattle and Buffalo Breeding (NPCBB) and it started functioning from 2004. The main objective of ALDA is to produce good quality semen, to improve training facilities for extending breeding network.

Vaterinary Biological

The Institute of Veterinary Biologicals, Khanapara is producing and procuring vaccines against economically important diseases of animals and birds to fulfill the need of the State. This institute is mainly responsible to make vaccines available in the local dispensaries/ hospitals at free of cost through district network. Beside mass immunization, emphasis has also been given in prevention, diagnosis and treatment if the diseases. Subsequently economically important diseases like Duck Cholera, Duck Plasma, Ranikhet, Swan Fever, F.M.D., etc. prevalent all over the state are also covering by this project.

Dairy Development

The Dairy Development in Assam was initiated in the latter part of the Second Five Year Plan period with the basic concept to develop the Dairy industry in the State through establishment of Town Milk supply scheme almost in all important towns of Assam to feed the consumers hygienic, clean milk at reasonable price. Till February 1982 the Dairy Development activities were carried out by the Director of A.H. & Veterinary Department. To expand the role of Dairy activities in the state economy, the Govt. of Assam created a separate Directorate of Dairy Development bifurcating it from the Animal Husbandry and Veterinary Department during the year 1982. The primary focus areas of Dairy Development, Assam are:

1. Procurement, processing and distribution of milk aiming at economic upliftment of rural milk producers and help urban consumers to get quality milk at a reasonable price.
2. Developing adequate infrastructure to ensure procurement and processing of milk produced in the State.
3. Organising milk producers for efficient procurement, processing and marketing.
4. Awareness among milk producers, traders and consumers regarding clean milk production and consumption.
5. To modernize the supply of inputs like A.I., Feed, Fodder, Animal Health coverage and Training etc. to the Dairy farmers in the milk shed areas linked with Milk Supply Schemes and Milk Plants.
6. To help the villagers in marketing their produce by setting up of suitable transport and marketing organization.

FISHERIES

Fishery sector contributes more than 2% of GSDP to the state economy and plays an important role in providing livelihood to a significant proportion of the population on the state. The state has vast and varied water resources suitable for development of inland fisheries. With about 3.9 lakh hectares of diversified water resources in the form of wetlands; low-lying and derelict water bodies, rivers, ponds & tanks, etc., there are vast opportunity for enhancing the fish production in the State is really great. However, the State yet to attain the level of fish production to meet the growing demands. There is a large gap in between demand for fish and production of fish in the State. The present per capita fish production is 7.8 kg/year which was 6 kg/year during 2001-02. Sustainable utilization of the available water resources will help to generate employment opportunities to thousands of unemployed youth and also contributing towards narrowing the production gap and demand in the State.

Considering the potential of the fishery sector on rural employment, income and livelihood, Government has been making a number of positive interventions for sustainable development of the sector and to meet the ever increasing demand for fish. The focus is on bridging the gap between the demand and supply of fish. Government is also taking various initiatives for conservation and propagation of local fish species including the indigenous fish having ornamental value. The fish seed production and its marketing are also regulated under the provisions of newly framed Assam Fish Seed Rules, 2010 to ensure quality fish seed to the farmers.

Mukhya Mantrir Matsyamitra Asoni Under Fishery Extension Service

Weather and climatic condition during the monsoon months make it difficult for the fishermen to go for fishing. Additionally, for conservation of indigenous fishes in the natural water bodies in Assam, a fishing ban period has been imposed from 1st April to 15th July as per Assam Fishery Rules 1953 and Assam Fishery Rules (Amendment) 2005. Thus, the poor fishermen earning their bread from fishing have to go through a distressed period during this lean season and practically they are left with no means of livelihood during this period.

It is, therefore, proposed to introduce the scheme—"Mukhya Mantrir Matsyamitra Asoni" under State Plan 2011-12 to relieve them from these sufferings. The main objective of the scheme is to provide one-time-financial assistance @ ₹ 10000/- to each fishermen for sustenance during the lean period. The respective District Fishery Development officer of State Fishery Department will select the beneficiaries, who are active fishermen by profession, living below poverty line and who had no other means of sustenance during the lean period.

State Fish Laboratory

A State Fish Laboratory has been established at the Directorate Complex, Guwahati under RKVY for testing of Soil and water quality parameters. Additionally the laboratory will also extend support to farmers for investigation on fish health and hygiene.

Live Gene Bank

Live Gene Bank, a joint venture of Department of Fisheries, Assam and National Bureau of Fish Genetic Research, Lucknow established at Ulubari Fish Seed Farm, Guwahati in 2007 has been continuing. Under this programme, conservation through breeding and propagation of local endangered economically important fish species has been taken up for future use and research. Species like Chital and Pavo has been successfully bred and reared in improved ponds in the farm.

FLORA AND FAUNA

Forest Area

Forestry is a vital sector of the State. The State Forest Department has been entrusted the maintenance and management of Forest, Forest Produce and Wild life in the State. In the recent past the importance of environment protection and conservation of natural resources has been given wide attention at state and national level. As a result various NGO's with the Forest Department has come forward to protect and maintain the Forestry sector of the State. The State of Assam is enriched with extensive forest area and wealth like valuable forest products and also rich with different species and strains of floras and faunas. People of Assam from time immemorial have also depended upon the forests to meet their daily needs.

Forest Cover

The forest cover in the state, as per India State Forest Report 2017, based on interpretation of satellite data, is 28,105 sq km, which is 35.83% of the State's geographical area. In terms of forest canopy density classes, the State has 2,797 sq km very dense forest, 10,192 sq km moderately dense forest and 15,116 sq km open forest.

Wildlife and National Parks & Sanctuaries

The Wildlife Act provided for setting up national parks and sanctuaries for Wildlife. The total Wildlife Protected Areas in the State of Assam is 3925 sq km. The category wise Wildlife Protected Area is as follows:

Area of the National Park and Wildlife Sanctuaries in Assam, (July, 2017)

Name of the National Park	Location (District)	Area in Sq. Km.
Kaziranga National Park	Golaghat, Nagaon & Sonitpur	858.98
Manas National Park	Chirang and Baksa	500.00
Orang National Park	Udalguri and Sonitpur	78.81
Nameri National Park	Sonitpur	200.00
Dibru-Saikhowa National Park	Dibrugarh and Tinsukia	340.00

Wildlife Sanctuaries (WLS)

Name of the Wildlife Sanctuaries	Location (District)	Area in Sq. Km.
Bhejan-Borajan-Padumoni WLS	Tinsukia	7.22
Panidehing WLS	Sivasagar	33.93
Gibbon WLS	Jorhat	20.98
Nambor-Doigurung WLS	Golaghat	97.15
Garampani WLS	Karbi Anglong	6.05
Nambor WLS	Karbi Anglong	37.00
East Karbi Anglong WLS	Karbi Anglong	221.81
Marat Longri WLS	Karbi Anglong	451.00
Burhachapori WLS	Sonitpur	44.06
Laokhowa WLS	Nagaon	70.13
Pabitora WLS	Morigaon	38.80
Sonai-Rupai WLS	Sonitpur	220.00
Barnadi WLS	Udalguri	26.22
Chakrasila WLS	Kokrajhar	45.56
Dihing-Patkai WLS	Dibrugarh and Tinsukia	111.19
Barail WLS	Cachar	326.25
Amchang WLS	Kamrup (Metro)	78.64
Deepor Beel Wildlife Sanctuary	Kamrup (Metro)	4.1
Proposed Wildlife Sanctuaries:		
North Karbi Anglong WLS	Karbi Anglong	96.00
Bardoibam Beelmukh WLS	Lakhimpur	11.25

Source: *Chief Conservator of Forest (WL), Assam.*

Protected Area

The protected area network in Assam includes five (5) National Parks and eighteen (18) Wildlife Sanctuaries covering an area of 3592.94 sq km constituting 4.6 per cent of the geographical area. During 12th five year plan a sum of ₹ 1550.00 lakh was proposed for implementation of development and management schemes for Wildlife National Parks and a sum of ₹ 180.00 lakh was proposed for 2012-13.

Project Tiger

The State has three Tiger Reserves, namely Kaziranga, Manas and Nameri. To ensure conservation of Tiger, Government has further notified the Tiger Conservation Rules, 2010 and Government of India has been requested for direct funding to these Tiger Conservation Foundations. However, most attentive issue is that the Tigers in these reserves have been decreasing to a larger numbers, as revealed by the Tiger Census Report. Kaziranga National Park and Manas Wildlife Sanctuary are in the list of World Heritage sites.

District-wise Forest Cover of Assam

(Area in km²)

District	Geo-graphical Area	Very Dense Forest	Mod. Dense Forest	Open Forest	Total	Per cent of GA	Scrub
Baksa	2,457	156	127	273	556	22.63	6
Barpeta	2,282	0	24	81	105	4.60	1
Bongaigaon	1,093	0	54	182	236	21.59	0
Cachar	3,786	93	1,077	1,053	2,223	58.72	19
Chirang	1,923	402	108	184	694	36.09	3
Darrang	1,585	0	11	75	86	5.43	1
Dhemaji	3,237	68	125	145	338	10.44	4
Dhubri	2,176	1	19	70	90	4.14	4
Dibrugarh	3,381	106	68	583	757	22.39	1
Dima Hasao	4,888	209	1,519	2,482	4,210	86.13	4
Goalpara	1,824	14	94	190	298	16.34	2
Golaghat	3,502	21	119	511	651	18.59	4
Hailakandi	1,327	13	366	394	773	58.25	5
Jorhat	2,851	12	103	439	554	19.43	4
Kamrup	3,105	50	421	448	919	29.60	3
Kamrup Metropolitan	955	0	225	235	460	48.17	1
Karbi-Anglong	10,434	586	3,801	3,596	7,983	76.51	76
Karimganj	1,809	3	300	513	816	45.11	47
Kokrajhar	3,296	438	267	453	1,158	35.13	1
Lakhimpur	2,277	29	86	180	295	12.96	1
Morigaon	1,551	10	42	122	174	11.22	4
Nagaon	3,973	50	363	497	910	22.90	9
Nalbari	1,052	0	19	75	94	8.94	0
Sivasagar	2,668	9	153	526	688	25.79	3
Sonitpur	5,204	109	259	687	1,055	20.27	3
Tinsukia	3,790	410	356	813	1,579	41.66	10
Udalguri	2,012	8	86	309	403	20.03	1
Grand Total	**78,438**	**2,797**	**10,192**	**15,116**	**28,105**	**35.83**	**217**

Forest Cover Change Matrix

(Area in km²)

Class	2017 Assessment					
	Very Dense Forest	Modest Dense Forest	Open Forest	Scrub	Non Forest	Total ISFR 2015
Very Dense Forest	1,102	234	9	0	80	1,425
Moderately Dense Forest	1,590	9,058	451	2	155	11,256
Open Forest	105	788	13,253	17	694	14,857
Scrub	0	24	102	171	71	368
Non Forest	0	88	1,301	27	49,116	50,532
Total ISFR 2017	**2,797**	**10,192**	**15,116**	**217**	**59,116**	**78,438**
Net Change	1,372	–1,064	259	–151	–416	

Major Types of Forests

1. Tropical Wet Evergreen,
2. Tropical Semi-Evergreen,
3. Tropical Moist Deciduous,
4. Sub Tropical Broad Leaved Hill,
5. Sub Tropical Pine and Littoral,
6. Swamp Forests.

Forest Education

Name of Forest Ranger's College—State Forest Service College, Burnihat

Name of Forester's School—Assam Forest School, Jalukbari, Guwahati

Name of Forest Guard's School—Forest Guards' Training School, Makum

POPULATION

According to the final result of Census of India, 2011 the population of Assam stood at 3,12,05,576 of which 1,59,39,443 are males and 1,52,66,133 females and the decadal growth being 17.1 per cent during the last decade 2001-2011.

As per 2011 census, the share of population of Assam to the total population of India is 2.58 per cent. Assam ranks fourteenth in size of population among all the States of India as per 2011 censuses. During inter-censual period 2001-2011 a decline of 1.99 per cent and 3.7 per cent of decadal growth rate have been observed in Assam and India respectively. Assam ranks fifteenth among all the States of India in terms of density of population.

The decadal growth rate of population for the State has abruptly come down to 17.1 per cent during 2001-2011. This variation has been observed predominantly in the districts of Kamrup Metropolitan (18.95%), Chirang (11.26 %), Dima Hasao (13.53%) and Kokrajhar (5.19%). The districts of Tinsukia, Sivasagar, Jorhat, Golaghat, Karbi-Anglong and Lakhimpur have, however, maintained a reasonable decrease during the last decade. Due to creation of four new districts the decade growth rates for 2001 have been affected in 12 districts. The density of population has gone up to 398 as against 340 in 2001 census. The density of population is highest in the district of Kamrup Metropolitan (1999) followed by Dhubri (1171) and Nalbari (764) and the lowest density is seen in Dima Hasao (44). The sex ratio in the State shows an improvement from 935 in 2001 to 958 in 2011. The highest sex ratio has been recorded in the district of Baksa (974) and the lowest in the district of Dima Hasao (932). The growth of literacy in Assam has shown an encouraging sign. The literacy rate for Assam as per Census 2011 comes to 72.2 per cent with 77.8 per cent for males and 66.3 per cent for females. The highest literacy rate at the district level is observed in Kamrup Metropolitan (88.7%) followed by Jorhat (82.1%) and Sivasagar (80.4%) while the lowest is in Dhubri (58.3%).

Area, Population and Headquarters of Districts

S.No.	District	Area (sq. km.)	Population	District Headquarters
1.	Dhubri	2,828	19,49,258	Dhubri
2.	Kokrajhar	3,129	8,87,142	Kokrajhar
3.	Bongaigaon	2,510	7,38,804	Bongaigaon
4.	Goalpara	1,824	10,08,183	Goalpara
5.	Barpeta	3,245	16,93,622	Barpeta
6.	Nalbari	2,257	7,71,639	Nalbari
7.	Kamrup	4,345	15,17,542	Guwahati
8.	Darrang	3,481	9,28,500	Mangaldoi
9.	Sonitpur	5,324	19,24,110	Tezpur
10.	Lakhimpur	2,277	10,42,137	North Lakhimpur
11.	Dhemaji	3,217	6,86,133	Dhemaji
12.	Morigaon	1,704	9,57,423	Morigaon
13.	Nagaon	3,831	28,23,768	Nagaon
14.	Golaghat	3,502	10,66,888	Golaghat

S.No.	District	Area (sq. km.)	Population	District Headquarters
15.	Jorhat	2,851	10,92,256	Jorhat
16.	Sivasagar	2,668	11,51,050	Sivasagar
17.	Dibrugarh	3,381	13,26,335	Dibrugarh
18.	Tinsukia	3,790	13,27,929	Tinsukia
19.	Karbi-Anglong	10,434	9,56,313	Diphu
20.	Dima Hasao	4,888	2,14,102	Haflong
21.	Karimganj	1,809	12,28,686	Karimganj
22.	Hailakandi	1,327	6,59,296	Hailkandi
23.	Cachar	3,786	17,36,617	Silchar
24.	Chirang	1,169.9	4,82,162	Kajalgaon
25.	Kamrup Metropolitan	1,528	12,53,938	Guwahati
26.	Baksa	2,400	9,50,075	Mushalpur
27.	Udalguri	1,852.16	8,31,668	Udalguri
28.	Biswanath	-	-	-
29.	Charaideo	-	-	-
30.	Hojai	-	-	-
31.	Majuli	-	-	-
32.	South Salmara Mankachar	-	-	-
33.	West Karbai Anglong	-	-	-
34.	East Kamrup	-	-	-
35.	South Kamrup	-	-	-

Population : At a Glance

	Head	Unit	2001 *Census, Assam*	2011 *Census, Assam*
1.	Population	Lakh	266	312
2.	Decadal Growth	Per cent	18.92	17.1
3.	Change in percentage of decadal growth	Per cent	(-) 5.39	(-) 1.99
4.	Density	Per Sq. Km.	340	398
5.	Sex-Ratio	Females per 1000 males	935	958
6.	Literacy	Per cent	63.3	72.2
7.	Urban Population	Per cent	12.9	14.1
8.	Rural Population	Per cent	87.1	85.92
9.	S.C. Population	Per cent	6.9	7.2
10.	S.T. Population	Per cent	12.42	12.4

Birth and Death Rates

The data obtained from the Sample Registration Bulletin published by the Registrar General of India depicts some idea about the trend in the birth and death rates and infant mortality rate in the State. According to this source, in most of the years from 1991 to 2002 birth rates, death rates and infant mortality rates were found to be higher in the State than that of the country as a whole. During the year 2014, the birth rates, death rates and infant mortality rates of Assam have been 22.4, 7.2 and 49 per thousand as against 25.0, 8.1 and 64 per thousand respectively at all-India level.

EDUCATION

As per 2011 Census, Literacy Rate of Assam is 72.2% with male literacy rate 77.8%, which is behind the National rate of 73.0% and male literacy rate 80.9% respectively. The female literacy rate with 66.3% stood above the National rate of 64.6%. To achieve the goal of Universal Elementary Education, educational programmes of Sarva Shiksha Abhiyan (SSA) along with various innovative schemes are being implemented by the State Government. The State Government equally gives emphasis in providing qualitative technical education to build technical skills to cater the needs of the economy. Keeping in view of importance of education in the socio-economic development, the State Government has been implementing various educational programmes.

Elementary Education

The Directorate of Elementary Education (DEE), Assam has been functioning to achieve the goal of Universalisation of Elementary Education in the State to provide useful and relevant elementary education to all children in the age group of 6 to 14 years. It aims to bridge all gender and social category gaps at primary stage with focus on elementary education of satisfactory quality. All schemes for elementary education are implemented through SSA.

SCERT

SCERT, Assam is the State Academic Authority engaged in academic resource development through various programmes such as organizing long and short term training, workshops, seminars, research and evaluation activities for teachers and teacher educators to make them professionally competent for effective teaching.

Higher Education

The Directorate of Higher Education and Directorate of Secondary Education is established to give primary focus on expansion and promotion of Higher

Education by granting financial assistance to the needy educational institutions besides implementing various programmes for development of general education and assisting for infrastructure development in general with special focus to rural and backward areas.

Number of Higher Educational Institutions in Assam as in 2015-16

Institutions	Numbers
Universities (including private and Deemed University)	12
Government Colleges	6
Provincialised Colleges	295
Non-Govt. Colleges	43
Provincialised Sanskrit & Pali Tols	97
Literary & Voluntary Organisations	19
Govt. Law College	1
Non-Govt. Law Colleges	19

Source: *Higher Education, Assam, Kahilipara, Guwahati-19*

Technical Education

The Directorate of Technical Education, Assam prepares, supervises and implements the plans and schemes for overall development of Technical Education in the State.

Medical Education

The Directorate of Medical Education, Assam is entrusted with the task of generating human resources like Doctors, Nurses, Technicians, Physiotherapists, Pharmacists and other Health personnel to meet the growing needs of not only the State but the entire North Eastern region.

The Directorate has a host of institutes under its control there are Assam Medical College (AMC) & Hospital, Gauhati Medical College (GMC) & Hospital, Silchar Medical College (SMC) & Hospital, Jorhat Medical College, Regional Dental College, Guwahati; Regional Nursing College, Guwahati; Govt. Ayurvedic College, Guwahati; S.J.N. Homeopathic Medical College, Guwahati; Dr. J.K. Saikia Homeopathic Medical College, Jorhat; Assam Homeopathic Medical College, Nagaon, three pharmacist institutes associated with AMC, GMC and SMC, Medical Institute at Jorhat and three Institute of Paramedical Sciences at Guwahati, Dibrugarh and

Silchar. The Srimanta Sankaradeva University of Health Services, Assam and Jorhat Medical College & Hospital have started functioning from 2009-10.

Besides the above institutes, steps have already been taken for establishment of three more medical college's viz. Fakaruddin Ali Ahmed Medical College, Barpeta; Tezpur Medical College Tezpur; Assam Hills Medical College and Research Institute, Diphu. Steps have also be taken to establish three more medical college at Lakhimpur, Kokrajhar and Dhubri.

List of Important Universities

1. Assam Agricultural University, Jorhat
2. Assam University, Silchar
3. Dibrugarh University, Dibrugarh
4. Guwahati University, Guwahati
5. Indian Institute of Technology, Guwahati
6. National Institute of Technology (Deemed University), Silchar
7. Tezpur University, Tezpur

The other major institutions are:

1. Regional Research Laboratory, Jorhat
2. Tocklai Tea Research Centre, Jorhat
3. Centre for Plasma Physics, Guwahati

LANGUAGE

With a majority of the total population using the tongue, **Assamese** is the major language of the State. Besides English, Assamese was accorded the status of the official language of the Brahmaputra Valley by the Official Language Act of 1960. However, Bengali and English were also simultaneously accorded the status of official language for the Barak Valley and the two Hill Districts by the same Act. The earliest specimen of the Assamese script is to be found in copper plates and inscriptions discovered in different parts of the region.

Scholars opine that the origin of Assamese goes back to the Magadhan-Prakrit script. By all standards it is a composite language into which words of Indo-Aryan and Indo-Chinese origins have made their way. Pre-Aryan and non-Aryan influences are also discernible not only in loan words but also in its grammar, syntax and pronunciation.

Speeches of the Tibeto-Burman, Austro-Asiatic and Tibeto-Chinese families abound among the tribal population. The widest variety of language found in the tribal popluation can however be attributed to the Tibeto-

Burman family. The Bodo language group with its Kachari, Lalung, Rabha, Moran and even Chutia variations, in turn dominate the Tibeto-Burman family. Other recognized Indian languages spoken in the State include Bengali, Hindi and Oriya. Oriya, Mundari, Santhal, Tamil and Telegu are mostly spoken by the tea garden labourers.

INDUSTRY

Assam continue to make efforts for gearing up industrial activities with a view to create a strong industrial base by harnessing the un-tapped resources available in the State through various growth inducing factors besides taking steps for removal of existing infrastructure inadequacies. The Industries and Commerce Department of the State as well as some other agencies like AIDC are closely associated with implementation of various promotional schemes meant for industrial development of the State. Despite various constraints a favourable industrial climate is gradually being created in the State as discernible from the increasing interest shown by investors of the State as well as from outside.

Industrial Estate and Industrial Growth Centre

The prime function of the Commissionerate of Industries and Commerce Department, Assam is to create environment for industrialization by setting up Industrial infrastructure in the perspective of industrial development and attract investment through proper planning. At present, there are 20 Industrial Estates, 17 Industrial Areas, 12 Growth Centers under the Industries and Commerce Department of Assam spread over an area of 2155 thousand sq.m land in different locations of the State. Apart from the aforesaid infrastructures, there are 11 Integrated Infrastructure Development (IID) Projects, 3 Industrial Growth Centers, 6 Mini Industrial Estates, One Export Promotion Industrial Park, two Food Processing Industrial Park spread over an area of 7343 thousand sq.m land also provided additional infrastructure facilities to the entrepreneurs of the State. The Growth Centres and IID Centres are facilitated with excellent connectivity, dedicated power lines, adequate water supply, central effluent treatment plants, etc.

Some Ongoing Infrastructure Projects

Industrial Growth Centre : The Industries and Commerce Department of Assam has undertaken three centrally sponsored projects known as Industrial growth Centre project at Chariduar, Matia and Chaygaon-Patgaon under Central sponsored scheme.

Export Promotion Industrial Park (EPIP) : The Export Promotion Industrial Park located at Amingaon in Kamrup district was approved by the Government of India with a total project cost of ₹ 1462.0 lakh and both the Central and State Governments jointly share the project costs. The objective of the project is to create high standard infrastructure. The project has already been completed with national standard infrastructure. As many as 38 industrial units are producing wide range export oriented products there.

Agro-Based Industries : The agro climatic weather of Assam is ideal for the growth of a variety of food crops as well as plantation of cash crops. Tea produced in Assam has high demand in the west particularly in Europe as a beverage. The abundant forest resources provide timber for industries like plywood, paper. Various kinds of fruits, vegetables as well as medicinal herbs available in the State are yet to be tapped for commercial purpose.

Food Processing Industry : As per available report of Agriculture Department, implementation of the Technology Mission for Integrated Development of Horticulture (TMIDH) in Assam has brought tremendous change in production of fruits, spices and vegetables in the State thereby opening ample scope for setting up of food processing industries in the State.

At present less than 30 per cent of agriculture produce are processed in the State. Among the total processed food, 80 per cent are of primary food products like packaged milk, milled flour, rice, tea, spices, etc. Processing and packaging of perishable fruits and vegetables, although it has ample potential to grow with increasing demand, does not have desired importance due to non-availability of sufficient storage facility.

Food Processing Industrial Park : The Government of India has approved for setting up of a Food Processing Industrial Park at Chaygaon in Kamrup district with a project cost (revised) of ₹ 496.00 lakh and the costs of the project will be borne by both the Central and the State Government. The ASIDC Ltd. is implementing the project.

Tea Industry

The Tea industry occupies an important place in Assam and plays a very special role in the State economy in particular and in the national economy in general. The first Indian tea was sent to United Kingdom for public sale in the year 1838. Although the tea cultivation was extended to other parts of the country between 50's and 60's of the last century, as of today, Assam Tea has maintained its international reputation and commands significant share in the World Tea Market. The tea industry in Assam also provides average daily employment to more than six lakh persons in the State, which is around 50 per cent of the total average daily number of labour employed in the country. Assam alone produces more than half of India's tea production.

The total area under tea cultivation in Assam is accounting for more than half of the country's total area under tea. In addition to existing big & large tea gardens owned by reputed both Indian and multinational companies, the profession of tea plantation in the State has been taken up by common people as business venture at present, especially by unemployed youths. "There are more than 84,577 small tea growers [STG] in Assam producing about twenty per cent of the State's total annual production in 78,203 hectares of land. Most of the STGs in the State are confined to Dibrugarh (52%) and Sivasagar (41%)". [State focus paper, Assam-2012-13 by NABARD].

According to the State Government reports, there are about 70000 small tea holdings covering approximately 117,000 acres of land in 14 out of 35 districts in Assam. It is important to note that 87 per cent of the cultivation is done in land area measuring less than three acres. Major concentration is in 5 Upper Assam Districts (64519) which is 94 per cent of the total number of Small Tea Growers in 14 districts of Brahmaputra valley.

In Assam, tea is grown both in the Brahmaputra and Barak plains. Tinsukia, Dibrugarh, Sivasagar, Jorhat, Golaghat, Nagaon and Sonitpur are the districts where tea gardens are mostly found. Assam produces 51% of the tea produced in India and about 1/6th of the tea produced in the world. In 1911 a **Tea Research Centre** was started at **Toklai** in **Jorhat** for developing more scientific and fruitful methods of cultivating tea plants, applying fertilizer, testing soil, selecting sites for garden and processing tea leaves. This is the oldest and largest Tea Research Centre in the world.

The Guwahati Tea Auction Centre is actively taking part in Tea trading of the Tea produced mainly in the North Eastern States since its establishment.

Forest and Wood Industry

Plywood, pulp and paper, safety match box making, etc. are the main forest based industries in the state. Plywood industry is the third largest industry in the state after tea and petroleum. The state forest is the source of raw material for above industries.

Important Paper Industries

	Industries	Area
1.	**Ashok Paper Mills**	Jogighopa (State Govt)
2.	**Kamrup Paper Mills**	Amingaon, Guwahati (Private Sector)
3.	**Hindustan Paper Corporation Ltd.**	Panchgram (Central Govt.)
4.	**Hindustan Paper Corporation Ltd.**	Kagaznagar Jagi Road (Central Govt.)

Important Match Box Industries

	Industries	Area
1.	**U.F. Mill.**	Dhubri (State Govt)
2.	**WIMCO Ltd.**	Dhubri (Private sector)

Agro-Based Industry

The 74% of state's population is engaged in agriculture and allied industries. Due to easy availability of products and fruits, several agro-based industries flourished in Assam.

Cottage Industry

Assam was traditionally famous for it's cottage industry, especially **spinning and weaving**. Pat or pure silk production is essentially confined to Assam. Assam produces about 10% of total natural silk of India. Assam also produces **Muga**, the golden silk. Assam is also the main producer of **Eri** or **Endi**. Weaving is an important cottage industry of Assam. It is a traditional industry which can be traced back to very ancient times.

Sericulture

Traditionally, sericulture is a major cottage industry in the State. Sericulture continues to be an important labour-intensive and agro-based cottage industry providing gainful occupation to around 2.50 lakh person in rural and semi-urban areas of Assam. Of this a sizeable number of male workers belong to the economically weaker section of the society and women. Moreover, sericulture is a sustainable farm-based economic enterprise positively favouring the rural poor in the un-organized sector because of its relatively low requirement of fixed capital and higher returns on investment.

Non-mulberry silk in general and Muga silk in particular has been closely associated with the rituals and traditions of Assam and thus, silk production and its usage has been an important household activity in the State over the years. Muga Silk and Eri Silk have a good demand in the national and international market. Rearing of Eri, Muga and Mulberry silkworm are playing an important role in the economic development of a large section of rural population of the State. It is practiced in 10740 villages at present and provides employment to more than 2.5 lakh family of the State. Muga culture is endemic to Assam in the world. The State accounts for highest production of non-mulberry silk, Muga and Eri in the country. Assam has the monopoly in the world in the production of Muga, the "Golden Silk", as more than 95 per cent of Muga Silk is produced in Assam. Assam has also achieved the right of 'Geographical Indication' for

Muga thread. The State is also a Major producer of Eri Silk (about 65 per cent).

A cocoon bank at Boko, Kamrup District is at an advanced stage of implementation. This will benefit primary growers, reelers and spinners of Eri and Muga. Efforts are being made to increase production of Muga, Eri and Mulberry in the State. State Government has taken initiative for revival of numerous defunct sericulture farms and centres in the State. The State has been given special emphasis for implementation of various schematic plans especially for augmentation of silk food plant plantation and rejuvenation of old silk food plants area. Besides this, organization of private graineurs for production of quality muga and eri seeds, construction of scientific silk worm rearing houses, setting up of a Sericulture College, etc. are also prioritized for development of sericulture in the State.

Handloom

In Assam, Handloom Weaving is a way of life. It is inexorably linked with Assamese Culture and Heritage. Handloom Industry of Assam is known for its rich glorious tradition of making handloom and handicraft products. It also plays a very important role in the socio-economic development of the State. Assam is a proud owner of more than 13.00 lakh looms out of the total 28.00 lakh looms in the country. In spite of being intensely connected with the culture of the State, the Handloom Industry has not flourished in commercial sphere to the required extent. At present about 2.05 lakh looms are being utilized for commercial weaving in the true sense. About 6.00 lakh looms run semi-commercially and earns subsidiary income. Rests are domestic looms and are run to meet the domestic requirements. Moreover, handloom weaving provides direct and indirect employment to about 25.0 lakh people in the State. The cooperative coverage is about 45 per cent of the State's weaver population which is far below the National coverage.

The Handloom and Textiles Department of Assam, at present, directly runs 102 Handloom Training Centres, 4 Handloom Training Institute and 1 powerloom Centre under Training Programme, 98 Weavers' Extension Service Units and 20 Handloom Production Centre, one Handloom Research and Designing Centre and one Production Procurement Centre under production programme to assist the weavers with skill upgradation backward and forward linkages in taking handloom as a self employment venture. The Assam Government Marketing Corporation is the State Level organization to look after the weavers of the State. The three-pronged Cooperative (organized) Sector consists of more than 3634 Primary Level, 22 District Level and 2 Apex Cooperative Societies covered about 33 per cent weaver population of the State.

Other Industries

Bell-metal work is a traditional cottage industry of Assam. The normal products of bell-metal are the traditional plates, cups, tumblers, pitchers, bowls, sarais (a tray with a stand), dwarf pitchers, pots, hookahs and musical instruments.

Brass-work is also an important traditional handicraft of Assam. Brass articles are produced not only for day-to-day use, but also for interior decoration. The total production of marketable finished goods annually is about 300 tonnes.

Apart from the above, some other cottage industries have come up in the State. These include **ivory work** of Barpeta; **pottery industry** of Hajo, Singimari, Mornoi; bamboo and cane work specially in the hills; goldsmithy, coir industry of Nalbari; hand-made paper industry of Chandkhuchi in Nalbari district; soap making in almost all important towns of the State, etc.

Border Trade Centre-Infrastructure Development

Assam is sharing international border with Bangladesh, Bhutan and Myanmar and thus has ample scope to enhance trade with these countries. To facilitate bilateral border trade with Bangladesh there are 8 Land Custom Stations (LCS) of India/Assam viz. Dhubri Steamer ghat, Mancachar, Golokganj, Silchar RMS, Karimganj Ferryghat, Sutarkandi, Mahisasan Railway Station and Guwahati Steamer ghat.

For bilateral trade with Bhutan there are 3 (three) Land Custom Stations-Daranga, Hatisar and Ultapani. The work of the Border Trade Centre project located at Daranga in Baksa District is in progress. Another Border Trade Centre project is taken up at Jagun in Tinsukia District.

POWER

Power is the basic infrastructural requirement for the growth of industries as well as over-all economy of the State. However, despite Assam possessing immense potential of power ranging from hydel to natural gas including oil and coal resources, the progress of this sector in the State has not taken place on a scale commensurate with the possibilities. As a result, there exists a big gap between availability and demand for power in the State.

In pursuance of the Indian Electricity Act 2003, and as a part of the Assam power sector development programme, the Government of Assam has set in motion the process of unbundling the Assam State Electric Board (ASEB) in 2004, into following government companies:

The Assam Power Generation Corporation Limited (APGCL),

The Assam Electricity Grid Corporation Limited (AEGCL), and

The Assam Power Distribution Company Limited (APDCL).

These initiatives are in the interest of all the stakeholders in the electricity sector in the State, *i.e.,* consumers, shareholders, suppliers, creditors, infrastructure builders and the Government of Assam. The scheme like externally aided project, rural electrification, accelerated power development and reform programme (APDRP) which are yet being executed under Assam State Electricity Board (ASEB).

The Assam Power Generation Corporation Ltd. (APGCL) was constituted to look after power generation in the State Sector. The final Transfer Scheme was implemented in August 2005. The company is mainly responsible for development of Thermal & Hydel Power Projects to Generate Electricity to meet the energy demand in the State to the extent feasible.

Power Projects Operational in Assam

(a) **Namrup Thermal Power Stations (NTPS) :** The power generation sources of Assam are basically thermal and hydro. After creation of ASEB with the sole objective of self-sufficient of power, foundation stone was laid as "Naharkatia Thermal Power Project" in 1960. In course of time the name of this Power Station was changed to Namrup Thermal Power Station.

(b) **Lakwa Thermal Power Stations (LTPS) :** Lakwa Thermal Power Station is one of the pioneer power stations in the North Eastern region. It is situated at Maibella in the district of Sivasagar, Assam. It was the day 22nd May 1977, then Hon'ble President of India, Sri Nilam Sanjeeva Reddy laid down the foundation stone of the power project and gave a major thrust for the upliftment of the area. After commissioning of the project in the year 1981, the power station has been serving to the nation and specially to the power starved state of Assam to a large extent.

(c) **Karbi Langpi Hydro Electric Project :** The river Borpani originates from Meghalaya in the name of Umkhen and flows into the Assam hill region in the name of Borpani (Langpi). The river has tremendous potential for Hydro Electricity generation. Assam State Electricity Board was entrusted the job of carrying out a detailed survey for harnessing power potentialities of Borpani basin during 1976-77.

The 2 × 50 MW Karbi Langpi Hydro Electric Project (KLHEP) is a run off the river project located in Karbi Anglong District of Assam. This is the last stage development of the Borpani River basin utilizing an average head of 235 m. The Karbi Langpi Hydro Electric Project was sanctioned by the Planning Commission during 1979. The construction of the project was started during 1979-80 with infrastructure development activities. However, due to different factors the project could not be completed even after 20 years from starting. However, the whole work was finally completed in January 2007.

Development of Hydro Electric Projects in Assam

Ongoing Projects under State Plan (Partial Funding)

1. **Myntriang Small Hydro Electric Project :** The Assam Power Generation Corporation Limited (APGCL) is implementing the Myntriang Small Hydro Electric Project on Myntriang river near Amtereng Village. The Myntriang Small Hydro Electric Project is located near Karbi Langpi Hydro Electric Project at Amtereng.
2. **Lungnit Small Hydro Electric Project :** The project is located 25 km away from Diphu, District Headquarter of Karbi Anglong, This is a two stage development of the river Lungnit *i.e.* Stage-I (3 MW) by utilizing head of 48 m and 2.83 cumec of discharge in two unit of 1.50 MW each and Stage-II (3 MW) by utilizing head of 43.00 m and 3.24 cumec of discharge in two unit of 1.50 MW each.

Installed Capacity and Generation of Power

The installed capacity of generating plants at present in the State is 379.7 MW which include Coal, Hydel and Gas plants of the state. The installed capacity for generating power has come down due to de-commissioning of Bongaigaon Thermal Power station (BTPs) and Mobile Gen. sets and de-rating of age-old units of Namrup (NTPS). The status of power generation in the state is not satisfactory from the point of power requirement of the consumer. There has been always a shortage of power supply in the state due to generation of less amount of power in comparison to its demand. However, the ASEB has been trying to meet the power shortage by importing power from other foreign sources.

Power Supply Position

The energy requirement in the State has been worked out at 379.7 Million Unit (MU) during the year 2015-16 as against 9104 MU in the previous year but the availability of energy during the periods was 7571 MU and 7165 MU respectively. However, the power generation was 1851 MU and 1894 MU during the years 2015-16 and 2014-15 respectively. The peak demand of electricity in the state has increased from 1423 MW in 2014-15 to 1526 MW during 2015-16, though shortage of power has come down from

229 MW in 2014-15 to 76 MW in 2015-16, the shortage in percentage being 16.09% in 2014-15 and 5% in 2015-16 respectively.

Number of Electricity Consumers

As per 2015-16, 37.0 per cent households in Assam, use electricity as a source of lighting compared to 67.0 per cent households at All-India level. The rural-urban difference in use of electricity as a source of light is very high in Assam. Only 28.0 per cent of rural households use electricity for lighting purposes in comparison to 84.1 per cent urban households in Assam.

Households using Electricity as Source of Lighting

Item	Assam			India		
	Rural	Urban	Total	Rural	Urban	Total
Total	53,74,553	9,92,742	63,67,295	16,78,26,730	7,88,65,937	24,66,92,667
Electricity	15,24,221	8,34,679	23,58,900	9,28,08,038	7,30,89,256	16,58,97,294
Households using Electricity (%)	28.0	84.1	37.0	55.0	93.0	67.0

TRANSPORT

Assam being the gateway to the other States of the North Eastern Region of the Country, the need for development of transport and communication sector in the State is of vital importance for speedy economic development of the region. Due to its geographical isolation, transport has been a major bottleneck in the process of economic progress of the State. The existing infrastructures and facilities of transport and communication in the State are hardly adequate enough to meet the requirements. The State is no doubt served by all the modern means of transport viz., roads, railways, waterways and airways but there is enough scope for further improvement of the facilities.

Roads

The principal function of the Public Works Department (PWD) is to develop the infrastructure for transport & Communication of the State and Residential & Non-residential accommodation facility in the State. The Assam PWD (Roads wing) is primarily responsible for improvement of road communication through construction and maintenance of roads, bridges and culverts for speedy development of the State.

(1019) NE-GK–7

The road network in Assam comprises of total 58202 Km of roads consisting of 3862.54 Km National Highways, 2530 Km State Highways, 4379 Km Major district roads, 1409 Km Urban roads, 36544 Km Rural Roads and 2443 Km. Rural Roads and the rest are Panchayats & Other Non PWD Roads. Prime Minister Narendra Modi on May 26, 2017 dedicated the longest river bridge (9.15 km) of India, Dhola-Sadia Bridge on Lohit river to the nation. He also named the bridge after Balladeer Bhupen Hazarika.

Road Network in Assam *(in Km)*

Item	2011-12	2012-13	2013-14	2014-15	2015-16
Surfaced Road	21200	22700	23747	23948	25546
Un-surfaced Road	24300	22800	21753	20914	19316
National Highway	2848	3069	3069	3834.68	3862.53
State Highway	3134	3134	3134	2530	2530
Major District Road	4413	4413	4413	4379	4379
Rural Road	36544	36544	36544	36544	36544
Urban Road	1409	1409	1409	1409	1409

Highway Development Project

Out of the total 100087 km length of NH in the Country, Assam's share is only 3.8 per cent. Compared to 30.44 km NH length per thousand sq.km geographical areas and 5.93 km NH length per lakh of population (2011 Census) of the country as a whole, Assam has 49.24 km per thousand sq.km geographical areas and 12.38 km NH per lakh of population in the State.

In addition, Government of India has proposed to construct/improve roads connecting Doboka (Assam) to Dimapur (Nagaland Border), Baihata-Chariali to Bandardewa, Bandardewa (Assam) to Arunachal Border, Assam/ Meghalaya Border to Assam Tripura Border and Silchar (Assam) to Mizoram Border under NHDP Phase-II.

Important National Highways of Assam

1	**31**	From W.B. Border-Gouripur-North Salmara-Bijni-Charali-Amingaon Junction with NH No. 37
2	**31B**	North Salmaria-Abhayapuri-Junction with NH No. 37 near Jogighopa
3	**31C**	From W.B. Border-Kochugaon-Sidli Ju. With NH-31 near Bijni
4	**36**	Nagaon-Dabaka-Amlakhi-Nagaland Border
5	**37**	Junction with NH No.31B near Goalpara-Paikan-Guwahati-Dispur-Nowgong-Numaligarh-Jorhat-Jhanzi-Dibrugarh-Tinsukia-Makum-Saikhoghat
6	**37A**	Kuwari Tal - Junction with NH. No. 52 near Tezpur

7	**38**	Makurm-Ledo-Likhapani
8	**39**	Numaligarh-Naojan-Bokajan-upto Nagaland Border
9	**44**	From Meghalaya Border- Badarpur-Karimganj-Patharkandi- upto Tripura Border
10	**51**	Paikan-upto Meghalaya Border
11	**52**	Baihata-Charali-Mangaldai-Dhekiajuli-Tezpur-Gohpur-Bander Dewa-North Lakhimpur-Dhemaji-Kulajan-Arunachal Border-Junction with NH. No. 37 near Saikhoaghat
12	**52A**	Gohpur-A.P. Border-Bander Dewa
13	**52B**	Kulajan-Dibrugarh
14	**53**	Junction with NH-44 near Badarpur-Silchar-Lakhimpur upto Manipur Border.
15	**54**	Dabaka-Lumding-Langting-Haplong- Silchar-Dwarband upto Mizoram Border
16	**61**	Jhanzi-Amguri-Nagaland border
17	**62**	Dudhnai-Damara upto Meghalaya Border
18	**151**	Karimganj-Bangladesh Border
19	**152**	Patacharkuchi-Hajua-Bhutan Border
20	**153**	Ledo-Lekhapani-Arunachal Pradesh Border
21	**154**	Dhaleshwar-Bhairabhi-Mizoram Border

Railways

As per information available from the N.F. Railway, Headquarters, Maligaon, Guwahati, Assam has total railway route length 2442.57 km. at present. This 2442.57 km. comprising of 2400.85 km. under Broad Gauge and 41.72 km. Meter Gauge. The proportion of Broad Gauge railway route length in the State, although, is 98.29 per cent, it shares only 3.69 per cent of the country's total broad gauge railway route length. As per Indian Railway Statistical Publication 2014-15, the total Railway Route length of India as on 31st March, 2015 is 66030 km. out of which Electrified Route length is 22224 km. Assam shares 3.7 per cent of the total Railway Route length of the country. The total number of passengers carried by N.F. Railway is 112 million Nos. and the total Cargo carried is 31.555 million Tonnes during 2015-16. The revenue generated from this goods carried is ₹ 1794.74 crores.

A "Rail Heritage Park" having railway museum was established in New Tinsukia Railway Station to showcase ancient memorials ranging from ancient turntable built during British period of 1892, railway wheels used by British Army during the Second World War to narrow gauge Steam Engine built in 1889. With the theme dedicated to Dibru-Sadyia Railways and Assam-Bengal Railways, the heritage park was developed at approximate cost of ₹ 2.0 crore.

Inland Water Transport

Inland water transport is generally accepted as the most efficient mode of transportation from the point of energy consumption. It is also considered as the cheapest mode of transportation as well as labour intensive and environment friendly in nature. Assam is a riverine State. As much as 32 per cent of the water resource of the country flow down through the river Brahmaputra, Barak and their myriad tributaries weave a vast network of waterways in the State. The Brahmaputra has 891 km navigable length of water ways from Sadiya to Dhubri while the Barak has 121 km length of navigable waterways. The Sadiya-Dhubri stretch of the Brahmaputra River has been declared as the No. 2 National waterways of the country in the year 1988 and afterwards the proposals to activate the Commercial service have been moved for overall economic development of the North-eastern Region.

Air Transport

Assam is well connected with the rest of the country through Air Transport. The State has the highest numbers of operational civil airports in the North-East and these are located at Guwahati, Tezpur, Jorhat, Dibrugarh, North Lakhimpur and Silchar. In addition, one more civil airport located at Dhubri (Rupshi) district of Assam is lying closed and non-functional for long time. The State Govt. has demanded to reopen the airport for passenger traffic for the benefit of the State which will further benefit the people of Meghalaya. All major airlines including private commercial airlines *viz.,* Indian Airlines, Spice jet, Indigo, Go-air etc. are operating their flights to and from Guwahati and intra-state air services regularly. In addition to these civil airports, small private airstrips in the interior areas are present in large numbers. Some small and remote airstrips are being operated under private operators like tea gardens and PSUs.

ADMINISTRATION

Assam is divided into **35 administrative districts**. More than half of these districts were carved out during 80s and 90s from original 1. Lakhimpur, 2. Jorhat, 3. Karbi Anglong, 4. Darrang, 5. Nagaon, 6. Kamrup, 7. Goalpara, 8. North Cachar and 9. Cachar districts, delineated by the British. Earlier, during 70s, Dibrugarh was separated out from original Lakhimpur district.

The local governance system is organised under the **Zila Parishad** (District Panchayat) for a district, panchayat for group of or individual rural areas and under the urban local bodies for the towns and cities. Presently there are 2202 village panchayats covering 26395 villages in Assam. The 'Town-committee' or Nagar-committee for small towns, 'municipal board' or **pouro-xobha** for medium towns and municipal corporation or pouro-nigom for the cities consist of the urban local bodies.

For the revenue purposes, the districts are divided into revenue circles and **mouzas**; for the development projects, the districts are divided into 219 'development-blocks' and for law and order these are divided into 301 police stations or thana.

Districts of Assam

1. Tinsukia
2. Dibrugarh
3. Sivasagar
4. Dhemaji
5. Jorhat
6. Lakhimpur
7. Golaghat
8. Sonitpur
9. Karbi Anglong
10. Nagaon
11. Marigaon
12. Darrang
13. Kamrup Rural
14. Nalbari
15. Barpeta
16. Bongaigaon
17. Goalpara
18. Kokrajhar
19. Dhubri
20. North Cachar Hills
21. Cachar
22. Hailakandi
23. Karimganj
24. Kamrup Metropolitan
25. Baksa
26. Chirang
27. Udalguri
28. Biswanath
29. Charaideo
30. Hojai
31. South Salmara-Mankachar
32. West Karbi Anglong
33. East Kamrup
34. South Kamrup
35. Majuli

Assam has a unicameral legislature. The State Legislative Assembly has **126 members** at present. Assam has **14 representatives** in the Lok Sabha, the lower house of the Parliament of India. It also has **seven representative** in the Rajya Sabha, the upper house of the Parliament.

Assam (Asom) Legislative Assembly

The Assam Legislative Assembly came into being on the day of its first sitting on April 7, 1937 in the Assembly Chamber at Shillong, the erstwhile Capital of the composite State of Assam. Assam under the provisions of India Council Act, 1861 did not have its own democratic institution but was tagged with East Bengal in 1905 and the Institution was then called "Legislative Council of Eastern Bengal and Assam", which started functioning from December 18, 1906. In 1909, the Council had a strength of 40 members and out of 40 seats, Assam was allotted 5 seats. In 1912, Assam was reconstituted into a Chief Commissioners' province. In the year 1913, after Assam was granted a Legislative Council under the Government of India Act. 1909, the Assam Legislative Council came into being with a strength of 34 members of which 13 were nominated by the Chief Commissioner and 21 were elected by the people. The Legislative Council of Assam first met on 6th January, 1913 at 11 a.m. at Shillong, which was presided over by Sir Archdale Easle, the Chief Commissioner of Assam. Under the Government of India Act, 1919, the strength of the Legislative Council was raised to 53 members with effect from 1st April, 1921 of which 41 were elected members and the remaining 12 were nominated.

The Government of India Act, 1935 was adopted by the British Parliament on 2nd August, 1935 and was implemented in 1937. The Government of India Act 1935 made provisions for a Legislative Assembly in each province and as a result the Legislature in Assam became bicameral. The Assam Legislative Assembly had the strength of 108 members and all of them were elected members. The strength of the Legislative Council (Upper House) was not less than 21 and not more than 22 members.

After the partition of India, Sylhet district of Assam was transferred to the then East Pakistan by a referendum and the strength of the Assembly was reduced to 71. However, after Independence, the strength of members were again raised to 108. The bicameral Assam Legislative Assembly became unicameral with the abolition of the Assam Legislative Council in 1947. In the years that followed, Assam was truncated to several smaller states. In 1963, Nagaland came into being as a separate State. With the passing of North Eastern (Reorganization Areas) Act in 1971 by the Parliament, Meghalaya became a full-fledged state. Subsequently, Mizoram and Arunachal Pradesh also followed suit. After the creation of Meghalaya as a separate state, Shillong continued to be the joint capital of both Assam and Meghalaya. However, in 1972, the Government of Assam decided to shift the Capital to Dispur, Guwahati. Accordingly, the first sitting of the Budget Session of the Assam Legislative Assembly was held at the temporary capital at Dispur on the 16th March, 1973.

With the changing geographical boundaries together with the shifts in the population graph of Assam, the strength of members of the Assam Legislative Assembly has fluctuated during the last sixty odd years. In 1952-57 it was 108, reaching still lower to 105 in 1957-62 (the Second Assembly) and then to 114 in 1967-72 (the third Assembly) until it reached a strength of 126 members in 1972-78 (the fifth Assembly).

The Guwahati High Court (Court of Assam, Nagaland, Mizoram, and Arunachal Pradesh)

The Guwahati High Court as of today emerged from the High Court of Assam. On 9th September, 1947, the Assam Legislative Assembly adopted a resolution that a High Court be established for the Province of Assam. In exercise of power conferred by sub-section (1) of section 229 of the Government of India Act, 1935, as adopted by the Indian Provincial

Constitution (Amendment) Order, 1948, the Governor General of India was pleased to promulgate on 1st March, 1948 the Assam High Court Order, 1948, establishing the High Court of Assam with effect from 5th April, 1948, for the then Province of Assam.

Sri Hiralal J. Kania, the then Chief Justice of India came to preside over the inauguration of the High Court at the invitation of His Excellency the Governor of Assam Sir Akbar Hydari and the Premier of the Province Late Gopinath Bardoloi. Sir R.F. Lodge was sworn in as the first Chief Justice of Assam High Court on 5th April, 1948. The Assam High Court initially had its sittings at Shillong but shifted to Guwahati from 14th August, 1948. Later on, the Assam High Court came to be known as the High Court of Assam and Nagaland on the constitution of State of Nagaland with effect from 1st December, 1963. On re-organization of the North-Eastern region by the North Eastern Area (Re-organization) Act, 1971, a common High Court was established for the five North-Eastern States Assam, Nagaland, Manipur, Meghalaya and Tripura and the two Union Territories (Union Territory of Mizoram and the Union Territory of Arunachal Pradesh) and called as the Guwahati High Court.

With the enactment of the State of Mizoram Act, 1986 (Act 34 of 1986) and the State of Arunachal Pradesh Act, 1986 (Act 69 of 1986), the States of Mizoram and Arunachal Pradesh attained statehood on 20.2.1987. By the State of Mizoram Act, 1986, from the appointed day, common High Court for the States of Assam, Nagaland, Meghalaya, Manipur, Tripura and Mizoram called the High Court of Assam, Nagaland, Meghalaya, Manipur, Tripura and Mizoram came into being. Under the State of Arunachal Pradesh Act, 1986, from the appointed day, *i.e.*, 20.2.1987, a common High Court for the State of Assam, Nagaland, Meghalaya, Manipur, Tripura, Mizoram and Arunachal Pradesh came into being.

The Guwahati High Court occupied a unique position of being a common High Court of seven States of North East India till 23/03/2013, before the date of functioning of separate High Courts in Meghalaya, Manipur and Tripura.

ARTS & CRAFTS

The people of Assam have traditionally been craftsmen from time immemorial. Though Assam is mostly known for its exquisite silks and the bamboo and cane products, several other crafts are also made here.

Cane and Bamboo

Cane and bamboo have remained inseparable parts of life in Assam. They happen to be the two most commonly-used items in daily life, ranging from household implements to construction of dwelling houses to weaving accessories to musical instruments. The **Jappi**, the traditional sunshade continues to be the most prestigious of bamboo items of the state, and it has been in use since the days when the great Chinese traveller Hiuen Tsang came to Assam and visitors are welcomed with a jaapi.

Cane and bamboo furnitures on the other hand have been a hit both in the domestic as well as the export market, while paati, the traditional mat has found its way into the world of interior decoration.

Metal Crafts

Bell-metal and brass have been the most commonly used metals for the Assamese artisan. Traditional utensils and fancy articles designed by these artisans are found in every Assamese household. The Xorai and bota have in use for centuries, to offer betel-nut and paan while welcoming distinguished guests. The entire population of two townships near Guwahati—Hajo and Sarthebari, are engaged in producing traditional bell-metal and brass articles. They have also used their innovative skills to design modern day articles to compete with the changing times. Gold, silver and copper too form a part of traditional metal craft in Assam and the State Museum in Guwahati has a rich collection of items made of these metals.

Handlooms

Assam is the home of several types of silks, the most prominent and prestigious being muga, the golden silk exclusive only to this state. **Muga** apart, there is **paat**, as also **eri**, the latter being used in manufacture of warm clothes for winter. Of a naturally rich golden colour, muga is the finest of India's wild silks. It is produced only in Assam.

The women of Assam weave fairy tales in their looms. Skill to weave was the primary qualification of a young girl for her eligibility for marriage. This perhaps explains why Assam has the largest concentration of Handlooms and weavers in India. One of the world's finest artistic traditions finds expression in their exquisitely woven 'Eri', 'Muga' and 'Paat' fabrics.

The traditional handloom silks still hold their own in world markets. They score over factory-made silks in the richness of their textures and designs, in their individuality, character and classic beauty. No two hand-woven silks are exactly alike. Personality of the weaver, her hereditary skill, her innate sense of colour and balance all help to create a unique product.

Toys

The toys of Assam have been broadly classified under four heads : (i) clay toys, (ii) pith, (iii) wooden and bamboo toys, and (iv) cloth-and-mud toys.

While the human figure, especially dolls, brides and grooms, is the most common theme of all kinds of toys, a variety of animals forms have also dominated the clay-toys scene of Assam. Clay traditionally made by the Kumhar and Hira communities, have often depicted different animals too, while gods, goddesses and other mythological figures also find importance in the work of traditional artist.

Pith or Indian cork has also been used for toy-making since centuries in Assam. Such toys are chiefly made in the Goalpara region and they include figures of gods, animals and birds, the last of which again dominate the over-all output.

Pottery

Pottery is probably as old as human civilisation itself. In Assam, pottery can be traced back to many centuries. The Kumhars and Hiras are two traditional potter communities of Assam and while the Kumhars use the wheel to produce his pots, the Hiras are probably the only potters in the world who do not use the wheel at all. Again, among the Hiras, only the women folk are engaged in pottery work, while their men help them in procuring the raw materials and selling the wares.

The most commonly-used pottery products include earthen pots and pitchers, plates, incense-stick holders, earthen lamps, etc. while modern-day decoratives have also found place in their latest designs.

Masks

With tribal art and folk elements form the base of Assamese culture, masks have found an important place in the cultural activities of the people. Masks have been widely used in folk theatres and bhaonas with the materials ranging from terracotta to pith to metal, bamboo and wood.

Jewellery

Jorhat in Upper Assam is one place where the traditional Assamese form of manufacture of jewellery is still in vogue, and people flock to Jorhat to get the exquisite Assamese jewellery. Assamese jewellery include the doog-doogi, loka-paro, bana, gaam-kharu, gal-pata, jon-biri, dhol-biri and keru, all of which have also encouraged the modern jewellers to producing similiar designs mechanically.

Traditional Paintings

The tradition of paintings in Assam can be traced back to several centuries in the past. Ahom palaces and satras and naam-ghar, etc. still abound in brightly-coloured paintings depicting various stories and events from history and mythology. In fact, the motifs and designs contained in Chitra-Bhagavata have come to become a traditional style for Assamese painters of the later.

Paintings

Painting is an ancient tradition of Assam. The ancient practices can be known from the accounts of the Chinese traveller **Xuanzang** (7th century AD). The account mentions that **Bhaskaravarma**, the king of **Kamarupa** has gifted several items to **Harshavardhana**, the king of Kannauj including paintings and painted objects, some of which were on Assamese silk. Many of the manuscripts available from the Middle Ages bear excellent examples of traditional paintings. The most famous of such medieval works are available in the **Hastividyarnava** (A Treatise on Elephants), the **Chitra Bhagawata** and in the **Gita Govinda**. The medieval painters used locally manufactured painting materials such as the colours of **hangool** and **haital**. The medieval Assamese literature also refers to **chitrakars** and **patuas**. Traditional Assamese paintings have been influenced by the motifs and designs in the medieval works such as the Chitra Bhagawata.

FAIRS AND FESTIVALS

Assam is a land of fairs and festivals. Most of the festivals celebrated in Assam have their roots in the diverse faith and belief of her inhabitants, but a spirit of accommodation and togetherness characterizes the celebration of all festivals. The perfect fusion of heritage of her numerous races has made Assam the home of the most colourful festivals which are passionate, compelling and mesmerizing reflecting the true spirit, tradition and lifestyle of the people of Assam.

Six festivals are organised by the Department of Tourism, Govt. of Assam, every year to encourage tourists to visit Assam. They are given below:

1. Majuli Festival
2. Elephant Festival
3. Brahmaputra Beach Festival
4. Dehing Patkai Festival
5. Tea Festival
6. Rongali or Bohag Utsav (The Spring Festival)

Besides these, the major festivals celebrated in Assam are **Bihu**, **Baishagu**, **Ali-Ai-Ligang**, **Baikho**, **Rongker**, **Rajini Gabra, Harni Gabra**, **Bohaggiyo Bishu**, **Ambubashi Mela** and **Jonbill Mela** and so on. The people of Assam also celebrate Holi, Durga Puja, Diwali, Saraswati Puja, Lakshmi Puja, Kali Puja, Eid, Muharram, Me-Dam-Me-Phi, the birth and death anniversaries of Vaishnava Saints Srimanta Sankardev and Madhabdev. The tribals of Assam have their own colourful festivals like the **Kherai Puja** of the Bodos, the **Baikho** and **Pharkantis** of the Rabhas, Ali-ai-ligang and Parag of the Mishing tribe, the Sagra-misawa wansawa and laghun of the Tiwas.

The Ahoms of Tai origin celebrate **Me-Dum-Me-Phi** on the 31st of January annually. The **Ojapali** dances of non-Vaishnavite origin are usually associated with the Serpent Goddess Manasa. Bathow festival is celebrated by the Kacharis through sacrifice of goats and chickens. The Bodos of the plains in general have an intricate pattern of indigenous dances associated with the primitive rituals like Kherai Puja. The Dimasas celebrate **Rangi Gobra** and **Harni Gobra** at the start of the cropping cycle for prosperity to ward off calamities. The Deoris observe **Bohagiya visu**—the Spring time festival.

Tea Festival

Celebrated every year in Jorhat, this festival is all about tea, music and merriment.

Elephant Festival

For conservation and protection of Asiatic elephant a festival is organized every year at Kaziranga National Park jointly by the Forest Department and Tourism Department, Govt. of Assam. The festival includes many activities by domestic elephants and various cultural programmes.

Bihu

Bihu is a series of three prominent festivals of Assam. Primarily a festival celebrated to mark the seasons and the significant points of a cultivator's life over a yearly cycle, in recent times, the form and nature of celebration has changed with the growth of urban centers. A non-religious festival, all communities—religious or ethnic—take part in it. Three Bihus are celebrated: **rongali**, celebrated with onset of spring and the beginning of the sowing season; kongali, the barren bihu when the fields are lush but the barns are empty; and the bhogali, the thanksgiving when the crops have been harvested and the barns are full. Rongali, kongali & bhogali bihu are also known as **'bohag bihu', 'kati bihu' & 'magh bihu'** respectively. The day before the each bihu, is known as '**uruka**'. There are unique features of each bihu. The first day of 'rongali bihu' is called 'Goru bihu' (the bihu of the cows). On this day the cows are taken to the nearby rivers or ponds to be bathed with special care. Traditionally, cows are respected as sacred animals by the people of Assam. Bihu songs and Bihu dance are associated to rongali bihu.

It is one of those festivals where the major tribes in the state celebrate, albeit with different names. While the Bodos celebrate Baisagu, the Rabhas celebrate Baikho. The Missings, Deuris and Morans on the other hand call the festival Bihu Utsav. Tribal groups like the Mishings, the Deoris, and the Morans celebrate "Bihu" with dances of their own distinctive style.

Ambubachi Mela

It is the most important festival of Kamakhya temple of Guwahati and it is held every year during monsoon (mid-June). It is a ritual of austerities celebrated with 'Tantric rites'. It is a common belief that the reigning diety, 'Kamakhya', 'The Mother Shakti' goes through her annual cycle of menstruation during this period.

During Ambubachi the doors of the temple remain closed for three days. It is believed that the earth becomes impure for three days. During this time no farming work is undertaken. Daily worship and other religious performances are suspended during this period. After three days, the temple doors are reopened after the Goddess is bathed and other rituals performed. It is believed that the mother earth regains her purity after that. This is purely a ritual of Tantric cult.

Me-Dum-Me-Phi

The most important Ahom festival which deserves mention is the **Me-Dum-Me-Phi,** *i.e.*, the ancestor worship festival which is observed by the whole Ahom community. This is performed annually on the 31st of January at some common venue. In this way, it helps to develop social contacts and community feelings among the Ahoms. Colourful processions with devotees in traditional finery are also taken out on the occasion.

Jonbeel Mela

This spectacular fair (mela) is held every year during winter at Jonbeel of Jagiroad, a lesser known township only 32 kms from Guwahati. A few days before the mela, tribes like the Tiwas, Karbis, Khasis, Jaintias from the Meghalaya hills come down with their various products for this mela. On the occasion of the 'mela' a big bazar is held here where these tribes exchange their products with local people in barter system which is very rare in a civilized modern society.

Before the 'mela' they perform fire worship or *agni* puja for the well-being of mankind. It is to be noted that during this mela the 'govaraja' or the king of the Tiwa tribe along with his courtiers visit this mela and collect taxes from his subjects. The significant point of this mela is its theme of harmony and brotherhood amongst various tribes and communities. During the 'mela' these communities perform their traditional dances and music to celebrate the mela in a befitting manner.

Baishagu

Famous for its myriad colours and merriment, 'Baishagu' is generally celebrated by the Bodo Kacharis during mid April. It is the most cherished festival of the Bodo tribe. The Bodos also celebrate it as a spring time festival at the advent of the new year.

Bohaggiyo Bishu

This is the most fascinating spring festival of the Deoris of Assam, one of the four divisions of the Chutiyas, who are believed to have been members of the great Bodo race. The term 'Bishu' might have originated from the Chutiya word 'Bishu'. 'Bi' means extreme and 'Su' means 'rejoicing' like other Spring time tribal festivals.

Bohaggiyo Bishu is also observed during mid-April at a stretch for seven days with unrestricted joy and merrymaking. It is to be observed that the Deoris Bishu do not always fall on the Sankranti Day. The Bishu must be preceded by a 'Than puja' and evidently it must start on a Wednesday. There is much socio-religious significance and arrangements to be made before the puja. Once in every four years a white buffalo is sacrificed which is considered a substitute for the traditional human sacrifice. The Deodhani dance is the most important and significant part of the festival. Husori or carol song party is the main attraction.

Rajini Gabra & Harni Gabra

This is the annual festival of the colourful Dimasa tribe. It is exclusively a socio-religious festival which is generally observed before starting a new cultivation. Rajini Gabra is celebrated during day time. The 'Kunang' or the village headman propitiates the family deity by closing the village gate on the worship date. On the same night in a function called 'Harni Gabra', the presiding deity is worshipped for the protection and welfare of the people.

It is very interesting to note that during the Rajini Gabra and Harni Gabra festival if any outsider enters the village inspite off seeing the closed gate, the entire function is considered to be spoilt. The intruders then have to bear the total cost for holding the festival a new.

Rongker and Chomangkan

Rongker and Chomangkan are the two most important festivals of the Karbis, an indeginous tribe of Karbi Anglong. Rongker is basically a spring time festival of merriment and is performed at the beginning of the New year, *i.e.,* April. To propitiate different gods and goddesses for the well being of the entire village, the elderly male folk organise Rongker so that people can be free from diseases and natural calamities for the entire year. They pray for a good harvest, too. The women are not allowed to enter the worship arena during this festival.

On the other hand, Chomangkan is the festival dedicated to the dead. It is primarily a death ceremony. There is no particular time for holding this funeral ceremony. It depends upon the convenience of the locality. This festival is a must for every Karbi. It is a non-stop four days and four nights celebration.

Ali-Ai-Ligang

Ali-Ai-Ligang, the spring festival of the Mishing tribe, is the most colourful festival held every year on the first Wednesday (Ligange lange) of the month of 'Ginmur Polo' (February-March). 'Ali' means root, seed; 'Ai' means fruit and 'Ligang' means sow. That is why 'ceremonial' sowing of paddy starts on this day. A dance is performed by the young boys and girls, characterized by brisk stepping, flinging and flapping of hands and swaying of hips reflecting youthful passion, reproductive urge and joie-de-vivre. "Poro Aapong" or rice beer, Pork and dried fish is essential for the feast. The festival continues for five days and during this festival certain taboos with respect to the cutting of trees, fishing, ploughing, burning jungles etc. are strictly observed.

IMPORTANT PLACES

1. **Guwahati**—gateway to the Assam and N.E. region & principal city of Assam, Kamakhya & Bhubaneshwari temples; Basistha Ashram; Navagraha Temple; State Zoo; Museum; Regional Science Centre; Planetorium; Tirupati Balaji Mandir; Srimanta Sankardev Kalakshetra; Umananda Temple; Shree Shyam Mandir, etc.
2. **Dispur**—capital of Assam.
3. **Diphu**—centre of Karbi art and culture.
4. **Sivasagar**—seat of Ahom rule in Assam—Shivdol, Vishnudol, Devidol, Rang Ghar, Talatol Ghar, Joysagar, Ahom Museum, Gargaon, Kareng Ghar, Charaideo, etc.

5. **Sualkuchi**—famous for Assamese silk-Muga and Pat.
6. **Chandubi**—a natural lagoon and picnic spot.
7. **Barpeta**—Vaishnava Monastery, Shrine of Shri Madhabdev.
8. **Hajo**—where three religions meet—Hinduism, Buddhism & Pao-Mecca, a mosque for Islam.
9. **Jorhat and Dibrugarh**—major tea producing areas.
10. **Tezpur**—temples, ancient ruins and monuments—Da Parbatia, Agnigarh, Bamuni Hills, Bhairavi and Mahabhairava temples and the twin tanks of Bar Pukhuri and Padum Pukhuri and Cole Park.
11. **Madan Kamdeva**—famous for erotic sculpture of 12th century.
12. **Sri Surya Pahar**—rock cut images.
13. **Digboi**—one of the world's oldest oil refinery.
14. **Majuli**—largest river island of the world, centre of Vaishnava culture. There are many satras, which are regarded as the main centres for Assamese art, music, dance, drama, etc.
15. **Jatinga**—famous for the bird mystery near Haflong.
16. **Haflong**—only hill station in Assam.
17. **Bhalukpong**—famous for scenic beauty, picnic and angling spot.
18. **Bhairavakunda**—a picnic spot at the border of Arunachal Pradesh, Assam and Bhutan.
19. **Daranga**—famous winter mela held every year.
20. **Bordoa**—birth place of Shri Sankardev, famous Vaishnavite reformer of Assam.

ASSAM : AT A GLANCE

- Area (in sq. km.) : 78,438
- Latitude : 24 to 28 degree North
- Longitude : 90 to 96 degree East
- Forest Area : 28,105 (35.83 per cent of total area)
- No. of Districts : 35
- Name of the Districts : Tinsukia, Dibrugarh, Sivasagar, Dhemaji, Jorhat, Lakhimpur, Golaghat, Sonitpur, Karbi Anglong, Nagaon, Marigaon, Darrang, Kamrup Rural, Nalbari, Barpeta, Bongaigaon, Goalpara, Kokrajhar,

		Dhubri, North Cachar Hills, Cachar, Hailakandi, Karimganj, Kamrup Metro-politan, Baksa, Chirang, Udalguri, Biswanath, Charaideo, Hojai, South Salamara-Mankachar, West Karbi Anglong, East Kamrup, South Kamrup, Majuli.
• Lok Sabha Constituencies	:	14
• Rajya Sabha Seats	:	7
• Vidhan Sabha Constituencies	:	126
• Nature of Legislature	:	Unicameral
• Capital	:	Dispur
• Languages	:	Assamese, Bengali, English
• Total Population-2011 census	:	3,12,05,576 (2.57 per cent of India's population)
• Male	:	1,59,39,443
• Female	:	1,52,66,133
• Decadal Growth (2001-2011)	:	17.1%
• Literacy Rate	:	72.2%
• Male Literacy Rate	:	77.8%
• Female Literacy Rate	:	66.3%
• Density (per sq. km.)	:	398
• Sex Ratio (per 1000 males)	:	958
• No. of Universities	:	7
• No. of National Parks	:	5 (Kaziranga, Manas, Dibru-Saikhowa, Nameri, and Rajiv Gandhi Orang National Parks)
• State Animal	:	One-horned rhinoceros
• State Bird	:	White-winged wood duck
• State Tree	:	Hollong (Dipterocarpus-macrocarpus)
• State Flower	:	Foxtail Orchids
• Important Tribes	:	Bodo represents nearly half of the total ST population of the state (40.9 per cent). Miri (17.8 per cent), Mikir (10.7 per cent), Rabha

		(8.4 per cent), Kachari (*i.e.*, Sonowal Kachari) (7.1 per cent) and Lalung (5.2 per cent) are other tribes.
• Major Festivals	:	Bihu, Baishagu, Ali-Ai-Ligang, Baikho, Rongker, Rajini Gabra, Harni Gabra, Bohaggiyo Bishu, Kherai Puja, Pharkantis, Parag.
• Name of the National Highways	:	NH-31,NH-36,NH-37,NH-38, NH-39,NH-44,NH-51,NH-52, NH-53,NH-54,NH-61,NH-62,NH-151,NH-152,NH-153,NH-154

OBJECTIVE QUESTIONS

1. What is the area of Assam?
A. 78,438 sq. km. B. 88,438 sq. km.
C. 98,000 sq. km. D. None of these

2. Assam is situated on latitude between
A. 24°N and 28°N B. 34°N and 36°N
C. 30°N and 35°N D. None of these

3. Assam is situated on longitude between
A. 90°E to 96°E B. 85°E to 90°E
C. 95°E to 98°E D. None of these

4. How many districts are in Assam?
A. 25 B. 20
C. 35 D. None of these

5. Assam Legislative Assembly consists of
A. 60 members B. 100 members
C. 126 members D. None of these

6. Capital of Assam is
A. Dispur B. Guwahati
C. Karimganj D. None of these

7. According to 2011 census, total population of Assam is
A. 3,12,05,576 B. 3,37,77,037
C. 2,28,78,491 D. None of these

8. According to 2011 census, decadal growth (2001-2011) of population of Assam is
A. 17.1% B. 28.92%
C. 38.62% D. None of these

9. According to 2011 census, total number of scheduled castes population of Assam is

A. 22,31,321 B. 12,87,491
C. 33,08,570 D. None of these

10. Percentage of SC population in Assam is

A. 7.9% B. 7.2%
C. 10.9% D. None of these

11. Percentage of ST population in Assam is

A. 12.4% B. 14.4%
C. 20.4% D. None of these

12. According to 2011 census, percentage of Urban population in Assam is

A. 13.9% B. 16.9%
C. 14.1% D. None of these

13. According to 2011 census, male population of Assam is

A. 1,59,39,443 B. 1,68,78,491
C. 1,87,77,037 D. None of these

14. According to 2011 census, literacy rate of Assam is

A. 80% B. 85%
C. 72.2% D. None of these

15. Male literacy rate in Assam is

A. 77.8% B. 84.63%
C. 81.44% D. None of these

16. Female literacy rate in Assam is

A. 66.3% B. 64.74%
C. 74.75% D. None of these

17. According to 2011 census, population density in Assam is

A. 398 per sq. km B. 540 per sq. km
C. 240 per sq. km D. None of these

18. Sex ratio (per 1000 males) in Assam is

A. 895 B. 958
C. 998 D. None of these

19. Main tribe of Assam is

A. Bodo B. Miri
C. Mikir D. Rabha

20. Who established the Koch kingdom in Assam

A. Malladeva B. Bishwas Singh
C. Birpal D. None of these

21. Largest river island in the world is

A. Majuli Island B. Barak
C. Barail D. None of these

22. Confluence point of Brahmaputra River is
A. Bay of Bengal
B. Arabian Sea
C. Indian Ocean
D. None of these

23. 'Noonmati' is famous for
A. Oil Refinery
B. Coal Reserve
C. Copper Reserve
D. None of these

24. The main crop of Assam is
A. Rice
B. Wheat
C. Mesta
D. None of these

25. The area coverage under Rabi crops in the State is around
A. 30%
B. 27%
C. 25%
D. None of these

26. In Assam, homestead gardens is locally known as
A. Aami
B. Bari
C. Kuli
D. None of these

27. The total area under forests in Assam is
A. 28,105 sq. km.
B. 30,541 sq. km.
C. 20,891 sq. km.
D. None of these

28. How many National Parks are there in Assam?
A. 5
B. 6
C. 7
D. None of these

29. 'Toklai' is famous for
A. Jute Research Centre
B. Tea Research Centre
C. Rice Research Centre
D. None of these

30. Assam State Electricity Board (ASEB) was constituted in
A. 1958
B. 1950
C. 1960
D. 1970

31. Lokpriya Gopinath Bordoloi International Airport is situated at
A. Tezpur
B. Guwahati
C. Dibrugarh
D. None of these

32. In Lok Sabha, total number of seats reserved for Assam is
A. 15
B. 14
C. 20
D. None of these

33. In Rajya Sabha, total number of seats reserved for Assam is
A. 8
B. 7
C. 10
D. None of these

34. Assam University is situated at
A. Silchar
B. Jorhat
C. Dibrugarh
D. None of these

35. 'Bihu' is the important festival of
A. Manipur
B. Assam
C. Arunachal Pradesh
D. None of these

36. Me-Dum-Me-Phi is famous
A. festival
B. dance
C. music
D. None of these

37. Which of the following is famous for gateway to the Assam and N.E. Region ?
A. Dispur
B. Guwahati
C. Barpeta
D. None of these

38. Capital of Ahom Kingdom was
A. Sibsagar
B. Guwahati
C. Jorhat
D. None of these

39. The first known ruler of Assam was
A. Mahiranga Danava
B. Hatakasur
C. Sambarsur
D. None of these

40. The first Varman King who performed the Ashwamedha Yagya was
A. Mahendra Varman
B. Pushya Varman
C. Bhaskar Varman
D. None of these

41. The last king of the Kachari kingdom was
A. Gobind Chandra
B. Jashanarayan
C. Pratap Narayan
D. None of these

42. In which year, Toklai Tea Research Centre was established?
A. 1922
B. 1911
C. 1933
D. None of these

43. Longest river of Assam is
A. Barak River
B. Brahmaputra River
C. Disang River
D. None of these

44. State tree of Assam is
A. Hollong
B. Neem
C. Peepal
D. None of these

45. State animal of Assam is
A. Tiger
B. Rhino
C. Elephant
D. None of these

46. State bird of Assam is
A. Asian Koel
B. Hill Myna
C. White-winged Wood Duck
D. None of these

47. State Flower of Assam is

A. Foxtail Orchids B. Lotus
C. Palash D. None of these

ANSWERS

1	2	3	4	5	6	7	8	9	10
A	A	A	C	C	A	A	A	A	B
11	**12**	**13**	**14**	**15**	**16**	**17**	**18**	**19**	**20**
A	C	A	C	A	A	A	B	A	B
21	**22**	**23**	**24**	**25**	**26**	**27**	**28**	**29**	**30**
A	A	A	A	B	b	A	A	B	A
31	**32**	**33**	**34**	**35**	**36**	**37**	**38**	**39**	**40**
B	B	B	A	B	A	B	A	A	A
41	**42**	**43**	**44**	**45**	**46**	**47**			
A	B	B	A	B	C	A			

●●●●●●●

4

MANIPUR

INTRODUCTION

Nestled on a plateau and surrounded by nine sub-Himalayan ranges of hills, Manipur is the place that gifted the game of Polo to the world. The martial tradition of Manipur is reflected in such indigenous games even today. Literally meaning "the jeweled land", Manipur is richly endowed with natural beauty and splendor. The first Prime Minister of India, Jawaharlal Nehru, described Manipur as a "Jewel of India", bewitching beholders with its natural beauty and its cultural paraphernalia. Decorated by innumerable beautiful flora and inhabited by a number of attractive fauna, Manipur shines with Nature's grace. It is made more enchanting with its unique natural setting, comprising of eye-catching waterfalls, lakes, streams and evergreen forests.

This is the place, where Rajashree Bhagyachandra created the famous Ras Lila, the classical dance of Manipur, out of his enchanting dream by the grace of Lord Krishna. Her folk dances reveal the mythological concept of creation of Manipur.

The Meiteis, who live primarily in the state's valley region, are one of the primary ethnic groups. Their language, Meiteilon (also known as Manipuri), is also the lingua franca in the state. It was recognized as one of India's national languages in 1992. The Kukis and Nagas live in the hills of the state. The Kukis too have their own kingdoms like the Chahsat, Aisan, Jampi, etc. and were close to the Meitei kings in the plain. The independent existence of the Meitei and Kuki kings can be proved by common practice of calling Kuki village headmens by Meiteis as "Ningthou", which means "King".

HISTORY

Manipur's history as a political entity is traced around 33 AD with the ascending of Pakhangba as the first king at the throne at Kangla. The royal chronicle, Cheitharol Kumbaba, narrates of different principalities ruled by different tribes in the Manipur valley and the adjoining hills. Though initially there were nine principalities in the valley, it was later merged into seven. Each principality was governed by different tribes. During the period from the first century AD to the tenth century AD, integration of these tribes took place under the military might of the Mangang tribe. With the transformation of a tribal political form to a feudal structure slowly and gradually over time, these tribes, who went through various layers of social interactions and changes, got renamed as clans through totem and taboo.

In addition to these, several hills tribes were also absorbed within these seven clans of the Meitei state. These largely took place through migration. This phenomenon took place as late as eighteenth century AD. Potsangbam as a locality and also as a pana (administrative division) was formed by the hills tribes (Tangkhuls) who settled in the valley. Similarly, there had been migration from the valley to the hills as well. Oinam in the Senapati district is inhabited by communities whose origins are traced to the valley.

The beginning of eleventh century marked watershed in the history of Manipur with the introduction of the written constitution in the state. Loiyamba Shinyen, the state decree, supposed to have been issued by King Loyamba in 1110 AD showed the level of political development of an Asiatic state. This also marked the consolidation of a feudal form of social system in the state. The next shift in state formation took place around 1698 AD with the coronation of Pitambar Charairongba (1698–1709 AD). Social transformation began with the process of hinduization, which came in full swing at the time of his son, Garib Nawaj. It is during this period that migration of the Brahmins from India took place in large scale. Consolidation of military power took place at the time of Garib Nawaj with his invasion of Burma and defeating the Toongoo dynasty. The next shift took place with Manipur's defeat at the hands of the British in 1891. That put an end to the ever-weakening state of Manipur of its sovereign power as a kingdom. The final shift came with end of colonial power in the state. Manipur experienced a brief period of independence as a sovereign nation between 15 August 1947 and 15 October 1949 when the nation was merged to Indian dominion as a Part–C state. Later on it was further degraded to the status of a union territory from 1956 onwards. In 1972, Manipur was elevated to the status of a state of Union of India.

GEOGRAPHY

Manipur has a total surface area of 22,327 sq. km. forming 0.7% of the total land surface of the Indian Union. It is situated between the latitude

23°50′N to 25°42′N and the longitude 92°58′E to 94°45′E. It has a border of 854 km of which 352 is international border with Myanmar on the east. The remaining 502 km long border separates her from the neighbouring states of Nagaland on the North, Assam on the west and Mizoram on the south and the south-west. Physiographically the land is divisible into a central valley and the surrounding mountains. The plain or the valley is approximately (2238 sq. km.) amounting to 10% of the total area. Out of this an area of 550 sq. km. is occupied by lakes, wetlands, barren uplands and hillocks.

Two river systems viz. the **Barak-Brahmaputra System** and the **Chindwin-Irrawaddi System** drained the entire State. The Barak River and its tributaries form the sub-system in the western hills and join the earlier system. Important tributaries under this sub-system are the Dzuko, the Leimatak, the Irang, the Makru and the Tuivai flowing in a NE-NW orientation.

The Imphal or Manipur River meanders through the Manipur valley in a NW-SE direction. Its important tributaries are the Kongba, the Iril, the Thoubal, the Heirok, the Sekmai, the Khuga and the Chakpi rivers. The Manipur River passes through a gorge flow out of the state to join the Chindiwin River in Myanmar.

The mountains are divided into the Western Hills comprising the Koubru-Laimaton, Makui-Longbi, Kala Naga and Vangai ranges, while the Eastern Hills comprise the Siroi, Mapithel and Yamodoung ranges. The highest peak in the state is **Mt. Essau** or **Tenipu** (9824 ft/2994 m).

Geological Features

Geologically, Manipur is said to belong to the young folded mountains of the Himalayan system. The rocks in the state vary from upper Cretaceous to the present alluvium. The oldest rocks found in the state are mainly confined in the eastern part of the state close to Indo-Myanmar border and the rocks are grouped as cretaceous rocks consisting of chromite (Epilates), serpentine etc. Availability of Asbestos, Chromite, Copper ore, Coal, Big iron, Lignite, Lime stone, Nickel ore and Petroleum is reported in some parts of the state.

In Ukhrul district limestone deposits are found which belong to upper cretaceous period. The sandstone, shale of the Disang group found over the eastern half of Manipur belong to the Eocene period. The rocks consisting of sandstone, shale, clay, etc. of the Barail group are confined to the rocks of Disang group and extend along the mid western portion of the state and they belong to the upper Eocene and Oligocene periods.

The shales and sandstone of the Tipam and Surma groups cover the western blanks of Manipur and they belong to Miocene period. Rocks of alluvial deposits found in the Manipur valley portion are of recent origin and further they can be grouped as older and younger alluvium. The state is mainly composed of tertiary rocks. In the Ukhrul area there are igneous rocks which contain quartz, sandstone, limestone, etc.

The soil of the state is of two major types – residual and transported, which cover both the hill and plain of the State. The residual soils are either laterized or non-laterized. The laterized red soils covering an area of 2,500 sq. km. in the Barak drainage on the Western slope of Manipur. It contains rich portion of nitrogen and phosphate, a medium acidity and lesser amount of Potash. The old alluvial is brought down by river Barak basin and Jiri river and their tributaries from their lateritic water ship hills. The compact and less permeable soils contain higher quantity of potash, fair amount of nitrogen and phosphorus with medium acidity. The transported soils are of two types – alluvial and organic. The alluvial soils cover 1600 sq. km. in the valley. These soils have general clayey warm texture and grey to pale brown colour. They contain a good proportion of potash and phosphate, a fair quantity of nitrogen and organic matter and are less acidic. The organic soils cover the low lying areas of the valley. With dark grey colour and clayey loam texture, these peaty soils have high acidity, abundance of organic matter, a good amount of nitrogen and phosphorus but are poor in potash. The hill soils are more or less rich in organic carbon (1 to 3%) in the top soil, but poor in available phosphorus and potash. They are acidic in nature.

Distribution and Classification of Soils

The soil of Manipur belongs to 4 orders, 8 sub-orders, 13 great-groups and 23 sub-groups. It is observed that the Inceptisols are the dominant soils followed by Ultisols, Entisols and Alfisols and occupy 38.4%, 36.4%, 23.1% of the total geographical area of the State, respectively. Lakes and marshy lands occupy 1.9 per cent. The area-wise distribution of soil at order and suborder levels of Taxonomy are given below.

S. No.	Soil order	Suborder	Area ('000 hect.)	Per cent of TGA
1.	Inceptisols		858.3	38.4
		Ocrepts	654.6	29.3
		Acrepts	203.7	9.1
2.	Ultisols		811.0	36.4
		Humults	374.0	16.8
		Udults	436.9	19.6

S. No.	Soil order	Suborder	Area ('000 hect.)	Per cent of TGA
3.	Entisols	Orthents	515.6	23.1
4.	Alfisols	Udalfs	3.8	0.2
5.	Miscellaneous Marshy land		42.4	1.9
		Total	**2231.0**	**100.0**

TGA: Total Geographical Area

MINERALS

There are not many minerals in Manipur but it has rich lignite seams in the southern hills. The other known minerals that Manipur possess but have to be exploited yet are limestone, copper, chromite, nickel, asbestos and salt. Poor communication facilities, inaccessibility and inclement climate have been the constraints in mineral explorations. However, the first attempt of systematic geological survey in Ukhrul district in the recent years have located quite a number of minerals whose mining potential needs be assessed after a detailed study.

Limestone

A substantial deposit of good quality limestone suitable for use in the manufacture of cement has been located during the recent years by the Geological Survey of India near Ukhrul. Limestone has also been located at a number of other areas *e.g.,* Hundung, Mova, Khonggoi, Lambui and Paoyi. In the Ukhrul area, limestone occurs in two bands. A reserve of 579 M tonnes has been proved by drilling to a depth of 105 meters. Other deposits are 0.26 M tonnes at Khonggoi and 1.88 M tonnes at Hundung. All these deposits taken, together are expected to be able to feed a cement plant of modest capacity of 200 tonnes per day for approximate 45 years. But the present installed capacity is only 50 TPD (tonne per day).

Evaporities

Evaporities are the mineralised salt sediments from the evaporation of saline waters specially the seawaters. These are used in fertilizer, chemical, drug and building industries. Minor occurrences of magnesium and other salts in Kongai area of Chingai sub-division of Ukhrul district have been located.

Chromite

Chromite deposits containing partly metallurgical grade ore have been located at Kwatha and Khudengthabi in Chandel district and near Siroi Peak in Ukhrul district.

Ferrous Alloy Metals

Nickeliferous magnetites, copper and cobalt have been located at Kwatha, Khudengthabi and Namphesha along the ultramaphic expositions near Moreh. The ore grade and size of deposit need further assessment with investigations extended into the northern strips of the ultramaphic belt. The possibility of locating platinum in this ophiolite belt has been observed.

Asbestos

Minor occurrences of these minerals have been reported from the ultramaphic suites of rocks particularly in the Ukhrul and Moreh areas.

Clay

The alluvial soils and some of the residual soils in the valley contain clay. The character of the clay is such that it can not be used in the manufacture of white-ware. Bricks, sanitary and channel pipes can be manufactured from it. The clay deposit at Kangvai (Churachandpur district) has been recommended for use in terracotta industries. This deposit has a reserve of 2.52 M tonnes. The clay deposits at Thongjao, Sekmai and some other villages are used in pottery. The rest are fit for brick industry.

FLORA AND FAUNA

More than 77 per cent of the state area is under forest and important forest products are obtained in Manipur. It is said that the forest of Manipur holds seventy different species of commercially valuable woods including teak. There are also bamboos and canes apart from firewood, which people collect for their daily use. Turpentine, wax, resin, gumfibre, the spicy dalchini, honey, and medicinal herbs are among the other products of Manipur's forests. There is, however, scope for raising the revenue of the state from its rich forests.

For a hilly State like Manipur, forest products are the most important natural resources for environmental protection and maintaining ecological balance. According to Forest Report, 2017 by Forest Survey of India (FSI), Dehradun, the forest cover of Manipur is 17,346 sq. kms. as against 16,994 sq. kms. in 2015.

Forest Cover within Green Wash

Very Dense Forest	898 sq km
Moderately Dense Forest	5,983 sq km
Open Forest	8,568 sq km
Sub Total	15,449 sq km

Forest Cover outside Green Wash

Very Dense Forest	10 sq km
Moderately Dense Forest	527 sq km
Open Forest	1,360 sq km
Sub Total	1,897 sq km
Total Forest Cover	17,346 sq km
Tree Cover	220 sq km
Total Forest & Tree Cover	17,566 sq km
Per Capita Forest & Tree Cover	0.61 ha
Of State's Geographical Area	78.68%
Of India's Forest & Tree Cover	2.19%

Classification of Forest

Area under forest includes all lands classed as forests under any legal enactment dealing with forests or administered as forests whether state owned or private and whether wooded or maintained as potential forest land. The area of crops raised in the forests and grazing lands or area open for grazing within the forests are generally included under the forests area.

District-wise Forest Cover of Manipur (State of Forest Report 2017)

(Area in km²)

District	Geographical Area	Very Dense Forest	Mod. Dense Forest	Open Forest	Total	Percent of GA
Bishnupur	496	0	1	21	22	4.44
Chandel	3,313	11	970	1,926	2,907	87.75
Churachandpur	4,570	42	1,663	2,464	4,169	91.23
Imphal East	709	0	61	217	278	39.21
Imphal West	519	0	16	38	54	10.40
Senapati	3,271	272	751	1,161	2,184	66.77
Tamenglong	4,391	390	1,754	1,809	3,953	90.03
Thoubal	514	0	2	71	73	14.20
Ukhrul	4,544	193	1,292	2,221	3,706	81.56
Total	**22,327**	**908**	**6,510**	**9,928**	**17,346**	**77.69**

The Shiroy Lily

It is grown at the peak of the Shiroy Kashang Mountain at a height of 8400 feet above sea level situated in Ukhrul district of Manipur. The Shiroy Lily belongs to Lilium family, but unique in character. By using a microscopic lens, seven colours which claimed its superiority to other lilies in the world can be seen light pink in colour. The height of the plant varies from 2 ft. to 3.5 ft. depending on the soils fertility. Shiroy Lily is not grown anywhere in the world accept Shiroy Kanhong of Manipur. It is said that Princess Chitrangoda of Manipur had own the heart of Arjuna in her first meeting by offering a Shiroy Lily. Arjuna was so impressed with the beauty and fragrance of the flower that he at once lost himself on her.

Fauna

Manipur is the only spot on earth in which the Brow-Antlered Deer (Cervus eldi eldi) locally known as Sangai is found. This rare deer is surviving in its natural habitat at the Keibul Lamjao. The habitat was declared as a National Park in the year 1977 covering an area of 40 sq. kms. It is unique in its own physical feature as the park lies submerged under water covered entirely on the surface by a floating entangled mass of vegetation like grass, shrubs and earth, called phumdi. The deer survives on top of this phumdi.

The other area already declared as protected area besides Keibul Lamjao national Park is the Yangoupokpi-Lokchao Wildlife Sanctuary with an area of 184.80 sq. km. It is situated at Chandel District and is located on the Indo-Malayan Zoo geographical Zone. The Malayan Sun Bear is found in this wildlife sanctuary.

National Parks and Wildlife Sanctuaries

S. No.	Conservation site	Location (District)	Area in sq. km
1.	Keibul Lamjao National Park	Bishnupur	40.00
2.	Yangoupokpi-Lokchao Wildlife Sanctuary	Chandel	184.80
3.	Bunning Wildlife Sanctuary	Tamenglong	115.80
4.	Zeliad Wildlife Sanctuary	Tamenglong	21.00
5.	Keilam Wildlife Sanctuary	Churachandpur	187.50
6.	Jiri-Makru Wildlife Sanctuary	Tamenglong	198.00
7.	Shiroi Hill National Park	Ukhrul	41.00

CLIMATE

The impact of terrain diversity, altitudinal variation and river regime has become eloquent in the seasonal variability of climate from one place to another. The Barak basin and lower foothills of Manipur Western hills have a warmer climate than the central valley and surrounding hills. Similarly, the western part of the state is more moist than the eastern because of its location on the windward slope of the hills.

The climate of Manipur can be broadly classified into—

1. Temperate prevailing in the higher altitude of hill where temperate fruits and vegetables can be grown throughout the year.
2. Sub-tropical prevailing in the lower altitudes hills and central valley plain where winter lasts from November to February and rainy season from May to September. The transition period of March, April and October can be described as spring and autumn though short.
3. Tropical prevailing in Jiri plains and foothills—during March. In this plain and foothills all the tropical crops can be raised. The temperature ranged from sub-zero to 36°C.

RAINFALL

The climate of the State is salubrious with approximate average annual rainfall varying from 933 mm at Imphal to 2593 mm at Tamenglong. Monsoon confers upon Manipur a very handsome rain as seen below—

1. South-West monsoon (June to Sept.)—825 mm
2. Post monsoon period (Oct. to Dec.)—151 mm
3. Winter monsoon (Jan. to Feb.)—52 mm
4. Pre monsoon (March to May)—407 mm

Although the State receives adequate rainfall, it suffers from temporal and location variations. There are great variations of rainfall in different districts. There is scarcity of water for economic activities in some districts.

IRRIGATION

Major and Medium Irrigation had been introduced in the State from 1980. So far 8 (eight) Major and Medium Irrigation & Multipurpose projects have been taken up viz;

1. Loktak Lift Irrigation Project
2. Khoupum Dam Project
3. Sekmai Barrage Project
4. Imphal Barrage Project
5. Singda Multipurpose Project
6. Thoubal Multipurpose Project
7. Khuga Multipurpose Project
8. Dolaithabi Barrage Project

Out of the above Khoupum Dam, Imphal Barrage, Sekmai Barrage, Loktak Lift Irrigation, Irrigation component of Singda project, Barrage component at Keithelmanbi and a part of the lift canal of Thoubal Multipurpose Project had been completed upto the end of VIIIth Plan. The Irrigation potential created from these projects upto the end of IXth Plan was 28,500 Ha. At present, three ongoing projects viz; (i) Khuga Multipurpose Project, (ii) Thoubal Multipurpose Project and (iii) Dolaithabi Barrage Project are in progress.

DRAINAGE SYSTEM

The state is drained by various streams which belong to three river systems. The Manipur river and its tributaries—Imphal, Thoubal, Nambul, Nambol, Khuga, Sekmai, and other smaller streams with **Loktak** and other associated lakes form the water resources of the valley having catchment of 6,332 sq. km about 28.4% area of the state. Discharging maximum quantity of water during the monsoon months (May-September), they frequently inundate the land along their banks. Every year Manipur experiences havoc of flood. **River Barak** and its tributaries Irang, Makru, Jiri and their associated streams which drain the Northern and Western hill areas, have a catchments of 9042 sq. km. about 40.5% area of entire state. The Eastern slope of Manipur eastern hills is connected by a number of small streams of the **Chindwin river** system, which have a catchment area of 6953 sq. km., about 31.1% area of the state. **River Axenglox** and its tributaries, – Chamu and Chingai and river Yu and its tributaries—Maklang, Tayungbi, Taretlok, Lokchao and Tuiyaag flow in sub-parallel pattern and their supply terminates in the valley of Myanmar.

AGRICULTURE

Agriculture and allied activities provide the backbone to the economy in both the hills and the valley of Manipur. It engages about 70% of the workers. The size of the cultivated area is, however, only 12.98% of the total geographical area of the State. Of this total cultivated area, 52% is confined to the valley. Therefore, half of the total valley area which accommodates 67% of the total population is occupied for agriculture purposes. The pressure on land in the valley is thus quite conspicuous.

Agriculture : At a Glance

1. Geographical area of the State	22,327 Sq. km.
2. Gross agricultural area	2,89,826 hect.
3. Net agricultural area	2,34,015 hect.
4. Percentage of gross agricultural area	12.98%

5.	Percentage of net agricultural area	0.48%
6.	Percentage of net agriculture area in the hills to net agricultural area of State.	3.00%
7.	Percentage of net agricultural area in the hills to geographical area	5.55%
8.	Percentage of net agricultural area in the valley to net agricultural area of State	47.00%
9.	Percentage of net agricultural area in the valley to geographical area	4.93%
10.	Cropping Intensity	123.84%

POPULATION

According to 2011 census, Manipur has a population of 28,55,794. The sex ratio was 985 females per 1000 males. The valley that is 12% of the total geographical area had 58.84% of the population while the hills (88%) were inhabited by 41.16%. This makes an impaired distribution of population between the hills and the plains having the population densities of 52 persons per sq. km. and 632 persons per sq. km. respectively even though the average density of 115 per sq. km. is much below the all India average.

Area, Population and Headquarters of Districts (2011 Census)

S. No.	District	Area	Population	Headquarters
1.	Senapati	3,271	4,79,148	Senapati
2.	Ukhrul	4,544	1,83,998	Ukhrul
3.	Chandel	3,313	1,44,182	Chandel
4.	Churachandpur	4,570	2,74,143	Churachandpur
5.	Tamenglong	4,391	1,40,651	Tamenglong
6.	Imphal (West)	519	5,17,992	Lamphel
7.	Imphal (East)	709	4,56,113	Porompat
8.	Thoubal	514	4,22,168	Thoubal
9.	Bishnupur	496	2,37,399	Bishnupur

Population by Religious Communities (2011 Census)

S. No.	Religious Communities	Percentage
1.	Hindu	41.4%
2.	Muslim	8.39%
3.	Christian	41.3%
4.	Sikh	0.05%

S. No.	Religious Communities	Percentage
5.	Buddhist	0.24%
6.	Jain	0.05%
7.	Other Religious Communities	2.98%

- Total Population—28,55,794 (2011 Census)
- Male Population—14,38,586
- Female Population—14,17,208
- Sex Ratio (Female per 1000 Male)—985
- Density of Population (Per sq. km.)—128
- Literate Population—76.9%
- Towns (including 5 Census towns)—33

The rate of growth of population in Manipur registers much higher rate than the All-India-rate from 1961. The decadal growth rate was 35.04 per cent during 1951-61, 37.53 per cent during 1961-1971, 32.46 per cent during 1971-81, 29.29 per cent during 1981-91, 24.86 per cent during 1991-2001 and 24.50 per cent during 2001-2011, much higher than the All India average as seen in the following table.

Growth of population, Manipur vis-a-vis India during 1951 to 2011 (in percentage)

Census Year	Manipur	All India
1951	12.80	13.31
1961	35.04	21.51
1971	37.53	24.80
1981	32.46	24.66
1991	29.29	23.85
2001	24.86	21.34
2011	24.50	17.07

Source: Census Operations, Manipur

Population by Occupation

The structure and character of economy is largely reflected in the occupational composition of the economy. In 2011 in Manipur people engaged in agricultural activities account for 70% of the total population indicating the marked importance of land-based primary activities. Remaining 30% were engaged in secondary and tertiary sector.

Density of Population

The density of population which exerts pressures on the environmental behaviours of the area, keeps on rising in the valley. The density of population increased from 64 in 1981 to 107 in 2001 and 128 in 2011 while even in 2001 it remains very low in the hills; only 44 per sq. km. In Imphal area it is more than 600 with all attendant consequences, giving rise to the problem of urban onslaught with huge accumulation of solid wastes and unplanned settlement.

Density of population in Manipur (per sq. km. area)

Year	Density
1981	64
1991	82
2001	107
2011	128

Source: Govt. of Manipur, Directorate of Economics and Statistics.

Growth of Urban Population in Manipur (1961-2011)

Year	No. of Towns	Urban Population	Percentage to Total Population
1961	1	67,717	8.68
1971	8	1,41,492	13.19
1981	32	3,75,460	26.42
1991	31	5,05,645	27.52
2001	33	5,76,410	25.12
2011	33	8,34,154	29.02

District-wise Population (2011 Census)

S. No.	State/Districts	Total Population	Males	Females	Density (per km.)	Sex ratio (females per 1000 males)
	Manipur	**2,855,794**	**1,438,586**	**1,417,208**	**128**	**985**
1.	Senapati	4,79,148	2,47,323	2,31,825	59	937
2.	Tamenglong	1,40,651	72,371	68,280	32	943
3.	Churachandpur	2,74,143	1,38,820	1,35,323	60	975
4.	Bishnupur	2,37,399	1,18,782	1,18,617	479	999
5.	Thoubal	4,22,168	2,10,845	2,11,323	821	1002
6.	Imphal West	5,17,992	2,55,054	2,62,938	998	1031
7.	Imphal East	4,56,113	2,26,094	2,30,019	643	1017
8.	Ukhrul	1,83,998	94,718	89,280	40	943
9.	Chandel	1,44,182	74,579	69,603	44	933

PEOPLE OF MANIPUR

There is not much of historical evidence available on the origin of the people of Manipur. There are different schools of thought regarding the origin. Some people considered Manipuris as the descendants of Tartar Colony from China. Others considered that the Manipuris were descendants of the surrounding hill tribes, *i.e.,* the big race of Nagas which was once in existence in many parts of the world. The Manipuris are related to the present Naga race of the hills also in respect of many customs still in existence in both groups. Some believe that Manipuris are a fine stalwart race descended from an Indo-Chinese stock, with some admixture of Aryan blood. Some scholars consider that the Manipuris are Kshatriyas as mentioned in the Epic, 'Mahabharatha'.

Another school of thought consider Manipuris the descendants of Kiratas. Another school of thought considers Manipuris to be descended from the stock of Dravidians who migrated from south India to Manipur and Naga hills through Burma.

The population of Manipur comprises different social groups. They are Meiteis, Nagas, Kukis and Miscellaneous groups. The entire population of Manipur is distributed into two regions: the hill population and the valley population. The valley people are supposed to be the descendants of four old tribes called Khuman, Luang, Moirang and Maithai. The hill people are broadly divided into Naga and Kuki tribes. The people of Manipur, both in the valley and the hills are having predominantly Mongoloid features. But it is not difficult to distinguish the valley and the hill people.

Meities

Physical Features

The Meiteis are mainly populating the main valley. Men are muscular and stout with well developed chest and hard limbs. They possess enormous stamina and muscular power. The improvised Mongol features distinguish them from other Mongolian races. Hairs are generally coarse and black. Very few grow beard, and moustache is not in fashion. The women are beautiful with improved Mongol features like slightly sharp facial features. Meitei women can be easily distinguished from a hill woman.

Profession

The common profession among men is agriculture. The educated folk seek official jobs and some engage themselves in different kinds of business. Women are hard working.

Kukis

The Kukis are also called Khongjois. They are distributed widely in Manipur, occupying the south-western, south and south-eastern hills which spread in the district of Churachandpur, Tangnoupal district and Sadar hills in the north Manipur. There are different beliefs about their origin. Some of the Kukis believe their origin is in the north at a place Maikel. Some traces the Kukis links with Zomi, who migrated from China. The term Zomi is an ancient and historical name of the Zo ethnic groups (Zo means cold region and Mi means men). With the reference to the alpine climate the people living on the hills could be named as Kuki. The Kukis who came to Manipur during 1830 and 1840 were a nomadic race. Some authorities consider them having traces to Malaya peninsula. There are different groups among Kukis. Those who migrated from Mizoram are called Mizos and are educationally advanced. Another group of those migrated from Burma side in 1830 is like the Paite. Manipuris consider Kukis to be of two groups, old Kuki and new Kuki. The new group of Kukis is the group comprising those who migrated to Manipur during the region of Raja Nar Singh. The old Kukis of Manipur are the Thadao and Vaipei.

Profession

The chief is the owner of the land and the forest of a certain area in that locality. The land is divided amongst the willing tillers. They have to give the chief a certain portion of paddy as tax. If the forest produce is utilized by any villager in his area then the user will have to pay the tax.

Naga Tribes

The Nagas occupy the northern, north-eastern, and north-western hills of Manipur. The different groups of Nagas are Thangkhuls, Mao, Muram Nagas, Tadubi, Kolya, Khoiras or Mayang Khong, Kabuis, Koirengs, Chirus and Marings. There are several stories about the origin of different groups of Nagas. It is believed that Nagas and Meiteis have common ancestors.

Profession

Nagas are expert in bow and arrow fight, spear throwing and in the use of Dao. All tribes keep Dao. It is made of iron blade which is set in a wooden handle. It is very useful and is kept always by men. It is used for clearing the way in thick forest. In the slash-and-burn method of agriculture the Dao plays an important role. The arrows are poisoned with the help of a herb extract called Acronite. These are used only on war or in hunting of big animals. Buffalo hide of oblong, round shapes are used for making shields for use during hunting and wars.

Basket making and other kind of bamboo work is done in every house. Cultivation is done by the slash-and-burn system called 'jhum' or dry cultivation. This is also termed as shifting cultivation. Their main hobby is hunting. Fishing is also done in hill streams, ponds and ditches. Both fishing and hunting are prohibited during cultivating seasons.

Lois

The Lois consider themselves as the oldest inhabitants. Lois means 'slaves or dependent'. These small tribals inhabit the valley of Manipur. They are called Singmei, Undro and Chairel. All of them speak different dialects but with a considerable mixture of Manipuri words.

Profession

The Lois are expert at agriculture and hold monopoly in the silk, iron smelting and other craft work. Now they have been given scheduled caste status and the state government is taking interest in their uplift. There is no caste system in Manipur but Lois are the victim of political dis-recognition from the past. They are not given recognition so as to avoid their political rising but they are not treated like scheduled castes. The Lois are not much involved in social activities and political affairs. Their cultural life is similar to that of the Meities. They celebrate Lai-Haraoba according to their own customs which only differ in minor details. In dress and food habit there is practically no difference with that of Meities.

Muslims

Muslims are living in several villages at Mayang, Imphal, Yaripok, Lylong, Thoubal etc. Their main occupation is agriculture. Some educated ones also seek official jobs in state and central government service. They are intelligent and hard-working persons. They have mixed characters of Mongoloid and Aryans in their features. They follows all norms of the Muslim society.

Maring

It is said that they had close relationship with the Meitei Kings and their name derived from mei (fire) and ring (start or produce). Meitei kings depended on them during wars with neighbours. There are three mains groups of Marings who identify themselves with different colours in their clothings: Black, Red, and Red and Black on the border. They participate actively in the State politics. If provided adequate road and communication infrastructure, they will be a very progressive group of tribes.

Sikhs

The Sikhs settled in Manipur are of Punjab origin but most of them have come from Burma where they had gone from Punjab in earlier times. Some of them entered Manipur after the Second World War and some others after the Burmese government disallowed them the citizenship. They have Gurudwaras at Imphal and Moreh. At these two places only they are largely concentrated. All Sikhs keep beard and wear turban. They are strict in keeping the five "ks", the kesha, kangha, kripan, kara, kachha *i.e.,* to grow hair, keep comb, keep sword, keep armlet and wear shorts. All Sikhs are businessmen dealing in transport, cloth, contracts, etc. They are pioneer transporters in Manipur. Salwar-kurta or sari-blouse is the common dress among Sikh women. They speak Punjabi among themselves but are also fluent in Meitei and even tribal languages. The Sikhs of Moreh also speak Burmese. They are an adaptable society. They keep their culture and are very particular about their faith and the ritualistic performances in the Gurudwaras and their homes. Sikhs believe in the gurus, the great religious teachers who got the inspirations from the God and taught the masses to follow the right path. For the Sikhs the guru is the guide to the religious path.

Nepalis

The Nepalis are the old settlers in Manipur. The contribution of Nepalis to the Manipuri society is valuable. Most of the Nepalis entered Manipur as servants and labourers and settled here. Some started cultivation of the tribal chief's land as tenants with sufficient share of the crops. They were known for cattle rearing. Most of the settlers started dairies along with their agriculture. Nepalis have scattered into small valleys in Mao, Maram, Karong and Kangpokpi areas. This is the main belt of Nepalis and they have improved agriculture and crops in Kangpokpi, Tomei-Tamenglong areas. Their thick population is between Tomei and Kangpokpi. The greatest contribution of the Nepalis is to transform the habitat to their advantage.

Bishnupuris

Some people of lower caste entered Manipur and they got good promises for their labour and jobs. Safaiwalas, cobblers, watermen, gardeners, washermen, etc. were not available. Manipur being a casteless society was unmindful of these requirements. In Manipur these jobs are done by all. There are some Sudra Manipuris who are supposed to be the descendants of immigrants who married Manipuri women. This is also a degraded class called Kalacheiya or Bishnupuris which consists of descendants of Doms and other Bengalis of low castes. They have played an important role in the society. In Manipuri society they are respected. There is no concept of untouchability. Those who are declared bonafide citizens of Manipur get the reservation benefits.

Biharis

Most of the labour class comprises people of Bihar and Uttar Pradesh. They have come here to earn their bread. They are fluent in Meitei as well as in Tribal dialects. They have established themselves throughout the valley on all routes. Biharis speak their Hindustani and also learn tribal dialects. This linguistic exchange is a great social advantage to both sides. The Biharis have maintained their culture. Their Hindustani dress will never change. They are all Hindus. Some are from upper castes and some from scheduled castes. Some Muhamadans have also migrated from Bihar in search of jobs or to run shops in Manipur. The curious character of Biharis is that they get adapted to any society. They are very good at business. They give due respect to the tribal and Meitei social custom and take part in the social ceremonies. The Biharis help each other and they are known for their unity.

Punjabis

There are some non-Sikh Punjabi traders settled at Imphal. Their contribution to Punjabi culture is worth mentioning. Their dishes are very tasty. They retain their habit of speaking Punjabi amongst themselves. They speak in a hilarious and jubilant mood. Their women wear salwar-kurta, sari and are very fond of cosmetics. Inside Punjabi house one finds several items of furniture and comfort. They believe in decent living and eating.

Marwaris

Marwaris are the dominating business community in the north-eastern region. They deal in big business and wholesale trade. Their concentrations are only in the established old towns and business centres like Imphal, Churachandpur and Moreh. They have entered Manipur in the late nineteenth and early twentieth century. They migrated from Rajasthan. Their religion is Hinduism, some observe Jainism and some Sanatan Dharm. Some have adopted Vaishnavite sect.

They marry within their community. Generally they live as joint family. Their food habits are very simple. They are vegetarian and refrain from meat, egg, chicken and alcoholic drinks. Their dress is unique. They wear white kurta pyjama without turban or with white turban. Their women wear sari and choli. During Hindu festival their women are dressed in costly saris. Their marriage parties are the occasions to display their rich clothes they wear. Their greatest contribution to Manipuri society is business mobilization in this isolated state. They have created a vital business line between Moreh, Imphal and Dimapur. There are Jains among Marwaris and also from Uttar Pradesh and other parts of the country.

South Indians

Moreh town of Manipur is the real settlement of Tamils and Keralites. Most of them are refugees from Burma. They have introduced Idli and Dosa, the famous snack dishes of South Indians to the Meiteis and tribals. The men dress in lungi and shirt. Office goers wear pants and shirts. The women wear sari and blouse. They are all Hindus and a few Christians may also be there. Moreh Tamils are all Hindus and have established several temples of Kali, Durga and Shiva in the town. They also celebrate their festivals with great pomp and show.

Bengalis

The Bengalis are the old settlers in Manipur. Due to the geographical closeness with Bengal the land has experienced a lot in respect of socio-cultural and socio-religious interaction between the two societies. The contribution of Bengalis to the Manipuri society is valuable. Bengalis are one of the most advanced and intellectually superb ethnical group of India. Bengali dress of the men is dhoti, kurta, shawl and turban which is same as of a Meitei man. The women wear sari and blouse. The food habits resembles those of Meiteis. Bengalis are rice eaters and fish is the main dish at every evening meal. They take keen interest in celebrations of Hindu festivals. They have maintained their Bengali culture with its finest heritage. They speak Bengali. Bengalis in Manipur are in almost all government offices, business and in teaching profession. Some of them have married Meitei girls.

Thus, Manipur is having all kinds of people and the society gets status of a cosmopolitan society and all groups are in harmonious relations.

Govt. Recognised Tribes

The Government of Manipur has recognised 32 tribes in the state. These are as follows:

1. Aimol	9. Anal	17. Angami	25. Chiru
2. Chothe	10. Gangte	18. Hmar	26. Kabui
3. Kacha Naga	11. Kharam	19. Koirao	27. Koireng
4. Kom	12. Lamgang	20. Lusai Tribes	28. Maram
5. Maring	13. Mao	21. Monsang	29. Mayon
6. Paite	14. Poumi Naga	22. Purum	30. Ralte
7. Sema	15. Simte	23. Sahlte	31. Tangkhul
8. Tarao	16. Thadou	24. Vaiphei	32. Zou

EDUCATION

The origin of the organized education in the state dates back to 1903 when Rev. W. Pettigrew, a British educationist and philanthropist became the first honorary inspector of schools under the Education Department of Assam. Prior to 1950, there was no education department in the state as such. In the year 1951-52, a new set up in the general administration of Manipur came into existence. The matter of educational activities was in the hands of the Territorial Council of Manipur till 1960. A full fledged education department came along with the attainment of statehood and since then considerable progress has been underway. Besides, numerous missionary schools, other private run schools have augmented the progress of education and literacy in the state in the recent years. Manipur is a small state in the north eastern part of India. The rate of literacy in Manipur is 76.9 per cent in 2011 which is of course above the national average of 73 per cent. There is, however, some difference in the levels of literacy among males and females. While the rate of literacy among males is 86.1 per cent, it is only 72.4 per cent among females.

The state's policy on education is based on the national policy that emphasizes on universalisation of elementary education. The Department of Education has the power of supervision and inspection, framing of curriculum and syllabi and selection of textbooks. At present, the Education Department of Manipur has four different entities viz.

1. Department of Education (University and Higher Education)
2. Department of Education (10+2)
3. State Council of Educational Research and Training, Government of Manipur and
4. Department of Adult Education.

The Manipur University came into existence on **June 5, 1980.** It is constituted under the **Manipur University Act, 1980.** In total, Manipur has **two universities,** one medical college and a number of professional colleges providing higher education to the students of the state.

Universities in Manipur

1. Manipur Central Agricultural University
2. Manipur University

ECONOMY

Agriculture and allied activities form the backbone of the economy of Manipur. Manipur is the first state which introduced **Oak Tasar** industry. While weaving and pisciculture are other important and traditional means of livelihood in the valley, logging, cultivation of a few cash crops, handloom and handicrafts are the traditional sources of additional income in the hills. Moreh has become an important business centre because of border trade with Myanmar.

Manipur, once a princely state became a part of India on the 15th of October 1949. Agriculture and allied activities provide the backbone to the economy in both the hills and the valley of Manipur. While weaving and pisciculture are other important and traditional means of livelihood in the valley, logging, cultivation of a few cash crops, handloom and handicrafts are the traditional sources of additional income in the hills.

Manipur is lagging much behind the national average in case of per capita income and in the recent few years the gap between the per capita income of the state and the nation has widen further. The state is heavily dependent on imports from outside for almost all items of everyday need.

Per Capita Income

Per Capita Income (PCI) is generally considered as the most effective indicator for ascertaining the economic welfare of a state. It enables one to know the average size of the income and the standard of living of the people. The net PCI of Manipur at current and constant (2011-12 = 100) prices in 2016-17 are estimated to be ₹ 61,535 and ₹ 46,563 respectively showing an increase of 8.70% and 3.90% over the previous year.

Net PCI at Current and Constant (2011-12=100) Prices (Manipur vis-à-vis India)

Year	At Current Prices (In ₹)				At Constant (2011-12 = 100) Prices (In ₹)			
	Manipur	Annual Growth Rate (%)	All India	Annual Growth Rate (%)	Manipur	Annual Growth Rate (%)	All India	Annual Growth Rate (%)
2011-12	39,762	-	63,460	-	39,762	-	63,460	-
2012-13	41,246	3.73	71,050	11.96	38,927	(-)2.10	65,664	3.47
2013-14	47,852	16.02	79,412	11.77	41,445	6.47	68,867	4.88
2014-15 (Q)	52,436	9.58	86,879	9.40	43,348	4.59	72,889	5.84
2015-16 (A)	56,610	7.96	93,293	7.38	44,815	3.38	77,435	6.24
2016-17 (P)	61,535	8.70	1,01,083	8.35	46,563	3.90	82,081	6.00

Q-Quick Estimates; A-Advance Estimates; P-Projected Estimates.

INDUSTRY

State Government has been making serious efforts for fostering conventional industrialization in the state. Apart from providing a package of incentives and concessions as laid out in its industrial policies and programmes in consonance with those of the Government of India, the State Government participated in the industrialization campaign with the incorporation of the Manipur Spinning Mills Corporation Ltd. in 1974 which started its commercial production in 1980. In order to facilitate growth of industries, the Manipur Small Industries Corporation was set up in 1969 and it was further upgraded to Manipur Industrial Development Corporation Ltd. (MANIDCO) in 1987. Manipur Handloom and Handicraft Development Corporation Ltd. was set up in 1976 to directly help production and marketing of handloom and handicraft products. Subsequently, State sponsored undertakings like, Manipur Electronics Development Corporation Ltd., Manipur Cements Ltd., Manipur State Drugs and Pharmaceuticals Ltd., Manipur Pulp and Allied Products Ltd. and Khandsari Sugar Factory as a Govt. factory came up in the State. Regional/State branch offices of Small Industries Service Institute, National Small Industries Corporation Ltd., Centre for Electronics Design & Technology and Central Institute of Plastic Engineering & Technology also, came up in the State to invigorate the growth of industries. District Industries Centres were set up in the districts in 1978-79 and decentralization of industrial growth in the rural areas began. Schemes like Seed Margin Money, Self Employment for Educated Unemployed Youths and Prime Minister's Rozgar Yojana were instrumented in the growth of industrial activities in the State. In tune with the present trend of economic reforms and given the limited capacity of the State government, the various corporations are looking for investors for expansion.

Industrial Corporations

There are ten State sponsored undertakings under the purview of the Department of Commerce & Industries, Manipur namely:

1. Manipur Handloom & Handicrafts Development Corporation Ltd.
2. Manipur Cements Ltd.
3. Manipur Spinning Mills Ltd.
4. Manipur Industrial Development Corporation Ltd.
5. Manipur Cycle Corporation Ltd.
6. Manipur Electronics Development Corporation Ltd.
7. Manipur Food Industries Corporation Ltd.
8. Manipur Pulp and Allied Products Ltd.

9. Manipur State Drugs and Pharmaceuticals Ltd.
10. Manipur Vanaspati and Allied Industries Ltd.

ENERGY

Manipur is endowed with a rich hydropower potential. With the commissioning of the Loktak Hydro Electric Project in 1983, the power position in Manipur has improved, though the state is still facing the plight of power shortage. A number of mini hydel plans and diesel-generating sets have been installed to electrify the administrative headquarters in the hill areas. Power distribution is not able to cope up with the requirements of the domestic consumption, street lightening and industry. About four-fifth of the villages are electrified but power supply in most of them is minimal. The per capita power consumption is only 140 KWh as against the all India average of 330.6 KWh. Non-conventional sources of energy like biogas, solar and wind energy are being explored to meet the power requirements in the state.

Therefore, the shortage of power is the major cause for the slow development in the state. Electric energy in the state continues to be insufficient. Purchases of power from outside the state have been rising at a higher rate. The following Table provides a picture of the power availability in the state.

Power Availability in Respect of Manipur State

Year	Power (Lakh KWH)				
	Requirement	Generated	Purchased	Free Energy from Loktak Hydro Electric Project	Total Available (Col. 3 to Col. 5)
2010-11	8,380	20.11	5,672.18	709.09	6,401.38
2011-12	6,150	15.64	5,633.70	610.49	6,259.83
2012-13	7,220	10.08	5,783.44	669.04	6,462.56
2013-14	8,240	10.10	6,064.02	736.86	6,810.98
2014-15	9,420	10.10	6,425.80	424.20	6,860.10
2015-16	10,800	Nil	7654.90*	579.30	8,234.20

* As on 31st January, 2016

After 1982-83, Manipur was connected to whereby power could be drawn from the NER grid. This was accompanied by a falling trend in the production of power in the state sector. There was a fall in the installed capacity after the mid 1980s, which is somewhat inexplicable. In 2001-02, the per capita consumption of electricity in Manipur was 68 KWh. The average level is dismally low and reflects the slow pace of industrialization in the state. The gap between Manipur and the all-India average is widening.

Manipur has a power generation capacity of about 48 MW at the state level. The diesel and micro-hydel projects owned by the state are run as a standby during peak load hours. The utilization of installed capacity in the state has declined substantially after the introduction of the grid system.

In addition, the Centre has set up seven micro-hydel projects in collaboration with private companies with a total capacity of 37.75 MW., namely, Ngeha, Inhu-I, Inhu-II, Bualkot, Chakpi, Sanalok and Makokching. On their completion the projects will be handed over to the state. The state is pinning its hopes on the completion of the Loktak Downstream Hydroelectric Project (HEP) and Tipaimukh HEP. Manipur depends mainly on the free power available from the Loktak hydro station of NHPC located in the state and the power purchased from central generating stations. In effect, the state is dependent entirely on the share of power allocated from central sector power plants, viz., Loktak HEP, Kopili HEP, Khandong HEP, Assam Gas Based Power Project at Kathalguri and Agartala Gas Turbine Power Project at Ramchandranagar, Eastern Regional Electricity Board, Meghalaya State Electricity Board, Ranganadi HEP and Doyang HEP in Nagaland.

The generation of all the central sector Power Project of North Eastern Region are shared among the states of the region as per the allocation made by the Govt. of India leaving 20% as unallocated share. During the year 2015-16, the allocated share of power for Manipur from the Central Sector Generating Stations in the North-Eastern Region of India is as given in the following Table.

Share of Power for Manipur from Central Sector, 2015-16

Sl. No.	Name of the Project	Installed Capacity MW	Share of Manipur (As on 30th Aug., 2015)	
			Per cent	MW
1.	Loktak Hydro Electric Project (NHPC)	105	36.57	38.4**
2.	Khongdong HPS	50	5.33	3
3.	Kopilli + Kopilli HPS	200	6.17	12
4.	Kopilli HEP Stage-II	25	6.0	2
5.	Kathalguri GPS	291	6.9	23
6.	Agartala GPS	84	7.0	6
7.	Agartala GPS Extra Unit-I	23	6.85	1.6
8.	Doyang HPS	75	6.7	5
9.	Ranganadi HPS	405	7.16	29
10.	Pallatana GPP	726	5.79	42
	Total	**1,984**	**94.47**	**162.00**

*** Inclusive of allocation of surrendered share 8 MW by Meghalaya to Manipur*

Source: Annual Administrative Report, 2015-16, Manipur State Power Company Limited

Renewable Energy

For implementation of renewable energy programme in the State, the Ministry of Non-Conventional Energy Sources, (MNES), renamed as National Solar Mission (NSM), Government of India have directed all the states to form State Nodal Agency (SNA). Accordingly, Manipur Renewable Energy Development Agency (MANIREDA) was established as the SNA for planning, development and implementation of various renewable energy programme in Manipur. The agency is placed under the control of the Power Department during 2014-15 for better integration and coordination of renewable energy with conventional energy. The cumulative achievements of the Agency are given below.

Solar Renewable Energy (RE) Projects and Biomass Gasifier Power Project

	Name of the Renewable Energy (RE) Projects	Number of System/Projects installed	Total installed capacity (in KW)
A.	Solar {Demonstration & Remote Village Electrification (RVE)}		
1.	Solar Home Lighting System	17,505	921
2.	Solar Street Lighting System	8,946	745
3.	Solar Lantern	8,139	77
4.	Solar Power Pack	305	37
5.	Solar Photo Voltaic (SPV) Power Plant	20	377.5
6.	1 KWp (each) Stand Alone type SPV Power Plant	399	399
7.	Solar Water Pump	30	27
8.	Implementation of energy awareness cum educational parks	10	20
9.	Implementation of 1 KWp	46	46
10.	Implementation of 5 KWp	67	335
B.	Biomass Gasifier Power Project	3	600

TRANSPORTATION

The State is included in the railway map of India with the opening of a rail head at Jiribam in May 1990. A railway line of 50 km connects it with Silchar (Assam) railway station. It is 255 km from Imphal. Dimapur, 215 km from Imphal is the nearest rail-head. The second railway line will be between Karong in Senapati District and Diphu in Assam through Dhansiri. The foundation stone was laid on November 17, 1998.

Another line to be connected with Silchar station with Toupul in Manipur was inaugurated in November 2004. The Jiribam - Toupul - Imphal Railway line has been declared as a National Project. Construction of the Line is in good progress and is targeted for completion by 2014 (upto Toupul) and 2016 (upto Imphal).

Imphal airport is the only airport which is linked with other stations in the region by Air India, Jet Airways and Alliance air. The Air India flights connect Imphal with Guwahati and New Delhi while Jet Airways flights connect Imphal with Guwahati and Kolkata. Alliance Air connects Imphal with Silchar and Kolkata. Inspite of the provision for subsidies on air transportation in the Northeast in general, it remains very costly. Thus, all the development activities of the state have come to depend heavily on road transport facilities.

ROAD TRANSPORT

Roads are the lifeline of the people of the state as the only means of transport for the state is the surfaced communication and road link in the accessible terrains. As such road has a special importance as vital infrastructure for economic development of the state. High priority is given in the plans and programme for construction of roads to develop the economy.

National Highway

National Highway is a highway which is declared as such under the National Highway Act, 1956. The National Highway system is the primary road grid of the state.

There are three national highways in Manipur viz.,

1. National Highway 39—Numaligarh-Dimapur-Kohima-Imphal-Moreh (214 km);
2. National Highway 53—Badarpur-Silchar-Jiribam-Imphal (222 km) and
3. (i) National Highway 150—Tipaimukh to Jessami via Imphal (523 km).
   (ii) National Highway 150A—15 km.

Highways and roads are regarded as arteries and veins of a state which are essential for its growth. The main artery of communication is the National High-way No. 39 connecting Imphal with Dimapur in the neighboring state of Nagaland. It runs through Mao in the extreme north of Manipur to the International border town of Moreh in the south-east. Dimapur is the railhead for road traffic to the state and in fact, this road is for so long her life line. The road passes through the hilly area of Senapati District and part of Nagaland Hill touching Kohima in between. The transport cost on this road is very high in view of frequent landslides on the hill tracts, restriction of transport services during night time due to unexpected events and one way trade movement because of little exports from Manipur.

Another road of considerable economic importance is the 225 kms. long National Highway No. 53 viz. New Cachar Road, connecting Imphal with Jirighat in Manipur Assam border. It passes through dense forests and difficult terrains of Tamenglong District which remained, by far, the most inaccessible district in the state. The opening of this road brings the District closer to other parts, helps in exploring untapped resources of the district and give incentives for more production and general development besides being a second life-line for the state. For this, State of Manipur, the road needs further development in order to be the main life-line of the state.

Following Table shows the differences in road density and the compound annual growth rates across districts during the period 1984-2002. The valley districts are definitely better served by roads than the hill districts, indicating that the development of road infrastructure for hills should be given more weightage to unleash the latent potential for development.

Inter-District Road Density (km per 100 sq.km)

District	1984	2002	CAGR in %
Senapati	13.44	23.73	3.45
Tamenglong	14.15	22.09	2.50
Churachandpur	6.58	21.23	6.72
Chandel	11.84	19.32	2.76
Toubal	91.61	143.97	2.54
Bishnupur	44.13	84.67	3.68
Imphal*	72.67	120.60	2.85
Ukhrul	14.47	24.47	2.96
Manipur	18.75	32.12	3.03

*Note: *Imphal East and Imphal West*

The Centre cleared the Northeast Express project proposed by the NEC that would interlink the capitals of the seven northeastern states. The 6907 km long road will consist of 4464 km of NH, 2060 km of newly declared NH and 393 km of NEC roads. It will have four lanes in the plains and two lanes in the hills. Another significant development is the proposal for a Transnational Highway linking India, Myanmar and Thailand, which will link Moreh to Mae Sot in Thailand through Bagan in Myanmar. Besides, the return of peace in the South Asian region may mean that the Northeast will regain its access to the sea and Kolkata via Bangladesh. It is hoped that it will restore to a large extent the disruption in infrastructure that occurred at the time of Independence and Partition.

State Highways and Major District Roads

The state Highways and major district roads form the secondary road system and take care of collection and distributary functions. The length of surfaced road of National Highways was 1,317 Kms in 2013 which was the same as in the previous year. On the other hand, the other roads like State Highways, PWD Roads, Rural Road, Urban Road and Project Road have changed over the years. The length of road according to category is presented in Table below:

Length of Road in Manipur

(In kms.)

Classification of Road	2012		2013	
	Total	Surfaced	Total	Surfaced
(1)	(2)	(3)	(4)	(5)
National Highways	1317	1317	1317	1317
State Highways	1137	1137	715	620
PWD Roads	8305	3475	9404	3407
Rural Road	6680	2964	7635	3919
Urban Road	212	156	166	111
Project Road	1600	1408	1601	1601

Sorces: Statistical Year Book, All India (MoSPI, GoI)

ADMINISTRATION

The total number of districts in Manipur is sixteen. A district of Manipur is headed by a Deputy Commissioner who is over all in-charge of the administration in the particular district. He has to perform triple functions as he holds three positions: at once he is the Deputy Commissioner, the district Magistrate and the Collector. As a Deputy Commissioner he is the executive head of the district with multifarious responsibilities. As the District Magistrate he is responsible for maintaining the law and order situation in the district. As the Collector he is the Chief Revenue Officer of the district, responsible for revenue collection and recovery. The Police administration in the district is under the control of Superintendent of Police (SP). To decentralize the authority in administrative set up a district is divided into one or more subdivisions, further divided into tehsils and blocks.

Districts and their Sub-divisions

Sl. No.	Name of District	Name of Sub-division
1.	Senapati	Tadubi, Paomata, Purul, Willong, Chilivai Phaibung, Song-Song, Lairouching
2.	Kangpokpi (Bifurcated from the erstwhile Senapati District)	Kangpokpi, Champhai, Saitu Gamphazol Kangchup Geljang, Tuijang Waichong, Saikul, Lungtin, Island, Bungte Chiru
3.	Tamenglong	Tamenglong, Tamei, Tousem

Sl. No.	Name of District	Name of Sub-division
4.	Noney District (Bifurcated from the erstwhile Tamenglong District)	Nungba, Khoupum, Longmei (Noney), Haochong
5.	Churachandpur	Churachandpur, Sangaikot, Tuibuong, Mualnuam, Singngat, Henglep, Kangvai, Samulamlan, Saikot
6.	Pherzawl (Bifurcated from the erstwhile Churachandpur District)	Pherzawl, Thanlon, Parbung-Tipaimukh, Vangai Range
7.	Chandel	Chandel, Chakpikarong, Khengjoy
8.	Tengnoupal District (Bifurcated from the erstwhile Chandel District)	Machi, Moreh, Tengnoupal
9.	Ukhrul	Ukhrul, Lungchong-Maiphai, Chingai, Jessami
10.	Kamjong District (Bifurcated from the erstwhile Ukhrul District)	Kamjong, Sahamphung, Kasom Khullen, Phungyar
11.	Imphal East	Porompat, Keirao Bitra, Sawombung
12.	Jiribam (Bifurcated from the erstwhile Imphal East District)	Jiribam, Borobekra
13.	Imphal West	Lamshang, Patsoi, Lamphelpat, Wangoi
14.	Bishnupur	Nambol, Bishnupur, Moirang
15.	Thoubal District	Thoubal, Lilong
16.	Kakching (Bifurcated from the erstwhile Thoubal District)	Kakching, Waikhong

The state follows a unicameral system of government *i.e.,* it has only one house–the Manipur Legislative Assembly (Vidhan Sabha) consists of 60 members. Manipur has two seats in the Lok Sabha—the lower house of Parliament. There is one seat in Rajya Sabha—the upper house of Parliament. Like all other states of India, the head of the state is the Governor, appointed by the President of India. His or her post is largely ceremonial. The Chief Minister is assisted by a group of ministers with independent power. The Chief Minister is the head of government and is vested with most of the executive powers.

Manipur Public Service Commission

Under Article 315(4) of the Constitution, the Union Public Service Commission (UPSC) agreed to function as the Public Service Commission of the State of Manipur till October 21, 1972. On October 3, 1972 the Governor of Manipur issued the order of constitution of the Manipur Public Service Commission under Article 318 with one Chairman and two Members.

SPORTS OF MANIPUR

The important sports of Manipur are:

1. **Yubi Lakpi (Manipuri Rugby) :** "Yubi" in Manipur means coconut and "Lakpi" means snatching. The oriental game is played on the lush green turf of the palace ground or at the Bijoy Govinda Temple ground. The coconut serves the purpose of a ball and is offered to the king or the judges who sit just beyond the goal line.
2. **Hiyang Tannaba (Boat Race) :** It is generally held in the month of November at Thangapat (Moat). The boats called Hiyang Hiren are regarded to be invested with spiritual powers and the game is associated with religious rites. The Meiteis believe that worship of the Hiyang Hiren will prevent one from evil omens.
3. **Mukna (Manipuri Wrestling) :** This game is the Manipuri style of wrestling played between two male rivals for trial of strength by sheer physical strength and skill. Mukna is a highly popular and prestigious game. In the olden days, the game enjoyed royal patronage.
4. **Sagol Kangjei (Manipuri Polo) :** The Sagol Kangjei has been adapted and adopted by the international enthusiasts of the game as Polo and now it's now being played worldwide. Today, the world has accepted that the game of Polo originated from Manipur.
5. **Kang :** Played on the mud floor of a big out-house fixed targets hit with "Kang" which is a flat and oblong instrument made of either ivory or lac. Played strictly during the period between 'Cheiraoba' (Manipuri New Year's day) and the Rath Yatra festival. Manipuri religiously adhere to its time-frame as popular belief holds that if the game is played beyond its given limit, evil spirits invaded the mind of players and spectators.
6. **Thang-Ta & Sarit Sarat :** These are the forms of Manipuri Martial Arts, the traditions of which had been passed down over the centuries.

FESTIVALS

Manipur is a land of festivities. Some of the important festivals are:

1. Yaoshang (Dol Jatra)
2. Rath Jatra
3. KUT (Festival of Kuki-Chin-Mizo)
4. Gang-Ngai (Festival of Kabui Nagas)
5. Chumpha (Festival of Tangkhul Nagas)

6. Christmas (Festival of Christians)
7. Cheiraoba (The Manipur New Year)

DANCE

Manipuri dance is the perfect representation of Manipuri culture. The dance is often devoted to religious themes, while the Raas Lila (love story of Radha and Krishna) dominating it. The 29 tribes of Manipur have different dances to offer—Lai Haroba (feast of dances, representing celebrations of Gods), Pung Cholem (Mridang dance), Mao Naga dance, the priestess dance of Malbe Jagoi, Thangal Surang dance etc. The vibrant culture of the Manipuris is reflected in their dance and drama.

IMPORTANT TOURIST PLACES

Singda : At an altitude of 921 meters, 16 kilometers from Imphal to west, Singda is a beautiful picnic spot with picturesque scenery. There is an inspection Bungalow here and an artificial lake as a manifestation of Singda Dam.

Red Hills (Maibam Lokpa Ching): This hillock about 17 kilometers in the south from Imphal is the thrilling spot where a fierce battle took place between the Allied Forces and the Japanese Forces in the World War II. Japanese war veterans have recently constructed a monument at the foot of this hill under the title of "India Peace Memorial."

Moirang: Moirang, 45 kilometers from Imphal is the ancient temple of the pre-Hindu deity, Lord Thanjing. In the month of May, men and women dressed in bright, traditional costumes, sing and dance in honour of the Lord here at the Moirang Lai Haraoba. It was from the village of Moirang that the graceful Khamba Thoibi dance originated. It was also in Moirang that the flag of the Indian National Army was first hoisted on Indian soil on April 14, 1944. There is an INA museum exhibiting letters, photographs, badges of ranks and other articles associated with INA, and a bronze statue of Netaji Subhash Chandra Bose in uniform.

Kaina: It is a beautiful hillock, about 29 kilometers from Imphal. Kaina is a sacred place of the Hindus. Beautiful hill shrubs and charming natural surroundings give the place a saintly solemnity. According to legend, one night, Shri Govindajee appeared to his devotee Bhaigyachandra, Maharaja of Manipur, in a dream and asked him to build a temple enshrined with his image carved out of a jackfruit tree which was then growing at Kaina. Ceremonial dances depicting the divine dream are performed as Ras at the Mandop.

Khongjom: Khongjom is a place of greatest historic importance, recognized as a symbol of patriotism and valour. It was here that Major General Paona Brajabashi and other Manipuri warriors proved their valour against the mighty force of the invading British Army in 1891. A war memorial stands on the tip of this scenic hill. Khongjom day is celebrated as a State function every year on April 23.

Tengnoupal: Sixty-nine kilometers from Imphal, this is the highest point on the Indo-Myanmar Road. From there, one can see full view of the valley of Manipur. When a visitor passes along the road, he will find himself above the clouds, but in natural surroundings.

Tamenglong: This regions is 156 kilometers from Imphal and is the district Headquarters of the Tamenglong district. Tamenglong is known for its deep gorges, mysterious caves, splendid waterfalls and exotic orchids. The Tharon Cave, Booming Meadow, Zeilad Lake, and Barak Waterfalls are interesting tourist spots in Tamenglong.

Mao: Mao is one of the oldest hill stations of Manipur, bordering Nagaland located midway between Dimapur and Imphal on the National Highway 39. It is 5762 feet above sea level. The Mao inspection bungalow built by the Royal Military Engineers in 1897 is more than a hundred years old.

Loktak Lake: Loktak lake is the largest freshwater lake in the northeast and much of it falls within the Keibul Lamjao National Park. Large areas of the lake are covered with thick matted weeds and on this unique floating habitat live the local fishing people and some rare species that include the sangai or Manipuri dancing deer.

Keibul Lamjao: Fifty three kilometers from Imphal and 5 kms from Sendra is located Keibul Lamjao, which is the only floating National Park in the world. There is a floating lodge.

Sendra: Sendra is a small islet in the middle of Loktak lake. It is the viewpoint overlooking the beautiful lake and its surroundings.

Khangkhui Cave: Khangkhui Cave is a remarkable natural lime-stone cave. The big hall in the cave is the darbar hall of the Devil King living deep inside while the northern hall is the royal bedroom, according to local folklore. During World War II, the villagers sought shelter in this cave.

Tamenglong: This region is known for its deep gorges, mysterious caves and splendid waterfalls and its exotic orchids. Besides interesting spots like Burning Meadow, Zailad Lakes, Barak waterfalls, etc., the Tharon cave is of great importance, having 34 joints, this cave is 655.6 meters in length. It has five exits and good ventilation system so that no symptom of exphyxia can be experienced.

Sekta: Sekta, the living museum, is an ideal place with a unique natural description.

Shaheed Minar: This 165 foot monument of Bir Tekendrajit Park at the heart of the Capital commemorates the indomitable spirit of Manipur martyrs who sacrificed their lives while fighting against the British in 1891.

MANIPUR : AT A GLANCE

• Area (in sq. km.)	:	22,327
• Latitude	:	23°50′N to 25°42′N
• Longitude	:	92°58′E to 94°45′E
• Forest Area (in sq. km.) (including tree cover)	:	17,346 (77.69% of the total geographical area of the State)
• No. of Districts	:	16
• Name of the Districts	:	Senapati, Tamenglong, Thoubal, Ukhrul, Bishnupur, Chandel, Churachandpur, Imphal East, Imphal West, Jiribam, Kangpokpi, Kakching, Tengnoupal, Kamjong, Noney and Pherzawl
• Lok Sabha Constituencies	:	2
• Rajya Sabha Seat	:	1
• Vidhan Sabha Constituencies	:	60
• Nature of Legislature	:	Unicameral
• Capital	:	Imphal
• Language	:	Meiteilon
• Total Population-2011 census	:	28,55,794
• Male	:	14,38,586
• Female	:	14,17,208
• Decadal Growth (2001-2011)	:	24.5%
• Literacy Rate	:	76.94%
• Male Literacy Rate	:	83.58%
• Female Literacy Rate	:	70.58%
• Density (per sq. km.)	:	128
• Sex Ratio (per 1000 males)	:	985
• No. of Universities	:	2 1. Manipur Central Agriculture University 2. Manipur University

- No. of National Parks : 2
  1. Keibul Lamjao National Park
  2. Shiroi Hill National Park
- State Animal : Sangai
- State Bird : Nongyeen
- State Flower : Siroi Lily
- State Game : Manipuri Polo
- Important Tribes : Thadou is the largest with 1.8 lakh population representing 24.6 per cent of the state's total ST population, followed by Tangkhul (19.7%), Kabui (11.1%), Paite (6.6%), Hmar (5.8%), Kacha Naga (5.7%), and Vaiphui (5.2%)
- Major Festivals : Yaoshang (Dol Jatra), Rath Jatra, KUT (Festival of Kuki-Chin-Mizo), Gang-Ngai (Festival of Kabui Nagas), Chumpha (Festival of Tangkhul Nagas), Christmas (Festival of Christians), Cheiraoba (The Manipur New Year)
- Name of National Highways : NH-39, NH-53, NH-150, NH-150A.

OBJECTIVE QUESTIONS

1. What is the area of Manipur?
A. 20,327 sq. km. B. 22,327 sq. km.
C. 32,327 sq. km. D. None of these

2. Manipur state is situated on latitude between
A. 23°50′N and 25°42′N B. 20°40′N and 30°50′N
C. 35°33′N and 36°50′N D. None of these

3. Manipur state is situated on longitude between
A. 90°03′E and 92°78′E B. 92°58′E and 94°45′E
C. 95°E and 96°E D. None of these

4. What percentage of the total geographical area of the Manipur state is under forest cover?
A. 80% B. 90%
C. 77.69% D. None of these

5. How many districts there are in Manipur?
A. 16 B. 10
C. 15 D. None of these

6. Total number of Lok Sabha constituency in Manipur is
A. 2 B. 1
C. 4 D. None of these

7. Total number of Rajya Sabha constituency in Manipur is
A. 3 B. 4
C. 1 D. None of these

8. Manipur Legislative Assembly consists of
A. 40 B. 80
C. 60 D. None of these

9. What is the name of the capital of Manipur state?
A. Dispur B. Imphal
C. Itanagar D. None of these

10. Official language of Manipur is
A. Meiteilon B. Hindi
C. Urdu D. None of these

11. According to 2011 census, total population of Manipur is
A. 32,76,000 B. 28,55,794
C. 52,56,000 D. None of these

12. According to 2011 census, male population of Manipur is
A. 14,38,586 B. 18,71,154
C. 15,71,639 D. None of these

13. According to 2011 census, female population of Manipur is
A. 14,17,208 B. 10,95,634
C. 12,46,739 D. None of these

14. During 2001-2011, the decadal growth of population of Manipur was
A. 30% B. 21.89%
C. 24.5% D. None of these

15. Highly populated district in Manipur is
A. Imphal East B. Chandel
C. Imphal West D. Senapati

16. Less density populated district in Manipur is
A. Tamenglong B. Imphal East
C. Thoubel D. Churachandpur

17. Which is the smallest district in Manipur?
A. Churachandpur B. Tamenglong
C. Bishnupur D. Imphal West

18. What proportion of total population of Manipur live in Urban area?
A. 50% B. 45%
C. 29.2% D. None of these

19. According to 2011 census, total literacy rate in Manipur is
A. 85% B. 76.9%
C. 95.5% D. None of these

20. According to 2011 census, male literacy rate in Manipur is
A. 90% B. 83.58%
C. 70% D. None of these

21. According to 2011 census, female literacy rate in Manipur is
A. 78.5% B. 70.26%
C. 90.5% D. None of these

22. In Manipur, population density (per sq. km.) is
A. 128 B. 304
C. 95 D. None of these

23. Sex ratio in Manipur is
A. 878 B. 985
C. 958 D. None of these

24. Total number of National Parks in Manipur is
A. 2 B. 4
C. 5 D. None of these

25. State animal of Manipur is
A. Elephant B. Deer
C. Sangai D. None of these

26. What is the name of state bird of the Manipur state?
A. Nongyeen B. Peacock
C. Cuckoo D. None of these

27. What is the name of state flower of the Manipur?
A. Siroi Lily B. Rohira
C. Lotus D. None of these

28. What is the name of state game of the Manipur?
A. Football B. Polo
C. Cricket D. None of these

29. Highest peak of the Manipur is
A. Tenipu B. Kangto
C. Gori Chen D. None of these

30. Major soil of Manipur is
A. Ultisols B. Inceptisols
C. Entisols D. None of these

31. The forest cover of Manipur is
A. 17,346 sq. km. B. 20,250 sq. km.
C. 12,549 sq. km. D. None of these

32. In which district Keibul Lamjao National Park is situated?
A. Chandel B. Bishnupur
C. Tamenglong D. Ukhrul

33. In which district Shiroi Hill National Park is situated?
A. Tamenglong B. Chandel
C. Ukhrul D. None of these

34. Important tribes of Manipur is
A. Thadou B. Tangkhul
C. Kabui D. None of these

35. ST population in Manipur is predominantly
A. Hindu B. Christian
C. Muslim D. None of these

36. Total number of notified scheduled tribes in Manipur are
A. 32 B. 49
C. 39 D. None of these

37. How many notified SCs are in Manipur?
A. 6 B. 7
C. 5 D. None of these

38. SCs population of Manipur is primarily concentrated in
A. Thoubal District B. Senapati District
C. Ukhrul District D. None of these

39. Manipur Industrial Development Corporation Ltd. (MANIDCL) was established in
A. 1987 B. 1990
C. 1985 D. None of these

40. Manipur Handloom and Handicraft Development Corporation Ltd. was set-up in
A. 1976 B. 1987
C. 1997 D. None of these

41. Longest National Highways of Manipur is
A. NH-39 B. NH-53
C. NH-150 D. None of these

42. Manipur State Road Transport Corporation (MSRTC) was established in
A. 1970 B. 1976
C. 1980 D. None of these

43. Manipur University came into existence on
A. June 10, 1990 C. June 5, 1980
B. August 15, 1985 D. None of these

44. According to area, the largest district of Manipur is
A. Senapati B. Churachandpur
C. Thoubal D. None of these

45. Name of the district headquarter of Imphal West district is
A. Porompat B. Lamphel
C. Bishnupur D. None of these

46. What is the name of only Floating National Park in the World?
A. Keibul Lamjao National Park B. Kaziranga National Park
C. Shiroi Hill National Park D. None of these

47. In Manipur 'Mao' is famous for
A. folk dance B. festival
C. hill stations D. None of these

48. Zeilad lake is situated in
A. Tamenglong district B. Bishnupur district
C. Senapati district D. None of these

49. The length of the international border shared by the Manipur state is
A. 352 kms B. 500 kms
C. 450 kms D. None of these

50. The biggest fresh water lake in eastern India is
A. Zeilad lake B. Loktak lake
C. Dal lake D. None of these

ANSWERS

1	2	3	4	5	6	7	8	9	10
B	A	B	C	A	A	C	C	B	A
11	**12**	**13**	**14**	**15**	**16**	**17**	**18**	**19**	**20**
B	A	A	C	C	A	C	C	B	B
21	**22**	**23**	**24**	**25**	**26**	**27**	**28**	**29**	**30**
B	A	B	A	C	A	A	B	A	B
31	**32**	**33**	**34**	**35**	**36**	**37**	**38**	**39**	**40**
A	B	C	A	B	A	B	A	A	A
41	**42**	**43**	**44**	**45**	**46**	**47**	**48**	**49**	**50**
C	B	B	B	B	A	C	A	A	B

●●●●●●●

5

MEGHALAYA

HISTORY

Tucked away in the hills of eastern sub-Himalayas is Meghalaya, one of the most beautiful state in the country. Nature has blessed her with abundant rainfall, sun-shine, virgin forests, high plateaus, tumbling waterfalls, crystal clear rivers, meandering streamlets and above all with sturdy, intelligent and hospitable people.

Advent of the British

The British came to Sylhet in 1765. At that time the Khasis used to come at Pandua on the border of Sylhet to trade in silk, cotton goods, iron, wax, honey and ivory in exchange for rice, salt and dried fish. Limestone from the Khasi hills used to fulfill the demand in Bengal then. Soon British officials of the East India Company began trading in limestone and thus came in contact with the Khasis. In 1824, the Burmese invaded Cachar and also appeared at the border of the Jaintia Hills. The British sent a small force to reinforce the Jaintia Rajah's troops. On 10th March 1824, a friendship treaty was signed by the Rajah accepting the protection of the British. Other Khasi chiefs also allowed the passage of the British troops through their territories. After the Burmese invasion was over, the British demanded a corridor through the Khasi and the Jaintia Hills to connect Assam valley with Surma valley. Most of the Khasi chiefs agreed, and the road was completed in March 1829, but only after quelling an upheaval by U Tirot Sing. The story that followed after putting down the uprising by U Tirot Sing was the signing of several treaties with different Khasi chiefs. The Khasi, Garo, and Jaintia tribes each had their own kingdoms, until they came under the British administration in the 19th century. Later, the British incorporated Meghalaya into Assam in 1835. In 1862, the Jaintias revolted under U Kiang Nongbah. By virtue of these treaties, the British gradually took control of the mineral deposits and side by side subjugated the chiefs and also took control of judiciary.

When Bengal was partitioned on 16 October, 1905 by Lord Curzon, Meghalaya became a part of the new province of 'Eastern Bengal and Assam'. However, when the partition was reversed in 1912, Meghalaya became a part of the province of Assam. On 3 January, 1921 in pursuance of Section 52A of the Government of India Act of 1919, the Governor-General-in-Council declared the areas now in Meghalaya, other than the Khasi States, as "backward tracts". Subsequently, however, the Government of India Act of 1935 regrouped the backward tracts into two categories, namely, "excluded" and "partially excluded" areas in place of backward tracts.

At the time of Independence of the country in 1947, the present day Meghalaya constituted two districts of Assam and enjoyed limited autonomy within the state of Assam. The Assam Reorganisation (Meghalaya) Act, 1969 accorded an autonomous status on the state of Meghalaya. The Act came into effect on April 2nd, 1970, and an Autonomous State of Meghalaya was created within the State of Assam. The Autonomous state had a Legislature in accordance with the Sixth schedule to the Constitution. The Legislature had 37 members.

In 1971, the Parliament passed the North-Eastern Areas (Reorganization) Act, 1971, which conferred full statehood on the Autonomous State of Meghalaya. The full-fledged State of Meghalaya came into existence on 21 January 1972. Emergence of Meghalaya as a full-fledged State marked the beginning of a new era of the geo-political history of North Eastern India. It also marked the triumph of peaceful democratic negotiations, mutual understanding and victory over violence and intrigue.

GEOGRAPHY

The State of Meghalaya is situated on the north east of India. It extends for about 300 kilometres in length and about 100 kilometres in breadth. Meghalaya lies between 20°1′N and 26°5′N latitude and 85°49′E and 92°52′E longitude. The boundaries of the state are demarcated by the Goalpara and Kamrup districts of Assam in the north, the south-western part of the district of Goalpara and a part of Rangpur district of Bangladesh in the west, the Mymensingh and Sylhet districts of Bangladesh in the south and the north Cachar and Karbi Anglong districts of Assam in the east. The total geographical area of the State is approximately 22,429 sq. km and consists of primarily steep hills and deep gorges with very limited areas covering valleys and plains land. The state is divided into three regions in terms of its physical features:

1. **The Central Plateau** includes the Khasi-Jaintia Hills, which is an imposing, plateau with rolling grasslands, hills and river valleys. The

Garo Hills forms the western part of the plateau. Its elevation varies between 150 m to 1961 m above the mean sea level. The highest point of the plateau and that of the entire state is the Shillong Peak whose elevation is about 1961 m. It serves as a catchment area for rivers and streams traversing the state. Comparatively, it has the largest area of grassland, which can be profitably utilised for animal husbandry, dairying and horticulture. It is the main centre of potato cultivation and vegetables for supply outside the state.

2. **The border area** begins where the southern face of the Central Plateau ends. Deep gorges and slopes at the foot of which a narrow strip of plain land runs along the international border with Bangladesh forms the southern region of the state. It is a region of the heaviest rainfall. The world-renowned Cherrapunji and Mawsynram, the wettest places in the world are located in this area. Nut plantations and subtropical and tropical fruits like mandarin, lemon, guava, pineapple and banana are grown in plenty in this region.
3. Like the border area, **the submontane region** also forms a continuation of the Central Plateau till it merges with the plains of Assam. But unlike the border area, which is generally steep and abrupt in certain places, it slopes gently downward until it merges with the plains of Assam in the north. It is a region of comparatively lower rainfall but has favourable scope both for agriculture and horticulture.

Shillong, the capital of Meghalaya is located at an altitude of 1496 metres above sea level. Shillong, which was made Assam's capital in 1874, remained so till January 1972, following the formation of Meghalaya. According to legends, Shillong derived its name from a deity named "Shyllong" whose dwelling is also known as Shyllong peak from whose niece the Syiem clan of Khyrim, Mylliem, Maharam, Malaisohmat, Bhowal and Langrin sprang up.

Shillong is connected by a good arterial road with the rest of the country through Assam. A good road connects Shillong with Sylhet in Bangladesh. It is also connected with other important towns of the state like Jowai and Tura. An airport at Umroi, about 30 Kilometres from Shillong, connects Shillong by air with the rest of the country. Shillong is also the headquarters of the North Eastern Council, the Eastern Air Command, the Assam Rifles, the Assam Regimental Centre and 101 Command Zone.

MINERALS

Meghalaya is endowed with great mineral wealth but its exploitation for development has been minimal. Small cottage-type coal mining is widely prevalent in different areas extending from Jaintia Hills, East and West Khasi Hills in the East ending in East Garo Hills in the West. The coal reserve in the state is estimated to be about 640 million tonnes but its production has been increasing at a snail's pace because mining is being carried on in an unscientific manner. Unlike other regions of the country coal mines in the state are entirely under the private ownership. The process of coal extraction here is so careless and indiscriminate that instead of giving suitable benefits it is creating serious problems for environment. Nonetheless coal from the state is the most important item of export both to other states of the country as well as to the neighbouring country.

Limestone is another major mineral item found in close proximity to coal. The total estimated reserve of limestone in the state is in the region of 5000 million tonnes. The cement grade limestone is used primarily in the cement plant of the region commissioned in 1966 at Cherrapunji. Limestone is also being exploited at Komorrah for the Chhatak cement plant of Bangladesh. Besides cement grade limestone, other good quality limestone deposits occur in Siju, Shella-Bholaganj and Lumshang-Nongkhlieh belts of the state.

Sillimanite is another important mineral, which was being produced in the Sonapahar area but now its production and exploitation has been stopped. The Geological Survey of India's reconnaissance has revealed promising Kyanite deposits and fire clay in Garo Hills. Uranium has recently been located in the Southern part of West Khasi Hills and the state has appeared on the uranium map of the country. However, the work on this project has not made headway as a result of the people's protest against it.

Mineral : At a glance

S. No.	Mineral	Area
1.	Coal	West Dadenggiri, Siju, Balpakram, Pyndengrei, Langrin, Mawlong-Shella, Laitryngew and Bapung
2.	Limestone	Cherrapunjee, Mawlong-Ishamati, Komorrah, Shella, Borsora in Khasi Hills, Siju and Nangwalbibra in Garo Hills, Lumshnong, Sutnga, Nongkhlieh, Syndai and Lakadong in Jaintia Hills
3.	Phospherite	Sung Valley at the border of Khasi and Jaintia Hills districts, besides, some Phosphatic nodules are also located in Rewak area of Garo Hills
4.	Clay	Mahadek in Khasi Hills, Larnai and Tongseng in Jaintia Hills and Nangwalbibra and Rongrengiri in Garo Hills
5.	Sillimanite	Sonapahar region of West Khasi

S. No.	Mineral	Area
6.	Glass-Sand	Laitryngew, Umstew and Kreit in Khasi Hills and Tura in Garo Hills
7.	Gypsum	Mohendraganj and Harigaon in West Garo Hills
8.	Iron-Ores	Aradonga, Athiabari and Nishangram
9.	Uranium	Domiasiat in West Khasi Hills district

CLIMATE

The climate of Meghalaya is moderate but humid. The average annual rainfall is about 2600 mm over western Meghalaya, between 2500 to 3000 mm over northern Meghalaya and about 4000 mm over south-eastern Meghalaya. Meghalaya is the wettest state of India. The western part of the plateau, comprising the Garo Hills Region with lower elevations, experiences high temperatures for most of the year. The Shillong area, with the highest elevations, experiences generally low temperatures. The maximum temperature in this region rarely goes beyond 28 degrees, whereas winters temperatures of sub-zero degrees are common. The town of **Cherrapunji (Sohra)** in the Khasi Hills south of capital Shillong holds the world record for most rain in a calendar month, while the village of **Mawsynram**, near town of Cherrapunji, holds the distinction of seeing the heaviest yearly rains. Best time to visit Meghalaya is during the months of March to July.

The state of Meghalaya is directly influenced by the south-west monsoon and the northeast winter winds. The four seasons of Meghalaya are: Spring - March and April, Summer (Monsoon) - May to September, Autumn - October and November and Winter - December to February. During March and April, the atmosphere gradually warms up with the advent of Spring. From the middle of April the temperature starts rising to the maximum in the month of June and then decreases gradually. This period may be termed as the Summer (Monsoon) season. The maximum temperature recorded is 34° Celsius at Tura in West Garo Hills District and 28° Celsius at Shillong. October and November are the two months when the climate is cool and temperate. After November, the winter season sets in and continues up to the end of February. During these months the temperature comes down to as low as 2° Celsius in the Khasi Hills. Rainfall starts by the third week of May and continues right up to the end of September and sometimes well into the middle of October. The maximum rainfall occurs over the southern slopes of the Khasi Hills. The average annual rainfall in the State is 12,000 mm.

RIVERS

Meghalaya has many rivers. Most of these are rainfed and are therefore seasonal. In the Garo Hills, the Manda, the Damring and the Janjiram, flow towards the north while the Ringge and the Ganol flow in the westerly direction. Those that flow to the south are the Simsang, which is the biggest river in Garo Hills, and the Bhogai.

In the Khasi and Jaintia Hills, the rivers that flow in a northerly direction include the Khri, the Umtrew, the Umiam, the Umkhen besides the Kopli on the border between Jaintia - Hills and North Cachar Hills. The Kynshi, the Umiam Mawphlang and the Umngot flow to the south into Bangladesh.

AGRICULTURE

Agriculture is the main stay of the people on which about 81 per cent of the total population still depends for their livelihood. The state covers both sub-tropical and temperate climate and therefore both natural vegetation and cultivated crops also ranges from sub-tropical to temperate. Soil is generally acidic in nature, average nitrogen content being medium to high, phosphate content generally low and potash medium.

The following four classes of Agro-climatic zones are found in Meghalaya :

1. The Upper Hill region from 1200 metre to 1500 metre in altitude and above
2. The Middle Hill region from 600 metre to 1200 metre high
3. The Lower Hill region between 300 metre and 600 metre in altitude
4. The Terai or Plain region upto 300 metre from mean Sea Level

The widely prevalent agricultural practice has been shifting cultivation known as jhum in the region but a marked transition from shifting to settled cultivation is observed throughout the state. According to one estimate the minimum area under shifting cultivation at one time or the other has been 2650 sq. km in the state involving around 52,200 families. While ecological hazards created by jhum cultivation and its economic non-viability provide external pressure to abandon the practice, increasing population pressure, reduction in jhum cycle and overall socio-economic transformation have created internal pressure against it. Consequently, the prevailing trend is towards a clear shift from shifting to permanent cultivation.

The major food crops grown in the state are rice, maize and potato. Besides vegetables, all kinds of horticultural crops such as citrus fruits, banana, pineapple, peach, plum, etc. are grown in abundance. Among the spice crops ginger, turmeric, cinnamons are grown commonly in different parts of the state. Jute, mesta and cotton are produced mainly in the Garo hills. In addition, many indigenous crops containing aromatic, medicinal and pesticidal properties are found in the state. It is also noted for the presence of various kinds of orchids. Meghalaya has about 300 of the world's orchid species growing in its rich, forest land, gardens and nurseries. These rare specimens include the insect-eating pitcher plant, Wild Citrus and Pigmy Lily. Likewise, analysis of juice volume and citric acid content of these species has indicated that some species contain very high percentage of citric acid and hence opens up potentiality for production of this important chemical. The oil from tezpatta *(Cinnamomum tarnata)* available in Meghalaya in large quantities, contains 70-80 per cent engenol suitable for preparation of perfumery chemicals.

The estimated irrigation potential of the State both from surface and ground water is about 2.18 lakh hectare, the potential created so far is 59,000 hectare.

District-wise percentage of Net Irrigated Area in Meghalaya

S. No.	District	Percentage of Net Irrigated Area
1.	East Khasi Hills	3.63
2.	East Garo Hills	10.06
3.	Jaintia Hills	9.60
4.	Ri-Bhoi	9.84
5.	South Garo Hills	2.49
6.	West Garo Hills	3.42
7.	West Khasi Hills	11.21

It is indispensable to examine the nature of land system and patterns of landownership because it is closely linked with social structure and agrarian practices. The land system in the tribal areas of Meghalaya is usually characterised as the customary land system, which has neither been codified nor a cadastral survey conducted except in small portion in the plains of West Garo Hills district to prepare records of rights on land except in small portion in the plains of West Garo Hills district. It has not only complicated the agrarian question but has also led to serious distortions in the system depriving common people from maintaining control over land. Whatever limited information is available in historical writings and government reports help us to identify the basic nature and operation of agrarian social structure. Based on these facts we find two main classes of land in the Khasi-Jaintia Hills namely, **Ri-Raid** land and **Ri-Kynti** land. While the former is community owned land, the latter refers to the privately-owned land. Besides there are many sub-classes of land under these two broader categories known either by the same name or different names in different areas of the state.

Ri-Raid are lands set apart for the community over which no one has proprietary, heritable and transferable rights except the right to use and occupancy. Nonetheless occupancy rights revert to the community when a person ceases to use and occupy the landholding consecutively for a period of three years. The heritable and transferable rights over ri-raid land accrue when the occupant has made permanent improvements on the land. But even these rights terminate if the person concerned completely abandons the holding over such a period, as the Raid Council deems long enough. The management and control of ri-raid land belonging to the community is within the jurisdiction of the concerned community. Such lands are normally located at three levels, namely, village (ri-raid shnong), a group of villages (ri-raid Raid) and a group of villages and Raid (ri-raid Hima). A plot of ri-raid is allotted to individuals for constructing a dwelling or for cultivation and for other uses. Customarily, no rent or tax of any kind is charged on land for enjoying occupancy rights. It is the ri-raid land that has faced serious distortions in the wake of fast socio-economic changes taking place in the area.

Ri-Kynti lands, on the other hand, are lands set apart from the time of the founding of the area for certain clans upon whom were bestowed the proprietary, heritable and transferable rights. They further include any part of ri-raid lands, which at later stages were bestowed upon person or family or clan for certain yeoman services rendered to the area. The same rights devolve on Khasis on whom such lands are disposed of by the original owners by way of sale and transfer on receipt of full consideration for the same. Ri-Kynti, considered essentially private lands, includes two broader categories: ancestral and self-acquired. While ancestral lands are customarily under the control of the clan and cannot be brought to the market for sale or purchase, the self-acquired lands are under the complete ownership of persons who have acquired them through their own earnings. There is however no uniformity among various clans so far the nature of management and control of the ri-kynti of the clan is concerned. It is recognised that each clan has its own system of management or if land has been divided among the branches of the clans, the branches concerned have developed their own ways or if a particular branch has divided its share among the different families, the family concerned has its own system. Nonetheless the basic principle of management and control is almost similar throughout the Khasi Hills under which the control is in the hands of male adults of the clans, uncles and the adult brothers.

FLORA AND FAUNA

Meghalaya is a treasure trove of Nature, with its richly varied and dense endemic, exotic and cultivated flora. Nature, in its generous abundance, had bestowed on Meghalaya a unique array of vegetation, ranging from tropical and sub-tropical to temperate or near temperate. This is due to the diverse topography, varied and abundant rainfall and differential climatic and edaphic conditions of the State, within small regions. Biotic factors have also played an important role, at places decisive. Geographical position of Meghalaya has it appears favoured immigration and introduction of different plant species from the neighbouring states of the North Eastern India and also countries like China, Tibet and Myanmar. Geological factors, like the connection of Meghalaya with the land masses of Peninsular India, the Pacific Islands, Madagaskar and some other portions of Africa might also have influenced Meghalaya's flora and fauna to some extent.

As per the State of Forest Report 2017, published by the Forest Survey of India, Meghalaya has a forest cover of 17,146 km², which is 77.08% of the total geographical area of the state. Except the reserved forest areas and protected forests in and around Shillong (being managed by the department in arrangement with the District Councils), the rest of the forest areas are subjected to the primitive agricultural practice of shifting cultivation or slash and burn method especially in Garo Hills. The Meghalayan subtropical forests have been considered among the richest botanical habitats of Asia. These forests receive abundant rainfall and support a vast variety of floral and faunal biodiversity. A small portion of the forest area in Meghalaya is under what is known as "**sacred groves**". These are small pockets of ancient forest that have been preserved by the communities for hundreds of years due to religious and cultural beliefs. These forests are reserved for religious rituals and generally remain protected from any exploitation. These sacred groves harbour many rare plant and animal species. The Nokrek biosphere reserve and the Balapakram National Park, both in the West Garo Hills are considered to be the most biodiversity rich sites in Meghalaya. In addition, Meghalaya has three Wildlife Sanctuaries. These are the Nongkhyllem Wildlife Sanctuary, the Siju Sanctuary and the Baghmara Sanctuary, which is also the home of the insect eating **Pitcher plant**, the *Nepenthes khasiana.*

District-wise Forest Cover of Meghalaya *(Area in km²)*

District	Geographical Area	Very Dense Forest	Mod. Dense Forest	Open Forest	Total
East Garo Hills[TH]	2,603	63	1,075	1,128	2,266
East Khasi Hills[TH]	2,748	3	1,012	736	1,751
Jaintia Hills[TH]	3,819	100	1,488	915	2,503
Ribhoi[TH]	2,448	132	1,096	915	2,143
South Garo Hills[TH]	1,887	45	1,014	629	1,688
West Garo Hills[TH]	3,677	0	1,244	1,593	2,837
West Khasi Hills[TH]	5,247	110	2,457	1,391	3,958
Grand Total	**22,429**	**453**	**9,386**	**7,307**	**17,146**

Types of Forests

The forests of Meghalaya can broadly be grouped under the tropical type and the temperate type.

1. Tropical Forests

These forests are met within areas upto an elevation of 1200 m and with an average rainfall of about 100-250 cm. There are numerous sub types within this category such as evergreen, semi-evergreen, moist and dry deciduous forest, etc.

(a) **Tropical evergreen forests:** These forests usually occur in high rainfall areas as well as near catchment areas. They seldom form continuous belts due to various exogenous factors. But still, they harbour very rich species diversity, where nature is at its extravaganza forming a closed evergreen canopy. The trees exhibit clear zonation with dense and impenetrable herbaceous undergrowth.

(b) **Tropical semi-evergreen forests:** This category of forests occupies the north-eastern and northern slopes of the State, typically upto elevations of 1200 m, where annual rainfall is 150-200 cm with a comparatively cooler winter. The numbers of species here are fewer than the evergreen zone. There are also a few species in these forests which are deciduous in nature, such as *Careya arborea, Dillenia pentagyna* and *Callicarpa arborea.* Again there is a clear stratification of the trees in these forests.

(c) **Tropical moist and dry deciduous forests:** This type of forests occurs where annual rainfall is below 150 cm and at comparatively low elevations. Typical natural deciduous forests do not occur anywhere in Meghalaya but are only sub climax or man-made forests. These forests are characterised by seasonal leaf shedding and profuse flowering of the trees. Recurrent forest fires are a common phenomenon here. Deciduous forests are much more extensive in their distribution in the State and include a host of economically important trees like *Shorea robusta, Tectona grandis, Terminalia myriocarpa, Sterculia villosa, Logerstroemia flos-reginae, Porviflora, Morus laevigatus, Artocarpus chaplasha,* and *Gmelina arborea* both as natural and as plantations. *Schima wallichii, Artocarpus gameziana, Tetrameles mudiflora, Lannea coromandelica, Salmalia malabarica, Erythrina stricta, Premna milliflora, Vitex peduncularis, Albizia lebbeck, Lucida, Terminalia bellirica* etc. is also in abundance. These trees of the deciduous canopy are always lofty and straight bole and with spreading crown.

2. *Temperate Forests*

The temperate forests occupy the higher elevations about 1000 m, mostly along the southern slope of Khasi and Jaintia Hills. The rainfall here is very high 200-500 cm with a severe winter during November to March. Ground frost is also common during December to January.

Grass and Savannas

Grasslands of Meghalaya are also not a climax type but are only as a result of removal of original forest cover. The rolling grasslands covering large areas can be seen throughout the Shillong plateau, around Riangdo, Ranikor, Weiloi, Mawphlang, Mawsynram, Cherrapunji, Shillong, Jowai, Jarain, and Sutnga in Khasi and Jaintia Hills and major parts of West Garo Hills.

Sacred Groves

The sacred groves of Meghalaya largely fall under the temperate type and are the relic type evolved through millions of years. These are rich storehouse of vegetation wealth incomparable to any other type of forests in the State. These isolated pockets are untouched due to the religious beliefs and myths attributed to them. Many of the endangered species of the State are presently confined to these pockets only. Fagacaea members dominate over others in these sacred forests. Epiphytic flora is quite abundant and again dominated over by ferns and orchids.

A Botanical Wonder

Meghalaya's endemic Pitcher Plant or *Nepenthes khasiana* Hk. remains till now an explicable phenomenon to the botanists. It occurs in the Jarain area of the Jaintia Hills and the Baghmara area of the Garo Hills. The people in the Khasi Hills where the plant grows call it Tiew-Rakot, which means demon-flower or devouring-plant. The Jaintias call it Kset Phare, Kset means net with a lid and Phare means fly. The Garos call the plant Memang-Koksi, which literally means the basket of the devil. The most interesting part of the Pitcher Plant is its leaf. The leaf is modified into different organs, such as the lamina, the tendril, the pitcher and the lid. Over the pitcher, a lid is formed. It is an outgrowth on the face of the leaf near its apex. The lid grows and then become sealed over the mouth of the pitcher. When the plant attains maturity, the lid opens up. The pitcher is designed to catch insects.

FAUNA

Meghalaya has a large number of wild animals the most common of which is the Asian Elephant. The elephant population is mainly concentrated in

Garo Hills though some can be found in parts of Jaintia Hills and Ri Bhoi District. There are a few Royal Bengal tigers here as well. Some of the other animals being the Himalayan Bear, the Bear Cat, Leopards, Wild Cat, Slow Loris, three species of Macaques, Common Langur, the Hoolock Gibbon and many species of Deer. The Hoolock Gibbon which can truly make the hills come alive with their call are heard in the jungles of Siju, Balpakram and Nokrek. The Garos, consider them sacred and if a group decides to stay near a village it is considered a good omen.

Meghalaya, has a number of rare birds endemic to the State. The terrain being hilly only a few wetland birds are found in the state. Migratory ducks can be spotted in the Umiam Lake and the Siju Bird Sanctuary. The Great Indian Hornbill, found in Garo Hills, is easy to spot in the Balpakram National Park. The lesser or Grey Hornbill is also seen around Siju. The Hill Myna is endemic to this area and can be observed during the nesting season. One interesting and rare bird is the Peacock Pheasant seen in Siju. Different species of bee eaters and bulbuls can be found in the southern slopes of Khasi and Jaintia hills. Just below the Shillong Peak is a patch of mixed forests which has been mentioned in some bird watching handbooks as a good place to observe a variety of birds in season.

The salt deposits found in Arebellagre village, about 45 kms from Tura, attract large number of green pigeons during the months of March/April.

Wildlife Sanctuaries and National Parks

To help preserve this ecological diversity the Government has declared two National parks, one biosphere reserve and three sanctuaries. These are:

1. Balpakram National Park
2. Nokrek National Park
3. Nokrek Biosphere Reserve
4. Siju Bird Sanctuary
5. Baghmara Pitcher Plant Sanctuary
6. Nongkhyllem Sanctuary

Balpakram National Park

This park has been established in the west Garo Hill district in an area of 220 sq km. The nearest town is William Nagar about 15 km. The vegetation consists of tropical moist deciduous type. The predominant species is moist hill sal. The fauna of this area includes elephants, wild buffaloes, gaur (Indian bison), sambar, barking deer, wild boar, capped langur as well as predators such as tigers, leopards, clouded leopards and the rare golden cat.

Nokrek National Park

This park is also located in the west Garo Hills District. Its area is 68 sq. km. The forests of the parks are tropical semi-evergreen and moist deciduous. Mammals found in the park are capped langur, clouded leopard, leopard cat, fishing-cat, golden cat, Pangolin, wild buffalo, elephant, serow and tiger.

List of National Parks in Meghalaya

S.No.	National Park	Year of Establishment	Area (km^2)	Districts
1.	Balphakram	1985	220.00	South Garo Hills
2.	Nokrek Ridge	1986	47.48	East Garo Hills

POPULATION

As per 2011 Census, the total population of the State is 29,66,889 as against 23,18,822 in 2001 indicating the highest decadal growth of 27.9 per cent. Around 79.92 per cent of the population of the State lives in rural areas.

The State's population is pre-dominantly tribal and constitutes 86.1 per cent of the total population. The Scheduled Caste population is barely 0.6 per cent and the Others form 13.6 per cent of the total population of the State.

The number of villages as per 2011 Census is 5,782 as against 5,484 in 1991 Census. The main workers constitute 32.6 per cent while the marginal workers constitute 9.2 per cent.

The following table shows the district-wise population of Meghalaya as per 2011 census:

District	Population	Increase	Sex Ratio	Literacy	Density
1. East Khasi Hills	825,922	24.96%	1011	84.15%	301
2. West Garo Hills	643,291	24.09%	984	67.58%	175
3. Jaintia Hills	395,124	32.10%	1013	61.64%	103
4. West Khasi Hills	383,461	29.53%	980	77.87%	73
5. East Garo Hills	317,917	26.87%	972	73.95%	122
6. Ri Bhoi	258,840	34.26%	953	75.67%	106
7. South Garo Hills	142,334	40.95%	945	71.72%	75

The rate of literacy has appreciably grown from 62.06 per cent in 2001 to 74.4 per cent in 2011 which is above from the national average of 73 per cent. There is, however, some difference in the levels of literacy among males and females. While the rate of literacy among males is 76.0 per cent, it is only 72.9 per cent among females.

Meghalaya Urban Population 2011

Out of total population of Meghalaya, 20.07% people live in urban regions. The total figure of population living in urban areas in 595,450 of which 297,572 are males and while remaining 297,878 are females. The urban population in the last 10 years has increased by 20.07 per cent.

Sex Ratio in urban regions of Meghalaya was 1001 females per 1000 males. For child (0-6) sex ratio the figure for urban region stood at 954 girls per 1000 boys. Total children (0-6 age) living in urban areas of Meghalaya were 77,944. Of total population in urban region, 13.09% were children (0-6). Average Literacy rate in Meghalaya for Urban regions was 90.79 per cent in which males were 92.46% literate while female literacy stood at 89.24%. Total literates in urban region of Meghalaya were 469,851.

RELIGION

Presently, Meghalaya's population is predominantly Christian; about 70 per cent of the total population. The next sizeable religious community is the Hindus. Some Khasis, Jaintias, etc believe in their original religion. The Muslim population is a little over 4 per cent. Sikhs, Buddhists and Jains are less than 0.5 per cent of the total population.

Religion-wise Distribution of Population in Meghalaya (Census-2011)

Religious Communities	Population (2011 Census)			Percentage-wise Distribution		
	Total	Male	Female	Population	Male	Female
All Religions	2966889	1491832	1475057	100.0000	100.0000	100.0000
Hindus	342078	183622	158456	11.5299	12.3085	10.7423
Muslims	130399	67827	62572	4.3951	4.5465	4.2420
Christians	2213027	1100492	1112535	74.5908	73.7678	75.4231
Sikhs	3045	1640	1405	0.1026	0.1099	0.0952
Buddhists	9864	5144	4720	0.3325	0.3448	0.3199
Jains	627	342	285	0.0211	0.0229	0.0193
Others	258271	127983	130288	8.7051	8.5789	8.8327
Religion not stated	9578	4782	4796	0.3228	0.3205	0.3251

IMMORTAL MARTYRS

U Tirot Sing

After concluding the treaty of Yandabu in 1826, the British had control over the Brahmaputra valley. They had already occupied the Surma valley by becoming "Diwan" of Bengal in 1765. Now the British wanted a strategic road to link up these two valleys under their occupation. The construction of this strategic road was possible only through the Khasi Hills. The Khasi Hills were also considered suitable for setting up sanatoria cantonment. The political agent of the British, David Scott approached U Tirot Sing, the king of Khadsawphra Syiemship for construction of the road project through his kingdom. David Scott promised U Tirot Sing that if the project was agreed upon, U Tirot Sing would be allowed complete control over Bordwar and that free trade would flourish along the proposed road.

U Tirot Sing convened a session of his Durbar in which the matter was debated for two days and two nights. David Scott who was invited to witness the proceedings was struck with the decency, decorum and the quality of the debate. When David Scott had given up all hope, the Durbar agreed to his proposals. Soon a British garrison with labourers for construction of the road was posted at Nongkhlaw. News came that the British army at Guwahati and Sylhet had been reinforced. U Tirot Sing sensed the ulterior motive of the British to ultimately grab the entire hill territory lying between the Surma valley and the Brahmaputra valley. Alarmed by the eventuality, U Tirot Sing convened the Durbar and with its decision served a notice to the British to quit Nongkhlaw, but the British did not pay any heed.

U Kiang Nongbah

Raja Rajendra Singh of Jaintiapur, a Jaintia king was deprived of his kingdom through deceit. His territory in the plains was taken away by the British, and he was left with the option to rule over his people in the hills which offered little scope for earning revenue for running the administration. Hence, he declined kingship. The British then offered rulership to the village headmen, Dolois and Sirdar. This worked well from 1835 to 1953, though the people secretly bore a grudge against the British. Then the British imposed a house-tax in 1860 which met with resentment and within a few months, the people rose in rebellion. But the same was easily put down, as the rebels were not organised.

Towards the close of 1860, income tax was also levied in addition to the house-tax. There was an apprehension in the air that tax would also be levied on betel and betel-nut. Imposition of these taxes created turmoil amongst the Jaintias and they rose again in a fierce rebellion in 1862. The magnitude of the upsurge was so much that as many as seven regiments and detachments of troops were put into action to suppress it. Jowai, which was besieged by the rebels for about 3 weeks, was thus reoccupied amidst heavy casualties. The leader and guiding spirit in this rebellion was a young man, U Kiang Nongbah. In the first rebellion he kept his identity secret and thus avoided arrest. He was extremely shrewd and a great organiser. He contacted all the Dolois and Sirdars without causing any suspicion. He managed to hoodwink the British Intelligence Service. They had no trace of his movements and activities. Yet, ultimately he was defeated because of the superior might of the British. In the unequal fight that ensured, hundreds of Jaintias were killed and U Kiang Nongbah was betrayed, captured and hanged publicly to strike terror into the hearts of the Jaintias on December 30, 1862. When he was put to the gallows, he said, in a clear voice: "If my face turns eastward when I die on the rope, we shall be free again within a hundred years. If it turns westwards, we shall be enslaved forever".

Pa Togan Sangma

In 1835, the British conquered the Jaintia kingdom. The Khasis were also subjugated a little later. In 1862, the fierce rebellion of the Jaintias led by U Kiang Nongbah was put down. Now the British wanted to establish their hegemony in the Garo Hills. In December 1872, the British sent out battalions to Garo Hills to establish their control in the region. The attack was conducted from three sides – south, east and west. The Garo warriors confronted them at Rongrenggiri with their spears, swords and shields. The battle that ensured was unmatched, as the Garos did not have guns or mortars like the British Army. Togan Sangma, a young man was in command of the valiant Garo warriors. He fell fighting with unmatched heroism and courage in December 1872. Pa Togan Sangma is immortalised at the martyr's column in Shillong, where his name is enshrined along with U Tirot Sing and U Kiang Nongbah, the gallant heroes of the Khasis and Jaintias.

EDUCATION

Meghalaya is a small state in the north eastern part of India. The rate of literacy has appreciably grown from 62.6 per cent in 2001 to 74.4 per cent in 2011 which is now above of the national average of 73 per cent. There is, however, some difference in the levels of literacy among males and females. While the rate of literacy among males is 76.0 per cent, it is only 72.9 per cent among females. According to the Census Report, 2011, East Khasi Hills District, has shown the highest rate of literate persons in the

State with literacy rate of 84.2%. The state has one central university located at Shillong. In addition to it there are few professional colleges including the premier "Shillong Engg. and Management" College located at Mawlai, Shillong.

North Eastern Hill University (Central University)

North-Eastern Hill University was set up as a **Central University** on **19 July 1973** to cater the needs of north eastern states of India. The university has its main campus in **Shillong**. The jurisdiction of the University extends to the state of **Meghalaya**.

Engineering Colleges in Meghalaya

1. Shillong Engg. and Management College

Nursing Colleges in Meghalaya

1. Repsbun School of Nursing East Khasi Hills, Laitum Khrah, Shillong

Law Colleges in Meghalaya

1. Department of Law, North Eastern Hill University
2. Tura Law College
3. Shillong Law College
4. Khad-Ar-Doloi Law College, Jowai

Polytechnic Institutes in Meghalaya

1. Jowai Polytechnic
2. Shillong Polytechnic
3. Tura Polytechnic

LANGUAGES

The principal languages in Meghalaya are Khasi and Garo with English as the official language of the State. Khasi and Garo languages and literature have developed mainly because of the initiative of the Christian Missionaries.

INDIAN ARCHAEOLOGY

Bong Laskar Memorial, Baghmara, South Garo Hills District: This monument is situated in the heart of Baghmara, the headquarters of South Garo Hills District, Meghalaya. The Monument was built in the memory of Bong Laskar, one of the most prominent Laskars of Baghmara. The monument is built of burnt bricks and has a tomb like structure. It is 3.60 m high and 4.30 m wide. The period of construction of this monument could not be determined accurately. It is believed that one Besing Laskar constructed this monument before the British annexation of Garo Hills at around 1874.

Mir Jumla's Tomb at Mankachar, West Garo Hills District: Mir Jumla was one of the capable Mughal Generals. He was appointed the Governor of Bengal by Aurengzeb at around 1659. In 1662 he invaded Assam in course of terrestrial expansion. His initial success was however foiled by the flood of the mighty Brahmaputra River. Many of his men perished from starvation and malaria. Mir Jumla decided to retreat to Bengal by boat. However, before he could set his feet on the soil of Bengal, he fell ill and died in the year 1663. His mortal remain was buried on a hillock at Mankachar in the West Garo Hills District of Meghalaya.

Nartiang Ancient Sites and Remains, Jaintia Hills District : Nartiang is about 30 km north to Jowai in the Jaintia Hills district of Meghalaya. Archeologically and historically the place is considered to be of great importance for the State and the country. Historically, by the end of the first half of the 16th century approximately, the Jaintia rulers had consolidated their conquest by subduing many local petty chiefs in both the fringes of the plains of the Brahmaputra valley and the Surma valley with their capital at Jaintiapur. The expansion of the kingdom northwards made Nartiang pivotal for both the administrative and commercial relations with the Ahom and the Kacheri kingdoms of the plain of the Brahmaputra valley. Taking the proximity and the strategic location of the place into consideration, the Jaintia rulers accordingly shifted their hill or summer capital from Sutnga to Nartiang sometimes during the second or the third quarters of the 16th century. The place is found to consist of many archaeological sites and remains. They are:

1. The Monoliths Site
2. The Ruin Royal Palace

The Borghat Historical and Archaeological Remains, Jaintia Hills District: Borghat is a beautiful little village situated on the east bank of the blue river Myntdu in the south of the Jaintia Hills district at about 80 kms from Jowai. The navigability of the Myntdu river with other parts of the Surma Valley had made the place into a prospective commercial depot where traders from the hills and the plain of the erstwhile Jaintia kingdom could meet for commercial transaction. Further, the place also situated midway between Jaintiapur, the capital and Sutnga, the hill capital of the kingdom. The commercial and the strategic importance of the place had prompted the mighty Jaintia Raja, U Bor Sing to convert it into the kingdom sub-headquarters and adorned it with temples, tanks and other structural splendour of that time. Even with the transfer of the hill capital from Sutnga to Nartiang sometimes during the 2nd or 3rd quarters of the 16th century, the importance of this place as a flourishing market still continued till the time of partition in 1947.

Megaliths or Monoliths Site at (lew, Shillong) Laitlyngkot, East Khasi Hills District : At Laitlyngkot, a place of about 25 kms. from Shillong by the side of the lew Shillong. There are groups of clustered menhirs (Mawbynna Shynrang) and dolmens (Mawbynna Kynthei) of very impressive sizes. The biggest of these menhirs is about 5 meters in height, 1.50 meters in breadth and 0.05 meters in thickness. The Largest of these dolmens is about 9.25 meters in length, 3.25 meters in breadth and 0.50 meters in thickness. Altogether, there are about 60 menhirs and 20 dolmens in a cluster. Historically, the monument is said to have been associated with the establishment of the lew Shillong market. Their date of construction could not be determined. The menhirs and the dolmens are examples of the unpolished stone technology or culture and may be of great help to the scholars in the study of stone technology transition.

Crematorium of the Ancient Sohra Chiefs (Syiems) at (Pomsohmen) Cherrapunjee, East Khasi Hills District : At Pomsohmen, a hamlet of Cherrapunjee (Sohra) situated at about 52 kms. from Shillong, exits two structures of cultural importance, one is the crematorium of the mother of the ruling Syiems (chiefs) known as 'Ka Syiem Sad'. The structures were built of fine stone masonaries and measuring about 20 feet in length,12 feet in breadth and 8 feet in height. These Crematoria were built around the year 1856. According to customs, the successor of the deceased Syiem/chief would have to perform cremation rituals of his predecessor. Until and unless this ritual was being performed or completed and which was usually done with the prescribed pomps and honours, the successors of the deceased Syiem (chief) would not be considered by the people of the chiefdom as the full-fledged Syiem (chief) but as acting Syiem. However, since 1926, this customary ritual could not be performed mainly because it involves enormous expenditure and time. This ritual is found only in Sohra chiefdom and not in any other chiefdoms of the Khasi tribe of Meghalaya.

CULTURAL HERITAGE OF MEGHALAYA

Meghalaya is the homeland of India's ancient hill communities. Dance, music and sports reflect their way of life. Festive sounds of merry making echo from hill to hill revealing the pulsating life of the tribal people. Mindful of their cultural heritage, these simple folks are jovial and hospitable. There are about twenty-four communities in the state amongst which fifteen are scheduled tribes that have migrated from other states. The non-tribal communities are twelve in number who have migrated to Meghalaya for trading and business purposes.

Majority of the population of the state belongs to the Indo-Chinese linguistic Community of which the two important sub-families are 'Monkhmer' and Tibeto-Burman. The 'Monkhmes' families include the Khasis and Jaintias whereas the Garos belongs to the 'Tibeto-Burman' groups. All the Hinduized Communities of Meghalaya—Rabha, Kuch, Hajong, Barai belongs to the Bodo groups of Assamese Burman family. One of the characteristics features of the tribes of Meghalaya is that they could preserve their independence and ancestral institutions for many centuries inspite of the distractions provided by the neo-cultures around them. In fact their social organizations provide the most perfect examples of the still surviving matriarchal institutions.

Amongst the many tribes in Meghalaya, the most dominant tribes are Khasi, Jaintia and Garo which are detailed as under:

Socio-Cultural Background of Khasis

The Khasis in Meghalaya belong to the Monkhmer group. The Khasi tribes includes—*Boi, War, Khynriams* and *Lyngans.* The *Boi's* reside in the North West part of Khasi hills, *War* in the hill and valley of the southern part, *Khynrians* in the central and highest part of Meghalaya, the *Lyngans* occupy the western part of Meghalaya.

The history of the Khasi people before the advent of the British is not well documented. Their folklore and oral traditions tell about their supernatural origin. It is generally believed that Khasis have migrated from south-east to the Brahmaputra valley where they resided before entering the hills. In course of time, their language and customs changed. They were believed to have named from Jaintia hills to Khasi hills in the practice of shifting cultivation and in search of iron-ore.

The Khasis are divided into a number of clans, which trace their descent from ancestresses or Kiaws. The descendants of one Common ancestress are called Shi Kur. A sub-clan is called Shi-Kpoh. The smallest division of the clan is the family. The clans are bound together by strictties of religion, ancestor worship and funeral rites for those who continue their traditional tribal religion.

The rule of succession is strictly matrilineal. Women have important status assigned to them; and women, and not the men, inherit the property. The rule amongst the Khasis is that the youngest daughter 'holds' the religion. The members of the household witness her performance in the family ceremonies. Hence, she gets the lion share of the family property.

Residence is matriarchal. Although, amongst the children, both the sexes get share of the family property, but the youngest daughter gets the largest share and she lives in the ancestral home along with her husband, children and her parents. The brothers' after marriage live in their wives home. A man married to the 'heiress' lives with his inlaws but his status is weak. The management of the property is done by the maternal uncle and the groom of the heiress has to work under the supervision of the maternal uncle. Marriages to non-heiress are more stable and successful.

Religion is one aspect, which had been misinterpreted by the colonials in trying to achieve mass proselytization. The Khasis worship a formless god and refer to their religion as *Niamtre.* The three basic values of *Niamtre* are : one must earn by one's own effort, one can know god when he knows his fellow men and one must know the paternal and maternal relations meaning marriage within the clan is forbidden. Converts to Christianity, naturally, do not observe the Khasi religion *Niamtre* but fear leads them to believe in Khasi sorcery.

In the olden days, Khasi men wore a dhoti, jacket and turban but today their traditional attire is used on ceremonial occasions only. The dress largely is westernized. Women still wear the traditional dress consisting of the undercloth, and two pieces of clothes above it. The jewellery is made of gold and silver artistically crafted by local smiths.

Khasi houses are clean. They are cottages with thach roof, with plank or stone walls raised or a plinth at a height of 2-3 feet from the ground. The windows allow light to enter the houses. There is always a fire burning on earthen or stove hearth in the centre. Khasi house is oval shaped, divided into three rooms—a porch, a centre room and a retiring room.

Like all tribal communities, the Khasis love to feast, sing, dance and enjoy life to the hilt. Festivals are invariably celebrated with pomp and gaity, cutting across the petty differences of caste, creed, colour or religion.

Socio-Cultural Background of Jaintias

Jaintia is the term used for *'Synteng'* or *'Pnar'* belonging to the land of twelve Doloi. As to the origin of Jaintias, there are two schools of thought: One says that Jaintia Kingdom got its name from 'Jaintiapur' because of the famous shrine of Jaintia Devi (an incarnation of goddess Durga) mentioned in the Puranic and tantric literature, the other says, the Jaintias derived its name from *'Synteng'* or *'Pnar'.* Like the Khasi and Garos, they too lack recorded history. We find a little information on the Jaintias from the history of Assam. In the recent past, a more detailed history could be found since the time of the advent of the British. The Jaintias use the Khasi script and language.

The Khasis and Jaintias can not be treated separately as they have many things in common. As per the history of migration, the Jaintia were supposed to have come from Southeast Asia, with the probability that they have started their migration westward from Mongolia and along the Foot hills of the Himalayas to Southeast Asia, and ultimately to their present habitat through Myanmar. One opinion is that the Jaintias entered the hills in batches under different names—*Amwi, Changpung, Jowai, Nartia, Raliana, Sutuga etc.*

The Jaintia do not have a script of their own. They speak their own language and dialects. In case of dress, the Jaintia and Khasi men wear the same dress, but for women, dress is some what different from the Khasi. She wears a cloth around her body above the chest and another thrown over the shoulders and crossed in front. Women put on earnings and other ornaments of gold and silver. On the festive occasions the women wear a large beads of lac and silver with ornamental headgear.

Mother's clan is adopted by children. Mother has important duties of performing family rites and ceremonies, though in actual practices, her brother performs the ceremonies and sacrifices of the house. The mother, father and maternal uncle have their own place in the Jaintia family. Property law is matrilineal. The inheritance passes from mother to the youngest daughter. If the youngest daughter dies, the property then is inherited by the next youngest daughter. The heiress has no right to handle the property matters, the actual control is in the hands of the mother and maternal uncle. Ancestral property can not be alienated without the consent of the whole family. As far as the self-acquired property is concerned, it can be disposed off according to the will of the beholder. Women are property holders, keepers of the family purse and other movable and immovable properties. In traditional system, except in politics, they are treated equally with men but are not allowed to behave as superior to men.

In matters of traditional religions belief, the Jaintias feel that their religion is god given and not founded by men. Their religious value system have the three common beliefs: God is omnipresent, omnipotent and omniscient. They have no temples or churches. They are Maothistic. But they evoke God by different names according to their needs.

The Jaintias have a very rich art and cultural heritage. Carving engraving are the most popular art. The people have their own indigenous way of maintaining their artistic pursuits. Weaving though has lost the importance and can hardly be termed as a sustained activity but is still continued in certain parts of the hills. The handicrafts of Jaintias include the beautiful pottery industry, craft work of cane, bamboo and wood in multifarious designs which attract the customers.

Socio-Cultural Background of the Garos

The Garo hills are predominently inhabitated by the Garos. The Garo society also divides themselves mainly into two clans *(chatchi)—Marak* and *Sangma*. But now a days, we find other divisions of clans such as *Momin, Shira, Arengh* added to the Garo clans.

Garo Society or community is divided into 12 (twelve) sub-dialectical groups who inhabit in different locations of Garo hills. Garo society is a matrilineal society and its descent is traced through the mother. The residence is also matriarchal. As such, the title is taken from the side of the mother which is known as *"Machong"* and never from the father.

The village administration and its organisation is democratic in character. Garos were originally ruled by the traditional chieftains known as *"Nokmas"*. In the ancient days, Garos settled all civil and criminal cases by the indigenous tribal chiefs like Nokmas and his council.

Garo marriages are arranged between the two localized lineage groups. It is a symmetrical cross cousin marriage arranged on the basis of localized lineage group. Both mother's brother's daughter and the father's sister's daughter stands as the category of a potential wife. Although decent, inheritence, succession as well as residence are on female line, yet women do not seem to enjoy more power than the patrilineal people. Effective power is exercised by a group of matrilineally related males.

The Garos strongly believe in the existence of a supernatural being. They use a general term *'mite'* for a supernatural being. All the beings are supposed to be endowed with living spirits. They believe *'mite's* are responsible for creation of world and man. They try to keep a good relation with the mites and try to appease them by making sacrifices.

The religious beliefs of the different groups of non-christian Garos appear relatively uniform, but the ceremonies performed are varied. Christianisation of the Garo began only after the British occupied the Garo hills in the mid-nineteenth century. The Garo Christians have given up the practice of traditional religious rites and supplication of the spirits or gods totally and have adopted Christianity in its pristine form.

Christianity is one of the major causes of change in the life and culture of the Garos. The christian Garos have practically abandoned all aspects of the Garo culture and religion related traditional practices, ceremonies, dance and music.

CAVING

Caving is an art which needs the skills of rock climbers and swimmers and of course plenty of physical endurance. Apart from this there are many technical details that need to be considered before going for a caving expedition. Meghalaya has been receiving plenty of cavers (Speleologist) from different parts of the world who are dedicated to the art of caving. There are more than 1000 caves in Meghalaya. Meghalaya is a dream destination for cavers from around the world. If one wants to go for caving in Meghalaya then experienced cave guides should be contacted. There are more than 1000 caves in Meghalaya. The longest cave is Krem Laitprah/ Um Im-Ladit which is 22.2 km long and is located in Nongkhlieh Elaka of Jaintia Hills. The well known caves are:

Name of the Cave	District	Length
Krem Laitprah/Um Im-Ladit	Jaintia Hills	22 km 200 mts
Krem Kotsati-Umlawan	Jaintia Hills	21 km 530 mts
Synrang Pamiang	Jaintia Hills	14 km 157 mts
Krem Umthloo	Jaintia Hills	12 km 661 mts
Krem Chympe	Jaintia Hills	9 km 660 mts
Krem Mawkhyrdop (Mawmluh)	Khasi Hills	7 km 185 mts
Krem Lymput	Khasi Hills	6 km 641 mts
Tetengkol Balwakol	Garo Hills	5 km 335 mts
Siju Dobhakol	Garo Hills	4 km 770 mts

ECONOMY

Meghalaya's economy is primarily agricultural engaging around 57.45 per cent of its total population. However, the contribution of agriculture to the State's NSDP is around 33 per cent only as against the contribution of around 55 per cent by the tertiary sector. With the increase in population over the years and the corresponding decrease in availability of land for agricultural purposes, the incidence of landless labour and the resultant poverty has risen substantially. Inadequate infrastructural facilities, poor road communication due to hilly terrain and unemployment have been the major constraints of economic growth. Despite possessing a fairly rich resource endowment which could provide the base for an adequate rate of economic growth, Meghalaya is still an industrially backward State.

Investment for industrial development for generating income and employment have been encouraged through a number of incentives in pursuance of the State's Industrial Policy, 1997 and recently a number of units have come up especially at the EPIP, Byrnihat and the Industrial area near Umiam lake. However, the impact of these industrial investments on the State's economy is yet to be ascertained.

Sectoral Income Distribution

Though Meghalaya is primarily an agriculture economy with agricultural activities engaging nearly 57.45 per cent of the total work force, yet the contribution of this sector towards the economy of the state during 1999-2000 to 2007-08 is between 18.70 p.c. and 23.96 p.c. according to NSDP estimates at current prices. The share of the Industrial sector being in the range of 21.09 p.c. to 26.42 p.c. On the other hand, the share of Service sector in terms of percentage contribution during the same periods, have been between 53.21 p.c. at the lowest and 54.95 p.c. at the highest.

Poverty

The National Tenth Plan document prepared by the Planning Commission indicates that the national percentage of population below the poverty line has declined from 54.88 per cent in 1973-74 to 26.1 per cent in 1999-2000 which is expected to decline further to 19.34 per cent in 2006-07. In respect of the State of Meghalaya, the figures of the Planning Commission indicate that the percentage of population below the poverty line was 50.20 per cent in 1973-74 and 33.87 per cent in 1999-2000 which was declined further to 17.1 per cent in 2009-10 with a B.P.L. population of 8.23 lakhs. The State Government does not have any reliable data in respect of population below the poverty line.

State Income

The Net State Domestic Product of the State at current prices increased from ₹ 3211.30 crores in 1999-2000 to ₹ 6707.03 crores in 2007-08 and the corresponding per capita income increased from ₹ 10270 in 1997-98 to ₹ 19572 in 2004-05. The Net State Domestic Product of the State at constant (1999-2000) prices was ₹ 3211.30 crores during 1999-2000 and increased to ₹ 5059.59 crores during 2007-08. The per capita NSDP at current prices rose from ₹ 14355 crore in 1999-2000 to ₹ 69516 crore during 2014-15.

INDUSTRY

Status of Industrial development in the state. Despite having enormous potential in power generation, surplus Agro-Horticulture produces large reserve of coal, limestone and other mineral resources, Meghalaya has made little progress in the field of industrialization. The reason being, the state of Meghalaya is a landlocked territory with hilly terrain connected only by serpentine roads to various villages, making transportation costlier when compared with other states. Moreover, absence of railhead in the state, besides distance from the port is another factor hindering movement of goods and materials in and out of the state. This acts as an impediment for the development of large manufacturing units with large marketing hinterland.

Majority of the population is involved in the unorganised sector of the industry. In addition to agriculture and allied sectors, small-scale unregistered units play an important role in providing employment opportunities. All the 116 large & medium manufacturing enterprises are located in rural sector. And out of the 2653 small scale manufacturing enterprises operating in the state, 1902 are located in rural areas and 751 in urban areas. Similarly for construction related enterprises, 971 are located in rural areas and 635 in urban areas. The share of manufacturing sector in the industrial enterprises is relatively greater for both rural and urban sector when compared with the construction units. Manufacturing sector accounts to nearly 80% of the total industrial enterprise sector in the state.

In recent years, due to the package of incentives offered by the State Government combined with the attractive subsidies offered by the Central Government, a good number of industrial units have come up particularly at the EPIP at Byrnihat, Ri-Bhoi District and as a result, there has been tremendous pressure on the supply of power, thus making Meghalaya a power deficit State. The real economic benefits being accrued to the State of Meghalaya as a consequence of these investments in industrial units are yet to be ascertained.

Industrial Infrastructure in Meghalaya

To obviate the problem of prospective entrepreneurs in acquiring site for industries, Industrial Estates and Areas and Export Promotion Industrial Park (EPIP) and Growth, Centers have been created and more are likely to come in the near future. The following are the existing Industrial Sites.

1. Barapani Industrial Area with an area spread of over 44 hectares.
2. Growth Centre at Mendipathar, in East Garo Hills District
3. Industrial Estate in Shillong, Jowai, Mendipathar, Tura and Nongstoin.
4. Export Promotion Industrial Park (EPIP) at Byrnihat with an area spread over 259.35 hectares was in operation from April, 2001.

Existing Industrial Estates and Areas

Location	Area in Acres
Industrial Estates	
Shillong	10.22
Mendipathar	7.00
Tura	19.83

Location	Area in Acres
Jowai	14.56
Williamnagar	51.30
Nongstoin	10.00
Total	112.91
Industrial Areas	
Barapani	109.67

Source: Meghalaya Industrial Dev. Corp. (MIDC)

POWER

As against the hydro power potential of around 35,000 MW in the North Eastern Region of India, Meghalaya have a potential of about 3000 MW of hydro electric power of which the tapped power potential is only 188.76 MW. The first power project in Meghalaya is a mini-hydel project in the northern part of Shillong established in 1925. The tapped potential constitutes only 6% of the available hydro power potential. The State of Meghalaya is directly influenced by the South-West Monsoon. The physical orientation and placement of the State with respect to the rain bearing monsoon winds has gifted Meghalaya with the wettest place on earth – Mawsynram and Cherrapunjee. The average annual rainfall of the State is 12000 mm. The rain water flows down the rugged slopes and narrow valleys and descends rapidly to the plains of Assam in the North and Bangladesh in the South. Thus, the hilly terrains and the heavy rainfall have made Meghalaya a State ideal for harnessing hydro-electric power. Moreover, the hills of Meghalaya are blessed with a stable geology and of an older formation than the Himalayas. As a result, they are more stable and present less technical problems in the construction of dams, reservoirs, tunnels and water conducting system.

The scope for generating hydel power is abundant due to the topography of the area in the state. The Khasi Hills region possesses a favourable condition for this purpose that led to the commissioning of the first hydel power project of the North Eastern Region in Shillong during the early part of the twentieth century. Although the Shillong Hydro Electricity Company stopped functioning in 1980s due to the aging of the machines, several new projects started operation subsequently. The Umtrew hydel project in the Khasi Hills and the Tura Diesel project in the Garo Hills were installed in 1957 which expanded electricity in uncovered areas of the state.

However, the Umiam Hydel project installed by harnessing mainly the Great Umiam Khwan river at a reservoir known as Umiam Lake has emerged as the foremost hydel project of the region. From the initial installed capacity of only 36.00 Mega Watts, it has now a total installed capacity of 17,400 MW. It provides power not only to the entire state but also sales electricity to other North Eastern states. The Meghalaya State Electricity Board has also executed the Nangal Bibra thermal project in the coal belt area of the eastern part of the Garo Hills with an installed capacity of 8.00 Mega Watts. Another major project is expected to be installed in the Myntdu river in Jaintia Hills.

Present Power Situation in Meghalaya

At present, Meghalaya is having only hydro generation. During non-monsoon period, availability of power becomes low and even the restricted load demand of the State has to be met through import of power from the NE grid. This is mainly due to the new liberalized industrial policy of Meghalaya that has triggered an unprecedented load growth in the industrial sector of Meghalaya, coupled with identical growth in other sectors due to accelerated power development and reform process.

As of October 2017, Meghalaya had a total installed power generation capacity of 558.32 MW, comprising 353.03 MW from state utilities and 205.28 MW from central utilities. Of the total installed power generation capacity, 387.19 MW was contributed by hydropower, 140.09 MW by thermal power, and 31.04 MW by renewable power. During 2015-16, 315 KW SPV power plants of different capacities were being installed across government buildings as well as rooftops in the state. Work on manufacturing of 10 KW wind solar hybrid system in the government college at Tura has also been taken up during 2015-16.

Meghalaya State Electricity Board

The Meghalaya State Electricity Board, or MeSEB as it is known, came into being on the 21st January, 1975, consequent upon the bifurcation of the erstwhile Assam State Electricity Board. The bifurcation was an offshoot of the emergence of Meghalaya as a State in 1972. The MeSEB was constituted under Section (5) of the Electricity (Supply) Act, 1948 by the Government of Meghalaya vide notification No. PE304/74 dated 21.12.74.

With the bifurcation, the MeSEB inherited 4 power stations, the connecting transmission and distribution lines including the distribution sub-stations. Out of the 4 power stations, the Umiam Stage-III power station was then under construction. The total installed capacity at the time of bifurcation in 1975 was 66.506 MW. The total installed capacity has since gone up to 185.20 MW with the addition of the 60 MW Umiam-Umtrew Stage-III Power Station in 1979 and the 60 MW Umiam-Umtrew Stage-IV Power Station in 1992. The Table below depicts the existing Power Stations of the Board.

Existing Power Stations of the Meghalaya State Electricity Board

S. No.	Power Stations	Location	Unit	Capacity	Commissioning
1.	Umiam Umtrew	Sumer	I	9 MW	21.02.1965
	Stage I		II	9 MW	16.03.1965
			III	9 MW	06.09.1965
			IV	9 MW	11.09.1965
2.	Umiam Umtrew	Sumer	I	9 MW	22.07.1970
	Stage II		II	9 MW	24.07.1970
3.	Umiam Umtrew	Kyrdemkulai	I	30 MW	26.01.1979
	Stage III		II	30 MW	30.03.1979
4.	Umiam Umtrew	Nongkhylem	I	30 MW	11.08.1992
	Stage IV		II	30 MW	16.09.1992
5.	Umtrew	Dehal	I	2.8 MW	01.04.1957
			II	2.8 MW	01.04.1957
			III	2.8 MW	01.04.1957
			IV	2.8 MW	01.04.1968

Rural Electrification

Out of the total number of 5,782 villages in the State, 2,762 of them have a population of less than 200. Though rural electrification in Meghalaya is not an economically viable activity, yet it is implemented from the social point of view. The Central and State Governments continued to give emphasis on this programme.

TRANSPORTATION

The partition of the country in 1947 created severe infrastructural constraints for the Northeastern region, with merely 2% of the perimeter of the region adjoining the rest of the country. A narrow strip of land, often called the Siliguri Corridor or the Chicken's Neck, connects the region with the state of West Bengal. Meghalaya is a landlocked state with a large number of small settlements in remote areas. Road is the only means of transport. While the capital Shillong is relatively well connected, road connectivity in most other parts is relatively poor. A significant portion of the roads in the state are still unpaved. Most of the arrivals into the Meghalaya take place through Guwahati in neighbouring Assam, which is nearly 103 km away. Assam has a major railhead as well as an airport with regular train and air services to the rest of the country.

When Meghalaya was carved out of Assam as an autonomous state in 1972, it inherited a total road length of 2786.68 km including 174 km of

National Highways with road density of 12.42 km per 100 square kilometre. By 2012-13, total road length has reached up to 8,428 km out of which 5,674 km were surfaced. The road density had increased to 41.69 km per 100 square kilometre by March 2011. However, Meghalaya is still far below the national average of 75 km per 100 km2. In order to provide better services to the people of the state, the Meghalaya Public Works Department is taking steps for improvement and up-gradation of the existing roads and bridges in phased manner.

Road Network

Meghalaya has a road network of around 8,428 km, out of which 3,691 km is black topped and remaining 3942 km is gravelled. Meghalaya is also connected to Silchar in Assam, Aizawl in Mizoram and Agartala in Tripura through National Highways. There are many private buses and taxi operators who carry passengers from Guwahati to Shillong. The journey takes around 3-4 hours. Day and night bus services are available from Shillong to all major towns of Meghalaya and also other capitals and important towns of Assam and north-eastern States.

Railway

Meghalaya has a railhead at Mendipathar and regular train service connecting Mendipathar in Meghalaya and Guwahati in Assam, has started on November 30, 2014. The Cherra Companyganj State Railways was a former mountain railway through the state. Guwahati (103 km from Shillong) is the nearest major railway station connecting the north-east region with the rest of the country through a broad gauge track network. There is a plan for extending the rail link from Guwahati to Byrnihat (20 km from Guwahati) within Meghalaya and further extending it up to state capital Shillong.

Aviation

State capital Shillong has an airport at Umroi 30 km from Shillong on the Guwahati-Shillong highway. A new terminal building was built at a cost of Rs.30 crore and inaugurated in June 2011. Air India Regional operates flights to Kolkata from this airport. There is also a helicopter service connecting Shillong to Guwahati and Tura. Baljek Airport near Tura became operational in 2008. The Airports Authority of India (AAI) is developing the airport for operation of ATR 42/ATR 72 type of aircraft.

Other nearby airports are in Assam, with Borjhar, Guwahati airport (IATA: GAU), about 124 km from Shillong. Indian Airlines, Jet Airlines and Sahara Airlines connect Guwahati to Delhi and Kolkata. Air India has flights connecting Guwahati-Bangkok.

National Highways of Meghalaya

1.	**40**	Meghalaya/Assam-Barni Hat-Nongpoh-Umsning-Barapani-Shillong-Meghalaya-Indo/Bangladesh border	216
2.	**44**	Nongstoin-Shillong-Meghalaya/Assam Border	277
3.	**51**	Meghalaya/Assam-Bajengdoda-Tura-Kherapara-Burengapara	127
4.	**62**	Damra-Dambu-Baghmara-Burengapara.	190
		Total	**810**

ADMINISTRATION

Meghalaya has 11 administrative districts, 16 towns and 6851 villages. Meghalaya has a unicameral legislature. The State Legislative Assembly has 60 members at present. Meghalaya has two representatives in the Lok Sabha, the lower house of the Parliament of India; one each from Shillong and Tura.

It also has one representative in the Rajya Sabha, the upper house of the Parliament. Meghalaya has its own high court located at Shillong from 2013.

West Jaintia Hills District: West Jaintia Hills is an administrative district in the state Meghalaya in India. Jowai is the headquarters of west Jaintia hill district. West Jaintia hill District came into existence on 31st July 2012. The total area of the district is 1693 km^2.

East Jaintia Hills District: East Jaintia Hills district is a district with its headquarters at Khliehriat. The district was carved out of Jaintia Hills district on 31 July 2012. Khliehriat and Saipung are the two community and rural development blocks of the district. The total area of the district is 2,126 km^2.

South West Garo Hills District: South West Garo Hills is an administrative district and Ampati is the headquarter of this district. The South West Garo Hills is curved out of Present West Garo Hills. The total area of the district is 822 km^2.

South West Khashi District: The South West Khashi Hills district was carved out of the West Khashi Hills district on 3 August 2012. The total area of the district is 1,341 km^2. The district headquarters is located at Mawkyrwat.

North Garo Hills District: The North Hills district was carved out of the erstwhile East Garo Hills district. The district headquarters are located at Resubelpara. The district occupies an area of 1113 km^2.

Name of the Districts

Sr. No.	District	District HQ	Population (2011)	Growth Rate	Sex Ratio	Literacy Rate	Density (/km²)
1	East Garo Hills	Williamnagar	3,17,917	26.87%	972	73.95	122
2	West Garo Hills	Tura	6,43,291	24.09%	984	67.58	175
3	North Garo Hills	Resubelpara	*	*	*	*	*
4	South Garo Hills	Baghmara	1,42,334	40.95%	945	71.72	75
5	South West Garo Hills	Ampati	*	*	*	*	*
6	East Jaintia Hills	Khliehriat	*	*	*	*	*
7	West Jaintia Hills	Jowai	3,95,124	30.10%	1013	61.64	103
8	East Khasi Hills	Shillong	8,25,922	24.96%	1011	84.15	301
9	South West Khasi Hills	Mawkyrwat	*	*	*	*	*
10	West Khasi Hills	Nongstoin	3,83,461	29.53%	980	77.87	73
11	Ri-Bhoi	Nongpoh	2,58,840	34.26%	953	75.67	106

Origin and Growth of Meghalaya Legislative Assembly

Meghalaya has a unicameral Legislature based on adult franchise consisting of 60 (sixty) Members. It is duly constituted upon the issue of a notification under Section 73 of the Representation of the People Act 1951. At present, there are 55 reserved Legislative Assembly seats and 5 unreserved Legislative Assembly seats.

The First Session of the Meghalaya Legislative Assembly was held on the 25th March, 1972 with the Acting Speaker (Shri Jor Manik Syiem) in the Chair at Shillong, assembled in the old Council Hall of the composite Assam State. Prior from 2nd April, 1970 to 21st January, 1972 when Meghalaya was an autonomous State, the first Session of the Provisional Meghalaya Legislative Assembly consisting of 41 (forty one) Members, 38 (thirty eight) Members indirectly elected and 3 (three) Members nominated met at the District Council Hall, Tura, on 14th April, 1970 with Shri Simon Jenkin Duncan (Acting Speaker) in the Chair.

Autonomous District Councils

To provide a simple and inexpensive form of local self-governance to the tribal population, the Sixth Schedule was appended to the Constitution on the recommendations of a sub committee formed under the leadership of Gopinath Bordoloi. The Sixth Schedule provided for the constitution of Autonomous District Councils (ADCs) in certain rural areas of the Northeast including some areas that now fall in Meghalaya. The Sixth Schedule carries detailed provisions for the constitution and management of Autonomous District Councils (ADCs) and laid down the powers of the ADCs. At present Meghalaya has three ADCs, viz., **Khasi Hills Autonomous District Council, Garo Hills Autonomous District Council and the Jaintia Hills Autonomous District Council.**

North-Eastern Police Academy

The North Eastern Police Academy (erstwhile the Regional Police Training College) is an establishment of the Govt. of India, under the Ministry of Home Affairs. It is situated in Ri-Bhoi District of Meghalaya and has been in existence since July, 1978. It is engaged in shaping Police Officers of North Eastern States for equitable, effective and sensitive policing. It is dedicated to teaching its police trainees that they exist to safeguard the value of freedom—freedom from disorder, criminal acts and criminals.

The Academy is located at Umsaw Village under the Ri-Bhoi District of Meghalaya, just west of Guwahati-Shillong National Highway. The Academy has a beautiful sprawling campus spreading over an area of 205 acres of land at a height of 976 metres (3500 ft).

FESTIVALS, DANCES, MUSIC AND CELEBRATIONS

The pulsating beats of the drums reverberate around the hills of Meghalaya bringing along joy, excitement, friendship and announcing the "coming of the Festivals". Although the cradle for the festivals is religious, dance, music and celebrations cannot be separated from the festivals of Meghalaya. Festivities also celebrate the ethnic art forms and culture. Hence, any festival in Meghalaya would mean dance, music, song, gorgeous costumes with ornaments, colourful procession, fun, food and heady wines. Eat, drink and be merry has been the life style of Meghalaya. Christmas is the most celebrated festival of Meghalaya.

Festivals & Music of the Khasis

Music is integral to Khasi life. Every festival and ceremony from birth to death is enriched with music and dance. It is probably the music from the nature such as the humming of the bees, chirping of the birds, call of a wild animals, the gurgling streams, etc., which make music a natural extension to Khasi way of life. One of the basic forms of khasi music is the 'phawar', which is more of a "chant" than a song and are often composed on the spot, impromptu, to suit the occasion. Other forms of a song include ballads & verses on the past, the exploits of legendary heroes and laments for martyrs. Whatever the Khasi music lacks in formal sophistication of established school *(Gharana)* is more than adequately compensated by the purity, beauty, spontaneity and certain complexity in skilful rendering. The musical instruments, as expected of a tribal community living in such a natural settings, are wind and percussion based. Drums, cymbals, flutes and trumpets of various types, shapes and sizes are the instruments of the Khasis.

Dance is at the very heart of khasi life, rich in repertoire, performed often as a part of the "rites de passage" the life-cycle of an individual in a society or the annual passage of the seasons. Dances are performed at the level of individual villages (Shnong), a group of villages (Raid) and a conglomeration of raids (Hima). Local or regional flavours and colours bring variations to the basic dance form, which is universal in Khasi folk culture.

The Major Festivals of Khasis

Ka Pom-Blang Nongkrem—Festivals of Nongkrem Dance : Pom-blang Nongkrem, popularly known as the Nongkrem dance is one of the most important festivals of the Khasis. It is a five day religious festival held annually at Smith about 11 km from Shillong, the Headquarters of the chief (Syiem) of Khyrim. The festival is celebrated as a thanks giving to god almighty for the good harvest and to pray for peace and prosperity. The Syiem who is the administrative head of the Hima (Khasi state), Ka Syiem Sad (literally the Syiem Priestess) who is the caretaker of all religion ceremonies of the Hima, the Myutri (council of Ministers), the priest and high priest and the people in general all join in this festival, which is a rhythmic form of prayer for the well-being of all. Nongkrem is amongst the most prominent of ancestral cultural revivals.

Ka Shad Suk Mynsiem Festival : This annual spring dance performed in April every year in Shillong is to celebrate harvesting and sowing. One of the most important festivals of the Khasis, 'Ka Shad Suk Mynsiem' (Dance of the joyful hearth) is ritualistic and symbolic of timeless fertility cult. The analogy is drawn to a women as receptacle of seeds and bearer of fruits and men as cultivators, who provide the seeds and protect and nurse them till the crop is harvested, the dance takes place at Raid and Hima levels usually celebrated by maidens dressed in traditional fineries and menfolk in colourful costumes in accompaniment of drums and flute.

Ka-Shad-Shyngwiang-Thangiap: A ceremonial dance to express sorrow performed on the occasion of a death in the family. Male musicians play music on the flute, drum and bamboo pole. The dance begins on the day of death at a place next to the kitchen of the house and continues till the last rites are performed on the cremation grounds.

Ka-Shad-Kynjoh Khaskain : A dance to commemorate "house warming" or when a family moves into a new built home. Once the ritual ceremonies are over, the dance is performed in three stages Ka-Shad Kyuntui, Ka Shad Khalai Miaw and Ka Shad Brap and lasts throughout the night till dawn of the next day.

Ka-Bam Khana Shnong : Nobody knows when this 'village community Feasting festival' began but it is an event that everyone—men, women and children, look forward to. It is a social get together, but at the back of it all, it is a time to thank the lord for the old year past and seek his blessing for the new year which is to come. The entire village would participate with each home contributing cash or kind.

Umsan Nongkharai: The five day festival is held in spring (April or May), commencing on Sugi Lyngka with a ceremonial sacrifice of a goat and two cocks before the supreme deity of the Khasis *Lei Shyllong.* It ends on Sugi-Shillong, with a prayers offered at midnight to establish person-to-person contact between the finite and the infinite.

Shad Beh Sier : This deer hunting dance is dedicated to occupational merry-making. In off-harvest season, male haunters roam the dense forest for deer prey.

The Major Festivals & Music of the Jaintias

The Jaintia music and dance is very rich in many respects. Their music and dances are accompanied by different musical instruments. Popular among these are the bhuri (a clarionet like flute), bom (big drum). These instruments are used, mainly for community dances. The music produced is very exciting and vigorously rhythmic. There is *Ka Chowiang,* a home made bamboo flute, which is used in expressing the intricate Jaintia melody.

Festivals of the Jaintia hills, like others contribute significantly to maintaining a balance between man, his culture and his natural environment or eco-system. At the same time it seeks to revive the spirit of cohesiveness and solidarity among the people.

Behdeinkhlam festival : Behdeinkhlam festival is one of Meghalaya's most colourful religious festivals. It is celebrated for three days during July at Jowai by the Jaintias, the festival focusses on praying for the property and good health of people and on invoking divine blessings for a bountiful harvest.

The word literally means driving away of evil (plague) by wooden sticks. It is very popular and colourful festival where only men, young and old, take part in the dancing to the pulsating beat of drums and tune of flutes. Women do not take part in the dancing.

In the afternoon, 'Datlawakor'—a kind of football game with wooden ball—is played between two teams; one representing the upper valley and the other the lower valley of the Myntdu river.

The Laho dance: This a festival devoted to entertainment. Both men and women participate in the dancing dressed in their colourful best. Usually, two young men on either side of a girl, linking arms together, dance in rhythmic steps.

The other festivals of the Jaintias are: **Tiger festival, Bam Phalar, Rong Belyngkan, Durga Puja** and **Seng Kut Snem.**

The Major Festivals & Music of the Garos

Music and dance form an integral part of the life of the Garos. They perform different kinds of folkdances on festive occasions. Styles and forms of dance vary according to the nature of the festival. They have a variety of wind and percussion based musical instruments like drums, trumpets & flutes. The major festivals of the Garos are :

Wangala: Wangala is celebrated during October, after the harvest season. The ritual continues for 4 days and nights, accompanied by dancing and merriment. It culminates in the warrior's dance—the dance of a hundred drums, on the final day, which is a spectacular and delightful sight.

Dore Rata dance festival: This dance is exciting and interesting to watch. In this dance, the women try to knock off the turbans of their male partners.

Mangona : Mangona is a post-funeral ceremony of the Garos. A small hut with a bamboo structure is erected on the courtyard of the house that is known as 'Delang'. During the performance of the last rites for the "spirit" of the dead, dancing and singing continue throughout the night with the chanting of the funeral dirge known as 'Mangtata or Kalee'.

Festivals of Garos that are related to *"Jhumming"* are—*AA-O-Pata, Den Bilsia or Gitchipong Roka, Mi-Amua, Rongchu Gala, Ja Megapa, Sa Sat Ra Chaka, Anaoea, Pomelo dance, Do Kru Sua.* The festivals like *Saram Cha A* and *A Se Mania* of the Attong sub-tribe are also festivals related to Jhoomimg.

FESTIVALS

Calender of Garos Festivals

Festivals	Local Months	Gregorian Months	Vedic Months	
			Solar	Lunar
Denbilsia	Polgin	February	Tapasya	Phalgun
Asiroka	Chuet	March	Madhu	Chaitra
Agalmaka	Pasak	April	Madhave	Vaisakha
Miamua	Asal	June	Sue hi	Asharha
Rongchugala	Bado	August	Nabhasya	Bhadra
Ahaia	Asin	September	Is ha	Ashwina
Wangala	Gate	October	Urje	Kartika
Christmas	Posi	December	Sahasya	Pausha

Calender of Khasis Festivals

Festivals	Local Months	Gregorian Months	Vedic Months	
			Solar	Lunar
Bamkhana	Kyllalyngkot	January	Tapas	Magha
Shad Suk Mynsiem	Laiongjylliew	April-June	Sue hi	Asharha
Shad Nongkrem	Naitung	July	Nabhas	Sravana
Seng Kut Snem	Naiweing	November	Sahas	Agrahayana
Christmas	Nohprah	December	Sahasya	Pausha

Calender of Jaintias Festivals

Festivals	Local Months	Gregorian Months	Vedic Months	
			Solar	Lunar
Tiger Festival	DuiyataraWisu	Jan-Mar	Tapas-madhu	Magha-Chaitra
Bam Phalar/Bam Doh	Duiyatara	January	Tapas	Magha
Rong Belyngkan	Naisau-Naiynhru	May-June	Sukra-Suchi	Jyeshtha-Asharha
Behdienkhlam	Naihynru-Naiynhnaiaw	June-July	Suchi-nabhas	Asharha-Sravana
Durga Puja	Naikhynde-khonchonglad	Sept.-Nov	Isha-Sahas	Ashwina-Agrahayana
Seng Kut Snem	Khonchonglad	November	Sahas	Agrahayana
Christmas /Bam Phalar /Bam Doh	Kmaichonglad	December	Sahasya	Pausha

THE ARTS & CRAFTS OF MEGHALAYA

One comes across engravings of human and animal figurines on the walls of houses in Jaintia and Garo villages which reflect the ethnic creative thoughts and skill of the people. The finely engraved domestic utensils seem to capture fleeting images of birds on the wing or temporal flowers. Rock carvings depicting horses and elephants are found in the southern outskirts of Jaintiapur, now in Bangladesh, probably sponsored and appreciated by Jaintia kings of Yore. The carving of a man and his beloved, near Jowai town, inspire admiration for artistic imagination and rendering.

Meghalaya's lively collection of woven, decorative, dyed and colourful silk and cotton cloth speak of the weaver's magic. The designs and motifs vary from tribe to tribe and are distinctive in style. Stripes and checks dominate the textile designs. The colours used are bright and vibrant.

In the Jaintia Hills, the Larnai area excels in the blue-grey earthen pottery that is shaped by hand, without the aid of a potter's wheel. And the "Kimas", beautifully carved and engraved wooden posts, erected as memorials for the deceased, and which, like the "totem poles" of the American Red Indians, are gorgeous examples of the wood carving skills of the Garos. The Khasi metal workers are known to have once cast cannons. One can still hear the hiss of a forge and the ringing strokes of a master blacksmith's hammer in Meghalaya.

Artistic creations in cane and bamboo for exquisite and utilitarian products, that range from sleeping mats to winnowing fans, rain-shields, fishing traps, bags and tube-storage containers are common sights in Meghalaya. The cane bridges suspended over deep gorges and roaring mountain streams bear visible proof of the craftsmanship and consummate skill of the Meghalayans.

Even the typical, oval-shaped, wood and stone houses of the Khasis with thatched roofs that look like "overturned boats", the stone-walled houses in the Cherrapunjee area, the "mud-plastered, red and white painted" walls of Jaintias, are all expressions of architectural skill and artistic sense. The remnants of old stone bridges and ruins of old fortresses are mute witnesses of the cromlechs of the Khasis and Jaintias.

The women folk of all the tribes of Meghalaya are fond of jwellery. While the Khasis and the Jaintias wear gold ornaments called Kynjri Ksiar, the Garos wear beads called Rigitok. The designs are however, robust and not very popular with the tourists. Meghalaya's heritage, its traditional treasures of beauty, lore, legend, festivals—all spring from this artistic vision of the people.

(1019) NE-GK–13

TOURISM

Natural Beauty: Whole of NE is endowed with unmatched natural beauty. Some of the destinations within NE are mentioned below as examples with their different promotable USPs and possible competitions.

(a) **Umiam Lake:** Biggest artificial lake in North East with water sports.

(b) **Cherrapunjee & Mawsynram:** Highest rainfall area, Gorges, luxurious, tropical vegetation and host of innumerable variety of fern, moss and orchid & waterfalls.

(c) **Tura:** Balpakram park, Nokrek peak, Nokrek Biosphere reserve, Siju caves, deep gorges and exotic orchid.

Heritage Tourism

Many destinations, which can be promoted as heritage sites, including famous pilgrimage sites are in NE. Some examples of positioning such sites are mentioned below.

Mairang: Memorial of Late U. Tirot Sing, Syiem of Nongkhlow, Who fought against British.

Adventure Tourism: NE is full spots where adventure tourism can also be promoted. Some of them are mentioned below.

(a) **Umiam lake:** Boating, para-sailing, water scooter, skiing, etc.

(b) **Ranikor, Simsang river Umtrew, Kynshi:** Angling, white water rafting.

(c) **Jowai:** Hang-gliding.

(d) **Siju, Cherrapunji, Mawsynram, Syndai:** Speleology.

Pilgrimage

NE is also full of Hindu and Buddhist pilgrimage sites. Some of the most promising ones are mentioned below.

Bhaitbari: Famous for archeological importance.

Krem Mawjymbuin cave: Hindu pilgrimage to natural *Shivalinga*.

The Major Tourist Destinations of Meghalaya

Shillong

Shillong termed as "Scotland of the East", the capital of Meghalaya and also the district head quarter of East Khasi Hills is the best known hill resort in North-East India and is considered as one of the best in the country.

Shillong has always been the meeting point of traditional cultures and cosmopolitian styles and has its very own charms and attractions and its own following of regular seasonal visitors.

Located at an altitude of 1600 mtrs above the sea level, Shillong is easily motorable throughout the year and serves as a base from which the rest of the region can be conveniently accessed. It is connected with Guwahati, the nearest railhead at a distance of 103 km with national highway 39.

According to the legends, Shillong derived its name from a deity named SHYLLONG whose dwelling is also known as Shyllong peak from whose nice, the Syiem (Chief) clan of Khyrim, Mylliem, Maharram, Malaisahmat, Bhowal and Langrin sprang up.

Shillong has its own charm distinct from other hill stations. Shillong has been the centre of excellence for education during the pre and post independence period. Shillong is set amidst a landscape of slopes covered with weather, orchids and forests of pine with their typical fragrance and pure air, quick flowing streams and majestic waterfalls. There are a number of beautiful sights to see and places to visit in and around Shillong. These are:

- **Meghalaya State Museum:** This museum exhibits the anthropological and cultural life of the people of Meghalaya.
- **All Saints Cathedral:** One of the oldest Churches in Shillong.
- **Lady Hydari Park and Mini Zoo:** Lady Hydari Park, extends for over a kilometer in length, is replete with roses and flowers of the most exquisite hue and fragrance and has an excellent mini Zoo-cum-deer park attached to it.
- **Golf course:** Nestled within tall and elegant whispering pines, the eighteen-hole Shillong Golf course is one of the finest golf course in the world.
- **Botanical Garden:** A secluded but captivating spot with plethora of indigenous and exotic plants is located just below the Ward's lake.
- **Spread eagle falls:** Located on the outskrits of the city, lies a sparkling waterfall which looks like an eagle with wings spread out. Hence, the name *Spread Eagle falls.* The falls has fairly steep cliffs on three sides with a very deep pool beneath—a soothing setting amidst calm nature.
- **Crinoline falls and swimming pool:** Close to the Hydari park is Crinoline falls over looping the Crinoline swimming pool.
- **Sweet falls:** It is a beautiful fall east of happy valley on the Umkhen stream. The area around the falls is most suitable for a day's outing.

- **Shillong Peak:** An ideal picnic spot, 10 kms from the city, 1,965 metres above sea level, offers a panoramic view of the scenic countryside and is also the highest point in the state. Homage is paid to U Shyllong at the sanctum sanctorum at the peak's summit every spring time, by the religious priest of Mylliem state. In the evening, the city lights below appear like a star-studded abyss.
- **Elephant Falls:** This exquisitely beautiful waterfall is located at about 10 km from Shillong off the Shillong-Mawphlang Road. It is one of the most frequented of the several waterfalls and tourist spots in and around Shillong. The surroundings of the Elephant falls and its subsidiary falls are lush green and the rivulet has thick moss and ferns covering its stony banks. Beautiful Rhododendrons and myriad species of ever chirping birds make the place an enchanting one.
- **Bishop and Beadon Falls:** Both cascade down the same escarpment into a deep valley, the mass of water dissolving into misty sparks.
- **Sohpetbneng Peak:** 1,343 metre, 20 kms from Shillong, regarded as sacred by the Hynniewtrep people, is set amidst a beautiful Scenic view against the backdrop of Sacred Forest. This 'Navel-of-Heaven' as per Khasi mythology, is a heavenly peak which offers to fill the spiritual void and emptiness, to those who seek and desire solace and peace of mind.
- **Kyllang Rock:** On the road from Mairang to Nongkhlaw lies a massive single granite stone at great height known as Kyllang Rock. It presents an appearance of a circular dome with a diameter of about 1,000 ft.
- **Rengthiam Falls:** At a distance of 15 kms from Shillong on the Shillong-Jowai highway is the awe inspiring Rengthiam Falls. Located in the Mawlyngad village, 2 kms. away at Pepdah, this spectacular waterfall untouched in its natural beauty and surroundings will give any visitor the excitement of visiting the unknown in this unique corner waiting to be discovered.
- **Lum Nehru Park:** Adjacent to the Orchid Lake Resort in one of the surrounding spurs, there is a charming park. Besides beautiful lawns and flowers, there is also an orchid-house and an aviary. Plans are afoot to construct an Aquarium and set-up Musical-Fountains nearby.
- **Ward's Lake:** Located in the heart of Shillong, stands a beautiful man-made lake known as Ward's lake. The lake and its gradually

undulating grounds are hemmed in by lush green slopes. It has a most pleasant, winding walk-way all around its parameter set in cobbled sand stone. The lake has striking arched bridge over it providing an exhilarating view of the piscicultural wealth.

- **Umiam lake:** By the side of the Guwahati-Shillong road,16 kms from Shillong Umiam lake is at present the biggest arificial lake in Meghalaya. It is a beautiful picnic spot and a favourite place for anglers and water sports. Orchid Lake Resort, a property of Meghalaya Tourism provides accommodation and water sports. Adjacent to the resort, there is an aviary and orchid house.
- **Archery Stakes:** Evolves from an ancient tribal sport, the archery stakes run everyday at Saw-furlong, polo ground. Archers from clubs belonging to the khasi Archery Association fire 1500 arrows within four minutes at a cylindrical bamboo target. The arrow which stick in the target are then remove and counted and recounted in the presence of betters and spectators.

There is ample scope to glamourise the sport by including it as a part of casino event to become a major tourist attraction of Shillong.

Cherrapunjee

Exposure of Shillong to the world started from Cherrapunjee located 56 km from Shillong at an altitude of 1300 metres above sea level. Cherrapunjee was the first British out post in the NE part of the country before being shifted to Shillong. Cherrapunjee, is famous for being the heaviest rainfall area in the world. With deep gorges it is the habitat for an innumerable varieties of ferns, mosses and orchids. It was here that the Welsh Missionaries and the Ram Krishna Mission started their services in the khasi hills. Khasi literature with Roman script was born here. It is a pleasant drive to see roaring waterfall leaping into deep gorges, including the famed Nohsngthiang falls. The lovely town is also famous for its limestone caves, orange and honey.

- **Noh Kalikai Falls:** A few kilometres to the west of Cherrapunjee, a clear bubbling stream emerges from its steep mountain bed to be hurled down a rocky precipice into a deep gorge, creating a captivating view of breathtaking beauty.
- **David Scott Memorial:** On the way to Mausami falls lies an obelisk in memory of David Scott an agent to the Governor-General on the North Eastern Frontier of Bengal and Commissioner of Revenue and circuit in the district of Assam, North Cachar, Part of Rangpur, Sharpore and Sylhet.

- **Mawsami Falls:** The Mawsami falls is 1 km south of Mawsami villages. A panoramic view of Bangladesh's rolling plains can be seen from the Mawsami falls.
- **Kynrem Falls:** Falling from a height of 1000 ft with a width of 50 ft, it is situated by the side of the Shillong-Shella road about 10 km beyond Mawsami.
- **Mawlong Syiem Peak:** The Mawlong Syiem Peak is meant for those tourists seeking adventure and mystery. The Mawsami caves are close to this peak, the rocky subterranean caves can be explored during the dry season. It is an ideal picnic spot and paradise for orchid lovers.
- **Dainthlen Falls:** Located near Cherrapunjee, there exists another gentle but beautiful waterfalls known as Dainthlen Falls or the falls where Thlen (Python) was butchered. Legend has it that once upon a time, the people in order to rid themselves of evil hunted down the Thlen and butchered it on the wide flat rocks overlooking a gentle waterfall. Ever since the waterfall at this place has been known as Dainthlen Falls.
- **Mawsynram:** 55 km from Shillong, it closely rivals Cherrapunjee in annual rainfall. Its major attraction is a picturesque cave of vast and unexplored depth, featuring a giant stalagmite in the shape of a natural *"Shivalinga"*. A place of piligrimage for the Hindus and a natural wonder for sightseers.
- **Dawki:** 96 km from Shillong is a border town, where one can have a glimpse of the neighbouring country of Bangladesh. The colourful annual boat race during spring at the Umgot river is an added attraction. An eye catching motorable suspension bridge spans the Dawki river connecting Khasi and Jaintia Hills.
- **Mawphlang:** This countryside 24 km away from Shillong is a famous picnic spot. It is also known for its distillary founded by Capt. Hunt.
- **Jakrem:** 64 km from Shillong, is a popular health resort having hot spring of sulphur water, believed to have curative medicinal properties.
- **Symer Peak:** 45 km South west of Shillong lies the Symer peak. This Peak has a unique feature which projects like a big monument in the middle of a table land. According to Khasi legend, it is said that in the remote past the Symer Peak had a big fight with the Kyland rock. In the fight the Symer peak was defeated. The few caves that are found in the peak today is believed to be the injury caused during the fight.

- **Ranikor:** 140 km from Shillong, located on the bank of the river Jadukata, Ranikor stands on the beautiful sunny-sands of the river, A ferry service carries one across. Ranikor is an excellent fishing ground and Jadukata has no shortage of huge golden mahseers. The deeply forested environs of the place produce a scenic background of unique beauty. Its abundance of wildlife transforms the place into a wildlife lovers' paradise.
- **Mairang:** 40 kms from Shillong on the Shillong-Nongstoin road, Mairang is the head quarters of Nongkhlaw Syiemship as well as of the Mairang Sub-Division. In the centre of the town stands the memorial of late U. Tirot Sing Syiem, Syiem of Nongkhlaw (Raja of Nongkhlaw) who fought against the British. He raised the battle cry on April, 1829 but was finally captured and died in captivity at Dhaka on July 17, 1855.
- **Nongstoin:** About 96 kms from Shillong, it is the HQ of the West Khasi hills. Nongkhnum island, which recently created history in Meghalaya as the second largest island in Asia is located only a few kilometer away from Nongstoin.
- **Jowai:** Jowai, the head quarters of the Jaintia hill district is situated 64 kms away from Shillong at 1380 metres MSL along the Shillong Silchar highway. A picturesque town circled by the majestic Myntdu river.
- **Thadlaskein Lake:** 56 kms from Shillong, the lake according to legend was dug with the end of bows by members of 290 clans of U Sajjar Niangli a rebel general of Jaintia Raja to commemorate the great exodus of the clans, now mainly settled in the Ri-Bhoi and West Khasi Hills District.
- **Kiang Nangbah Monument:** Located on the banks of Syntu Ksiar alongside the river Myntdu there is a vast field known as Madadiah Kmal Blai. At the centre of this field stands the elegant Kiang Nangbah Monument erected by the Jaintia people in honour of U Kiang Nangbah, the Jaintia patriot who died a martyr to the cause of Jaintia freedom. The monument is a grateful people's tribute to their immortal martyr.
- **Nartiang:** 65 kms from Shillong was the summer capital of the Jaintia kings of Sutnga state. Huge monoliths form the striking landmarks of the village, said to be erected by Mar Phalyngki, a Goliath of Yore. The Nartiang menhir measure 27 feet in height above the ground, 6 ft in breadth and 2 feet 6 inches in thickness. The monoliths represent the megalithic culture of the Hynniewtrep

people. A 500 year old temples of Goddess Durga is another attraction at Nartiang.

- **Monument of U Kiang Nongbah:** This monument was erected in the honour of U Kiang Nongbah who fought against the British. He used to hold meeting at this place. He was eventually betrayed by one of his subjects and was hung on this very same spot.
- **Stone Bridge at Thiumuwi:** Located sixteen kms on the Jowai-Muktapur-Dawki road at a place called Thiumuwi a stone bridge was built. The bridge was made of immense slabs of stone supported upon huge tall stone pillars. The banks of the Thiumuwi stream with the cascading Thiumuwi Waterfalls which overlooks the stone bridge presents a memorable scenic-panorama to every visitor.
- **Syndai:** An important village located in the Jowai-Dawki road dotted with a number of caves and caverns. Till date eleven independent caves have been discovered near Syndai. Collectively these are known as Syndai caves. Caves are used as hide out during war times between the Jaintia kings and foreign intruders. The eleven caves are the Amsohmahattang cave, the Rupasor cave, the Kriah cave, the Amkoi cave, the Amkhloo cave, the Amlashriah cave, the Amthymme cave, the Amkari cave, the Lyngngohmah cave, the Kynda cave and the Chair cave. The caves have always been tourist attraction. There are also some relics of the past, such as the old brick temple, ruins of stone bridge, a pool of water which was fed through the trunk of curved stone elephant-standing still to this day and a rock with 'carving of Ganesh'.
- **Syntu Ksiar:** A vast pool of calm water the flow of the meandering river Myntdu which almost encircles the Jowai town, appears to come to a sudden halt is known as Syntu Ksiar which means Golden flower.

Tura

Tura, the district head quarter of West Garo hills is situated 323 km from Shillong via Guwahati at an altitude of 657 metres. Its original name was DURA the part name of DURAMA IMBAMA believed to be the youngest of the three most powerful goddesses who lived there in the past. The highest point being NOKREK PEAK at 1412 metres which provides an interesting range of orchids including wild life like wild elephant, rare varieties of birds etc. Tura provides some of the finest views of the hills against a backdrop of the low-lying plains and the sweeping curve of the mighty Brahmaputra. A sunset view can be best seen from Tura peak at 1400 metres and its summit can be reached by a 5 km trek which is a part hiking and part rock climbing.

- **Nokrek Biosphere Reserve:** 2 km away from the Nokrek peak is the Nokrek Biosphere reserve. This first Biosphere reserve in the North-Eastern region was declared as the National Gene Citrus Sanctuary in 1985. The park covers a vast area of 47 sq. km of dense forests. The park and Biosphere is famous for having abundance of traditional herbs and medicines. Mysterious and large gorilla like animal has been sighted inside the National park time and again.
- **Bhaitbari:** Located on the western frontier of the state, Bhaitbari is a small village of west Garo Hills District. The site is famous for the archaeological finds having been uncovered after protected 'excavations' on the area. The finds are of artefacts which reveals the existence of planned places of worship.
- **Siju Bird Sanctuary:** Just across the Siju cave on the other side of Simsang river in the South-Garo Hills is the bird sanctuary where one can spot many rare and protected wild birds. During winters, some migrating birds have been visiting this place. The area is a heaven for ornithologists.
- **Siju caves:** Located on the cliff overhanging the right bank of the Simsang River in South Garo Hills district, the cave is locally known as *Dobakhol* or the cave of Bats. The caves consists of innumerable internal chambers and labyrinths which have not yet been fully explored. The depth of the cave is yet to be fathomed. The cave is totally dark with a perennial stream flowing out of it, which abounds with different forms of aquatic life. The formation of stalagmites and stalactites in these caves resemble those of Blue Grotto in the Isle of Capri.
- **Chibrage:** A confluence of two rivers is just about 25 minutes drive from Tura. An ideal picnic spot with its lush green surrounding and breath taking beauty. The traditional hanging bamboo cane bridge suspended over the Ganoi river from bank to bank lures many tourists.
- **Balpakram National Park:** 167 km away from Tura town, Balpakram valley is known for the sanctuary of the typical fauna of the region. The Balpakram Wild Life Sanctuary has gained the status of a National Park. The Balpakram plateau is created by an awe inspiring mini grand canyon which separates the Garo hills from the Khasi hills across the Sib-bari rivulets. The plateau commands an enchanting view of the beautiful plains of Bangladesh. The literal meaning of Balpakram is the land of perpetual wind.

- **Milchang Dare:** It is a waterfall of immense beauty. The deep green surroundings with large ferns, tall creepers and elegant climbers make Milchang Dare a nature's beauty. The deep, wide pool at the bottom of the falls with its wide and expansive surrounding make it an exciting natural swimming pool full of fish of varied size and colour.
- **Sisobibra:** 12 km away from William Nagar, Sisobibra is a historical place where the Garo warriors fought the last battle against the British under the command of Pa Togan Nengminja Sangma.
- **William Nagar:** The head quarter of East Garo Hills district has all the amenities of a modern town and is the largest growth centre in Garo Hills next to Tura. This township has been named to honour first Chief Minister of Meghalaya Capt Williamson A. Sangma.
- **Rongbang Dare:** This sprightly fall, though perennial, is at its best during the monsoon months. It presents a romantic visual of lasting satisfaction to the motorists driving from Asanangre towards William Nagar. Clustered on either side by vast evergreen bamboo bushes, the falls itself appears to be on the sway, leaving the viewer with memories of ecstatic joy.
- **Baghmara:** Baghmara is the growing head quarter of South Garo Hills district. It is situated on the banks of the Simsang river and is famous for its tasty fish. The rare carnivorous pitchers plants locally called *Memang Koksi* grow abundantly in and around Baghmara.

Monoliths

Strange and awe inspiring ancient stone structures—are scattered abundantly through the Khasi & Jaintia Hills. They speak of ancient, may be even pre-historical links with races that extended to far away places. No one knows how many monoliths, ossuaries, funerary mounds (kped), cenotaphs, 'menhirs' have been destroyed by natural calamities or by man - but it was the handiworks of the original settlers of the land, the ancestors of the Meghalayans today. Many more may probably be hidden in shrubbery. Whatever they are, they are part of the "mystic" origins of the tribes who lived here. Like "stone henge" in the British isles, they are a part of Meghalaya's legacy, frozen forever in stone relics from a timeless past.

MEGHALAYA : AT A GLANCE

- Area (in sq. km.) : 22,429
- Latitude : 24°57′N and 26°10′N

- Longitude : 89°46′E and 92°53′E
- Forest Area (in sq. km.) : 17,146 (76.45% of the total geographical area of the state)
- No. of Districts : 11
- Name of the Districts : East Garo Hills, East Khasi Hills, East Jaintia Hills, Ri-Bhoi, South Garo Hills, West Garo Hills and West Khasi Hills, North Garo Hills, South West Garo Hills, West Jaintia Hills and South West Khasi Hills.
- Lok Sabha Constituencies : 2
- Rajya Sabha Seat : 1
- Vidhan Sabha Constituencies : 60
- Nature of Legislature : Unicameral
- Capital : Shillong
- Language : Khasi, Garo and English
- Total Population (as per 2011 census) : 29,66,889
- Male : 14,91,832
- Female : 14,75,057
- Decadal Growth (2001-2011) : 27.9%
- Literacy Rate : 74.4%
- Male Literacy Rate : 76.0%
- Female Literacy Rate : 72.9%
- Density (per sq. km.) : 132
- Sex Ratio (per 1000 males) : 986
- No. of Universities : 1 [North Eastern Hill University (Central University)]
- No. of National Parks : 2
  1. Nokrek National Park
  2. Balpakram National Park
- State Animal : Clouded Leopard
- State Bird : Hill Myna
- State Flower : Lady Slipper Orchid
- State Tree : Gamar
- Important Tribes : Khasi, Garo, Synteng, Hajong, Raba, Koch

- Major Festivals : Wangala, Rongchugala, Ahaia, Miamua, Bamkhana, Shad Nong-krem, Seng Kut Snem, Rong Belyngkan, Behdienkhlam
- Name of National Highways : NH-40, NH-44, NH-51, NH-62

OBJECTIVE QUESTIONS

1. Area of the Meghalaya state is
A. 20,429 sq. km. B. 22,429 sq. km.
C. 30,400 sq. km. D. None of these

2. What is the latitude of Meghalaya?
A. 19°N to 20°N B. 21°N to 24°N
C. 24°57′N to 26°10′N D. None of these

3. Meghalaya is situated on longitude between
A. 89°46′E and 92°53′E B. 80°50′E and 90°50′E
C. 75°40′E and 85°50′E D. None of these

4. Total number of districts in Meghalaya are
A. 11 B. 8
C. 9 D. None of these

5. What are the total number of Lok Sabha Constituencies in Meghalaya?
A. 2 B. 3
C. 1 D. None of these

6. Total number of Rajya Sabha constituencies in Meghalaya are
A. 1 B. 2
C. 4 D. None of these

7. Meghalaya Legislative Assembly consists of
A. 60 members B. 50 members
C. 30 members D. None of these

8. What is the name of the capital of Meghalaya?
A. Itanagar B. Shillong
C. Ziro D. None of these

9. According to the 2011 census, total population of Meghalaya is
A. 40,10,822 B. 29,66,889
C. 25,16,822 D. None of these

10. According to the 2011 census, total male population of Meghalaya is
A. 13,90,000 B. 16,56,432
C. 14,91,832 D. None of these

11. According to 2011 census, total female population of Meghalaya is

A. 14,75,057
B. 12,76,087
C. 13,56,432
D. None of these

12. In Meghalaya, decadal growth of population during 2001-2011 was

A. 40%
B. 27.9%
C. 35%
D. None of these

13. In 1824 which among the following invaded *Cachar* and appeared at the border of the Jaintia Hills?

A. Nepalese
B. Burmese
C. Bhutanese
D. Chinese

14. National Highway which not passes through Meghalaya is ....

A. NH-40
B. NH-43
C. NH-51
D. NH-52

15. The parliament passed the North-Eastern Areas (Reorganisation) Act, which conferred full statehood on the autonomous state of Meghalaya in ....

A. 1971
B. 1972
C. 1975
D. 1978

16. What proportion of total population of Meghalaya live in urban area?

A. 30%
B. 25%
C. 20.1%
D. None of these

17. According to 2011 census, total literacy rate in Meghalaya is

A. 74.4%
B. 70%
C. 80.36%
D. None of these

18. According to 2011 census, male literacy rate in Meghalaya is

A. 75%
B. 76.0%
C. 85.16%
D. None of these

19. What is the female literacy rate in Meghalaya?

A. 82.3%
B. 72.9%
C. 75%
D. None of these

20. According to 2011 census, density of population in Meghalaya is

A. 132 per sq. km.
B. 203 per sq. km.
C. 150 per sq. km.
D. None of these

21. According to 2011 census, sex ratio (per 1000 males) in Meghalaya is

A. 870
B. 986
C. 990
D. None of these

22. How many National Parks there are in Meghalaya?
A. 2 B. 3
C. 4 D. None of these

23. What is the name of the state animal of Meghalaya?
A. One horned rhino B. Wild buffalo
C. Clouded Leopard D. None of these

24. What is the name of state bird of Meghalaya?
A. Hill Myna B. Sarus Crane
C. Himalayan Monal D. None of these

25. What is the name of state flower of Meghalaya?
A. Lotus B. Brahm Kamal
C. Lady Slipper Orchid D. None of these

26. 'Mawsynram' is famous for
A. World record for most rain in a calendar month
B. Jute industry
C. Forest product
D. None of these

27. Manda river flows towards the
A. North direction B. South direction
C. West direction D. None of these

28. In which district, Balpakram National Park is situated?
A. West Garo Hills district B. West Khasi Hills district
C. Jaintia Hills district D. None of these

29. What is the name of headquarter of East Garo Hills district?
A. William Nagar B. Shillong
C. Jowai D. None of these

30. District headquarter of East Khasi Hills district is
A. Shillong B. Nongpoh
C. William Nagar D. None of these

31. Headquarter of Jaintia Hills district is located at
A. Nongpoh B. Jowai
C. Baghmara D. None of these

32. What is the name of headquarter Ri-Bhoi district?
A. Baghmara B. Nongpoh
C. Shillong D. None of these

33. Headquarter of South Garo Hills district is located at
A. William Nagar B. Jowai
C. Baghmara D. None of these

34. What is the name of the headquarter of the West Garo Hills district?
A. Tura B. Baghmara
C. Nongpoh D. None of these

35. 'Nongstoin' is the headquarter of
A. West Garo Hills district B. West Khasi Hills district
C. South Garo Hills district D. None of these

36. 'Ri-Raid' land means
A. Community owned land B. Privately owned land
C. Both A and B D. None of these

37. 'Ri-Kynti' land means
A. Community owned land B. Privately owned land
C. Both A and B D. None of these

38. According to area, the largest district of Meghalaya is
A. West Khasi Hills district B. Ri-Bhoi Hills district
C. West Garo Hills district D. None of these

39. North Eastern Hill University was set up on
A. 20 July, 1970 B. 19 July, 1973
C. 15 June, 1980 D. None of these

40. The first power project in Meghalaya was established in
A. 1925 B. 1930
C. 1945 D. 1950

41. Meghalaya State Electricity Board (MeSEB) was established in
A. 1975 B. 1980
C. 1985 D. None of these

42. What is the name of the airport of Meghalaya?
A. Umroi B. Jowai
C. William Nagar D. None of these

43. 'Jainsem' is a
A. dress C. song
B. dance D. None of these

44. North Eastern Police Academy is situated in
A. Ri-Bhoi district C. East Khasi Hills district
B. Jaintia Hills district D. None of these

45. Longest National Highway of Meghalaya is
A. NH-40 C. NH-44
B. NH-51 D. None of these

ANSWERS

1	2	3	4	5	6	7	8	9	10
B	C	A	A	A	A	A	B	B	C
11	**12**	**13**	**14**	**15**	**16**	**17**	**18**	**19**	**20**
A	B	B	B	A	C	A	B	B	A
21	**22**	**23**	**24**	**25**	**26**	**27**	**28**	**29**	**30**
B	A	C	A	C	A	A	A	A	A
31	**32**	**33**	**34**	**35**	**36**	**37**	**38**	**39**	**40**
B	B	C	A	B	A	B	A	B	A
41	**42**	**43**	**44**	**45**					
A	A	A	A	B					

●●●●●●●

6

MIZORAM

HISTORY

The word Mizo means highlander, a collective name given by their neighbours to a number of tribes which settled in the area. They are originally believed to have come from North-western China and gradually pushed themselves towards their present homeland, less than 300 years ago. The origin of the Mizos, like those of many other tribes in the North Eastern India is shrouded in mystery. They generally accepted as part of a great Mongoloid wave of migration from China and later moved out to India to their present habitat. It is possible that the Mizos came from Shinlung or Chhinlungsan located on the banks of the river Yalung in China. They first settled in the Shan State and moved on to Kabaw Valley to Khampat and then to the Chin Hills in the middle of the 16th century.

The earliest Mizos who migrated to India were known as Kukis, the second batch of immigrants were called New Kukis. The Lushais were the last of the Mizo tribes migrate to India. The Mizo history in the 18th and 19th Century is marked by many instances of tribal raids and retaliatory expeditions of security. Mizo Hills were formally declared as part of the British-India by a proclamation in 1895. North and south hills were united into Lushai Hills district in 1898 with Aizawl as its headquarters. The process of the consolidated of the British administration in tribal dominated area in Assam stated in 1919 when Lushai Hills along with some other hill districts was declared a Backward Tract under government of India Act. The tribal districts of Assam including Lushai Hills were declared Excluded Area in 1935.

It was during the British regime that a political awakening among the Mizos in Lushai Hills started taking shape the first political party, the Mizo Common People's Union was formed on 9th April 1946. The Party was later renamed as Mizo Union. As the day of Independence drew nearer, the Constituent Assembly of India set up an Advisory Committee to deal with matters relating to the minorities and the tribals. A sub-Committee, under the chairmanship of Gopinath Bordoloi was formed to advise the Constituent Assembly on the tribal affairs in the North East. The Mizo Union submitted a resolution of this Sub-committee demanding inclusion of all Mizo inhabited areas adjacent to Lushai Hills. However, a new party called the United Mizo Freedom (UMFO) came up to demand that Lushai Hills join Burma after Independence.

Following the Bordoloi Sub-Committee's suggestion, a certain amount of autonomy was accepted by the Government and enshrined in the Six Schedule of the constitution. The Lushai Hills Autonomous District Council came into being in 1952 followed by the formation of these bodies led to the abolition of chieftainship in the Mizo society. The autonomy, however, met the aspirations of the Mizos only partially. Representatives of the District Council and the Mizo Union pleaded with the States Reorganization Commission (SRC) in 1954 for integrated the Mizo-dominated areas of Tripura and Manipur with their District Council in Assam.

The tribal leaders in the North East were laboriously unhappy with the SRC Recommendations. They met in Aizawl in 1955 and formed a new political party, Eastern India Union (EITU) and raised demand for a separate state comprising of all the hill districts of Assam. The Mizo Union split and the breakaway faction joined the EITU. By this time, the UMFO also joined the EITU and then understanding of the Hill problems by the Chuliha Ministry, the demand for a separate Hill state by EITU was kept in abeyance.

Mautam Famine

In 1959, the Mizo Hills was devastated by a great famine known in Mizo history as 'Mautam Famine'. The cause of the famine was attributed to flowering of bamboos which resulted in a boom of the rat population. After eating bamboos seeds, the rats turned towards crops and infested the huts and houses and became a plague to the villages. The havoc created by the rats was terrible and very little of the grain was harvested. For sustenance, many Mizos had to collect roots and leaves from the jungles. Others searched for edible roots and leaves in the jungles. Still others moved to far away places, and a considerable number died of starvation. In this hour of darkness, many welfare organizations tried their best to help starving villagers. Earlier in 1955, the Mizo Cultural Society was formed with Pu Laldenga as its secretary. In March 1960, the name of the Mizo Cultural Society was changed to 'Mautam Front'. During the famine of 1959-1960, this society took the lead in demanding relief and managed to attract the attention of all sections of the people. In September 1960, the Society adopted the name of Mizo National Famine Front (MNFF). The

MNFF gained considerable popularity as a large number of Mizo Youth assisted in transporting rice and other essential commodities to interior villages.

Insurgency

The Mizo National Famine Front dropped the word 'famine' and a new political organisation, the Mizo National Front (MNF) was born on 22nd October 1961 under the leadership of Laldenga with the specified goal of achieving sovereign independence of Greater Mizoram. Simultaneous large scale disturbances broke out on 28th February 1966 government installations at Aizawl, Lunglei, Chawngte, Chhimluang and other places. The Government of India bombed the city of Aizawl with Toofani and Hunter Jet fighters. This was the first time that India had used its air force to quell a movement of any kind among its citizens. While the MNF took to violence to secure its goal of establishing a sovereign land, other political forces in the hills of Assam were striving for a separate state. The search for a political solution to the problems facing the hill regions in Assam continued. The Mizo National Front was outlawed in 1967. The demand for statehood gained fresh momentum. A Mizo District Council delegation, which met prime minister Indira Gandhi in May 1971 demanded fullfledged statehood for the Mizos. The union government on its own offered the proposal of turning Mizo Hills into a Union Territory (U.T.) in July 1971. The Mizo leaders were ready to accept the offer on the condition that the status of U.T would be upgraded to statehood sooner rather than later. The Union Territory of Mizoram came into being on 21st January, 1972. Mizoram got two seats in Parliament, one each in the Lok Sabha and in the Rajya Sabha.

Birth of Mizoram State

Rajiv Gandhi's election to power following his mother's death signaled the beginning of a new era in Indian politics. Laldenga met the prime minister on 15th February, 1985. Some contentious issues which could not be resolved during previous talks were referred to him for his advice. With Pakistan having lost control of Bangladesh and no support from Pakistan, the Mizo National Front used the opportunity that had now presented itself. New Delhi felt that the Mizo problem had been dragging on for a long time, while the Mizo National Front was convinced that bidding farewell to arms to live as respectable Indian citizens was the only way of achieving peace and development. Statehood was a prerequisite to the implementation of the accord signed between the Mizo National Front and the Union Government on 30th June, 1986. The document was signed by Pu Laldenga on behalf of the Mizo National Front, and the Union Home Secretary R.D. Pradhan on behalf of the government. Lalkhama, Chief Secretary of Mizoram, also signed the agreement. The formalization of the state of Mizoram took place on 20th February, 1987. Chief Secretary Lalkhama read out the proclamation of statehood at a public meeting organised at Aizawl's parade ground. Prime Minister Rajiv Gandhi flew in to Aizawl to inaugurate the new state. Hiteshwar Saikia was appointed as Governor of Mizoram.

GEOGRAPHY

Mizoram predominantly a christian populated state, is towards southern most tips of the north eastern states, sharing boarders of Manipur, Assam, Tripura then jutting down between Myanmar and Bangladesh. Mizoram is a mountainous region which became the 23rd state of the Indian Union in February, 1987. It was one of the districts of Assam until January 21, 1972 when it became a Union Territory. Sandwiched between Myanmar in the east and south and Bangladesh in the west, Mizoram occupies an area of great strategic importance in the northeastern corner of India. It has a total of 722 km boundary with Myanmar and Bangladesh. It is situated between 21.58 to 24.35 degrees north latitude and 92.15 to 93.29 degrees east longitude, extending over a land area of 21,081. The Tropic of Cancer passes by the capital city, Aizawl. The length of the state from north to south is 277 km. At the broadest from east to west, it is 121 km. Its major length in the west borders the Chittagong Hill Tracts of Bangladesh, spanning 318 km. In the east and the south, its border with the Chin Hills and Northern Arakans of Myanmar extends to about 404 km. On the Indian side, Mizoram is bounded by the states of Assam, Manipur and Tripura. The length of its borders with these states extends over 123 km, 95 km and 66 km, respectively.

Mizoram has the most variegated hilly terrain in the eastern part of India. The hills are steep (avg. height 1000 metres) and separated by rivers which flow either to the north or south creating deep gorges between the hill ranges. The highest peak in Mizoram is the Blue Mountain (Phawngpui) with a height of 2210 metres.

Hills

Mizoram is a land of rolling hills, rivers and lakes. As many as 21 major hills ranges or peaks of different heights run through the length and breadth of the state, with plains scattered here and there. The average height of the hills to the west of the state are about 1,000 metres. These gradually rise up to 1,300 metres to the east. Some areas, however, have higher ranges which go up to a height of over 2,000 metres. The Blue Mountain, situated in the southeastern part of the state, is the highest peak in Mizoram.

Hill Ranges and Peaks in Mizoram

S.No.	Name of Range/Peak	Height (in Metre)
1.	Blue Mountain (Phawngpui)	2,210
2.	Lengteng	2,141
3.	Surtlang	1,967
4.	Lurhtlang	1,935
5.	Tantlang	1,929
6.	Vapartlang	1,897
7.	Chalfithlang	1,866
8.	Hranturotlang	1,854
9.	Zopuitlang	1,850
10.	Tawitlang	1,837

Note: Tlang in Mizo Language means hills.

MINERALS

Mizoram has no known mineral resources, which are commercially exploitable. The few surveys that the Geological Survey of India and the Oil and Natural Gas Commission have conducted so far did not find any. The present main mineral of Mizoram is a hard rock of Tertiary period formation. This is mainly utilized as building material and for road construction work.

CLIMATE

Mizoram as a whole receives an average rainfall of about 3000 mm a year, with Aizawl getting 2,380 mm and 3,178 mm for Lunglei in the south. Rainfall is usually evenly distributed throughout the state. During rains the climate in the lower hills and river gorges is highly humid and exhausting for people, whereas it is cool and pleasant in the higher hills even during the hot season. A rather peculiar characteristic of the climate is the incidence of violent storms during March-early May. Strong storms arise from the north-west and sweep over the entire hills, often causing extensive damages to 'kacha' (temporary) dwellings and flowering perennials. Temperature varies from about 12°C in winter to 30°C plus in summer. Winter is from November to February, with little or no rain during this period. Spring lasts from end February to mid-April. Heavy rains start in June and continue up to August. September and October are the autumn months when the rain is intermittent.

RIVERS

Although many more rivers and streamlets drain the hill ranges, the most important and useful rivers are the Tlawng (also known as Dhaleswari or

Katakhal), Tut (Gutur), Tuirial (Sonai) and Tuivawl which flow through the northern territory and eventually join the Barak River in Cachar District. The Koldoyne (Chhimtuipui) which originates in Myanmar, is an important river in the south of Mizoram. It has four tributaries and the river is in patches. The western part is drained by Karnaphuli (Khawthlang tuipui) and its tributaries. A number of important towns, including Chittagong in Bangladesh, are situated at the mouth of the river. Before Independence, access to other parts of the country was only possible through the river routes via Cachar in the north, and via Chittagong in the south. Entry through the latter was cut off when the subcontinent was partitioned and ceded to East Pakistan (now Bangladesh) in 1947.

Rivers of Mizoram

S. No.	Name of River	Length in Kilometer (in Mizoram)
1.	Tlawng (Dhaleshwari)	185.15
2.	Tiak	159.39
3.	Chhimtuipui (Koldoyne)	128.08
4.	Khawthlangtuipui (Karnaphuli)	128.08
5.	Tuichang	120.75
6.	Mat	90.16
7.	Tuipui (Khawchhak)	86.94
8.	Tuivawl	72.45
9.	Teirei	70.84
10.	Tuirini	59.57
11.	Serlui	56.35

Lakes

Lakes are scattered all over the state, but the most important among these are Palak, Tamdil, Rungdil, and Rengdil. The Palak lake is situated in Chhimtuipui District which is part of southern Mizoram and covers an area of 30 hectares. It is believed that the lake was created as a result of an earthquake or a flood. The local people believe that a village which was submerged still remains intact deep under the waters. The Tamdil lake is a natural lake. Legend has it that a huge mustard plant once stood in this place. When the plant was cut down, jets of water sprayed from the plant and created a pool of water, thus the lake was named '*Tamdil* which means of 'Lake of Mustard Plant'. Today the lake is an important tourist attraction and a holiday resort. However, the most significant lake in Mizo history Rih Dil is ironically located in Myanmar, a few kilometres from the India-Myanmar border. It was believed that the departed souls pass through this lake before making their way to "Pialral" or heaven.

IRRIGATION

The ultimate surface irrigation potential is estimated at 70,000 hectares of which 45,000 hectares is under flow and 25,000 hectares by construction and completing 70 pucca minor irrigation projects and six lift irrigation projects for raising double and triple crops in a year.

AGRICULTURE

Agriculture is the mainstay of the people of Mizoram. Seventy per cent of the total population is engaged in Agriculture. The age old practice of Jhum cultivation is carried out annually by a large number of people living in rural areas. The climatic condition in the state with well distributed rainfall of 1900 mm to 3000 mm spread over eight to ten months in the year and location in tropic and temperate zone with various soil types have contributed to the occurrence of a wide spectrum of rich and varied flora and fauna. These natural features and resources also offer opportunities for growing a variety of horticultural crops.

Cropped Area

Mizoram has a total geographical area of 21,08,700 ha. The forest cover is about 86.27% of the total area. The gross cropped area of the state is 221.43 thousand ha. which is only 6.72% of the total area. Due to hilly terrain potential area for Wet Rice Cultivation (WRC) is very limited. It is estimated that there are 74,644 ha. of area having a slope of 0-25% out of this, only 15,308 ha. are currently under Wet Rice Cultivation, the remaining 79% of land needs to be exploited for increased production and productivity.

HORTICULTURE

More than 70% of the population of Mizoram depends on land based activities for their livelihood and horticulture plays as a vital role and occupies a very important place in the economy of Mizoram and contributes substantially to the State Gross Domestic Products. Out of the total horticulture potential area of 11.56 lakhs ha. only 1.21 lakhs is covered under horticulture plantation which shows that 10.35 lakhs ha *i.e.* (89.54%) of horticulture potential area is still lying untapped indicating vast scope for settlement of jhumia families into permanent settlement as well as development of horticulture in the state. Because of its hilly terrain horticulture is the only sustainable land base activities for development of the state and its farmers.

The main horticultural produce are Orange, Banana, Pineapple, Passion Fruit, Assam Lemon, Hatkora, which grows abundantly in all parts of the state. Oranges, Pineapples and Bananas are supplied to neighbouring states. Other fruits such as pear, plum, guavas, are also grown. Fruit preservation and processing units have been set up at Chhingchhip, Sairang and Vairengte. The state government is giving high priority to upgrade the agro-horticulture sector.

FLORA AND FAUNA

Mizoram is rich in flora and fauna and many kinds of tropical trees and plants thrive in the area. According to the report (2017) of the Department of Environment and Forests, 86.27 per cent of the total area of the state (18,186 sq. km.) is covered by forests. However, due to the traditional practice of shifting cultivation called 'jhuming', uncontrolled fire, unregulated felling and arbitrary allotment of land to individuals, two-third of the area is reported to have been partly depleted and degraded.

District-wise Forest Cover of Mizoram

(Area in Km^2)

District	Geographical Area	2017 Assessment			Total	Per cent of GA
		Very Dense Forest	Mod. Dense Forest	Open Forest		
Aizawl[TH]	3,576	18	1,092	1,984	3,094	86.52
Champhai[TH]	3,185	56	1,012	1,535	2,603	81.73
Kolasib[TH]	1,382	0	172	1,010	1,182	85.53
Lawngtlai[TH]	2,557	0	704	1,518	2,222	86.90
Lunglei[TH]	4,536	1	1,195	2,826	4,022	88.67
Mamit[TH]	3,025	43	772	1,885	2,700	89.26
Saiha[TH]	1,399	0	548	657	1,205	86.13
Serchhip[TH]	1,421	13	366	779	1,158	81.49
Grand Total	**21,081**	**131**	**5,861**	**12,194**	**18,186**	**86.27**

List of Existing and Proposed National Parks in Mizoram

Existing

1. Murlen National Parks (200 sq. km.)
2. Phawngpui Blue Mountain National Parks (50 sq. km.)

Proposed

1. Dampa (240 sq. km.)

DAIRY DEVELOPMENT

Besides a sizeable milk production from the private sector, the State Government has implemented 4 (four) Dairy Development Projects which were initiated under Central Scheme of I.D.D.P. (Intensive Dairy Development Project). Government's food policy for self-sufficiency in the project envisages establishment of infrastructures for collection, pasteurization, storage and distribution of the good quality milk. People's participation through Dairy Co-operative Societies is highly encouraged. Five such projects are implemented under this scheme. Dairy Plants at Aizawl, Champhai and Kolasib have been handed over to the District Dairy Co-operative Union and the Dairy project at Lunglei is being maintained by State Government.

FISHERIES

The State has a coastline of about 104 kms. It has 250 kms of Inland waterways and also a number of small tanks of fish ponds covering an area of 100 hectares. The coast is full of creeks and estuaries which provides excellent nurseries for major fishes as well as good shelter for fishing crafts. The share of fisheries in GSDP was around 2 per cent in 2015-16 (Q). During the year 2015, the marine fish production of 1,08,240 tonnes and inland fish production of 4,648 tonnes was achieved.

POPULATION

As per 2011 Census, the total population of the State is 10,97,206 indicating a decadal growth of 23.5 per cent. The State has the density of 52 persons per sq. km. Literacy in the state has grown rapidly, and Mizoram literacy at 91.3 per cent today, is the second highest in the country. The state government is striving hard to attain the top position in the near future. Female literacy of the State is 89.3 per cent. While male literacy rate is 93.3 per cent.

District-wise Population of Mizoram

District	Persons	Male	Female
Mamit	86,364	44,828	41,536
Kolasib	83,955	42,918	41,037
Aizawl	4,00,309	1,99,270	2,01,039
Champhai	1,25,745	63,388	62,357
Serchhip	64,937	32,851	32,086
Lunglei	1,61,428	82,891	78,537
Lawngtlai	1,17,894	60,599	57,295
Saiha	56,574	28,594	27,980
Mizoram	**10,97,206**	**5,55,339**	**5,41,867**

Population: At a glance

- Total Population : 10,97,206
- Sex Ratio : 976 : 1000
- Density : 52 persons per sq. km.
- Decadal Growth Rate : 23.5%
- Literacy Rate : 91.3% (male : 93.3% and female : 89.3%)

District-wise record of population as per 2011 census

S. No.	District	Headquarters	Population	Area
1.	Aizawl	Aizawl	4,00,309	3,576.31
2.	Champhai	Champhai	1,25,745	3,185.85
3.	Mamit	Mamit	86,364	3,025.75
4.	Lunglei	Lunglei	1,61,428	4,538.00
5.	Lawngtlai	Lawngtlai	1,17,894	2,557.50
6.	Saiha	Saiha	56,574	1,399.90
7.	Kolasib	Kolasib	83,955	1,282.51
8.	Serchhip	Serchhip	64,937	1,421.50

EDUCATION

In Mizoram, there are two universities (Mizoram University and ICFAI University). The history of higher education in Mizoram started only with the establishment of one private college in 1958, which is now constituent college of Mizoram University. There are 25 colleges, and 22 of them teach conventional subjects of general education and three others are professional colleges such as College of Teacher's Education, Hindi Training College, and Mizoram Law College. There are 10 government colleges and 14 others are called "deficit college" and there is one constituent College of Mizoram University. Seven Colleges offer Science stream along with arts and one college is a Science College. Bachelor of Computer Science (BCA) Course/Programme is opened in two Government Colleges.

Technical Education in Mizoram is in a fledgling stage. There are two polytechnic institutes of diploma standard (2006). Of which one is a Women Polytechnic. There is also one Veterinary College financed by the North-Eastern Development Council (NEDC). The growth is visible with the fact that only six colleges existed before 1975 and all others were established after 1980. There are 14 colleges recognised by the UGC eligible to receive development grants.

Technical Education is where Mizoram is lagging behind from other states. The State does not have even a single Technical College. This is the area where a thrust is given by the State Government ICFAI University has taken initiatives in Mizoram in the field of management. Now a BBA Programme has been started. To promote Technical Education, the Mizoram State Council for Technical Education was established in 1998 under the chairmanship of Minister of State, Higher & Technical Education and Director, Higher & Technical Education as the Member Secretary. The Technical Cell of the Directorate of Higher & Technical Education functions as the administrative unit of the Council. AICTE Norms and pay scales have been adopted for Technical Education in Mizoram. The Government has proposed to establish one Engineering College during the 11th Plan.

Mizoram University (Central University)

Mizoram University was established on 2nd July 2001 by the Mizoram University Act, 2000. The jurisdiction of the Mizoram University extends to the whole of Mizoram, the erstwhile jurisdiction of Mizoram Campus of North Eastern Hill University, Shillong, which functioned till 1.7.2001. Initially, the University had 7 academic departments inherited from NEHU, but now has a total of 28 academic departments.

ECONOMY

In terms of economic development, Mizoram has lagged behind in comparison to the rest of the country. Cottage industry and other small-scale industries play an important role in its current economy. The people of Mizoram have not taken a keen responsibility for the development of industry due to lack of raw materials.

The economic life of the Mizos has always been centered around jhum or shifting cultivation. During the rule of the Chiefs, the chiefs distributed jhum land every year from the land under their control to their subjects. The Village Councils now do the allocation of jhum land by letting the villagers draw lots. The sizes of the plots used to be usually between 1.5 and 3 hectares per family, depending on the number of able-bodied persons in a family. However, as land available for jhuming is becoming less due to allotment of lands to individuals, plot sizes in recent years have become smaller. Besides, the earning per man day in this practice of farming is so low that many young people now prefer to work as wage earners in services and other sectors. Jhum sites selection is done in November/ December and by mid February, felling of the vegetation is usually finished. The dried vegetation must be set on fire preferably before the early rains in mid March. After the unburned debris of trees and bamboos are cleared, the plot is ready for cultivation. The crops grown in the plots are mixed. Paddy remains the principal crop and others that are inevitably grown are common vegetables and pulses for household consumption. Now a days, cash crops such as ginger, turmeric, bird's eye chilly, oil seeds, maize, sugarcane, etc are grown. A variety of spices, herbs, flowers, fruits and oil seeds like sesame, soyabeans and mustard and cotton can grow well in Mizoram. The basic problem is the method of farming the land, that is, the practice of shifting cultivation, which causes depletion of forests and biodiversity, soil erosion as also a complex of environmental damages. Crop yields from unlevelled lands cannot be very high either and new scientific thinking says that it is better to improve them through scientific methods than through replacement with plantations which represent an alien interaction into a scientific pro-environmental as well as silk zone. It is important to better jhum restrict its spread and involve micro-credit agencies and give better alternative markets.

Banking and Finance

The common people in Mizoram seldom use banking instruments for their financial transactions. They mostly use cash money. Those who use banks do it mainly for saving or term deposits. Taking loans from banks against collaterals is also popular. The number of 'bad loans' is said to be high, particularly those loans extended by the first financial institution set up by the State, Zoram Industrial Development Corporation (ZIDCO).

ZIDCO was set up by the State government in collaboration with the Industrial Development Bank of India (IDBI) to foster the start up and the growth of industries in Mizoram. Another semi-financial institution, Mizoram Khadi and Village Industries Board (KVI) in 1986, was set up to promote various types of small scale and cottage industries. These two institutions extend credits to individuals and cooperative bodies for starting small industries. Part of the funding for the loans comes from the central credit institutions for development.

Mizoram Cooperative Apex Bank Ltd.

This Bank was established in 1981 and play vital role in the upliftment of the poor economy of the State. The Bank is running 12 Branches in various places of Mizoram for providing credit for Agriculture and other productive purposes.

INDUSTRY

Due to its topographical and geographical disadvantage, coupled with underdeveloped infrastructure and transport bottleneck, growth in industry is very modest. However with the opening up of border trade with Myanmar and Bangladesh, the 'Look East Policy' of the Government of India and the peaceful condition of the state, industrialisation is gaining momentum in the state.

Small industries dominate the industrial scenario acquiring prominent place in the socio-economic development of the state. With the objective of promoting industries in rural areas, the State Government has been running two common facility centres and one Regional Industrial Development like Industrial Growth Centre (IGC) at Luangmual, Aizawl, Export Promotion Industrial Park (EPIP) at Lengte, Integrated Infrastructural Development Centre (IIDC) at Pukpui, Lunglei and Food Park at Chhingcehip are nearing completion.

Scientific cultivation of tea has also been taken up. Establishment of Apparel Training and Design Centre, gems cutting and polishing are in the pipeline to encourage setting up of Export Oriented Units (EOUs). Of the cottage industries, Handloom and Handicrafts are given high priority and the two sectors are flourishing to meet consumers' demand in the state and in the neighbouring states of Meghalaya, Nagaland, etc.

Handlooms and Handicrafts

Mizo women typically use a handloom to make clothing and other handicrafts, such as a type of bag called *Pawnpui* and blankets. The Mizo rarely did much craft work until the British first came to Mizoram in 1889 when a demand for their crafts was created with this exposure to foreign markets. Currently, the production of handlooms is also being increased, as the market has been widening within and outside Mizoram.

ENERGY

In spite of abundant hydro-electric power potential available in the State (4500.0 MW approx.), only 0.66% of its potential has so far been harnessed, through Small & Mini Hydel Projects. The State's power demand is presently worked out to be 201 MW as per 18th Power Survey of India. The bulk of the State's power requirement is met from Central Sector Generating Stations in which the share of Mizoram is 103.09 MW. But, as these generating stations are mostly hydel stations which depend on rainfall, power availability from these stations are, therefore, seasonal. So, in dry seasons, inherent generation shortfall compelled the Department to resort to load shedding at various places.

The status of power in the state at a glance is –

1. **Demand** – 201 MW.
2. **Allocated share** – 103.09 MW (Real time available power is normally 60 MW due to reduction of generation from Central Generating Station, Transmission Failure etc.).

3. Local generation installed capacity – 29.35 MW Hydel.

The allocated power is wheeled to the State through NE grid at 132 kV level through the following lines:

1. 132 kV SC Jiribum (Manipur) to Aizawl (PowerGrid) line.
2. 132 kV S/C Badarpur (Assam) to Aizawl (PowerGrid) line.
3. 132 kV S/C Kumarghat (Tripura) to Aizawl (PowerGrid) line.

In Mizoram power is generated by two types viz. Hydel & Diesel. Due to its high generation cost, use of Diesel is avoided as far as possible. The Potential availability of hydro power of Mizoram is estimated at 4500 MW (approx.), out of which only 0.66% is presently harnessed.

Only 5.0% of the total energy available for the state is met within the state and the remaining 95.0% was imported mainly from Central Sector Projects.

Solar City Scheme for Aizawl

The Ministry of New and Renewable Energy (MNRE) has approved to develop Aizawl as a Solar City, and the Aizawl Solar City Master Plan has since been prepared and submitted to the Ministry. The Ministry had already approved and sanctioned ₹ 48.09 lakhs for preparatory activities to develop Aizawl as a Solar City, out of which ₹ 17.09 lakhs has already been released by the Central Government. The amount so released is being utilized for preparation of Aizawl Solar City Master Plan, promotional activities and for setting up of Aizawl Solar City Cell.

TRANSPORT

Transport Infrastructure

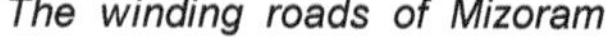

The winding roads of Mizoram

A close up of a road near Aizawl.

The state is the southernmost in India's far northeast, placing Mizoram in a disadvantageous position in terms of logistical ease, response time during emergencies, and its transport infrastructure. Prior to 1947, the distance to Kolkata from Mizoram was shorter; but ever since, travel through Bangladesh has been avoided, and traffic loops through Assam an extra 1,400 kilometres to access the economic market of West Bengal. This remoteness from access to economic markets of India is balanced by the state's closeness to Southeast Asian market and its over 700 kilometres of international boundary.

Road Network

The total length of all types of roads in Mizoram is 7632 km having a road density of about 36.463 km/100 sq km which is much below the national average of 129 km/100 sq km. Out of the total road network, National Highways covers 1465 km, BRO Roads covers 896 km and State Roads covers 6127 km which were constructed by the State government.

Mizoram PWD is presently looking after and maintaining the National Highways having a total length of 1465 km within the State. The fund required for the Highways is funded by the Ministry of Roads, Transports & Highways (MoRTH), Government of India.

Airport

Mizoram has an airport, Lengpui Airport (IATA: AJL), near Aizawl and its runway is 3,130 feet long at an elevation of 1,000 feet. Aizawl airport is linked from Kolkata—a 40-minute flight. Inclement weather conditions mean that at certain times the flights are unreliable. Mizoram can also be reached via Assam's Silchar Airport, which is about 200 kilometres (120 miles), around 6 hours by road to Aizawl.

Railway

There is a rail link at Bairabi rail station but it is primarily for goods traffic. The nearest practical station to Mizoram is at Silchar in Assam. Bairabi is about 110 kilometres (68 miles) and Silchar is about 180 kilometres (110 miles) from the state capital. The Government is now planning to start a broad gauge Bairabi Sairang Railway connection for better connectivity in the state.

Helicopter

A Helicopter service by Pawan Hans has been started which connects the Aizawl with Lunglei, Lawngtlai, Saiha, Chawngte, Serchhip, Champhai, Kolasib, Khawzawl and Hnahthial.

Water Ways

Mizoram is in the process of developing water ways with the port of Akyab Sittwe in Burma along its biggest river, Chhimtuipui. It drains into Burma's Rakhine state, and finally enters the Bay of Bengal at Akyab, which is a popular port in Sittwe, Burma. The Indian government considers it a priority to set up inland water ways along this river to trade with Burma. The project is known as the Kaladan Multi-modal Transit Transport Project. India is investing $103 million to develop the Sittwe port on Burma's northern coast, about 160 kilometres (99 miles) from Mizoram. State Peace and Development Council of Burma has committed $10 million for the venture. The project consists of two parts. First, river Kaladan (or Kolodyne, Chhimtuipui) is being dredged and widened from the port at Sittwe to Paletwa, in Chin province, adjacent to Mizoram. This 160 km inland waterway will enable cargo ships to enter, upload and offload freight in Paletwa, Myanmar.

As second part of the project, being constructed in parallel includes a 62 km two-lane highway from Paletwa (also known as Kaletwa or Setpyitpyin) to Lomasu, Mizoram. Additionally, an all-weather multilane 100 km road from Lomasu to Lawngtlai in Mizoram is being built to connect it with the Indian National Highway 54. Once complete, this project is expected to economically benefit trade and horticulture exports of Mizoram, as well as improve economic access to 60 million people of landlocked northeast India and Myanmar.

List of National Highways in Mizoram

1. **NH-44A** — Mizoram/Tripura Border-Tukkalh-Mamiti-Sairang-Aizawl.
2. **NH-54** — Mizoram/Assam Border-Chhimlung-Bilkhawthr-Kolasis-Bualpui-Mualvum-Aizawl-Zobawk- Pangzawl-Leite-Zobawk-Sairep-Saiha-Kaladan-Tuipang.
3. **NH-54A** — Lunglei and connecting on NH-54 near Zowawk
4. **NH-150** — Mizoram/Manipur Border-Thingsa-Ratn-Darlawn-Phaileng-Seling.
5. **NH-154** — Meghalaya/Assam Border-connecting on NH-54 near Bualpui.

ADMINISTRATION

Districts of Mizoram		
S.No.	**Districts**	**Headquarters**
1.	Aizawl	Aizawl
2.	Kolasib	Kolasib
3.	Champhai	Champhai
4.	Serchhip	Serchhip
5.	Mamit	Mamit
6.	Lunglei	Lunglei
7.	Saiha	Saiha
8.	Lawngtlai	Lawngtlai

After the 1986 signing of the Historic Memorandum of Settlement between the Government of India and the Mizo National Front, Mizoram was granted Statehood on February 20, 1987 (as per the Statehood Act of 1986). Mizoram became the 23rd State of the Indian Union. The capital of Mizoram is Aizawl. Mizoram has a unicameral legislature like most other Indian states. The Mizoram State Legislative Assembly has 40 seats. Mizoram is now represented at the Parliament by two MPs, one in the Lok Sabha and the other in the Rajya Sabha. Mizoram has witnessed vast constitutional, political and administrative changes in recent years. The traditional chieftainship was abolished and the District and Regional Councils (created under the Sixth Schedule of the Constitution of India) gave a substantial measure of local control. Today the Lais, Maras, and the Chakmas have separate Autonomous District Councils. The Village Councils are the grassroots of democracy in Mizoram.

Legislative Assembly

Mizoram was one of the districts of Assam State till it attained a status of Union Territory in 1972. Mizoram Legislative Assembly started functioning on 10th May of the same year with thirty elected and three nominated Members. Mizoram attained Statehood on 20th February 1987 and the first State Assembly was instituted in March, 1987 with a total membership of forty. The Mizoram Legislative Assembly celebrated its Silver Jubilee in May 1997. Mizoram Legislative Assembly has been a full-fledged member of the Commonwealth Parliamentary Association since 1987. Mizoram Legislative Assembly has a powerful Committee System. At present it has twenty standing Committees. Shri Hiteshwar Saikia was the first Governor and Ch.Chhunga was the first chief minister of the state.

The Aizawl Permanent Bench, Guwahati High Court

The Aizawl Permanent Bench of the Guwahati High Court was established on 5th July, 1990 and was inaugurated by the then Chief Justice of India, Mr. Justice S.B. Mukherjee, in the presence of the then the Chief Justice of the Guwahati High Court, Hon'ble Mr. Justice A. Raghuvir, His Excellency the then Governor of Mizoram, Mr. Swaraj Kaushal and the then Hon'ble Chief Minister Mr. Lal Thanhawla.

ART AND CULTURE

Festivals

Important festivals of Mizoram are:

- **Mim Kut:** The Mim Kut festival is usually celebrated during the months of August and September, after the harvest of maize. Mim Kut is celebrated with great fanfare by drinking rice-beer, singing, dancing, and feasting.
- **Chapchar Kut:** Chapchar Kut is another festival celebrated during March after completion of their most arduous task of Jhum operation *i.e.*, jungle-clearing. This is a spring festival celebrated with great fervour and gaiety.
- **Pawl Kut:** Pawl Kut is a festival celebrated in December to commemorate the end of harvest season. It is the greatest Mizo festival.

Dances

Important dances of Mizoram are:

- **Cheraw :** The most colourful and distinctive dance of the Mizo is called Cheraw. Long bamboo staves are a feature of this dance and it is known to many as the Bamboo Dance.
- **Khuallam :** Khuallam was originally a dance performed by honoured invitees while entering into the arena. Khuallam is performed by a group of dancers, the more the merrier, in colourful profiles to the tune of gongs and drums.
- **Chheih Lam :** Chheih Lam is the dance done over a round of rice-beer in the cool of the evening. The lyrics in triplets are usually spontaneous compositions, recounting their heroic deeds and escapades and also praising the honoured guests present in their midst.

Folk Songs

The folksongs of Mizoram are: Bawh Hla, Hlado, Thiam Hla & Dawi Hla, Dar Hla, Puipun Hla, Lengzem Zai.

SPORTS & YOUTH SERVICES

- Rajiv Gandhi Stadium at Mualpui.
- Indoor Stadium at Pitarte Tlang, Republic Veng, Aizawl.
- Champhai Indoor Stadium (Vanlallawma Indoor Stadium).
- Cricket Stadium at Sihhmui.
- Indoor Stadium, Bungtlang.
- Indoor Stadium, Keitum.
- State Sports Academy, Zobawk.
- Mini Sports Complex, Lengpui.
- Regional Sports Training Centre, Saidan, Kolasib.
- Indoor Stadium at Electric Veng, Aizawl.
- Astro Turf at A.R. Lammual, Aizawl.
- Astro Turf at Thuamluaia Mual, Lunglei.
- Astro Turf Hockey Playground at Boys Hockey Academy, Kawnpui.
- Multi-purpose Hall at Mualpui, Aizwal.
- Indoor Stadium at Chanmari, Lunglei.

GOVERNMENT HOSPITALS

1. Civil Hospital, Aizawl
2. Kulikawn Hospital, Aizawl
3. Civil Hospital, Lunglei
4. District Hospital, Champhai
5. District Hospital, Serchhip
6. District Hospital, Saiha
7. District Hospital, Kolasib
8. District Hospital, Mamit
9. District Hospital, Lawngtlai
10. Referral Hospital, Falkawn
11. Cancer Hospital (RCC), Zemabawk

MIZORAM : AT A GLANCE

- Area (in sq. km.) : 21,081 (0.6% of the country)
- Latitude : 21.58 to 24.35 degrees north

- Longitude : 92.15 to 93.29 degrees east
- Forest Area (in sq. km.) : 18,186 (86.27% of State's Area)
- No. of Districts : 8
- Name of the Districts : Aizawl, Kolasib, Champhai, Serchhip, Mamit, Lunglei, Saiha, Lawngtlai
- Lok Sabha Constituencies : One
- Rajya Sabha Seat : One
- Vidhan Sabha Constituencies : 40
- Nature of Legislature : Unicameral
- Capital : Aizawl
- Language : Mizo, English, Kuku
- Total Population (as per 2011 census) : 10,97,206
- Male : 5,55,339
- Female : 5,41,867
- Decadal Growth (2001-2011) : 23.5%
- Literacy Rate : 91.3%
- Male Literacy Rate : 93.3%
- Female Literacy Rate : 89.3%
- Density (per sq. km.) : 52
- Sex Ratio (per 1000 males) : 976
- No. of Universities : One [(Mizoram University) (Central University)]
- No. of National Parks : 2
  1. Murlen National Parks
  2. Phawngpui Blue Mountain National Parks
- State Animal : Serow (Saza)
- State Bird : Hume's Bartailed Pheasant (Vavu)
- State Flower : Dancing Girl (Aiting)
- State Tree : Mesual Ferrea/Nahar (Herhse)
- Important Tribes : Any Mizo (Lushai), Chakma, Pawi, Lakher, Any Kuki and Hmar

- Major Festivals : Mim Kut, Chapchar Kut, Pawl Kut
- Name of National Highways : NH-44A, NH-54, NH-54A, NH-54B, NH-150, NH-154

OBJECTIVE QUESTIONS

1. What is the area of Mizoram?
A. 19,000 sq. km. C. 21,081 sq. km.
B. 20,000 sq. km. D. None of these

2. What is the latitude of Mizoram?
A. 15°16′N to 20°15′N C. 21°58′N to 24°35′N
B. 25°N to 27°N D. None of these

3. Mizoram is situated on longitude between
A. 90°E and 95°E C. 85°E and 88°E
B. 92°15′E and 93°29′E D. None of these

4. How many districts are there in Mizoram ?
A. 8 C. 9
B. 10 D. None of these

5. Mizoram Legislative Assembly consists of
A. 40 members C. 60 members
B. 70 members D. None of these

6. What is the name of the capital of Mizoram?
A. Aizawl B. Shillong
C. Dispur D. None of these

7. According to 2011 census, total population of Mizoram is
A. 10,97,206 B. 9,99,543
C. 7,88,432 D. None of these

8. Total male population of Mizoram is
A. 5,55,339 B. 5,29,464
C. 5,49,2011 D. None of these

9. According to 2011 census, total female population of Mizoram is
A. 5,41,867 B. 5,49,269
C. 6,29,212 D. None of these

10. In Mizoram, decadal growth of population during 2001-2011 was
A. 23.5% B. 27.52%
C. 43.21% D. None of these

11. According to 2011 census, total STs population of Mizoram is
A. 8,54,263 B. 10,36,115
C. 5,49,312 D. None of these

12. Percentage of scheduled tribes population in Mizoram is
A. 85% B. 94.4%
C. 90% D. None of these

13. According to 2011 census, percentage of urban population in Mizoram is
A. 55% B. 69%
C. 52.1% D. None of these

14. According to 2011 census, total literacy rate in Mizoram is
A. 94% B. 97%
C. 91.3% D. None of these

15. What is the male literacy rate in Mizoram?
A. 95.9% B. 93.3%
C. 96.7% D. None of these

16. What is the female literacy rate in Mizoram?
A. 89.3% B. 95%
C. 92.64% D. None of these

17. According to 2011 census, population density in Mizoram is
A. 100 per sq. km. B. 52 per sq. km.
C. 80 per sq. km. D. None of these

18. According to 2011 census, sex ratio in Mizoram is
A. 960 B. 875
C. 976 D. None of these

19. Mizoram University is a
A. Central University B. State University
C. Private University D. None of these

20. Total number of National Parks in Mizoram, is ....
A. 2 B. 3
C. 4 D. None of these

21. What is the name of the state animal of the Mizoram?
A. Chinkara B. Red Panda
C. Serow D. None of these

22. What is the name of the state bird of the Mizoram?
A. Hume's Bartailed Pheasant B. Great Hornbill
C. Emerald dove D. None of these

23. What is the name of the state flower of the Mizoram?
A. Kachnar B. Palash
C. Dancing Girl D. None of these

24. The length of the Mizoram state from north to south is
A. 277 km. B. 377 km.
C. 400 km. D. None of these

25. Highest peak in the Mizoram is
A. Blue Mountain (Phawngpui) B. Gorichen Peak
C. Nyegi Kangsang D. None of these

26. Largest (in length) river of Mizoram is
A. Tiak B. Tlawng
C. Mat D. None of these

27. Palak lake is situated in
A. Chhimtuipui district B. Aizawl district
C. Mamit district D. None of these

28. According to the report (2017) of the Department of Environment and Forests, what percentage of the total area of the state is covered by forests?
A. 86.27% B. 90%
C. 70% D. None of these

29. What is the name of the headquarter of Saiha district?
A. Saiha B. Aizwal
C. Kolasib D. None of these

30. Mizoram University was established in
A. 1980 B. 1998
C. 2001 D. None of these

31. Mizoram was granted statehood on ....
A. February 20, 1987 B. March 20, 2001
C. June 5, 1989 D. None of these

32. Who was the first Governor of Mizoram ?
A. Shri Hiteshwar Saikia B. Shri Baldeo Singh
C. Shri Balram Jakhar D. None of these

33. The Aizawl Permanent Bench of Guwahati High Court was established in ....
A. 2001 B. 1990
C. 1988 D. None of these

34. Main National High way of Mizoram is ....
A. NH-54 B. NH-150
C. NH-154 D. None of these

35. 'Cheraw' is famous for ....

A. folk dance
B. folk music
C. festival
D. None of these

ANSWERS

1	2	3	4	5	6	7	8	9	10
B	B	C	A	A	A	A	A	A	A
11	**12**	**13**	**14**	**15**	**16**	**17**	**18**	**19**	**20**
B	B	C	C	B	A	B	C	A	A
21	**22**	**23**	**24**	**25**	**26**	**27**	**28**	**29**	**30**
C	A	C	A	A	B	A	A	A	C
31	**32**	**33**	**34**	**35**					
A	A	B	A	A					

●●●●●●

7

NAGALAND

HISTORY

The early history of Nagaland is largely undocumented and unknown. The earliest references to Nagaland are found in the Mahabharata. Several characters from the region, such as Princess Ulupi and Prince Iravan, were referred to as Naga people in the epic. Nagaland before the arrival of the British Raj was part of Manipur under the Manipuri administration as Thibomei and Thimbong districts. The word Naga is perhaps a misnomer derived from Bengali meaning naked as most people were semi-naked when the British explored this hill districts of Manipur. The people were originally referred to as Chingmee (Hill People) or Hao (Tribes) in the history of Manipur. With the permission of Manipuri king, the East India Company explored deep inside the naga hills in search of trade route, etc. The British brought the Assamese and Bengali traders from whom the Naga adopted their dialect called Nagamese which is a mixture of Assamese and Bengali dialects.

Early history of Nagaland is the customs, economic activities of the Naga tribes. The Naga tribes had socio-economic and political links with tribes in Assam and Myanmar—even today a large population of Naga inhabits Assam. Following an invasion in 1816, the area along with Assam came under direct rule of Myanmar. This period was noted for the oppressive rule and turmoil in Assam and Nagaland. When the British East India Company took control of Assam in 1826, they steadily expanded their domain over modern Nagaland. By 1892, all of modern Nagaland except the Tuensang area in the northeast was governed by the British. It was politically amalgamated into Assam, which in turn was for long periods a part of the province of Bengal.

The Naga territory remained split between Assam and the North East Frontier Agency after independence in 1947, despite a vocal movement advocating the political union of all the Naga tribes; one faction called for secession from India. Sectarian and political violence increased throughout the state—extremist groups damaged government and civil infrastructure, and attacked government officials and Indians from other states. The Union government sent the Indian Army in 1955, to restore order. In 1957, the Government began diplomatic talks with representatives of Naga tribes, and the Naga Hills district of Assam and the Tuensang frontier were united in a single political entity that became a Union territory—directly administered by the Central government with a large degree of autonomy. This was not satisfactory to the tribes, however, and soon agitation and violence increased across the state—included attacks on Army and government institutions, as well as civil disobedience and non-payment of taxes. In 1960 the Union government agreed to make Nagaland a self-governing state within India; the state was officially inaugurated in 1963 and the first state-level democratic elections were held in 1964. Naga separatists, however, continued to show violent opposition; they have been demanding autonomy and creation of a single administrative unit comprising all the Naga inhabited areas spanning across some of the north eastern states. Naga rebels and the Indian government have agreed on a ceasefire and peace talks are going on.

GEOGRAPHY

Nagaland, the 16th State of the Indian Union, was established on 1st December, 1963. Nagaland is a vibrant hill state located in the extreme north eastern end of India, bounded by Myanmar in the east; Assam in the west; Arunachal Pradesh and a part of Assam in the north with Manipur in the south. The State consists of eleven administrative districts, inhabited by 16 major tribes along with other sub-tribes. Each tribe is distinct in character from the other in terms of customs, language and dress. It lies between 25°6′ and 27°4′ latitude, north of equator and between the longitudinal lines 93°20′E and 95°15′E. The state capital is Kohima, and the largest city is Dimapur. With a population of nearly two million people, it has a total area of 16,579 sq. km. (0.5% of India's geographical area).

Nagaland is a state of high mountains, deep gorges, lush valleys, and winding streams. The dominant geographic feature of the landscape is the Naga Hills, which run all the way through the state and contribute to the mountainous terrain. The Naga Hills rise from the Brahmaputra Valley in Assam to about 2,000 feet and rise further to the southeast, as high as 6,000 feet. **Mount Saramati** at an elevation of 12,552 feet is the state's highest peak—this is where the Naga Hills merge with the Patkai Range in Myanmar. **Rivers** such as the **Doyang** and **Dhiku** to the north, the **Barak** river in the southwest and the **Chindwin** river of Myanmar in the southeast, dissect the entire state.

MINERALS

Coal occurs in Nazira coalfields (North of Dikhu River) in Borjan and Tiru Valley, Mon district. Limestone occurs in Phek district. Nickel, ferrous chromite ore occurs in ultrabasic belt at Pokhpur, Tuensang district. Occurrences of thin lenses of chrysotile asbestos near Panchimi and Kurani in the Tugu valley and Pyrites in Mokokchung and Tuensang districts are reported. For petroleum and natural gas, ONGC has delineated a number of prospective oil structures in the foothills where sufficient prognosticated resources (600 million tonnes) hydrocarbon have been forecasted. Out of these, a reserve of over 20 million tonnes with recoverable reserves of approx. 6 million tonnes has been established from Changpang oil fields. In Chumukedima area, three oil exploratory wells have been completed with no commercial outflow. The entire oil exploration work, however, is suspended presently by ONGC.

Minerals: At a glance

1. **Coal:** Borjan and Tiru Valley (Mon district), Konya (Tuensang district), Jhansi-Desai Valley (Mokokchung district)
2. **Lime stone:** Wazeho, Satouza (Phek district), Nimi belt (Tuensang district)
3. **Nickel, Cobalt and Chromium:** Pokhpur (Tuensang district)

CLIMATE

Nagaland's mountainous terrain has a profound effect on the state's climate. Nagaland has a largely monsoon climate with high humidity levels. During the winter months (October–February), temperatures range from about 39ºF to 75ºF (4ºC-24ºC); summer months (March–June) bring temperatures up into the 60ºF-90ºF (16ºC-31ºC) range. Filling the gap between those months, the monsoon season sees heavy rains and temperatures slightly cooler than the summer. Annual rainfall averages around 70-100 inches—concentrated in the months of May to September.

SOILS

The soils of Nagaland are derived from tertiary rocks belonging to Barail and Disang series. Though the state is small, due to large variation in topography and climate, the following kinds of soils occur in the state:

(i) Alluvial soils : (a) Recent alluvium (Entisol), (b) Old alluvium (Oxizols and Ultisol) and (c) Mountain valley soil (Entisol).

(ii) Residual soils : (a) Laterite soils (Oxizols and Ultisol), (b) Brown forest soils (Mollisols and Inceptisols) and (c) Podzolic soils (Spodesols).

(i) Alluvial Soils

Recent alluvium which is also known as Entisol occurs mostly in the western and southwestern part of the state whereas old alluvium is chiefly found in the northwestern part of Nagaland bordering Sivasagar District of Assam. Mountain valley soil (Entisol) covering about 224.8 sq. kms occurs mostly in the valleys of the central and eastern part of the State. Though alluvial soils are more fertile, their formations are mostly confined to the low-lying areas in the west and to the banks of the rivers.

(ii) Residual Soils

Residual soils which are generally porous and have light textures dominate a major landscape of Nagaland. Laterite soil (Oxizol) is the most widespread and occurs in the mid-southern part and the eastern part of the state. It covers 4,495.8 sq. kms of the total area of the State. Brown forest soil (Mollisol), is found mainly in the intermediate high hill ranges covering a total area of 4,952.7 sq. kms. Podzolic soil (Spodosol) covers an area of about 4,835.0 sq. kms and occurs at high altitude with humid and temperate climate in the central, southern and eastern part of the state. Major part of the Tuensang District is occupied by this type of soil.

Soils are generally fertile and responsive to application of fertilizer. Nagaland soils are acidic, very rich in organic carbon but poor in available phosphate and potash content.

RIVERS

Nagaland is dissected by a number of seasonal and perennial rivers and rivulets. The major rivers of Nagaland are Doyang, Dikhu, Dhansiri, Tizu, Tsurong, Nanung, Tsurang or Disai, Tsumok, Menung, Dzu, Langlong, Zunki, Likimro, Lanye, Dzuza and Manglu. All these rivers are dendritic in nature. Of the rivers, Dhansiri, Doyang and Dikhu flows westward into the Brahmaputra. The Tizu river, on the other hand, flows towards east and joins the Chindwin River in Burma (now Myanmar).

Doyang: It is the longest river in the state originating from the Japfü Hill near the southern slope of Mao in Manipur and moves in a south west direction passing through Kohima district and flows northward into Zunheboto and Wokha District. It passes through a great part of Wokha District and flows south westerly into Dhansiri in Sivasagar District of Assam. The main tributaries of Doyang are Chubi river which flows southward from Mokokchung District and Nzhu River, originating from Nerhema area of Kohima district and flows through Miphong in Tseminyu area and finally pours itself to Doyang.

Dikhu: River Dikhu which has a total length of about 160 kms originates from Nuroto Hill area in Zunheboto district. The river traverses towards north along the border of Mokokchung and Tuensang districts. The main tributaries of river Dikhu are Yangyu of Tuensang district and Nanung in the Langpangkong range in Mokokchung district. The river flows further northward and leaves the hill near Naginimora and finally merges with the Brahmaputra River in the plains of Assam.

Dhansiri: Dhansiri flows through the southwestern part of the state through Rangapahar-Dimapur Plains of Dimapur District. This river receives almost all the western and southern drainages of Nagaland. Its main tributaries are river Dzuza and Diphu. At the extreme southwest of the state, it assumes a northwardly course forming a natural boundary with North Cachar Hills of Assam which finally drains into the Brahmaputra.

Tizu: The Tizu River forms an important drainage system in the eastern part of the state. It originates from the central part of the state and runs through a northeast direction flows through *Zunheboto, Phek* district and empties itself in the Chindwin River of Myanmar. The main tributaries of River Tizu are river Zunki, Lanye and Likimro.

Milak: Milak is another important river which flows through Mokokchung District. One of its main tributary is Tsurong.

Zungki: The Zunki river which is the biggest tributary of Tizu, starts from the northeastern part of Changdong forest in the south of Teku and flows in southernly direction towards Noklak, Shamator and Kiphire and finally joins Tizu below Kiphire.

IRRIGATION

Nagaland is basically an agricultural state, and all the resources depend upon the agricultural output. Water is evidently the most vital element in the plant life and is normally supplied to the plants by natural rain. However, the total rainfall in a particular area may be either inadequate or is ill-timed. Therefore in order to get the maximum yield from a crop, it is essential to supply optimum quantity of water to the crop and to maintain correct timings of water. This is possible only through a systematic irrigation system by collecting water during rainfall and from natural sources and to release it to the crops as and when it is needed.

In Nagaland, State Government has made considerable investment in irrigation. There is no major or medium irrigation project so far constructed in the State. However, the State is in the process of taking up some medium irrigation projects also. The department of Irrigation and Flood Control in the state has undertaken the Minor Irrigation schemes which are most vital and very suitable for the state. The total area in the state under irrigation is 1,22,880 hectares. The irrigation works are mostly meant to divert small hill streamlets to irrigate valleys used for rice cultivation. Most of the villages are scattered and perched on the hilltop and the cultivators traditionally cultivate the hill slopes either by making terraces or by jhumming. Irrigation is provided only in terraced fields wherever the facilities exist to bring water from the sources by gravity system through M.I. Channels. Due to non-availability of well organized irrigation system, a vast area of land both under forest and jhumlands, which if brought under permanent irrigation, the foodgrain production in the state could be raised enormously.

AGRICULTURE

Nagaland is basically a land of agriculture. About 70 per cent of the population depends on agriculture. The contribution of agricultural sector in the state is very significant. Rice is the staple food. It occupies about 70 per cent of the total area under cultivation and constitutes about 75 per cent of the total food production in the state. Cultivation on terraced fields, and in some cases **Jhum** or the shifting system of cultivation, is followed by the people in this state. The widespread practice of *jhum* has led to soil erosion and loss of fertility, particularly in the eastern districts. Only the Angami and Chakesang tribes in the Kohima and Phek districts use terracing techniques. Nagaland is not self-sufficient in foodgrains as the farmers do not take up cultivation on a large scale basis, and application of modern advance technologies is not viable due to the reasons which are as follows :

1. Most of the cultivated lands are steep sloped marginal land.
2. The land holdings of the cultivation are fragmented and scattered.
3. Most of the agriculture are mixed and single season cropping, consequently the yield per unit of area is low.
4. Also the deplorable inadequacy of link roads, to the steep terrain lands and hill ranges, the vast inaccessible agriculture area can not be put to full utilization for lack of all infrastructure facilities.
5. Cultivation is done with the help of spade, hoe and scrapes and not plough, as the region is hilly.

The other main crops of the state are Maize, Beans, Peas, Yam, Brinjal, Chilly, Pumpkin, Ginger, Tomato, Bitter-gourd etc. Horticulture products consist of Orange, Banana, Pineapple, Papaya, Mosambique, Guava, Plum, Pear etc. The district supply certain surplus produce from agriculture and horticulture like Beans, Yam, Brinjal, Chilly, Ginger, Tomato, Bitter-gourd etc. and Orange, Pineapple etc. beside varieties of wild vegetables.

FLORA AND FAUNA

Nagaland is very rich in bio-diversity, both flora and fauna. Even today some pockets of forests are covered with gigantic trees, where sun-rays can not penetrate. Due to reckless and uncontrolled cutting of trees for timber, firewood, continued Jhum cultivation and annual fire in vast tracts of land, forests got degraded and barren, which accelerated diminishing of the most of the original characteristics of the forests. About one-sixth of Nagaland is under the cover of tropical and sub-tropical evergreen forests—including palms, bamboo and rattan as well as timber and mahogany forests. While some forest areas have been cleared for jhum cultivation many scrub forests, high grass, reeds and secondary dogs, pangolins, porcupines, elephants, leopards, bears, many species of monkeys, sambar, deers, oxen and buffaloes thrive across the state's forests. The Great Indian Hornbill is one of the most famous birds found in the state. World tallest Rhododendron tree, which is recorded in the Guinnese Book, has been found in Japfu Mountain of Kohima district.

Nagaland has 75.33 per cent of forest cover, which is way above the recommended 33% for good ecological balance. What is even more unique is that 88.3% of the Forest Areas are owned by the various tribe communities and not by the government. This also creates problems, sometimes, because holistic planning becomes difficult. This may be part of the reason why although the State has rich mineral deposits—including petroleum, lime stone, marble and decorative stones, nickel, cobalt, chromium, basalt, spilite, etc.—the entire forest and mineral contribution to the State Domestic Product has been negligible so far (around 4%).

Types of Forest

Though Nagaland is a small state but as far as types of forests are concerned it has been endowed with a wide variety of forest types. This is mainly due to the fact that though it is mainly in tropics, Nagaland has land elevation ranging from a few hundred meters up to about four thousand meters.

(i) **Northern Tropical Wet Evergreen Forests :** These forests once covered the Namsa-Tizit area but now only a small vestige is found in the Zankam area. It is found only in Mon District. The dominant species in this type of forest are Hollong *(Dipterocarpus macrocarpus)*, Makai *(Shorea assamica)*, Nahor *(Mesua ferae)*, etc.

(ii) **Northern Tropical Semi Evergreen Forests :** This type of forests are found in the foothills of Assam-Nagaland border in Mokokchung, Wokha and Kohima Districts. The Species that make up these forests are similar to those of the Northern Tropical Wet Evergreen Forests. The only difference is that in the former case the evergreen species dominate though there are deciduous species like Bhelu, Paroli, Jutuli, etc. whereas in the present case, the number of ever-green species decreases and the deciduous species are dominant.

(iii) **Northern Sub-tropical Broad Leaved Wet Hill Forests :** This type of forests are found in the hill areas below 1800 m and above

500 m in all the districts of Nagaland. The wet evergreen species are conspicuous by their absence and the dominant species are mostly semi-deciduous. Some of the important timber species in this type are—Koroi, Pomas, Sopas, Gamari, Gogra, Khokan, Hollok, Sam, Am, Badam, Betula, etc.

(iv) Northern Sub-tropical Pine Forests: This types of forests are found in hill elevation of 1000 meters to 1500 meters in parts of Phek and Tuensang Districts of Nagaland. Pine is the dominant species and is found mixed with Quercus, Schima, Prunus, Betula and Rhododendron.

(v) Northern Montane Wet-temperate Forests: This type of forests are found on the higher reaches of the tallest mountains in Nagaland above 2000 meters in—Japfu, Saramati, Satoi, Chentang ranges. The species are typically evergreen with Quercus, Michelia, Magnolia, Prunus, Schima, Alnus and Betula.

(vi) Temperate Forests: This type of forests are found in peaks of the tallest mountains (above 2500 meters) like Saramati and Dzukou area. The species that dominate are Rhododendron, Patches of Juniperus coxie and Birch.

Forest Cover Change Matrix

(Area in km^2)

Class	2017 Assessment					
	Very Dense Forest	Modest Dense Forest	Open Forest	Scrub	Non Forest	Total ISFR 2015
Very Dense Forest	1,277	0	0	0	7	1,284
Moderately Dense Forest	2	4,575	11	2	100	4,690
Open Forest	0	12	6,448	13	492	6,965
Scrub	0	0	76	476	65	617
Non Forest	0	0	88	12	2,923	3,023
Total ISFR 2017	**1,279**	**4,587**	**6,623**	**503**	**3,587**	**16,579**
Net Change	–5	–103	–342	–114	–564	

Wildlife Sanctuaries and National Parks

1. Intangki National Park, Dimapur
2. Fakim Wildlife Sanctuary, Kohima
3. Rangapahar Wildlife Sanctuary, Dimapur
4. Puliebadze Wildlife Sanctuary, Kohima
5. Zoological Park, Kohima

DEMOGRAPHY

The population of Nagaland is 19,78,502 (0.16% of India's population) according to 2011 census and is scattered over 11 districts and 1278 villages. The State has the density of 119 persons per sq. km. As against decadal growth rate of 17.7% at the national level, the population of the State has negatively grown by –0.6% over the period 2001-2011. The sex ratio of Nagaland at 931 females to 1000 males is lower than the national average of 943. Female literacy of the State rose to 76.1% from 61.92% in 2001. There are many distinct tribes and a number of sub-tribes inhabiting the area such as Angamis, Zeliangs, Rengmas, Kukis, Semas, Aos, Lothas, Chang, Sangtam, Koyaks.

Area, Population (2011) and Districts Headquarters

S.No.	District	Area (sq. km.)	Population	Headquarters
1.	Kohima	3,144	2,67,988	Kohima
2.	Mokokchung	1,615	1,94,622	Mokokchung
3.	Mon	1,876	2,50,260	Mon
4.	Tuensang	4,228	1,96,596	Phek
5.	Zunheboto	1,255	1,40,757	Tuensang
6.	Wokha	1,628	1,66,343	Wokha
7.	Dimapur	927	3,78,811	Dimapur
8.	Phek	2,026	1,63,418	Phek
9.	Longleng	—	50,484	Longleng
10.	Kiphire	—	74,004	Kiphire
11.	Peren	—	95,219	Peren

District-wise Sex Ratio & Density

District	Sex Ratio	Density
Dimapur	919	409
Kiphire	956	66
Kohima	928	211
Longleng	905	89
Mokokchung	925	121
Mon	899	140
Peren	915	56
Phek	951	81
Tuensang	929	90
Wokha	968	102
Zunheboto	976	112

CULTURE AND PEOPLE

The population of Nagaland is entirely tribal. The Nagas belong to the Indo-Mongoloid family. The fourteen major Naga tribes are the Angami, Ao, Chakhesang, Chang, Khemungan, Konyak, Lotha, Phom, Pochury, Rengma, Sangtam, Sema, Yimchunger and Zeliang. The Chakhesangs were earlier known as Eastern Angamis and are a combination of the Chakri, Khezha and Sangtam sub-tribes. Now the Chakhesang tribe is spilt further; Pochury's who were earlier a part of it now claim a distinct entity. Each tribe has their own languages and cultural features. The Naga's have different stories about their origin. The Angamis, Semas, Rengams and the Lotha's subscribe to the Kheza-Kenoma legend. It is said that the village had a large stone slab having magical properties. Paddy spread on it to be dried doubled in quantity by evening. The three sons of the couple who owned the stone used it by rotation. One day there was a quarrel between the sons as to whose turn it was. The couple, fearing bloodshed, set fire to the stone which as a result cracked. It is believed that the spirit in the stone went to heaven and the stone lost its miraculous properties. The three sons thereafter left Kheza-Kenoma, went in different directions and became the forefathers of the Angami, Sema and the Lotha tribes. According to another legend, to which the western Angamis subscribe, the first man evolved from a lake called Themiakelku zie near Khonoma. The Rengmas believe that until recently they and Lothas formed one tribe. The Aos and the Phoms trace their origin to the Lungterok (six stones) on the Chongliemdi hill. Some people believe that these Indo-Mongoloids are 'kiratas' frequently mentioned in the old Sanskrit literature of whom 'Nagas' were a sub-tribe.

The hill tribes in the areas now known as Nagaland had no generic term applicable to the whole race. The word 'Naga' was given to these hill tribes by the plains people. This proved to be a great unifying force to the tribes now classified as Naga. Nagas are of sub-medium height, the facial index is very low, the nasal index corresponds to a medium nose, the hair is generally straight, the skin is brownish yellow. The eyes significantly do not show Mongolian form.

It could broadly be said that they are straight forward people, honest, hardworking, sturdy and with a high standard of integrity. They are lacking in humility and are inclined to equate a kind and sympathetic approach with weakness. The Nagas have a very strong sense of self respect and would not submit to anyone riding roughshod over their sentiments. The Angamis are politically the most conscious group. The Zeliang and Pochury tribes in Kohima district are comparatively simple and unsophisticated. The Tuensang tribes are un-spoilt children of nature. A striking characteristic of the Naga tribes is their hospitality and cheerfulness. To be greeted with a smiling face while travelling on the roads is a common experience. A visitor to Naga village is heartily received and entertained with a surfeit of rice-beer, which is generally served by the lady of the house or her young daughter with a warmth which is unforgettable.

Each of the major tribes has its own unique designs and colours, producing shawls, shoulder bags, decorative spears, table mats, wood carvings and bamboo works. Tribal dances of the Nagas give an insight into the inborn reticence of the people. War dances and dances belonging to distinctive tribes are a major art form in Nagaland. Some of these are Moatsu, Sekrenyi, Tuluni and Tokhu Emong. Nagaland is a rural state. More than four-fifths of the population lives in small, isolated villages. Built on the most prominent points along the ridges of the hills, these villages were once stockaded, with massive wooden gates approached by narrow, sunken paths. The villages are usually divided into khels, or quarters, each with its own headmen and administration. Dimapur, Kohima, Mokokchung, and Tuensang are the only urban centres with more than 20,000 people.

Nagas speak 60 different dialects belonging to the Sino-Tibetan family of languages. Nagamese, a variant language form of Assamese and local dialects is the most widely spoken language. One interesting part is every tribe has their own mother tongue and these tribes communicate with each other in Nagamese. As such Nagamese is not a mother tongue of any of the tribes and nor is it a written language. English, the official state language is widely spoken in official circles and is the medium for education in Nagaland.

SCHEDULED TRIBES

Nagaland has five communities notified as STs. These are Garo, Kachari, Kuki, Mikir, and Naga. Naga is a generic name for several groups, each having distinct identity.

There are sixteen tribes in Nagaland, each occupying a distinct area. Each Naga tribe has its own legend to give some indication of the course from which its migration took place, though some Naga tribes, such as the **Khiamungan, Pochury, Sangtam,** and **Chang** regard themselves as original inhabitants of these hills. The **Angami, Chakhesang, Lotha, Rengma and Sema** tribes have common traditions and myths of origin, and thereby they are said to have originated from a single stock but later on got separated and gradually required separate identities after occupying distinct hill ranges.

Gradually, after occupying separate eco-environmental zones, the smaller Naga tribes established permanent settlements. Some larger tribes, such as the **Ao** and the **Angami** however kept on shifting their habitats during the initial stage by encroaching into the territories of smaller tribes. Later on economic compulsions forced them also to settle down in specific territories and to maintain solitary groups of Kins following the principles of patrilocal residence and patrilineal descent. The practice of village endogamy followed even today almost universally by all Naga tribes, big or small is a direct result of the reliance on descent principles (and prevalence of 'local warfare' in the Naga hills until the recent past). Under such circumstances almost each major village emerged as a "tribe". It is indeed well known that until the beginning of the century there was no clear recognition of any multi-village interacting ethnic entity and there never existed a wider multi-village political system among the Nagas. Each localized Naga tribe and a vague idea about the maximal limits of its tribal boundary. Besides 'self-name', each tribe was differently identified by its neighbouring tribes.

The **Phom** form yet another small Naga tribe. They are also known as **Kahha.** The **Phom** area always remains enveloped by clouds. The cloud in local dialect is called **Phom.** Thus, these people came to be called as **Phom.** The **Pochury** who are the last group to be given recognition, form one of the smallest Naga tribes. Till 1987 they were the part of the **Chakhesang** Naga tribal category. The term **Pochury** is an acronym formed by amalgamation of letters derived from three place names—**Sapo, Kechuri** and **Khury.** The British described the **Pochury** as the eastern **Sangtam** or eastern **Rengma** interchangeably. The **Pochury** population is distributed in twenty-four villages. Unlike most of the Naga tribes the **Pochury** have some such clans, which have pan-tribal distribution. In the Meluri area the **Pochury** people had a monopoly over salt water, spinning, wooden work, leather work and stone work.

The **Rengma** are divided into two major territorial groups, **Ntenye** (northern) and **Nzong** (southern) groups. The **Rengma** occupy the spur of the ridge running from the **Nidzukru** hill to the Wokha hill. These two groups of the **Rengma** speak different dialects. The facts remain that one section of the **Rengma,** which had migrated to **Mikir** hills in Assam gradually, abandoned many aspects of the Naga culture and language. The **Rengma** in the past maintained certain institutionalized interrelationships at inter-village level mainly by arranging a special feast called **gwa-tho.** The **Rengma** depended on the **Lotha, Angami** and **Sema** for salt, but the former produced cotton in plenty and traded the same with the **Angami.** The **Rengma** have been famous as expert smiths and their spear heads daos were traded over the whole of the Naga Hills areas.

The **Sangtam** are also divided into two main territorial groups located in Chare circle and Kiphire and Tuensang District in eastern Nagaland, and speak two forms of same dialect. The **Sema** are one of the major and widely scattered Naga tribes of Nagaland. They are mainly concentrated in the Zunheboto District of Nagaland but their settlements may also be found in Kohima, Mokokchung and Tuensang districts, besides in neighbouring Assam.

The **Yimchunger** Nagas form a small community. This tribe is divided into three main sub tribes—the **Tikir Makware,** and the **Chirr** speaking different dialects. Endogamy at sub-tribal level is maintained in respective territories. Unlike the term **Zeliangrong** now increasingly being used by the members of three tribes, the **Zemi, Liangmei** and **Rongmei,** to identify and project themselves as a single ethno-cultural entity, the term **Zeliang** is used and recognized at administrative level in Nagaland. Thus the **Kabui** or the **Rongmei** tribe in Nagaland is separately recognized at administrative level. The fact that the **Zemi, Liangmei** and the **Rongmei** tribesmen who live scattered in distant places in the past, had broken the genealogical base and the moiety system of the **Zeliangrong** people in the long run. The processes of tribalisation, detribalisation and sanskritisation have affected the **Zeliangrong** people in different habitats, in the hills and the plains in different degree.

It was **Jadoniang** who revive and reformed the **Rongmei** religion and started the heraka cult in 1925, by amalgamating the Zemi, Liangmei and the **Rongmei.** After his death, Rani **Gaidinliu** popularized this cult. Besides this cult the rituals like **nga-ngai** (and also **chaga**) provide a symbol and basis for tribal solidarity. Like **Zeliangrong** the word **Chakhesang** is also an acronym formed by letters derived from the names of three tribes. The **Chakhru** and the **Khezha,** who form the main ethnic segments within the **Chakhesang,** are linguistically and culturally close to the **Angami** proper or the **Tengima** (western Angami). These two tribes, located in Phek District, were called as the eastern **Angami** during the British period. The **Chakhesang** people do not form a single endogamous group. Endogamy continues to be maintained at the sub tribal level. The three tribal segments (**Chakhru, Khezha,** and **Sangtam**) live in their respective territories, speak their own dialects, and variously practice and follow endogamy and other institutional principles of tribeship. But the **Zeliangrong** are clan exogamy by the customary law. Occupying a particular hill range the **Zounuo-Keyhonuo** was markedly conscious of their tribal identity even in the historical past in a number of ways. The tribe was regarded by the people as the largest unit of internal peace. Killing of a non-**Zounuo-Keyhonuo** Naga was not regarded as a crime. It was rather admired. Outside the **Zounuo-Keyhonuo** territory lived tribes such as the **Chakhru, Kheza, Mao** and others, occupying their own territories, and maintaining their distinct identities.

Distributed in ten original tribal villages the **Zounuo-Keyhonuo** tribes' men regard their tribal territory as their ancestral land. They believe that their villages were established by the descendants of their tribal ancestors **Zounuo** and **Keyhonuo** who themselves had established **Kigwema** and **Viswema** villages respectively. This believe is buttressed by the existence of a tribal genealogical chart linking the founders of all the villages of the tribe with the tribal ancestors on the one hand and connecting through moieties the numerous clans/lineages of each village within the same genealogical/segmentary (pyramidal) structure, on the other. The persistence of tribe depended indeed as much upon the conviction of the **Zunuo-Keyhonuo** people on this genealogical connectedness at maximal tribal level, as on their possession of common kinship, ritual, dialectical and cultural traits and oral traditions, besides their territorial affiliations.

Of the five communities notified as STs in Nagaland, the Naga constitutes 98.2 per cent. Sema, Konyak, Ao, Lotha, Chakhesang, Angami, Phom, etc. are major Naga sub-tribes, each having more than one lakh population. Kuki is the second largest ST in the state.

EDUCATION

The literacy rate for Nagaland in 2011 works out to 79.6% for the population 7 years and above. The corresponding figures for males and females were 82.8% and 76.1%, respectively, in 2011. In Nagaland, there are two Universities.

Administrative Training Institute, Kohima

The Administrative Training Institute, Kohima is the Apex Training Institute in the State of Nagaland. It was established in 1972 with the objective to keep updating and enhancing professional knowledge and skills needed for better performance of individuals and organizations, to promote better understanding of professional requirements and bringing about the right attitudinal orientation. The Administrative Training Institute aspires to identify the training needs of all categories of government servants, design appropriate training programmes and impart training effectively to the civil servants in the State.

Nagaland University (Central University)

Nagaland University was established on 6.9.1994. Though the act was passed in 1989. Its Head Quarters is at Lumami, Nagaland. It has jurisdiction over the whole of the State of Nagaland. It has affiliated 39 colleges. It has campuses in Kohima, Lumami and Medsiphema (School of Agricultural Sciences and Rural Development, SASRD), 25 Departments and 4 Schools of Studies.

The Global Open University, Nagaland

The Global Open University, Nagaland has been established under the provisions of The Global Open University Act 2006 (Act 3 of 2006) of the Government of Nagaland with a view to introducing vocational, job oriented and employment centric education in the North-East in general and in the State of Nagaland in particular. The State Government of Nagaland has taken bold steps in strengthening the activities of The Global Open University, Nagaland for enabling the World Institution Building Programme (WIBP) to develop adequate infrastructure in Nagaland in general and at Wokha, Kohima and Dimapur in particular.

ECONOMY

Nagaland is predominantly an agrarian economy with more than 70 per cent of the population dependent on agriculture for their livelihood with agriculture and allied activities contributing 28.07 per cent of the Gross State Domestic Product (GSDP). The Gross State Domestic Product (GSDP) which is defined as the total value of all goods and services produced within the State economy at a given time period (usually a year) is an important indicator broadly used to study the progress and growth of the economy. It portrays the sectoral composition and its contribution to the economy of the State.

The Gross State Domestic Product (GSDP) 2016-17 (A.E) at current prices is estimated to grow at 9.91 per cent as against 5.35 per cent achieved in 2015-16 (Q.E). In absolute terms, the GSDP at current prices is estimated to have increased from ₹ 19,214 crore to ₹ 21,119 crore during the corresponding years. At constant price the GSDP 2016-17 (A.E) is estimated to increase to ₹ 14,917 crore from ₹ 14,337 crore in 2015-16 (Q.E) registering a growth of 4.04 per cent.

GSDP Current and Constant at Market Prices *(₹ in Crore)*

GSDP	2011-12	2012-13	2013-14	2014-15 (P)	2015-16 (Q.E)	2016-17 (A.E)
Current	12177	14121	16584	18237	19214	21119
Constant	12177	12868	13793	14234	14337	14917

P-Provisional, Q.E-Quick Estimates, A.E-Advance Estimates

Growth Rate of GSDP Current and Constant at Market Prices

(In percentage)

GSDP	2012-13	2013-14	2014-15 (P)	2015-16 (Q.E)	2016-17 (A.E)
Current	15.97	17.44	9.97	5.35	9.91
Constant	5.68	7.19	3.20	0.72	4.04

P-Provisional, Q.E-Quick Estimates, A.E-Advance Estimates

INDUSTRY

Until the early 1970s, only cottage industries (*e.g.*, weaving, woodwork, basketry, and pottery) existed in the state. Lack of raw materials, financial resources, and power, as well as poor transport and communications, all hindered the industrial growth. Dimapur, the state's leading industrial centre, now has a sugar mill and distillery, a brick factory, and a television assembly plant. Other industries in the state include a khandsari (molasses) mill, rice mills, fruit-canning plants, a paper and pulp factory, a plywood factory, and cabinet and furniture factories.

Industrial Growth Centre

An Industrial Growth Centre with high standard infrastructure is being set up at Ganeshnagar near Dimapur. The Growth Centre would provide dedicated Power, sufficient water supply and communication facilities besides other facilities like banks, post offices, fire station, police station, etc. in an industry friendly environment.

Export Promotion Industrial Park

An Export Promotion Industrial Park with state of the art and environment friendly industrial infrastructure and facilities is being set up at Ganeshnagar near Dimapur. The Park, spread over an area of around 80 acres and adjacent to the Industrial Growth Centre, would provide industrial plots as well as ready built Standard Design Factories, state of the art Convention Centre with hi-tech communication services, secretarial services, besides other facilities.

Nagaland Industrial Development Corporation Limited (NIDC)

The Nagaland Industrial Development Corporation Limited (NIDC) is a Government of Nagaland undertaking, incorporated on March 26, 1970 with a mandate to assist, develop and promote industrial growth in the State. Besides funding long-term needs of industrial ventures by way of loans and capital infusion, NIDC is instrumental in development of infrastructure, providing technical and commercial know-how to entrepreneurs. In the backdrop of the liberalized National economy, NIDC is undergoing organizational and operational restructuring to meet the demands of a dynamic economy.

Large and Medium Industries of Nagaland

1. Nagaland Sugar Mill Company Limited, Dimapur
2. Nagaland Pulp & Paper Company Limited, Tuli, Distt.—Mokokchung

3. Citronella Oil Industries, Mongsuyuyumi Village, Distt.—Mokokchung
4. Pineapple Fibre Plant, Baghty Village, Distt.—Wokha
5. Mechanised Brick Plant, Tolumi Village, Distt.—Dimapur
6. Nagaland Plywood Factory, Distt.—Mon

Industrial Estates of Nagaland

1. Dimapur Industrial Estates
2. Kohima Industrial Estates
3. Tuensang Industrial Estates

POWER

The State is still dependent on the neighbouring States of Meghalaya and Assam for its power requirement. With the commissioning of the 75 MW Hydel Project at Doyang, 24 MW Hydel Project at Likhimro the power availability in the state is expected to improve and supply of adequate power to industry available. Preliminary surveys have revealed the potential of generating 2000 MW in the Tizu-Zungki basin.

Doyang Hydro Electricity Project (Neepco Ltd.)

It is a new addition to the Tourist spots in Wokha district. This Hydel Project has a large quantity of water impounded in a dam. This dam is visible from many hilltop villages in the surrounding areas. Doyang Hydro Electric Project of the North Eastern Electric Power Corporation Ltd. is situated in Wokha Sadar, 26 kms from the Wokha district Hqrs., and is under the administrative jurisdiction of the Addl. Deputy Commissioner, Doyang, which is presently being administered by the Deputy Commissioner, Wokha.

Oil and Natural Gas Commission (ONGC, Changpang)

Changpang situated in the Lower Lotha Range in the Bhandari Sub-Division. Changpang is situated around 120 kms away from the Wokha District Hqrs. ONGC started survey works as early as 1963 in the Changpang area of Nagaland under Wokha District. The survey report indicated that there are sufficient Hydro Carbon (Crude Oil) deposits all along the Nagaland Foothill adjoining Assam. This belt is geographically known as "SCHUPPEN BELT". ONGC discovered oil in the Changpang area and the trial production started in March, 1981. The area of the SCHUPPEN BELT was found to be highly oil prospective. The Nagaland State Government stopped all ONGC activities on the 2nd of May, 1994, on matters of Government policy. However, presently there are on-goings talks between, the Lotha Public and the Government of Nagaland, and the Government of Nagaland and the ONGC, for the resumption of operation for exploration and production of petroleum products in the Changpang oil fields.

TRANSPORTATION

Roads

The major mode of transportation in Nagaland is by road. Pliable road network and State Highways link with all districts as well as far-flung areas. Nagaland is also connected to the rest of the country by National Highways. Development of roads specifically in the notified industrial zones is being accorded priority. The total length of roads in Nagaland is 12079.8 km which includes national highway, state highways, district and village roads. 996 villages have been linked by roads. The length of National Highway roads is 1546.70 km.

Important National Highways

1. NH-36—Dhansiripur-Dimapur
2. NH-39—Kohima-Dimapur-Chumukedima-Medziphema
3. NH-61—Kohima-Narhema-Tseminya-Wokha-Mokokchung-Chantongia-Merang-Kong-Nagaland/Assam Border
4. NH-150—Kohima-Chizami-Nagaland/Manipur Border
5. NH-155—Mokokchung-Tuensang-Sampurre-Akhegwo-Meluri upto Manipur Border

Railways

The foundation stone for construction of the Dimapur-Zubza railway line was laid by the union minister of Railway in August 2016. Although declared a national project in 2010 work could not start as stipulated due to land issues. A committee has now been constituted to oversee the construction of Dimapur-Zubza connecting Kohima, the State capital (90.54 km). Survey for rail link in the the foot hills of the State from Dimapur—Tizit (246.25 km) has been completed. Construction of the railway up to Kohima will not only ease transportation of goods and passenger but will also boost tourism and other facilities.

Airways

- Name of the airport—Dimapur
- Distance from the State Capital—70.0 km

ADMINISTRATION

In January 1961 the Government of India conferred the status of a state on Nagaland but the state of Nagaland was officially inaugurated on December 1, 1963. It has 60 seats of legislative assembly. One member each represents the state in the Lok Sabha and the Rajya Sabha. The Capital of Nagaland, Kohima is beautifully located in the north-eastern hilly area. The state has 11 administrative districts, 52 blocks and 7 census towns, covering 1428 villages. Unlike most Indian states, Nagaland has been granted a great degree of state autonomy, as well as special powers and autonomy for Naga tribes to conduct their own affairs. Each tribe has a hierarchy of councils—at the village, range and tribal levels dealing with local disputes. There is a special regional council for the Tuensang district, elected by the tribes of the area.

Name of the Districts

1. Dimapur District
2. Kiphire District
3. Kohima District
4. Longleng District
5. Mokokchung District
6. Mon District
7. Peren District
8. Phek District
9. Tuensang District
10. Wokha District
11. Zunheboto District

GAMES OF NAGALAND

The most popular sport in the state by far, is an indigenous form of wrestling. The bouts start with the contestants holding each other's waist girdles. As soon as the signal is given, both the wrestlers try to throw off each other. A combination of various leg tricks and sheer brawn are employed to achieve victory, but the use of hands on an opponent's legs is considered a foul, though hands can be used to hold other parts of the body, waist upwards.

A wrestler is declared the winner if he can throw off his opponent, and in the process, get the trunk of the opponent to touch the ground, taking care not to let his own trunk do so. The wrestler who succeeds in pulling or thrusting down his opponent, or forces him into a kneeling position with both knees and one hand, or one knee and both hands touching the ground simultaneously, also wins. It takes three bouts to decide the result. Naga wrestling is quite popular amongst the Angami, Chakhesang, Zeliang, Rengma and Mao tribes. The sport has acquired an all - Nagaland sports status, and each alternate year a competition is held.

The other prominent sport in Nagaland is—fighting. This sport consists of kicking, solely, with the legs, and is quite similar in technique to Tae-Kwan-Do. The contestants stand apart on their marks and exchange kicks. The use of hands to hit or catch is absolutely forbidden. The barrage of kicks goes on until one party or the other surrenders. The kicks can be inflicted on any part of the body except the groin. This game, most popular amongst the Sema tribe, demands superb strength and agility, speed and awesome leg work.

FESTIVALS

Nagaland is a land of festivals. All the tribes celebrate their distinct seasonal festivals with a pageantry of colour and a feast of music. All the tribes have their own festivals which they hold so dear. They regard their festivals sacrosanct and participation in celebration is compulsory. They celebrate their distinct seasonal festivals with a pageantry of colour and a feast of music. Most of these festivals revolve round agriculture, it being the main-stay of Naga society. About 70 per cent population of Nagaland is directly dependent on agriculture and lives in a thousand and odd villages situated on high hill tops or slopes overlooking verdant valleys humming with murmuring streams. In this blissful setting Nagas enjoy the blessing of Nature with rare gusto striking the onlookers with awe and admiration. In most of the places agriculture consists of monocrop.

Although some religious and spiritual sentiments are inter woven into secular rites and rituals, the pre-dominant theme of the festivals is offering of prayers to a Supreme Being having different names in different Naga dialects. At these festivals, the spirit of Gods is propitiated with sacrifices by the Village Shaman for a bountiful harvest either before the sowing or on the eve of harvest. Some of the important festivals are Sekrenyi, Moatsu, Tuluni and Tokhu Emong.

ART AND CRAFTS

The various crafts and art that were known to the early Nagas and are still carried out to this day are:

Basketry

Naga storage and carry baskets women from fine strips of cane and bamboo are well known and sought after for their utility as well as aesthetic value. The cane baskets of Khonoma village are particularly well known for their intricate weaves. The cane baskets and containers woven by the Khiamngan weavers in the Tuensang District are also known for their fineness and delicacy of work that gives it a lace-like appearance. Headgears and mats are also woven from fine bamboo and cane strips. In the recent years, entrepreneurs have utilized the skills of these craftsmen to weave beautiful cane furniture that are being marketed in the local as well as outside market.

Weaving

Naga women are excellent weavers and the colourful shawls, bags and jackets woven by them are extremely popular. The loin loom is commonly used for weaving, although, in recent years the fly shuttle loom has become popular with the weavers. Each tribe uses distinguishing colours and motifs that are often based on tribal folklore. Earlier, natural dyes extracted from barks, roots and plants were used for dyeing cotton yarn and woven fabrics. In addition, woven cloth was embellished with beads, cowries shells and goats hair to denote the wealth and status of the weaver. Body cloth symbolizing Feast-giving and Head-taking added to the variety of clothes woven on the backstrap loom. The art of weaving is still popular amongst the Naga women, especially in the rural areas and the woven products of Nagaland have found its way into the National as well as International marker.

Woodcarving

Nagas are excellent woodcarvers. Making using of simple rudimentary tools and implements such as the local dao, hand drill and chisel, skilled craftsmen produce great works of art that local adorn village gates and house posts as well as objects of utility like the common wooden dish. One of the finest specimens that epitomize the skill of the Naga craftsman is to be found at Shangnyu village in Mon District. The work of art at Shangnyu consists of a massive wooden panel that has carvings depicting objects of art as well as those of ritual and utility value. Woodcraft has now been commercialized and craftsmen have been able to use their traditional skills to generate income for themselves. The Diezephe Craft village in Dimapur District is a good example of a craft concentrated village where the major source of income is from woodcraft.

Metal Work

Iron tin and brass were used to produce weapons as well items of utility and ornaments. The Konyak blacksmiths were famous for their works in the early days and their products were in great demand in the plains of

Assam. To this day, the local dao, spears, chisels, ornaments and other items of utility are still made by local blacksmith whose skills are highly valued in society. In addition, jewellery and beadwork is also popular with local craftsmen. Naga festivals are a testimony to the fascination and love the Naga tribesmen have for art and craft. The colour and beauty of the traditional attires symbolize the wealth and status of the wearer as well as the skill of the maker. The abundance of raw material, the splendid environment and the inherent skills of the people have all played a role in generating a rich history of art and craft in Nagaland. The resurgence of art and craft in recent times has enabled the traditional craftsman and artisan to earn as he creates.

PLACE OF INTEREST

The Second World War Cemetery, Kohima

War Cemetery, a symbolic memorial raised as a citation for the supreme human sacrifices made by the officers and men of the allied forces, to halt the tide of the Japanese onslaught during the Second World War. This was their lost post. The Commonwealth War Graves Commission meticulously maintains this Cemetery.

Kohima Village (Barra Basti)

This is where Kohima began, according to Naga belief. Barra basti, the big village, is reputedly the second ranking village in all Asia for its sheer size but there is a lot more to the village than its dimensions. There is, for instance, a ceremonial gateway—the traditional entrance to all Naga Villages—carved with defensive motifs of warriors and guns, and the symbols of prosperity the Mithun. Further up and to the side of the road, the old gate still stands in its own little shelter, still respected in its retirement. And still further into the heart of the steeply—rising Alage is a house built in the traditional Naga style with the upthrust crossed 'horns' crowning the gable, carved Mithun heads to indicate the status of the owners, a huge basket granary in the Verandah, and a trough in which to make rice beer for the whole community.

Khonoma Village

The pride of Khonoma is its ancient bastion approached through a traditional carved gate, up a flight of steep stone steps, and on to the highest point in the village. Here the Naga warriors made their last stand against the British in 1879. A simple white pillar commemorates G.H. Damant, Maj. C.R. Cook, Lt. H.H. Forbes and Sub. Maj. Nurbir Sai who died in fighting the Nagas in Khonoma.

Mount Tiyi

It is a hill with mysterious legends. It is believed by all Nagas that it is the abode of the departed souls. In local folklores, it is said that there once existed an orchard which could be traced by the lucky ones only. Colourful Rhododendrons are found clasping the rocks and cliffs. The peak offers a panaromic view of the villages, hills and valleys.

Dzukou Valley

This interesting valley, behind Japfu Peak, looks like a mown lawn from a distance and is watered by a meandering stream which often freezes in winter. In spring it is rich with wild flowers and pink and white rhododendrons. There are also interesting caves in the low hillocks that cluster inside the valley. The best time for trekking is November to March.

The State Museum, Kohima

A fascinating place filled with dioramas showing the lifestyles of the many individual tribes of Nagas, carved gateposts, status pillars to record feasts of honour, and traditional jewellery. An essential item used in Naga jewellery is the seashell. Visitors should also examine the ceremonial drum housed in a shed of its own in the grounds of the museum. The drum not only looks like a huge, dugout war canoe, but it also has a figurehead on its stem, stylised waves painted on its prow and paddle-like drum-strikers. These cultural pointer lend support to a Naga belief that their ancestors came from the sea. Scholars speculate that the ancestors of the Nagas were venture some seafarers from Sumatra who settled in the mountains of North-East India after a long migration but still retained memories of their Island's past in their legends, ceremonial jewellery and their great village drums.

Dimapur

Dimapur, from a Kachari word 'Dimasa' after the river which flows through it, is the gateway to Nagaland and its only railhead. The only airport of the state is also here. It is an important trade and commercial Centre on National Highway No. 39, and wears a rather cosmopolitan look. In the medieval ages, it was the capital of the Kachari rulers. In the heart of the town there is an old relic of the Kachari Kingdom which speaks about the once prosperous era. Among other places of interest for the tourist are Ruth's and Haralu emporia where one can see women weaving exquisite Naga shawls on traditional looms, and also make purchases of traditional handicrafts.

Other Places of Interest are: Mokokchung, Satoi range, Wokha, Phek, Zunheboto, Japfu Peak and Mount Totsu.

SOBRIQUETS/NICKNAMES

- "Gateway of Nagaland", "The Commercial Hub of Nagaland", "Melting Pot"—Dimapur
- "Highland City", "Misty City"—Kohima
- "Cultural Capital of Nagaland", "Picture Perfect City", "Aomolung", "Nagaland's Trendsetter"—Mokokchung
- "Rice Bowls of Nagaland"—Jalukie Valley; Tsurang-Changki Valley
- "Serpentine Town"—Tuensang

NAGALAND : AT A GLANCE

- Area (in sq. km.) : 16,579 sq. km. (0.5% of India's area)
- Latitude : 25°6′N to 27°4′N
- Longitude : 93°20′E to 95°15′E
- Forest Area (in sq. km.) : 12,489 (75.33% of State's Geographic Area)
- No. of Districts : 11
- Name of the Districts : Dimapur, Kiphire, Kohima, Longleng, Mokokchung, Mon, Peren, Phek, Tuensang, Wokha, Zunheboto
- Lok Sabha Constituencies : one
- Rajya Sabha Seat : one
- Vidhan Sabha Constituencies : 60
- Nature of Legislature : Unicameral
- Capital : Kohima
- Languages : English, Angami, Ao, Chang, Konyak, Lotha, Sangtam etc
- Total Population (as per 2011 census) : 19,78,502 (0.16% of India's population)
- Male : 10,24,649
- Female : 9,53,853
- Decadal Growth (2001-2011) : –0.6%
- Literacy Rate : 79.6%
- Male Literacy Rate : 82.8%

• Female Literacy Rate	:	76.1%
• Density (per sq. km.)	:	119
• Sex Ratio (per 1000 males)	:	931
• No. of Universities	:	2
		1. Nagaland University (Central University)
		2. The Global Open University
• No. of National Parks	:	One (Intangki National Park, Dimapur)
• State Animal	:	Mithun
• State Bird	:	Blyth's tragopan
• State Flower	:	Rhododendron
• State Tree	:	Alder
• Important Tribes	:	Angami, Ao, Chakhesang, Chang, Chirr, Khiemnungan, Konyak, Lotha, Phom, Rengma, Sangtam, Sema, Tikhir
• Major Festivals	:	Sekrenyi, Moatsu, Tuluni and Tokhu Emong
• Name of National Highways	:	NH-36, NH-39, NH-61, NH-150, NH-155

OBJECTIVE QUESTIONS

1. What is the area of Nagaland?
A. 15,459 sq. km. B. 16,579 sq. km.
C. 17,000 sq. km. D. None of these

2. Nagaland is situated on the latitude between
A. 20°6′N to 25°5′N B. 25°6′N to 27°4′N
C. 30°5′N to 32°5′N D. None of these

3. What is the longitude of the Nagaland state?
A. 90°5′E to 92°2′E B. 91°6′E to 92°5′E
C. 93°20′E to 95°15′E D. None of these

4. Total number of districts in Nagaland is
A. 12 B. 11
C. 15 D. None of these

5. Nagaland Legislative Assembly consists of
A. 70 members B. 60 members
C. 50 members D. None of these

6. What is the name of the capital of Nagaland?
A. Kohima B. Dimapur
C. Wokha D. None of these

7. Representation of Nagaland in Lok Sabha is
A. one B. two
C. three D. None of these

8. Representation of Nagaland in Rajya Sabha is
A. two B. three
C. one D. None of these

9. According to 2011 census, total population of Nagaland is
A. 19,78,502 B. 29,50,541
C. 17,51,231 D. None of these

10. According to 2011 census, total male population of Nagaland is
A. 9,42,000 B. 10,24,649
C. 12,43,214 D. None of these

11. According to 2011 census, total female population of Nagaland is
A. 9,00,000 B. 9,53,853
C. 5,43,214 D. None of these

12. Number of National Parks in Nagaland is ....
A. 4 B. 1
C. 2 D. None of these

13. Percentage of forest in Nagaland is
A. 75.33% B. 80.8%
C. 65.4% D. None of these

14. Decadal growth of population in Nagaland (2001-2011) is ....
A. 25.4% B. –0.6%
C. 20% D. None of these

15. According to 2011 census, total literacy rate in Nagaland is
A. 90% B. 75.5%
C. 79.6% D. None of these

16. What is the female literacy rate in Nagaland?
A. 68% B. 73%
C. 76.1% D. None of these

17. In Nagaland, male literacy rate is
A. 82.8% B. 88.6%
C. 85.5% D. None of these

18. According to 2011 census, density of population in Nagaland is
A. 320 per sq. km. B. 119 per sq. km.
C. 90 per sq. km. D. 11 per sq. km.

19. According to 2011 census, sex ratio in Nagaland is
A. 931 B. 850
C. 950 D. None of these

20. What is the name of the state animal of Nagaland?
A. Mithun B. Hoolock gibbon
C. Black buck D. None of these

21. What is the name of the state bird of Nagaland?
A. Black-necked crane B. Peacock
C. Himalayan monal D. Blyth's tragopan

22. What is the name of the state tree of Nagaland?
A. Alder B. Deodar
C. Sandal D. None of these

23. What is the name of the highest peak of the Nagaland?
A. Mount Saramati B. Blue Mountain
C. Tantlang D. None of these

24. Main crop of the Nagaland state is
A. Rice B. Maize
C. Wheat D. None of these

25. Nazira coal fields is situated in
A. Mon district B. Peren district
C. Phek district D. None of these

26. Nagaland Industrial Development Corporation Limited (NIDC) was established in
A. 1970 B. 1980
C. 1975 D. None of these

27. Longest National Highway of Nagaland is
A. NH-39 B. NH-61
C. NH-36 D. None of these

28. In Nagaland, airport is situated in
A. Dimapur B. Kohima
C. Wokha D. None of these

29. In Nagaland, Administrative Training Institute is located at
A. Kohima B. Dimapur
C. Wokha D. None of these

30. Nagaland University was established in
A. 1994 B. 1990
C. 2001 D. None of these

31. Dimapur is also known as
A. Gateway of Nagaland
B. Rice Bowls of Nagaland
C. Cultural Capital of Nagaland
D. None of these

32. Cultural capital of Nagaland is
A. Mokokchung
B. Kohima
C. Dimapur
D. None of these

33. Which of the following city is also known as 'Highland City' of Nagaland?
A. Kohima
B. Dimapur
C. Tuensang
D. None of these

34. Majority of population of Nagaland is
A. Hindu
B. Muslim
C. Christian
D. Sikh

35. In Nagaland, total forest area is
A. 12,489 sq. km.
B. 7,452 sq. km.
C. 5,432 sq. km
D. None of these

ANSWERS

1	2	3	4	5	6	7	8	9	10
B	B	C	B	B	A	A	C	A	B
11	**12**	**13**	**14**	**15**	**16**	**17**	**18**	**19**	**20**
B	B	A	B	C	C	A	B	A	A
21	**22**	**23**	**24**	**25**	**26**	**27**	**28**	**29**	**30**
D	A	A	A	A	A	B	A	A	A
31	**32**	**33**	**34**	**35**					
A	A	A	C	A					

●●●●●●

8

SIKKIM

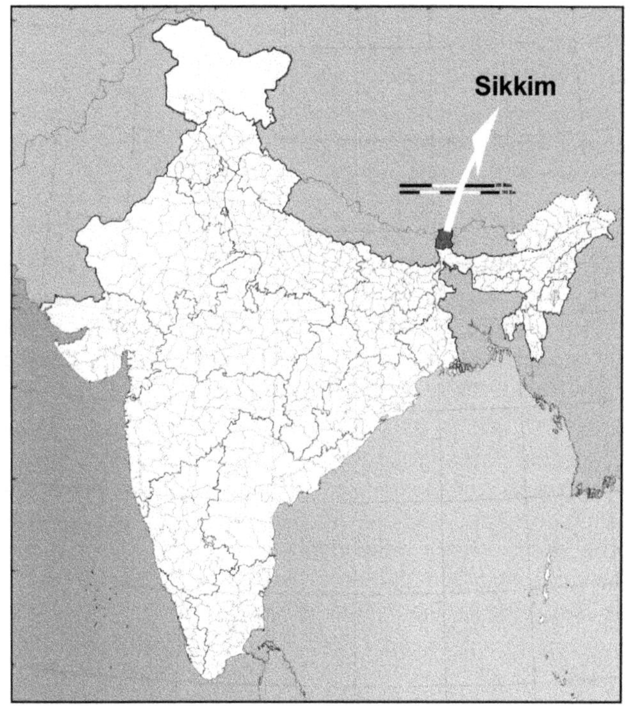

Location of Sikkim in India

Sikkim is a landlocked Indian state located in the Himalayan mountains. The state is bordered by Nepal to the west, China's Tibet Autonomous Region to the north and east, and Bhutan to the east. The Indian state of West Bengal lies to the south.

With 610,577 inhabitants as of the 2011 census, Sikkim is the least populous state in India and the second-smallest state after Goa in total area, covering approximately 7,096 km^2 (2,740 square mile). Sikkim is nonetheless geographically diverse due to its location in the Himalayas; the climate ranges from subtropical to high alpine, and Kangchenjunga, the world's third-highest peak, is located on Sikkim's border with Nepal. Sikkim is a popular tourist destination, owing to its culture, scenery and biodiversity. It also has the only open land border between India and China. Sikkim's capital and largest city is Gangtok.

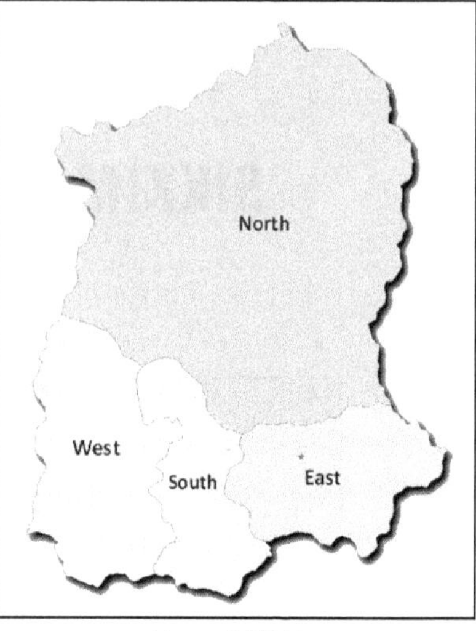

Map of Sikkim

According to legend, the Buddhist guru Padmasambhava visited Sikkim in the 8th century AD, introduced Buddhism and foretold the era of the Sikkimese monarchy. Sikkim's Namgyal dynasty was established in 1642. Over the next 150 years, the kingdom witnessed frequent raids and territorial losses to Nepalese invaders. In the 19th century, it allied itself with British India, eventually becoming a British protectorate. In 1975, a referendum abolished the Sikkimese monarchy, and the territory was merged with India.

Sikkim has 11 official languages: Nepali (which is its lingua franca), Sikkimese, Lepcha, Tamang, Limbu, Newari, Rai, Gurung, Magar, Sunwar and English. English is taught in schools and used in government documents. The predominant religions are Hinduism and Vajrayana Buddhism. Sikkim's economy is largely dependent on agriculture and tourism, and as of 2014 the state had the third-smallest GDP among Indian states, although it is also among the fastest-growing.

TOPONYMY

The most widely accepted origin theory of the name Sikkim is that it is a combination of two Limbu words: su, which means “new”, and khyim, which means “palace” or “house”. The name is believed to be a reference to the palace built by the state's first ruler, Phuntsog Namgyal. The Tibetan name for Sikkim is Drenjong, which means “valley of rice”, while the Bhutias call it Beyul Demazong, which means “the hidden valley of rice”. The Lepcha people, the original inhabitants of Sikkim, called it Nye-mae-el, meaning “paradise”. In History, Sikkim is known as Indrakil, the garden of the war god Indra.

HISTORY

Founding of the Monarchy

Statue of Guru Rinpoche

Little is known about Sikkim's ancient history, beyond the fact that its original inhabitants were the Lepcha. The earliest historical mention of Sikkim is a record of the passage of the Buddhist saint Padmasambhava, also known as Guru Rinpoche, through the land in the 8th century AD. The Guru is reported to have blessed the land, introduced Buddhism, and foretold the era of monarchy that would arrive in Sikkim centuries later. According to legend, Khye Bumsa, a 14th-century prince from the Minyak House in Kham in eastern Tibet, received a divine revelation instructing him to travel south to seek his fortunes. A fifth-generation descendant of Khye Bumsa, Phuntsog Namgyal, became the founder of Sikkim's monarchy in 1642, when he was consecrated as the first Chogyal, or priest-king, of Sikkim by the three venerated lamas at Yuksom.

Phuntsog Namgyal was succeeded in 1670 by his son, Tensung Namgyal, who moved the capital from Yuksom to Rabdentse. In 1700, Sikkim was invaded by the Bhutanese with the help of the half-sister of the Chogyal, who had been denied the throne. The Bhutanese were driven away by the Tibetans, who restored the throne to the Chogyal ten years later. Between 1717 and 1733, the kingdom faced many raids by the Nepalese in the west and Bhutanese in the east, culminating with the destruction of the capital Rabdentse by the Nepalese. In 1791, China sent troops to support Sikkim and defend Tibet against the Gorkha Kingdom. Following the subsequent defeat of Gorkha, the Chinese Qing Dynasty established control over Sikkim.

Sikkim During the British Raj

The 1876 map of Sikkim, depicting Chomto Dong Lake in northern Sikkim. However, the whole of Chumbi and Darjeeling are not depicted as part of Sikkim in the map.

Following the beginning of British rule in neighbouring India, Sikkim allied with Britain against their common adversary, Nepal. The Nepalese attacked Sikkim, overrunning most of the region including the Terai. This prompted the British East India Company to attack Nepal, resulting in the Gurkha War of 1814. Treaties signed between Sikkim and Nepal resulted in the return of the territory annexed by the Nepalese in 1817. However, ties between Sikkim and the British weakened when the latter began taxation of the Morang region. In 1849, two British physicians, Sir Joseph Dalton Hooker and Dr. Archibald Campbell, the latter being in charge of relations between the British and Sikkimese governments, ventured into the mountains of Sikkim unannounced and unauthorised. The doctors were detained by the Sikkimese government, leading to a punitive British expedition against the kingdom, after which the Darjeeling district and Morang were annexed to British India in 1853. The invasion led to the Chogyal of Sikkim becoming a titular ruler under the directive of the British governor. In 1890, Sikkim became a British protectorate, and was gradually granted more sovereignty over the next three decades.

After Indian Independence

In 1947, when India became independent, a popular vote rejected Sikkim's joining the Indian Union. Although a treaty was made between India and Sikkim in 1950, in the interest of Prime Minister Jawaharlal Nehru. That Indo-Sikkim treaty made Sikkim an Indian protectorate status. Sikkim came under the suzerainty of India, which controlled its external affairs, defence, diplomacy and communications, but Sikkim otherwise retained administrative autonomy.

A state council was established in 1953 to allow for constitutional government under the Chogyal. Meanwhile, the Sikkim National Congress demanded fresh elections and greater representation for Nepalis in Sikkim. Palden Thondup Namgyal, the Chogyal at the time, proved to be extremely unpopular with the people, and in 1973, riots in front of the Chogyal's palace led to a formal request for protection from India.

In 1975, the Prime Minister of Sikkim appealed to the Indian Parliament for Sikkim to become a state of India. In April of that year, the Indian Army took over the city of Gangtok and disarmed the Chogyal's palace guards. Thereafter, a referendum was held in which 97.5 per cent of voters supported abolishing the monarchy, effectively approving union with India. Although the union was presented as the will of the people by the Indian authorities, the merger was widely criticized as an annexation and India was accused of exploiting the ethnic divide and rigging the referendum. On 16 May 1975, Sikkim became the 22nd state of the Indian Union, and the monarchy was abolished. To enable the incorporation of the new state, the Indian Parliament amended the Indian Constitution. First, the 35th Amendment laid down a set of conditions that made Sikkim an "Associate State", a special designation not used by any other state. Later, the 36th Amendment repealed the 35th Amendment, and made Sikkim a full state, adding its name to the First Schedule of the Constitution.

Recent History

In 2000, the seventeenth Karmapa, Urgyen Trinley Dorje, who had been confirmed by the Dalai Lama and accepted as a tulku by the Chinese government, escaped from Tibet, seeking to return to the Rumtek Monastery in Sikkim. Chinese officials were in a quandary on this issue, as any protests to India would mean an explicit endorsement of India's governance of Sikkim, which China still recognised as an independent state occupied by India. The Chinese government eventually recognised Sikkim as an Indian state in 2003, on the condition that India officially recognise Tibet as a part of China; New Delhi had originally accepted Tibet as a part of China in 1953 during the government of Jawaharlal Nehru. The 2003 agreement led to a thaw in Sino-Indian relations, and on 6 July 2006, the Sikkimese Himalayan pass of Nathu La was opened to cross-border trade, becoming the first open border between India and China. The pass, which had previously been closed since the 1962 Sino-Indian War, was an offshoot of the ancient Silk Road.

GEOGRAPHY

Nestling as it does in the Himalayan mountains, the state of Sikkim is characterized by mountainous terrain. Almost the entire state is hilly, with an elevation ranging from 280 metres (920 feet) to 8,586 metres (28,169 feet). The summit of Kanchenjunga—the world's third-highest peak—is the state's highest point, situated on the border between Sikkim and Nepal. For the most part, the land is unfit for agriculture because of the rocky, precipitous slopes. However, some hill slopes have been converted into terrace farms. Numerous snow-fed streams have carved out river valleys in the west and south of the state. These streams combine into the major Teesta River and its tributary, the Rangeet, which flow through the state from north to south. About a third of the state is heavily forested.

Sunrise over Kanchenjunga, as seen from Sikkim. Standing 8,586 metres (28,169 ft) tall, it is the second-highest peak in India and the third-highest on the Earth.

The Ban Jhakri Waterfall

Park near Gangtok.

The Himalayan mountains surround the northern, eastern and western borders of Sikkim. The Lower Himalayas, lying in the southern reaches of the state, are the most densely populated. The state has 28 mountain peaks, more than 80 glaciers, 227 high-altitude lakes (including the Tsongmo, Gurudongmar and Khecheopalri Lakes), five major hot springs, and more than 100 rivers and streams. Eight mountain passes connect the state to Tibet, Bhutan and Nepal.

Sikkim's hot springs are renowned for their medicinal and therapeutic values. Among the state's most notable hot springs are those at Phurchachu, Yumthang, Borang, Ralang, Taram-chu and Yumey Samdong. The springs, which have a high Sulphur content, are located near river banks; some are known to emit hydrogen. The average temperature of the water in these hot springs is 50°C (122°F).

Geology

The hills of Sikkim mainly consist of gneissose and half-schistose rocks, producing generally poor and shallow brown clay soils. The soil is coarse, with large concentrations of iron oxide; it ranges from neutral to acidic and is lacking in organic and mineral nutrients. This type of soil tends to support evergreen and deciduous forests.

The Kanchengyao Himalayan mountains of northern Sikkim

Most of Sikkim is covered by Precambrian rock, which is much younger in age than the hills. The rock consists of phyllitesand schists, and is highly susceptible to weathering and erosion. This, combined with the state's heavy rainfall, causes extensive soil erosion and the loss of soil nutrients through leaching. As a result, landslides are frequent, often isolating rural towns and villages from the major urban centres.

Climate

The state has five seasons: winter, summer, spring, autumn, and a monsoon season between June and September. Sikkim's climate ranges from sub-tropical in the south to tundra in the north. Most of the inhabited regions of Sikkim experience a temperate climate, with temperatures seldom exceeding 28°C (82°F) in summer. The average annual temperature for most of Sikkim is around 18°C (64°F).

Sikkim is one of the few states in India to receive regular snowfall. The snow line ranges from 6,100 metres (20,000 feet) in the north of the state to 4,900 metres (16,100 ft) in the south. The tundra-type region in the north is snowbound for four months every year, and the temperature drops below 0°C (32°F) almost every night. In north-western Sikkim, the peaks are frozen year-round; because of the high altitude, temperatures in the mountains can drop to as low as –40°C (–40°F) in winter.

During the monsoon, heavy rains increase the risk of landslides. The record for the longest period of continuous rain in Sikkim is 11 days. Fog affects many parts of the state during winter and the monsoons, making transportation perilous.

GOVERNMENT AND POLITICS

State Symbols

State Day	16 May (Day of Accession to India)
State Animal	Red panda
State Bird	Blood pheasant
State Tree	Rhododendron
State Flower	Noble orchid

According to the Constitution of India, Sikkim has a parliamentary system of representative democracy for its governance; universal suffrage is granted to state residents. The government structure is organized into three branches:

1. **Executive:** Like all states of India, a governor stands at the head of the executive power of state, just like the president is the head of the executive power in the Union, and is appointed by the President of India. The governor's appointment is largely ceremonial, and his or her main role is to oversee the swearing-in of the Chief Minister. The Chief Minister, who holds the real executive powers, is the head of the party or coalition garnering the largest majority in the state elections. The governor also appoints cabinet ministers on the advice of the Chief Minister.

2. **Legislature:** Sikkim has a unicameral legislature, the Sikkim Legislative Assembly, like most other Indian states. Its state assembly has 32 seats, including one reserved for the Sangha. Sikkim is allocated one seat in each of the two chambers of India's national bicameral legislature, the Lok Sabha and the Rajya Sabha.

The White Hall complex in Gangtok houses the residences of the Chief Minister and Governor of Sikkim.

3. **Judiciary:** The judiciary consists of the Sikkim High Court and a system of lower courts. The High Court, located at Gangtok, has a Chief Justice along with two permanent justices. The Sikkim High Court is the smallest state high court in the country.

In 1975, after the abrogation of Sikkim's monarchy, the Indian National Congress gained a majority in the 1977 elections. In 1979, after a period of instability, a popular ministry headed by Nar Bahadur Bhandari, leader of the Sikkim Sangram Parishad Party, was sworn in. Bhandari held on to power in the 1984 and 1989 elections. In the 1994 elections, Pawan Kumar Chamling of the Sikkim Democratic Front became the Chief Minister of the state. Chamling and his party have since held on to power by winning the 1999, 2004, 2009 and 2014 elections.

SUBDIVISIONS

Sikkim has four districts—East Sikkim, West Sikkim, North Sikkim and South Sikkim. The district capitals are Gangtok, Gyalshing, Mangan and Namchi respectively. These four districts are further divided into subdivisions; Pakyong and Rongli are the subdivisions of the East district, Soreng is the subdivision of the West district, Chungthang is the subdivision of the North district and Ravongla is the subdivision of the South district.

Each of Sikkim's districts is overseen by a Central Government appointee, the district collector, who is in charge of the administration of the civilian areas of the district. The Indian Army has control over a large part of the state, as Sikkim forms part of a sensitive border area with China. Many areas are restricted to foreigners, and official permits are needed to visit them.

FLORA AND FAUNA

Sikkim is situated in an ecological hotspot of the lower Himalayas, one of only three among the eco-regions of India. The forested regions of the state exhibit a diverse range of fauna and flora. Owing to its altitudinal gradation, the state has a wide variety of plants, from tropical species to temperate, alpine and tundra ones, and is perhaps one of the few regions to exhibit such the diversity within such a small area. Nearly 81 per cent of the area of Sikkim comes under the administration of its forest department.

Noble orchid is Sikkim's state flower

Sikkim is home to around 5,000 species of flowering plants, 515 rare orchids, 60 primula species, 36 rhododendron species, 11 oak varieties, 23 bamboo varieties, 16 conifer species, 362 types of ferns and ferns allies, 8 tree ferns, and over 424 medicinal plants. A variant of the Poinsettia, locally known as "Christmas Flower", can be found in abundance in the mountainous state. The Noble Dendrobium is the official flower of Sikkim, while the rhododendron is the state tree.

Rhododendron is state tree; about 40 species of Rhododendron bloom late April - mid May across the state.

Orchids, figs, laurel, bananas, sal trees and bamboo grow in the Himalayan subtropical broadleaf forests of the lower altitudes of Sikkim. In the temperate elevations above 1,500 metres (4,900 feet) there are Eastern Himalayan broadleaf forests, where oaks, chestnuts, maples, birches, alders, and magnolias grow in large numbers, as well as Himalayan subtropical pine forests, dominated by Chir pine. Alpine-type vegetation is typically found between the altitude of 3,500 to 5,000 metres (11,500 to 16,400 feet). In lower elevations are found juniper, pine, firs, cypresses and rhododendrons from the Eastern Himalayan sub-alpine conifer forests. Higher up are Eastern Himalayan alpine shrub and meadows, home to a broad variety of rhododendrons and wildflowers.

The red panda is the state animal of Sikkim.

The fauna of Sikkim include the snow leopard, musk deer, Himalayan tahr, red panda, Himalayan marmot, Himalayan serow, Himalayan goral, muntjac, common langur, Asian black bear, clouded leopard, marbled cat, leopard cat, dhole, Tibetan wolf, hog badger, binturong, and Himalayan jungle cat. Among the animals more commonly found in the alpine zone are yaks, mainly reared for their milk, meat, and as a beast of burden.

The avifauna of Sikkim include the impeyan pheasant, crimson horned pheasant, snow partridge, Tibetan snow cock, bearded vulture and griffon vulture, as well as golden eagles, quails, plovers, woodcocks, sandpipers, pigeons, Old World flycatchers, babblers and robins. Sikkim has more than 550 species of birds, some of which have been declared endangered.

Sikkim also has a rich diversity of arthropods, many of which remain unstudied; the most studied Sikkimese arthropods are butterflies. Of the approximately 1,438 butterfly species found in the Indian subcontinent, 695 have been recorded in Sikkim. These include the endangered Kaiser-i-hind, the Yellow Gorgon and the Bhutan Glory.

ECONOMY

Elaichi, or cardamom, is the chief cash crop of Sikkim.

Sikkim's nominal state gross domestic product (GDP) was estimated at ₹ 2224791 lakh in 2017-18, constituting the third-smallest GDP among India's 29 states. The state's economy is largely agrarian, based on the terraced farming of rice and the cultivation of crops such as maize, millet, wheat, barley, oranges, tea and cardamom. Sikkim produces more cardamom than any other Indian state, and is home to the largest cultivated area of cardamom. Because of its hilly terrain and poor transport infrastructure, Sikkim lacks a large-scale industrial base. Brewing, distilling, tanning and watchmaking are the main industries, and are mainly located in the southern regions of the state, primarily in the towns of Melli and Jorethang. In addition, a small mining industry exists in Sikkim, extracting minerals such as copper, dolomite, talc, graphite, quartzite, coal, zinc and lead. Despite the state's minimal industrial infrastructure, Sikkim's economy has been among the fastest-growing in India since 2000; the state's GDP expanded by 89.93 per cent in 2010 alone. Sikkim has become the first state in India to transition its agriculture to entirely organic cultivation.

Terraced rice paddy fields of Sikkim

In recent years, the government of Sikkim has extensively promoted tourism. As a result, state revenue has increased 14 times since the mid-1990s. Sikkim has furthermore invested in a fledgling gambling industry, promoting both casinos and online gambling. The state's first casino, the Casino Sikkim, opened in March 2009, and the government subsequently issued a number of additional casino licenses and online sports betting licenses. The Play-win lottery has been a notable success in the state.

The opening of the Nathu La pass on 6 July 2006, connecting Lhasa, Tibet, to India, was billed as a boon for Sikkim's economy. Trade through the pass remains hampered by Sikkim's limited infrastructure and government restrictions in both India and China, though the volume of traded goods has been steadily increasing.

TRANSPORT

Air

Pakyong Airport

Prime Minister Narendra Modi on September 24, 2018 inaugurated Sikkim's first-ever airport at Pakyong. Prior to this airport, Sikkim was only state in India remaining without functional airport. Pakyong airport is India's 100th functional airport and one of the country's five highest airports.

The airport is spread over 201 acres and was constructed by Airports Authority of India (AAI). It is located on top of hill about two km above Pakyong village at 4,500 feet above sea level. It was carved from mountain side using massive geo technical 'cut and fill' engineering works. It is located around 60 km from Indo-China border and around 30km away from Gangtok, capital city of Sikkim. It has 1.75 km long runway. It has capacity to handle 50 in-bound and as many out-bound passengers flights. Initially, this airport will cater only to domestic flights, but later provide international flight services connecting Sikkim with other countries (especially neighbouring) like Paro (Bhutan), Kathmandu (Nepal) and Dhaka (Bangladesh).

Roads

A mountain road through Temi Tea Garden.

National Highway 31A and National Highway 31 link Siliguri to Gangtok. Sikkim National Transport runs bus and truck services. Privately run bus, tourist taxi and jeep services operate throughout Sikkim, and also connect it to Siliguri. A branch of the highway from Melli connects western Sikkim. Towns in southern and western Sikkim are connected to the hill stations of Kalimpong and Darjeeling in northern West Bengal. The state is furthermore connected to Tibet by the mountain pass of Nathu La.

Sikkim's roads are maintained by the Border Roads Organisation (BRO), an offshoot of the Indian Army. The roads in southern Sikkim are in relatively good condition, landslides being less frequent in this region. The state government maintains 1,857 kilometres (1,154 miles) of roadways that do not fall under the BRO's jurisdiction.

Rail

Sikkim lacks significant railway infrastructure. The closest major railway stations are Siliguri and New Jalpaiguri in neighbouring West Bengal. However, the New Sikkim Railway Project has been launched to connect the town of Rangpoin Sikkim with Sevoke on the West Bengal border. The five-station line is intended to support both economic development and Indian Army operations, and was initially planned to be completed by 2015, though as of 2013 its construction has met with delays. In addition, the Ministry of Railways proposed plans in 2010 for railway lines linking Mirik to Ranipool.

INFRASTRUCTURE

Sikkim receives most of its electricity from 19 hydroelectric power stations. Power is also obtained from the National Thermal Power Corporation and Power Grid Corporation of India. By 2006, the state had achieved 100 per cent rural electrification. However, the voltage remains unstable and voltage stabilisers are needed. Per capita consumption of electricity in Sikkim was approximately 182 KWh in 2006. The state government has promoted biogas and solar power for cooking, but these have received a poor response and are used mostly for lighting purposes. In 2005, 73.2 per cent of Sikkim's households were reported to have access to safe drinking water, and the state's large number of mountain streams assures a sufficient water supply.

On 8 December 2008, it was announced that Sikkim had become the first state in India to achieve 100 per cent sanitation coverage, becoming completely free of public defecation, thus attaining the status of "Nirmal State".

DEMOGRAPHICS

Population Growth History

Sikkim is India's least populous state, with 610,577 inhabitants according to the 2011 census. Sikkim is also one of the least densely populated Indian states, with only 86 persons per square kilometre. However, it has a high population growth rate, averaging 12.9% per cent between 2001 and 2011. The sex ratio is 890 females per 1,000 males, with a total of 3,23,070 males and 2,87,507 females recorded in 2011. With around 98,000 inhabitants as of 2011, the capital Gangtok is the most significant urban area in the mostly rural state; in 2011, the urban population in Sikkim constituted around 25.2 per cent of the total. In 2017, the average per capita income in Sikkim stood at ₹ 291373.

Sikkimese woman with child in Gangtok.

Ethnicity

Due to a centuries-long population influx from Nepal, the majority of Sikkim's residents are of Nepali ethnic origin. The native Sikkimese consists of the Bhutias, who migrated from the Kham district of Tibet in the 14th century, and the Lepchas, who are believed to have migrated from the Far East. Tibetans reside mostly in the northern and eastern reaches of the state. Migrant resident communities include Biharis, Bengalis and Marwaris, who are prominent in commerce in South Sikkim and Gangtok.

Religion (2011)

Hinduism has been the state's major religion since the arrival of the Nepalis; an estimated 57.8 per cent of the total population are now adherents of the religion. There exist many Hindu temples. Kirateshwar Mahadev Temple is very popular, since it consists of the chardham altogether. Sikkim's second-largest religion is Buddhism, which accounts for 27.3 per cent of the population. Sikkim has 75 Buddhist monasteries, the oldest dating back to the 1700s. Christians in Sikkim are mostly descendants of Lepcha people who were converted by British missionaries in the late 19th century, and constitute around 6.6 per cent of the population. As of 2014, the Evangelical Presbyterian Church of Sikkim is the largest Christian denomination in Sikkim. Other religious minorities include Muslims of Bihari ethnicity and Jains, who each account for roughly one per cent of the population. Traditional religions of the native Sikkimese account for much of the remainder of the population.

Religion in Sikkim (2011)

Religion	Percent
Hinduism	57.8%
Buddhism	27.3%
Christianity	9.9%
Islam	1.4%
Others	3.7%

The Rumtek monastery is among Sikkim's most famous religious monuments.

Although tensions between the Lepchas and the Nepalese escalated during the merger of Sikkim with India in the 1970s, there has never been any major degree of communal religious violence, unlike in other Indian states. Traditional religion of the Lepcha people is Mun, an animist practice which coexists with Buddhism and Christianity.

Languages

Nepali is the lingua franca of Sikkim, while Sikkimese and Lepcha are spoken in certain areas. English and Hindi are also spoken and understood in most of Sikkim. Other languages include Dzongkha, Groma, Gurung, Limbu, Magar, Majhi, Majhwar, Nepal Bhasa, Rai, Sherpa, Sunuwar, Tamang, Thulung, Tibetan, and Yakha.

Culture

Sikkim's Nepalese majority celebrate all major Hindu festivals, including Diwali and Dussera. Traditional local festivals, such as Maghe Sankranti and Bhimsen Puja, are also popular. Losar, Loosong, Saga Dawa, Lhabab Duechen, Drupka Teshi and Bhumchu are among the Buddhist festivals celebrated in Sikkim. During the Losar (Tibetan New Year), most offices and educational institutions are closed for a week. Sikkimese Muslims celebrate Eid ul-Fitr and Muharram. Christmas has also been promoted in Gangtok to attract tourists during the off-season.

The traditional Gumpa dance is being performed in Lachung during the Buddhist festival of Losar.

Western rock music and Indian pop have gained a wide following in Sikkim. Indigenous Nepali rock and Lepcha music are also popular. Sikkim's most popular sports are football and cricket, although hang gliding and river rafting have also grown popular as part of the tourism industry.

Dro-dul Chorten Stupa in Gangtok.

Cuisine

Noodle-based dishes such as thukpa, chowmein, thanthuk, fakthu, gyathuk and wonton are common in Sikkim. Momos—steamed dumplings filled with vegetables, buffalo meat or pork and served with soup—are a popular snack. Beer, whiskey, rum and brandy are widely consumed in Sikkim, as is tongba, a millet-based alcoholic beverage which is also popular in Nepal and Darjeeling. Sikkim has the third-highest per capita alcoholism rate amongst all Indian states, behind Punjab and Haryana.

Media

The southern urban areas of Sikkim have English, Nepali and Hindi daily newspapers. Nepali-language newspapers, as well as some English newspapers, are locally printed, whereas Hindi and English newspapers are printed in Siliguri. Important local dailies and weeklies include Hamro Prajashakti (Nepali daily), Himalayan Mirror (English daily), the Samay Dainik, Sikkim Express (English), Sikkim Now (English), Kanchanjunga Times (Nepali weekly), Pragya Khabar (Nepali weekly) and Himalibela. Furthermore, the state receives regional editions of national English newspapers such as The Statesman, The Telegraph, The Hindu and The Times of India. Himalaya Darpan, a Nepali daily published in Siliguri, is one of the leading Nepali daily newspapers in the region. The Sikkim Herald is an official weekly publication of the government. Online media covering Sikkim include the Nepali newspaper Himgiri, the English news portal Haalkhabar and the literary magazine Tistarangit. Avyakta, Bilokan, the Journal of Hill Research, Khaber Khagaj, Panda, and the Sikkim Science Society Newsletter are among other registered publications.

Internet cafés are well established in the district capitals, but broadband connectivity is not widely available. Satellite television channels through dish antennae are available in most homes in the state. Channels served are largely the same as those available in the rest of India, although Nepali-language channels are also available. The main service providers include Dish TV, Doordarshan and Nayuma.

EDUCATION

In 2011 Sikkim's adult literacy rate was 81.4 per cent: 86.6 per cent for males and 75.6 per cent for females. There is a total of 1,157 schools in the state, including 765 schools run by the state government, seven central government schools and 385 private schools. Twelve colleges and other institutions in Sikkim offer higher education. The largest institution is the Sikkim Manipal University of Technological Sciences, which offers higher education in engineering, medicine and management. It also runs a host of distance education programs in diverse fields. There is two state-run polytechnic schools, the Advanced Technical Training Centre (ATTC) and the Centre for Computers and Communication Technology (CCCT), which offer diploma courses in various branches of engineering. ATTC is situated at Bardang, Singtam, and CCCT at Chisopani, Namchi. Sikkim University began operating in 2008 at Yangang, which is situated about 28 kilometres (17 miles) from Singtam. Many students, however, migrate to Siliguri, Kolkata, Bangalore and other Indian cities for their higher education.

GOVERNMENT SCHEMES/PROGRAMS

Sikkim voluntarily adopted to go organic under the guidance of the Hon'ble Chief Minister. The State, thus, remains a foremost democratic model in the world on organic farming.

The process for bringing the total cultivatable land of 58,168 hectares under organic farming commenced at ground levels from 2010. Agencies accredited by Agriculture and Processed Food Products Export Development Authority are certifying the organic process in Sikkim in three phases.

Organic produce of Sikkim, mostly vegetables, would not only fetch more value for the Sikkimese farmers but also offers multiple benefits to the State. Organic status is going to supplement the ecotourism of Sikkim, another visionary initiative of the Hon'ble Chief Minister.

CHIEF MINISTER'S RURAL HOUSING MISSION

The Chief Minister's Rural Housing mission aims to make Sikkim the first Kutcha House-Free State in the country by 2013. The mission, popularly known as Chief Minister Rural Housing Mission (CMRHM), is one of flagship projects of the fourth-term Sikkim Democratic Front Government. It was launched on September 22, 2010 for eradicating poverty from Sikkim, a target which only the Government of Sikkim can convincingly dream and achieve among all States in the country.

Under the CMRHM, a total of 6,000 Pakka houses for poor Sikkimese families of rural areas are being constructed. The Kutcha houses of the identified beneficiaries living in rural areas converted into Pakka houses costing Rs. 3 lakhs each along with material support in 50 GCI sheets. The selection process starts from Ward in villages from which the nominees are screened at all levels of governance.

Aiming to Make Sikkim a Dairy Hub

Another path-breaking initiative of the State government is the Sikkim Dairy Mission that 2009-2012 envisages multiple long term benefits to the farmers and to open up livelihood avenues for unemployed rural people. The mission was launched with the primary objective to enhance milk production level making Sikkim a milk-surplus State. It also aims to make dairy enterprise a sustainable source of income for the rural populace of Sikkim.

Dairy development is a vital tool to uplift the socio-economic status of the rural farmers. The Sikkim Dairy Mission has a mandate to enhance milk procurement by the dairy cooperatives to substantial volumes per day. Young entrepreneurs are also encouraged to take up dairy farming as an attractive commercial activity.

Among the strategies outlined in the mission, high yielding crossbreed cows are provided to farmers and dairy cooperatives. Sikkim Milk Union is one of the exemplary dairy cooperative in the State and a successful venture of the State government in dairy farming expansion.

FORESTRY & ENVIRONMENT MISSION SIKKIM 2015

Scientific Management of Biodiversity for Posterity

The biodiversity hotspot, Sikkim is famed both within and outside the country for its exemplary measures to protect and preserve its rich flora and fauna. The Himalayan State is blessed with more than 4,500 flowering plants and several globally endangered wildlife species.

Expansion and success of flagship participatory greening programmes of the State government comes under the mission. The State Green Mission, a flagship progamme of the State government, would be made more participatory in coming years under the Forestry and Environment Mission focusing more on flowering and wild fruit varieties.

Creation and management of propagation nursery is another component of the mission. New nurseries will be established in both lowland and highland areas for the purpose of ex-situ conservation and distribution of important indigenous plant species for cultivation, multiplication and trading. The nurseries will be used to propagate rare and endangered plant species with high medicinal and economic values.

MISSION: HEALTHY SIKKIM

Reaching Healthcare Services at People's Doorsteps

The Mission Healthy Sikkim 2015 has been introduced for sustainable development by ensuring equality in healthcare throughout the State and facilitating everyone to attain the highest standard of health. To achieve this aim, the mission has some path-breaking initiatives to comprehensive the health indicators of people in Sikkim with their participation.

The mission is mandated to make available healthcare in socially equitable, accessible and affordable manner within reasonable timeframe, creating partnership between the public, voluntary and private health sector.

SOCIAL SECURITY MISSION

The State government from 1994-95 onwards, has initiated several path-breaking schemes in the field of social justice and security for the vulnerable sections of the Sikkimese society. These landmark initiatives have greatly empowered women, aged, infirm and destitute sections of the society.

Taking social justice a step further, the Social Security Mission 2015 aims to save the succeeding generations from the scourge of poverty, injustice and unemployment. The mission, has time-bound programmes to be completed and achieved by 2015.

In the field of social justice, the State government set up a Sikkim State Commission for Women in 2001 to safeguard the rights and legal entitlements of women in the State. The State government implemented the Prevention of Domestic Violence Act 2005 in 2007 and provided the landmark 40 per cent reservation of seats for women in panchayats and other local bodies. This reservation was increased to 50 per cent ensuring that Sikkimese women have equal representation at the grassroots governance.

Equality for women was also facilitated under the initiative of the Sikkim Succession Act 2008 that mandate equal property rights to Sikkimese daughters. The Sikkimese women are already enjoying 30 per cent reservation in government jobs. Other measures for women implemented by the State government are welfare of destitute women, hostel for working women, widow remarriage scheme and training for women to develop skills for employment.

A major initiative is the Small Family Scheme launched in 1997 which has a package of incentives for women. Grants are provided to 13-years girls to join school and understand the advantages of marrying at a proper age.

Pension to senior citizens, widows and ex-servicemen, crèches for working women's children, inter-caste marriage award scheme and allowances for the differently abled are also a part of the Social Security Mission 2015. The mission implemented the Juvenile Justice Scheme along with Juvenile Justice Act to protect the rights and interests of children in Sikkim. A policy document for improvement and better management of the six existing destitute homes is being framed.

HUMAN RESOURCE DEVELOPMENT MISSION

The Sikkim Human Resource Development Mission aims to empower Young Sikkimese with high quality education and provide access to them to a range of activities and experiences that will help them to make constructive choices and gain skills. The Government of Sikkim is the most youth-friendly government in the country and the Mission represents such connection between the government and youth.

The Mission would be covering the age-bracket of 14 to 35 years further divided into three sub-groups having different concerns and responsibilities.

Sikkim Entrepreneur Centres are to be established and tasked to find placements for skilled youths of Sikkim within and outside the State. Trained youths will be supported in self-entrepreneurship and forming youth self-employment groups by ensuring credit access at affordable and reasonably low interest rates.

SIKKIM CO-OPERATIVE MISSION

Diversifying cooperative activities in Sikkim

The Sikkim Cooperative Mission 2015, helmed by the Cooperation Department, aims to provide a vibrant, self-sustaining and eco-friendly economy with emphasis on employment generation, economic growth and organic agriculture. The mission comprise of various indicators of growth that would be dealt with individually and in general as well.

The Sikkim Cooperative Mission 2015 aims to diversify the cooperative activities in different fields. It emphasizes on establishing Multi-Purpose Cooperative Society (MPCS) at every gram panchayat level. Focus is also on developing cooperatives on construction, handloom, handicraft, animal husbandry, organic farming, tourism and other sectors. These cooperatives would be primarily involved in mobilization of educated unemployed youth.

POVERTY FREE MISSION

The Government vision of eliminating poverty in the State during the formal launch of the Mission "Poverty Free Sikkim 2013". This mission has time-bound and quantified targets for addressing poverty in its many dimensions including income, essential infrastructure and services, governance and exclusion.

UNIVERSAL FINANCIAL INCLUSION

The Chief Minister's Rural Universal Financial Inclusion Programme was launched during the Independence Day Celebration on 15th Aug. 2010. The programme aims to provide universal access to formal banking services to rural Sikkim, provide easy access to formal financial services, ensure inclusive and equitable, growth and empower rural women and to accelerate economic development in rural areas in general. It will also provide insurance services related to house and personal accident to the beneficiary families. Under this programme, about 70,000 rural families in the State will be benefited by opening a savings bank account in the name of the mother of the nuclear family.

SKILL DEVELOPMENT MISSION

The Skill Development Initiative was launched in 2003 and apart from the Directorate of Capacity Building, the State Institute of Capacity Building at Karfectar with state of the art facilities for residential training have been established. Under the Chief Minister's Self-Employment Scheme 5,780 youths have been covered for self-vocational ventures encompassing various agro-based activities and IT and Tourism related vocations. As a pioneering step, livelihood schools have been established in every constituency. Many boys and girls primarily from rural areas are undergoing different kinds of vocational upgradation trainings in such institutes across the state.

CHIEF MINISTER'S SELF RELIANT MISSION (CMSRM)

Government of Sikkim has launched a scheme called CMSRM with objective to empower Sikkimese youth to realise their full potential and understand their roles and responsibilities in making meaningful contribution to the development of scheme. This mission plays the significant role in creating employment opportunity thereby making financial independent by setting micro, small and medium enterprise in the state.

TOTAL LITERACY MISSION

The Total Literacy Mission, seeks to achieve 100 per cent literacy in Sikkim by 2015. Educational system in Sikkim is being revamped as per the Mission.

The Total Literacy Mission is being vigorously implemented across the State and involves every section of the society.

The Hon'ble Chief Minister has termed the Total Literacy Mission as a 'People's Mission' since it would have active participation of panchayats and elected representatives of the constituencies. Services of pre-primary and primary teachers are being engaged extensively by the Mission. One Adult Education Centre is set up in each Gram Panchayat Ward to bring under the education system those adult members of the village who missed school education for various reasons.

The mission further involves each literate person to take responsibility of teaching one illiterate person to achieve the 2015 target.

Computer literacy is another important responsibility tasked to the mission to equip students and teachers at par with rest of the country in terms of information technology.

The mission has formulated a school infrastructure project to strengthen the existing infrastructure of the schools. The target is to provide pucca buildings to all schools, adequate number of toilets, drinking water facilities, continuous power supply, quality laboratories, library facilities and playgrounds as per the school's requirements.

Quality higher and technical education is another priority under the mission by setting up more colleges and polytechnics.

SIKKIM AT A GLANCE

- Coordinates (Gangtok) : 27.33°N 88.62°E
- Country : India
- Admission to Union* : 16 May 1975
- Capital : Gangtok
- Largest City : Gangtok
- No. of Districts : 4
- Name of the Districts : East Sikkim, North Sikkim, South Sikkim, West Sikkim

  Legislature : Unicameral (32 seats)

  Lok Sabha constituencies : 1

  Rajya Sabha Seat : 1

  High Court : Sikkim High Court
- Area

  Total : 7,096 km^2 (2,740 square miles)
- Population (as per census 2011)

  Total : 610,577

  Density : 86/km^2 (220/square mile)
- Literacy : 81.4% (13th)

- Official languages : Nepali (lingua franca), English, Sikkimese, and Lepcha (since 1977), Limbu (since 1981), Newari, Gurung, Magar, Sherpa and Tamang (since 1995), Sunwar (since 1996)

*Assembly of Sikkim abolished monarchy and resolved to be a constituent unit of India. A referendum was held on these issues and majority of the voters voted yes. On May 15, 1975 the President of India ratified a constitutional amendment that made Sikkim the 22nd state of India.

OBJECTIVE QUESTIONS

1. Sikkim is a landlocked Indian state located in the Himalayan Mountain. The state is bordered by Nepal to the west, China's Tibet Autonomous Region to the north and east, and Bhutan to the east. Which Indian state lies to the south.

A. Assam B. West Bengal
C. Tripura D. Manipur

2. Which state is the least populous state in India and the second-smallest state after Goa in total area, covering approximately 7,096 km^2 (2,740 square mile).

A. Sikkim B. Manipur
C. Tripura D. Meghalaya

3. Sikkim is nonetheless geographically diverse due to its location in the Himalayas; the climate ranges from subtropical to high alpine, and......................, the world's third-highest peak, is located on Sikkim's border with Nepal.

A. Nilgiri B. Nandadevi
C. Karakoram D. Kangchenjunga

4. Sikkim is a popular tourist destination, owing to its culture, scenery and biodiversity. It also has the only open land border between India and...............

A. Nepal B. Bhutan
C. China D. Bangladesh

5. According to legend, the Buddhist guru Padmasambhava visited Sikkim in the..............., introduced Buddhism and foretold the era of the Sikkimese monarchy.

A. 8th century AD B. 8th century BC
C. 7th century AD D. 7th century BC

6. Sikkim's Namgyal dynasty was established in .... Over the next 150 years, the kingdom witnessed frequent raids and territorial losses to Nepalese invaders. In the 19th century, it allied itself with British India, eventually becoming a British protectorate.
   A. 1489 B. 1567
   C. 1642 D. 1768

7. When a referendum was abolished the Sikkimese monarchy, and the territory was merged with India.
   A. 1975 B. 1980
   C. 1983 D. 1985

8. How many official languages Sikkim has:
   A. 10 B. 11
   C. 12 D. 13

9. The most widely accepted origin theory of the name Sikkim is that it is a combination of two Limbu words: su, which means "new", and khyim, which means.
   A. Palace B. Good
   C. Way D. Distant

10. The earliest historical mention of Sikkim is a record of the passage of the Buddhist saint Padmasambhava, also known as ....
    A. Guru Rinpoche B. Guru Nimpoche
    C. Guru Simpoche D. Guru Kampoche

11. Where is the tallest statue of the saint in the world, at 36 metres (120 feet) found?
    A. Namchi B. Gangtok
    C. Dispur D. Rangiya

12. Following the beginning of British rule in neighbouring India, Sikkim allied with ....against their common adversary, Nepal.
    A. Germany B. France
    C. Holland D. Britain

13. When Sikkim became a British protectorate, and was gradually granted more sovereignty over the next three decades?
    A. 1880 B. 1885
    C. 1890 D. 1895

14. In 1947, when India became independent, a popular vote rejected Sikkim's joining the Indian Union. Although a treaty was made between India and Sikkim in..........., in the interest of Prime Minister Jawaharlal Nehru.
    A. 1947 B. 1950
    C. 1952 D. 1962

15. That Indo-Sikkim treaty made Sikkim an Indian protectorate status. Sikkim came under the suzerainty of India, which controlled its external affairs, defence, diplomacy and ...., but Sikkim otherwise retained administrative autonomy.

A. Road B. Health
C. Communications D. None of these

16. When a state council was established to allow for constitutional government under the Chogyal.

A. 1953 B. 1962
C. 1971 D. 1975

17. When Sikkim became the 22nd state of the Indian Union, and the monarchy was abolished. To enable the incorporation of the new state, the Indian Parliament amended the Indian Constitution. First, the 35th Amendment laid down a set of conditions that made Sikkim an "Associate State", a special designation not used by any other state. Later, the 36th Amendment repealed the 35th Amendment, and made Sikkim a full state, adding its name to the First Schedule of the Constitution.

A. On 16 June 1975
B. On 16 May 1975
C. On 16 April 1975
D. On 16 March 1975

18. In 2000, the seventeenth Karmapa, Urgyen Trinley Dorje, who had been confirmed by the Dalai Lama and accepted as a .... by the Chinese government, escaped from Tibet, seeking to return to the Rumtek Monastery in Sikkim. Chinese officials were in a quandary on this issue, as any protests to India would mean an explicit endorsement of India's governance of Sikkim, which China still recognised as an independent state occupied by India. The Chinese government eventually recognised Sikkim as an Indian state in 2003, on the condition that India officially recognise Tibet as a part of China.

A. monk B. tulku
C. guru D. acharya

19. The 2003 agreement led to a thaw in Sino-Indian relations, and on 6 July 2006, the Sikkimese Himalayan pass of .... was opened to cross-border trade, becoming the first open border between India and China. The pass, which had previously been closed since the 1962 Sino-Indian War, was an offshoot of the ancient Silk Road.

A. Nathu La
B. Rohtang pass

C. MacMahoan
D. None of these

20. The summit of .... the world's third-highest peak, is the state's highest point, situated on the border between Sikkim and Nepal.
A. Nandadevi
B. Karakoram
C. Kangchenjunga
D. Shivalik

21. Numerous snow-fed streams have carved out river valleys in the west and south of the state. These streams combine into the major .... River and its tributary, the Rangeet, which flow through the state from north to south.
A. Brahmaputra
B. Mandakini
C. Teesta
D. None of these

22. The Himalayan Mountains surround the northern, eastern and western borders of Sikkim. The Lower Himalayas, lying in the southern reaches of the state, are the most densely populated. The state has 28 mountain peaks, more than 80 glaciers, 227 high-altitude lakes (including the Tsongmo, Gurudongmar and Khecheopalri Lakes), five major hot springs, and more than 100 rivers and streams. How many mountain passes connect the state to Tibet, Bhutan and Nepal?
A. 8
B. 7
C. 6
D. 5

23. Sikkim's hot springs are renowned for their medicinal and therapeutic values. Among the state's most notable hot springs are those at Phurchachu, Yumthang, Borang, Ralang, Taram-chu and Yumey Samdong. The springs, which have a high .... content, are located near river banks; some are known to emit hydrogen. The average temperature of the water in these hot springs is 50°C (122 °F).
A. Potassium
B. Calcium
C. Sulphur
D. None of these

24. Most of Sikkim is covered by Precambrian rock, which is much younger in age than the hills. The rock consists of ...., and is highly susceptible to weathering and erosion. This combined with the state's heavy rainfall, causes extensive soil erosion and the loss of soil nutrients through leaching. As a result, landslides are frequent, often isolating rural towns and villages from the major urban centres.
A. chyllitesand schists
B. shyllitesand schists
C. phyllitesand schists
D. thyllitesand schists

25. According to the Constitution of India, Sikkim has a parliamentary system of representative democracy for its governance; universal suffrage is granted to state residents. The government structure is organized into three branches:

A. Executive B. Legislature
C. Judiciary D. All of these

26. Which complex in Gangtok houses the residences of the Chief Minister and Governor of Sikkim.

A. The White Hall B. The Black Hall
C. The Red Hall D. The Green Hall

27. Sikkim has four districts—East Sikkim, West Sikkim, North Sikkim and South Sikkim. The district capitals are .... These four districts are further divided into subdivisions; Pakyong and Rongli are the sub-divisions of the East district, Soreng is the subdivision of the West district, Chungthang is the sub-division of the North district and Ravongla is the sub-division of the South district.

A. Gangtok, Pakyong, Mangan and Namchi respectively
B. Gangtok, Gyalshing, Rongli and Namchi respectively
C. Gangtok, Gyalshing, Mangan and Namchi respectively
D. None of these

28. Sikkim is situated in an eco-logical hotspot of the lower Himalayas, one of only three among the eco-regions of India. The forested regions of the state exhibit a diverse range of fauna and flora. Owing to its altitudinal gradation, the state has a wide variety of plants, from tropical species to temperate, alpine and tundra ones, and is perhaps one of the few regions to exhibit such the diversity within such a small area. Nearly .... per cent of the area of Sikkim comes under the administration of its forest department.

A. 71 B. 76
C. 81 D. 86

29. The Noble is the .... official flower of Sikkim, while the .... is the state tree.

A. Dendrobium, Rhododendron B. Juniper, Pine
C. Firs, Cypresses D. None of these

30. Sikkim's nominal state gross domestic product (GDP) was estimated at .... in 2014, constituting the third-smallest GDP among India's 29 states. The state's economy is largely agrarian, based on the terraced farming of rice and the cultivation of crops such as maize, millet, wheat, barley, oranges, tea and cardamom.

A. US$1.57 billion B. US$1.87 billion
C. US$1.97 billion D. None of these

ANSWERS

1	2	3	4	5	6	7	8	9	10
B	A	D	C	A	C	A	B	A	A
11	**12**	**13**	**14**	**15**	**16**	**17**	**18**	**19**	**20**
A	D	C	B	C	A	B	B	A	C
21	**22**	**23**	**24**	**25**	**26**	**27**	**28**	**29**	**30**
C	A	C	C	D	A	C	C	A	A

●●●●●●

9

TRIPURA

INTRODUCTION

Tripura, one of the seven sister states of Northeast India, is the smallest state of the region and the second most populous state after Assam, with a total population of about 3.67 million, as per 2011 Census. The state is divided into eight districts – North Tripura, South Tripura, West Tripura, Dhalai Shepahijala, Khowai, Gomati and Unokati. Nearly two-thirds of the area is hilly, leaving very little cultivable land to meet the requirement of burgeoning population of the state.

HISTORY

The Origin of the name Tripura is a highly debated issue. According to Rajmala, Tripura's celebrated court chronicle, Tripura was once ruled by King Tripur after whom the state has been named. This opinion has been challenged by many historians and scholars as well. They claim that the King Tripur was an imaginary figure and no historical basis can be ascribed to this fact. Some writers have observed that the name Tripura derives from the Goddess Tripura Sundari—the presiding deity of the land. Another opinion is that the name Tripura originated from the two words—'tui' means water and 'pra' means near. Together, it conveys the meaning of Tripura as a land adjoining the waters. This version seems to be relevant as the hill people of Tripura still call the state as Tipra and not Tripura. Some scholars hold the opinion that the name Tripura was a Sanskritised version of Tipra, a hill tribe to what the then ruling family belonged.

Tripura finds mention in the Mahabharata, the Puranas and pillar inscriptions of Emperor Ashoka. In the 1300 AD, Tripura came under the control of the Manikya dynasty, a family of Indo-Mongolian origin. In the early part of 17th century AD, Tripura came under the administration of the Mughals. But the local rulers (the Manikyas) continued to retain some of their power. After the British established their colonies in Kolkata, they conquered some parts of modern Tripura but applied no administrative control for more than a century. To the British, Tripura was known as Hill Tippera. Even when a representative was appointed in the year 1871 AD, the Manikya Maharajas had enough independence, though they were asked to seek British approval on the accession of a new ruler.

One of the greatest of the Manikya rulers was Bir Chandra Manikya Bahadur of the 19th century AD. He was a great poet and musician and made an attempt to modernise and organise Tripura's administration, and abolish the practice of slavery and sati. The last ruling Maharaja of Tripura was Bir Bikram Kishore Manikya. Maharaja Bir Bikram Kishore succeeded his father aged fifteen in 1923, reigning under the guidance of his powerful uncles. For several years he ruled under a Council of Regency, a form of rule which usually prompted a deeper interest in state affairs by British officials. A series of administrative and other reforms were encouraged, education expanded, communications and infrastructure improved. When the young Maharaja assumed full control, the state was on a par with other princely states. His keen interest in military affairs were to stand in good stead, particularly when the war in Burma reached India's borders and the Japanese threatened invasion. The small Tripura army served with distinction and honour, winning several decorations for gallantry. Amongst the latter, the Maharaja's own younger brother.

After the death of Maharaja Birbikram Kishore Manikya Bahadur in May 1947, a Council under the leadership of his widowed wife Maharani Kanchan Prabha Devi took over the charge of the administration on behalf of minor prince Kirit Bikram. The monarchy came to an end on 9th Sept, 1947 and Tripura was merged with the Indian Union as a part 'C' State, administered by the Chief Commissioner. Tripura became a Union Territory on 1st November 1956. The territorial council was formed on 15th August 1959, which was later dissolved and a Legislative Assembly with a council of ministers was formed in July, 1963. Tripura became a full fledged state in 1972. Till 31st August 1970 the district administration was run by one Deputy Commissioner. On 1st September 1970, Tripura was divided into three districts, namely, North Tripura, South Tripura and West Tripura. Later the fourth district called Dhalai was created which started functioning from 16th April, 1995. For administrative purposes, the state has been divided into 8 districts, 23 sub-divisions and 58 development blocks—with effect from 21 January 2012, after a Government of Tripura Decision, out of which the newly created districts are 4, sub-divisions 6, development blocks 5. The four new Districts are Khowai, Unakoti, Sipahijala and Gomati.

GEOGRAPHY

Tripura, a landlocked hilly state in the north-eastern India is surrounded on the north, west and south by Bangladesh. It is accessible to the rest of the country only through the Cachar district of Assam and Aizawl district of Mizoram in the east. The state extends between 22°56' and 24°32' N latitudes and 90°09' and 92°10'E longitudes. Its maximum stretch measures about 184 km from north to south and about 113 km from east to west. With an area of 10,486 sq. km or 0.32% of the total geographical area of India, Tripura is the third smallest state of the country. It has an international land frontier with Bangladesh of about 856 km, which constitutes nearly 84% of the total perimeter of the state. On the other hand, the land frontier with Cachar district is only 53 km and that of Mizoram 109 km. The hills of the state which have added beauty to its landscape run from north to south parallel to one another till they disappear in the plains of Sylhet in Bangladesh. From the east the principal hill ranges are the Jampui, Sakhan Tlang, Langtorai, Athara Mura and Bara Mura. The highest peak of the state is as Betling Shiv (3200ft./1000m.) in the Jampui hill range. Known popularly as the "orange basket" of Tripura, Jampui Hills is a hill station 3,000 feet above sea level, 250 km from Agartala. It is inhabited by the Lushai and Reang tribes, who almost entirely live on orange cultivation. Stone and rock-cut images belonging to 7th-9th centuries can be seen at Unakoti.

Climate

Tripura has a tropical climate and receives rainfall during the monsoons. People in Tripura generally experience very hot and humid climatic conditions. Summer season commences in March and continues until May with average temperature of 35°C. Winter has an average temperature of 10.5°C and continues from December to January. Monsoon season extends from May to August and the average rainfall recorded in and adjoining Tripura is 230 cm per annum.

RIVERS

Important rivers of Tripura are: 1. Gomati, 2. Muhuri, 3. Manu, 4. Dhalai, 5. Burima, 6. Khowai, 7. Haora.

The largest and the most sacred river of Tripura is the "Gomati" which accepts myriad south-following streams, before cutting across the ranges in a steep sided valley from east to west and emerging out of the hills near Radhakishorepur. The source of the river is thought to be Tirthamukh where also lies the most alluring "Dumbur" falls considered as a very pious and chaste place for the people to take a holy dip in the water. This place portrays the religious sentiments associated with the river Gumti and its source Dumbur. The riverbeds here are generally sandy in the hills and clayey in the plains. There is however no artificial canal system in the state.

FLORA AND FAUNA

Tripura has a geographical area of 10,486 sq. km. of which 7,726 sq. km. (73.68%), is the forest area as per legal classification in the state, the remaining forest areas are degraded. Due to 856 km long international borders with Bangladesh, the trans-border-conservation is one of the most serious problems leading to degradation of existing forest.

Recorded Forest Area (2016)

- Reserved Forest (RF): 3,588.18 sq. km.
- Protected Forest (PF): 1.59 sq. km.
- Unclassed Forest (UF): 2,117 sq. km
- Total: 6,294 sq. km.
- Of State's Geographic Area: 59.99%
- Of Country's Forest Area: 0.82%

Types of Forest

Tripura is divided into two major forest types. These are:

1. Evergreen forest
2. Moist deciduous forest

Moist deciduous forests are further divided in two distinct categories, namely (i) moist deciduous Sal forests and (ii) moist deciduous mixed forest. Moist deciduous Sal forest covers parts of Belonia, Udaipur, and Sonamura and Sadar sub-divisions.

Evergreen Forest

Evergreen forests can be seen in Dharamnagar and Kailashahar area, Jampui and Sakhan hill ranges, and in part of Belonia, Sabrum, Kamalpur and Sadar sub-division. Once occupying a large area, evergreen forest has now been reduced significantly and exist in patches along hill slopes, sandy river banks, etc. Species of Dipterocarpus, Artocarpus, Amoora, Elaeocarpus, Syzygium, Eugenea dominated the top canopy.

Sal Forest

The dominant species, Sal or Shorea robusta provides more than 60% of the top canopy in this type of forest. Found in southern and northern low hills, extending up to the border of Bangladesh, Sal forest has undergone significant changes in some areas like Sonamura, due to expansion of paddy cultivation. Locally, Sal forest can still be found in Belonia, Udaipur, Sonamura and part of Sadar sub-division.

Moist Deciduous Mixed Forest

Characterized by absence or scarce, Sal trees, mixed forest offer dense and even canopy reaching a height of as long as 25 meters. Such forest can be seen in Amarpur, Sonamura, Udaipur and Sadar areas and in fragmented patches in Dharmanagar, Kailashahar and Kamalpur areas.

Wildlife Sanctuaries

The state of Tripura has four wildlife sanctuaries. They are:

1. Sipahijala Wildlife Sanctuary
2. Gomati Wildlife Sanctuary
3. Trishna Wildlife Sanctuary
4. Roa Wildlife Sanctuary

Name of the Wildlife Sanctuary

S.No.	Name of the Sanctuary	Area in km²	Important Fauna
1.	Sipahijala Wildlife Sanctuary	18.54	Birds and primates, migratory birds in the winter.
2.	Gomati Wildlife Sanctuary	389.54	Elephant, samber, barking deer, wild goats, serrow etc.
3.	Trishna Wildlife Sanctuary	194.71	Bison, leopard, barking deer, wild dog, capped langur, king cobra, spectacled monkey, slow lorries, etc.
4.	Roa Wildlife Sanctuary	0.86	Many species of birds and primates.

MINERALS

Important Minerals of Tripura

S.No.	Mineral	Location	Uses
1.	Hard Rock	Jampui Hills, Longatari Hill	Road metals
2.	Limestone	Sakhan & Jampui Range and Manpui area	Suitable for inferior quality of Lime Puzzolana mix.
3.	Clay	All over the State generally in river bank deposit	Sanitary ware, Stone wares, Sewerage pipes, Electric insulator
4.	Glass Sand	Bishramganj, Old Agartala, Jogendranagar, Sekerkota, Dasharambari, Mohanpur	Many uses

In Tripura, the mineral resources are mainly glass sands, limestone, plastic clay and hard rock; all these material are being used to a variable degree. However, the single most important resource in the state is oil and natural gas. ONGC or Oil and Natural Gas Commission has initiated massive exploration programme in the State.

AGRICULTURE

Tripura is basically an agrarian state with about 27% of the land area available for farming. Agriculture and allied activities is the mainstay of the people of Tripura and provides employment to about 42% of the population. There is a preponderance of food crop cultivation over cash crop cultivation in Tripura. At present about 62% of the net sown area is under food crop cultivation. Paddy is the principal crop, followed by oilseed, pulses, potato and sugarcane. Tea and rubber are the important cash crops of the State. Tripura has been declared the Second Rubber Capital of India after Kerala by the Indian Rubber Board.

Special initiatives have been taken by the State Government to increase flow of credit to agriculture through Kisan Credit Card (KCC), which includes sponsoring of eligible farmers to banks. Total number of farmers in the state is about 4.90 lakh, out of which about 4.26 lakh farmers have been covered under KCC. The State Agriculture Department has drawn up a plan in-consultation with Banks to cover all eligible farmers under KCC with-in next three years.

Land Utilisation Statistics

Sl. No.	Area	Area in Ha
1.	Geographical area	10,49,169
2.	Land not available for agriculture use	1,44,440
3.	Net cropped area	2,55,490
4.	Gross cropped area	4,90,540
5.	Cropping intensity (%)	186

Cropping Pattern

The Cropping pattern in Tripura acquires typical character of hill agriculture in the North Eastern Region where two distinct and parallel farming system viz., (i) shifting cultivation in the hill slopes (ii) settle farming cultivation in the plains are in vogue. Rice is the pre-dominant crop in both the systems. The state grows three seasonal rice crops viz. aush, aman and boro in the settled farming areas including wide range of food and non-food crops.

The undulating topography of the State favours the fruit cultivation. As a result more than 40% of area is under different fruit crops. The important fruit crops are pineapple, banana, mango, orange, jackfruit, litchi and papaya.

Vegetables in Tripura have already shifted from tiny home stead to large scale commercial cultivation over the State. Now-a-days; hybrids are being admired by most of the farmers of the State. Off-season vegetables like summer cabbage, cauliflower and tomato which provide much higher return per unit area has been introduced in the state and the progressive growers are also coming forward to adopt the production technique.

Plantation crops constitute a large group of crops. The major plantation crops in Tripura include the coconut, arecanut, oil palm, cashew, tea, coffee and rubber. Plantation crops which are dealt by the State Horticulture Department are coconut, arecanut and cashew only.

Floriculture is a sunrise sector in Tripura. Owing to steady increase in demand of cut flower, commercial approach of floriculture has become one of the important sectors in the State. Its area is fast expanding and commercially produced flowers are marigold, gladiolus, tube rose, cheri gold in open field condition and some exotic flowers like gerbera, orchids and anthurium are being cultivated under controlled condition.

IRRIGATION

Tripura is a small state in the North East with a cultivable land of 2,80,000 hect. and irrigation potential of 1,17,000 hect. Out of the available water resources; 79,933 hect. can be brought under assured irrigation through surface water and remaining 38,000 hect. through ground water.

The ultimate aim of the State Government is to provide assured irrigation to the entire irrigable land of 1,17,000 hector for achieving self-sufficiency in food. Accordingly, the Government of Tripura has constituted a taskforce for implementing the programme within the above time schedule. The work of three medium irrigation projects at Gomati, Khowai and Manu are in progress.

POPULATION

Tripura is the second most populous state in North-East India, after Assam. According to the census of 2011, Tripura has a total population of 36,73,917, with a density of 350 persons per square kilometer, and ranks 18th among Indian states. It constitutes 0.30% population of India. In the 2011 census of India, Bengalis represent almost 70% of Tripura's population and the native tribal populations represent 30% of Tripura's population. The literacy rate of Tripura is 87.2%, higher than the national rate of 73%. The literacy rate among the women is 82.7% as compared to 91.5% among the men.

Districts	Area in sq. km.	Total population	Literacy	Sex ratio (females per 1000 males)	Density (per sq.km)
West	942.55	918200	91.07	970	974
Shepahijala	1044.78	483687	84.68	952	463
Khowai	1005.67	327564	87.78	957	326
Gomati	1522.8	441538	84.53	959	290
South	1534.2	430751	84.68	956	281
Dhalai	2400	378230	85.72	944	158
Unokati	591.93	276506	86.91	972	467
North	1444.5	417441	87.90	963	289
Tripura	10486.43	3673917	87.22	960	350

The distribution of population in Tripura is highly uneven. West Tripura is by far the most populated district of the state. More than 45% of the total population of the state has been concentrated in this district. The eastern part of Tripura (Dhalai district) is more hilly and heavily forested and contains only 10% of the total population of the state.

During the first half of 20th century Tripura registered a high growth rate of population. The growth rate during 1901-1951 varied between 25% and 34%. After 1951 particularly during 1951-1961 the growth rate was astounding, 7.69% per annum. During the period 1952-1956, 1.9 lakh displaced people from erstwhile East Pakistan entered the state. This large-scale migration had an immediate effect on the population density and growth of population of Tripura. Growth rate of population during 2001-2011 was 14.84%.

Density

Tripura ranks 18th position in terms of density of population at all India level. Among the North-eastern states, Tripura is now the second highest populated state after Assam. The population density of Tripura in 2011 is 350 persons per sq. km., which means that now 45 more people live in a sq. km. area in the state then they lived a decade ago. The population density for all India in 2011 is 382.

Sex Composition

The Census 2011 data reveals that the sex ratio was 960 in the state (per 1000 males) against all India sex ratio of 943 (per 1000 males). This is a positive improvement in sex ratio in the state and it rose from 948 (per 1000 males) in 2001 to 960 (per 1000 males) in 2011.

Population Census: 2011-Census

Sl.	Item	Unit	Tripura	All India
1.	Area	Sq. Km.	10,491.69	32,87,263
2.	Population	In Lakhs	36.73	12,108.00
3.	Males	In Lakhs	18.74	6,232.03
4.	Female	In Lakhs	17.99	5,875.22
5.	Sex ratio (female per thousand male)	Nos.	960	943
6.	Literacy rate	In %	87.27	73.0
7.	Male Literacy rate	In %	91.5	80.9
8.	Female Literacy rate	In %	82.7	64.6

TRANSPORTATION

Roads

The state has 853 km of National Highway, 329 of State Highway, 90 km of major district roads and 1,099 km of other district roads and 10,472 km of village roads.

Roads in Tripura

S.No.	Item	Unit	Tripura (2015-16)
1.	National Highway	Km	853
2.	State Highway	Km	329
3.	Major Districts Road	Km	90
4.	Other Districts Road	Km	1,099
5.	Village Road	Km	10,472
6.	IBP Road	Km	834
7.	Total Roads	Km	—
8.	Total Railway Lined	Km	66

NH of Tripura

1. NH.44—Tripura/Assam Border-Ambassa-Chandrasadhubari-Barjala-Udaipur-Sabrum.
2. NH.44A—Tripura/Mizoram Border-Sakhan-Manu.

Railways

The total length of lines within the State is 66 km. It has been extended up to Manughat. Work of extension of railway line up to Agartala is in progress.

Aviation

The main airport at Agartala is connected with Kolkata, Guwahati. The state has other three small airports at Khowai, Kamalpur and Kailashahar where small chartered planes can land after prior information.

ECONOMY

Economy of Tripura is basically agrarian and characterized by high rate of poverty, low per-capita income, low capital formation, inadequate infrastructural facilities, geographical isolation, communication bottleneck, inadequate exploitation, inadequate use of forest and mineral resources, low progress in industrial field and high un-employment problem. More than 42 per cent of its population now directly depends on agriculture & allied activities.

The latest Gross State Domestic Product (GSDP) with a more recent new 2011-12 base with the revised methodology, data base and additional area coverage shows that contribution of primary sector has been increased to 45 per cent in 2015-16, although the land available for agricultural cultivation is relatively restricted in the State.

This trend is observed in both the estimates prepared by Central Statistics Office, New Delhi and the Directorate of Economics & Statistics, Tripura.

The average annual growth rate in real terms of Gross State Domestic Product (GSDP) at new 2011-12 prices or in real terms for 2015-16(P) was 9.3 per cent in 2015-16. There is no denying the fact that the State has put efforts for ensuring sustainable growth during last couple of years by augmenting better fiscal consolidation and economic development, which has also been appreciated by the Government of India. The State's economy anticipated similar growth trends of over 9 per cent in real terms during 2016-17 also.

The Gross State Domestic Product (GSDP) at current prices with a recent new 2011-12 base at current prices increased from ₹ 19,208.41 crore in 2011-12 to ₹ 21,663.20 crore in 2012-13 and to ₹ 25,592.83 crore in 2013-14 and to ₹ 34,368.32 crore in 2015-16 (P).

The per capita income of the State with a recent new 2011-12 base also rose steadily from ₹ 47,079 in 2011-12 to ₹ 52,434 in 2012-13 and to ₹ 61,570 in 2013-14 and to ₹ 80,027 in 2015-16 (P).

Gross/Net State Domestic Product with 2011-12 Base

The estimates at current prices are worked out by evaluating all goods cost prevailing in a particular year. The estimates at constant prices are worked out by using the base year price to eliminate the effect of price changes/ inflation and thereby, reflect real growth/development of the economy.

At Current Prices

According to new base of 2011-12 with revised methodology and data base, GSDP at current prices increased from ₹ 19,208.41 crore in 2011-12 to ₹ 21,663.20 crore in 2012-13 and ₹ 25,592.83 crore in 2013-14 and ₹ 34,368.32 crore in 2015-16 (Provisional). On the other hand, the NSDP at current prices increased from ₹ 17,419.05 crore in 2011-12 to ₹ 19,631.14 crore in 2012-13 and ₹ 23,328.98 crore in 2013-14 and ₹ 31,058.33 crore in 2015-16 (Provisional).

(₹ in crore)

Year	GSDP at current prices	NSDP at current prices
2012-13	21,663.20	19,631.14
2013-14	25,592.83	23,328.98
2014-15	27,422.39	24,532.28
2015-16 (P)	34,368.32	31,058.33

Source: DES, Tripura.

At Constant Prices

The GSDP at constant prices increased from ₹ 19,208.41 crore in 2011-12 to ₹ 20,872.97 crore in 2012-13 to ₹ 22,819.11 crore in 2013-14 and ₹ 27,820.32 crore in 2015-16 (Provisional). The NSDP at constant prices has also increased from ₹ 17,419.05 crore in 2011-12 to ₹ 18,857.21 crore in 2012-13 to ₹ 20,623.06 crore in 2013-14 and ₹ 24,905.59 crore in 2015-16 (Provisional).

(₹ in crore)

Year	GSDP at constant prices	NSDP at constant prices
2012-13	20,872.97	18,857.21
2013-14	22,819.11	20,623.06
2014-15	24,814.24	22,255.63
2015-16(P)	27,820.30	24,905.59

Source: DES, Tripura

Per Capita Income with New Base Year 2011-12

The per capita income at current prices has been increased from ₹ 47,079 in 2011-12 to ₹ 52,434 in 2012-13 and ₹ 61,570 in 2013-14 and to ₹ 80,027 in 2015-16 (Provisional) with new base of 2011-12. The per capita national income at current prices during the said period rose from ₹ 63,460 in 2011-12 to ₹ 71,050 in 2012-13, ₹ 79,412 in 2013-14 and ₹ 94,130 in 2015-16.

13th Finance Commission

The 13th Finance Commission had grossly under assessed the commited requirements of the State Government as specially the expenditure relating to the salary and pension. As a result the State Finance have come under severe fiscal stress and strain since the State has also limited scope for generation of additional resources for meeting such committed liabilities.

Approach of 13th Finance Commission was different from previous Finance Commissions because a normative formula has been applied for computation of salary on the base year of 2005-06. On base of 2005-06, 35 per cent increase for pay revision has been considered to work out figure for 2006-07. For subsequent years, 6 per cent increase has been considered for increment and DA with 1 per cent attrition. Moreover, while assessing salary expenditure, 13th Finance Commission applied another criterion that salary should not exceed 35 per cent of revenue expenditure net of interest and pension. Salary above this ceiling will have to be reduced by 10 per cent every year till it is brought down below 35 per cent. All these factors have actually hurt the State where-in traditionally salary expenditure has been contributing large proportion of non-plan revenue expenditure.

Tripura Fiscal Responsibility and Budget Management Act, 2005

The State Government continued to pursue fiscal correction and consolidation for overall improvement of the financial health of the State. The State Government has enacted the Tripura Fiscal Responsibility and Budget Management Act, 2005 on 25th June 2006 during the fiscal year 2005-06.

The Act provides the responsibility of the Government of Tripura to ensure prudence in fiscal management and fiscal stability by progressive elimination of revenue deficit, reduction in fiscal deficit, debt management consistent with fiscal sustainability.

The prime objectives of the FRBM Act are as follows:

(i) To ensure prudence in Fiscal Management.

(ii) Fiscal stability by maintaining revenue positive status.

(iii) Gradual reduction of fiscal deficit up to 3% of GSDP.
(iv) Prudence in debt management.
(v) Greater transparency.
(vi) Conduct of fiscal policy in a medium term frame-work.

12th Five Year plan

The State has adopted multi-pronged strategy which focuses on building infrastructure, strengthening social infrastructure, inclusive and sustainable growth, social and regional equity, improving quality of life, capacity building and skilled development, widening livelihood opportunities, etc. For this, emphasis has been laid on the following:

(i) **Reducing Infrastructural deficit**—There is a need to bridge the infrastructural gaps to meet the growing aspiration of the people. Further, growth in economic activities is to be supported by robust infrastructure. The plan approach in Tripura has taken note of the vital infrastructural needs like roads, power, drinking water, irrigation, etc.

(ii) **Sustaining growth in agricultural and allied sector**—Dependence of large population on agri and allied activities and its contribution to the State Domestic Product make it a priority sector in Planning process. The sectoral plans have been re-oriented for greater public investment and capacity building.

(iii) **Expanding and Strengthening capacity of key social sector**—Health, education, women and child welfare, nutrition and food security are critical pillars of sustainable development. Attention has therefore been paid to the key sectors like health, education and rural development.

(iv) **Inclusiveness**—Flow of adequate benefits to historically disadvantage is one of the key under lying theme of the plan document. Thrust has been laid for public investment for creating equal opportunities for SC/ST/OBCs and Minorities. This is necessary for there empowerment and greater participation in development process.

(v) **Social and regional equity**—There is a need for closing the gap between the deprived local population and the rest of the country. It is therefore necessary that there is enough investment for expansion of social infrastructure for covering the disadvantaged sections, backward,remote and border areas.

(vi) **Greater convergence for improvement in livelihood and income opportunities**—Strengths of strong social capital and vibrant democratic institutions is being laveraged for converging scheme in social sector such that it leads to sustained livelihood opportunities for the poor and deprived.

(vii) Capacity building and skill development—Developing capacity and building strong human resource base is fundamental necessity for multiplying the returns from public investment in infrastructural development. Emphasis is being laid in building capacity of human resources for greater employment opportunities.

(viii) Institutional decentralization—Focus on better governance and deeper involvement of people through net work of decentralized institutions at village and Block level.

Priority Sector

The Government of Tripura identified seven priority sectors for overall development of the State, these are:

(i) Agriculture and Irrigation.

(ii) Drinking water.

(iii) Housing

(iv) Road connectivity

(v) Education

(vi) Healthcare and

(vii) Rural Electrification.

INDUSTRY

Although, industrial development always remains a thrust area in the State Government's economic policies. The State's endeavour is to provide efficient and cost effective infrastructure, skilled human resources, stable environment and good governance which are the prerequisites for creating a proper investment environment for sustainable industrial growth. Unfortunately, Tripura has not been able to attract desired private investments in this industrial sector from rest of the country and therefore, remained an industrially backward state due to its unique economic disadvantages arising out of remoteness and poor connectivity, hilly terrain, weak resource base, poor infrastructure, as well as shallow markets.

The State has the potentiality for industrial opportunities and improvement which in turn will increase employment generation in the State. One of the main thrust areas of the State Industries & Commerce Department is to promote and develop the rural, micro, small and medium enterprises, agri-based food processing industries and also promoting export and import business with the neibouring country of Bangladesh. Tea and rubber based industries are taken into consideration for the development of industrial base in Tripura. Although the State is backward in industrilisation but has the potentiality for industrial opportunities and improvement which in turn will increase employment generation in the State.

Tea Industry

Tea industry in the state occupies an important place in its economy. Tea cultivation in Tripura was started as far back as 1919 during the reign of Maharaja Birendra Kishore Manikya. The state has suitable agro-climatic conditions for development of tea plantation. The soils are generally fertile, and have no major problems of toxicities or deficiencies. The state is also categorized as a traditional tea-growing state—with about 60 Tea Estates and 3,000 small tea growers, producing about 7.5 million kg. of tea every year. This makes Tripura the 5th largest, among the 14 tea producing states, after Assam, West Bengal, Tamil Nadu and Kerala.

Other Industries

Tripura's handicrafts in structure, beauty and variety is of great demand outside. For improving the design and quality of the products the All-India Handicraft Board has set up a research unit at Agartala.

Handloom weaving is the single largest industry. Another age-old industry of the state is silk. The Sericulture industry is developing fast. During the reign of Maharaja Birendra Kishore Manikya (1909-23), a school was opened at Agartala for giving training in Sericultural weaving. A jute mill set up in Agartala under public sector produces about 20 tonnes of jute products per day. Tripura is abundant in natural gas and a number of gas-based industries have sprung up.

Industrial Estates and Industrial Centres

In order to provide common facilities and services to the entrepreneurs, the state government is running six industrial estates. One each at Arundhutinagar, Dhwajanagar, Dukli, Kumarghat, Badharghat and Dharmanagar. Besides the state has three industrial centres viz. Udaipur in south Tripura, Kailashahar in north and one at Agartala. The department of industries also runs 4 industrial centres—two at Indranagar, one each at Jatanbari and Kailashahar; three industrial development centres viz. at Malaynagar and Takmacherra in West Tripura district and Uttakhali in North Tripura district.

Industrial Training Institute (ITI)

Presently, there are 13 ITIs in the State.

Sl. No.	Name of ITI	Total capacity	
		No. of Trades	No. of Trainees
1.	ITI Indranagar	13	250
2.	Women's ITI Indranagar	7	140
3.	ITI Kailashahar	12	260
4.	ITI Jatanbari	9	180
5.	ITI Udaipur	7	135
6.	ITI Belonia	7	135
7.	ITI Ambassa	7	195
8.	ITI Dharmanagar	7	135
9.	ITI Khumulwng	4	160
10.	ITI Manubankul	4	160
11.	ITI Boxanagar	4	160
12.	ITI Khowai	4	160
13.	Pvt. ITI Ramkrishna Mission	3	120
	Total		**2190**

Information Technology

In Tripura, IT activities were initiated in a serious manner in April, 1999 with setting up of a separate State Directorate of Information Technology (DIT) and Tripura State Computerisation Agency (TSCA).

Tripura State Wide Area Network (SWAN): SWAN is a State-wide computer (data/voice/video) network setup to the block level for running of e-governance applications across the State. There are 66 Points of Presence (POPs). IP phones for voice communication are installed in almost all sites. The network is working smoothly. The project has been implemented by NIC and BSNL is the bandwidth provider. Tripura was the sixth State in the country and first State in the Eastern and North Eastern Region to complete SWAN.

Agartala City Area Network (ACAN): Agartala City Area Network (ACAN) has been setup to connect different offices at Agartala through OFC backbone. The ACAN is envisaged as the backbone network for delivering various e-Governance applications, information to citizens through data, video and voice communications.

CO-OPERATION

Co-operative movement is taking an important role for socio-economic development of the valuable un-organised section of the people of the state both in agriculture and non-agriculture sector. Co-operative movement was launched in Tripura in 1949 back by registration of "Swasti Samabaya

Samity Ltd.," under Bombay Co-operative Societies Act, 1925. The movement has acquired a comprehensive character with the enactment of Tripura Co-operative Societies Act, 1974 and Tripura Co-operative Societies Rules, 1976.

The co-operative movement in Tripura has passed through several phases of development and is yet to achieve it's desired goal due to proliferation of uneconomic and dormant co-operatives. However, emphasis has given for development of the co-operative movement for achieving self-sustaining Co-operative structure in the state. Agricultural allied activities like fishery, animal husbandry, village and cottage industries play significant role in the rural economy of the state. The cooperative are not limited to the agricultural credit societies and non-agricultural credit societies but encompass marketing, milk supply, weavers, farming, fishery, etc. Therefore, co-operative movements in the state need to play a crucial role for upliftment of rural poor and creation of rural assets.

The co-operative societies are classified into two sectors, one credit societies and other non-credit societies. The credit societies consist of agriculture credit societies (LAMPS, PACS, services, farmers, small farming) T.S.C.B Ltd., T.C.A.R.D.B Ltd., A.C.U.B Ltd. and employees credit societies. The non-credit societies consist of marketing, weavers, other industries, fisheries, milk consumers and transport, etc.

Women Co-operative Societies

There were 142 No. of Women Co-operative Societies in the State as on 31.3.2017. Out of this, 58 Societies were in West Tripura District, 8 societies were in Khowai District, 15 Societies in Shipahijala District, 17 Societies in Gomati districts, 7 Societies where in South Tripura District, 9 Societies were in North Tripura District, 12 Societies in Unokoti District, and remaining 16 Societies were in Dhalai District.

Tripura State Co-operative Bank (TSCB): Tripura State Cooperative Bank Ltd. (TSCB) was established in the year 1957 under the Bombay Cooperative Societies Act. TSCB is an Apex Co-operative Bank in the State channelising funds as per the guidelines of Reserve Bank of India (RBI) to LAMPS and PACS for effecting disbursement of credit to the cooperative members at a nominal rate of interest.

Presently, TSCB has 59-branches and 4-extension counters in the State. In the recent past, the credit sector faced constraints of credit business due to non-realisation of substantial over dues from the cooperative members of LAMPS/PACS.

With a view to revamp the sector, stringent action was initiated which has resulted in the improvement of recovery climate. Apart from extending the institutional credit support, TSCB Ltd. also provides different kinds of loans to the individual borrowers. Further, working capital of the Bank has been improving gradually over the years. The TSCB has been implementing various Government sponsored schemes like Swabalamban, Tripura State Support Project for SHG's (TSSPS) and other banking services including old age pensions, MREGA payment, and disbursement of salaries to the employees.

Tripura Co-operative Agriculture and Rural Development Bank Ltd.: Tripura Cooperative Agriculture & Rural Development Bank was registered in February, 1960. Presently, it has five branches with head office at Agartala. The Bank is mainly serving the credit needs of small and marginal farmers for development of agriculture and allied activities in the State. Besides, the Bank is also financing non-farm sector activities *e.g.*, small transport loans, self-employment trades, small business based trades in rural areas.

Agartala Co-operative Urban Bank (ACUB): The ACUB is governed by an elected board of management with 11 Board of Directors since its functioning from 1979. The ACUB raises deposits from members and non-members and also advances loans. The ACUB has been disbursing short-term loans for different purposes like—education, medical treatment, house repairing, repayment of old debts and purchase of durable goods, etc. In addition, it provides mid-term loans for the purchasing of scooter/motor bike and for medical treatment outside Tripura. The Bank also provides long term (LT) loan for purchase of houses/flats, vehicles, auto rickshaws, vans, jeep, and buses, etc.

The State Marketing Federation of Tripura Ltd. (TMARKFED): Marketing is also an important thrust area in the co-operative movement of Tripura. The Tripura Apex Marketing Co-operative Society Ltd. as a State level Apex Society is functioning since 1957. There has been a substantial growth of marketing of agricultural and minor forest produces (MFP). It procures agricultural produce and forest produce under price support operations through different LAMPS/ PACS and Primary Marketing Co-operative Societies in the State.

EDUCATION

Literacy and education are reasonably good indicators of development in a society. The literacy rate for Tripura in 2011 works out to 87.2% for the population 7 years and above, which was 73.20% in 2001. The corresponding figures for males and females were 91.5% and 82.7%, respectively, in 2011. The gap in male-female rate in the state observes at 9.2 %. The literacy rate at all India level stood at 73% in 2011.

The State Government has been attached highest priority to education since it attained the statehood in 1972. The State has been spending 12-14 per cent of its annual budget for school education sub-sector.

The "Right of Children to Free and Compulsory Education Act, 2009" has come into effect from April 2010 to provide free and compulsory education to children in the age group of 6-14 years in a neighbourhood school. Elementary education, consisting of primary (I-V) and upper primary or middle (VI-VIII) is the main basis of education, which is successfully covered under "Sarva Shiksha Abhiyan" and "Mid-day meal" schemes in the State. The secondary (IX-X) education is covered through "Rashtriya Madhyamik Shiksha Abhiyan" and higher secondary education (XI-XII) is also witnessed a phenomenal expansion in the State.

Higher Education

The state has one Central University and one Private University, 24 General Degree Colleges, 1 Institute of Advanced Studies in Education, 3 Engineering College, 5 Polytechnic, Inst., 1 Govt. Law College, 1 Music College, 1 Art and Craft College, 1 Tripura Joint Entrance Board, 1 Oral Coaching Centre, 1 Govt. Musuem, 1 State Archieves, 1 State Kala Academy, 1 Rabindra Satabarshiki Bhavan, 25 Public Libraries including Birchandra State Central Library.

In 2005-06 a government medical college has been started from August 2006, which is the first medical college in the state, and named as Agartala Government Medical College (AGMC).The Tripura Engineering College has been transformed into the National Institute of Technology (NIT) in 2005-06 after strong persuation of the State Government with the Ministry of Human Resource Development, Government of India.

Tripura University

Tripura University is the only state run University of Tripura. The Bill for converting the Tripura University into a Central University has been passed into the Parliament in December, 2006.

POWER

The development in Power Sector in Tripura despite geographical, economic and infrastructural hindrance has come a long way till now. Performance of all important sectors in the economy, ranging from agriculture to commerce and industry, as also the performance of social sectors like health, depends largely on the availability, cost and quality of power.

The State has two sources of generation mainly, hydro and thermal. The State is endowed with natural gas, which enhances potentially for thermal power generation. Out of the two major sources of power generation, thermal power accounts for 93% while remaining 7% is generated from Hydel power (*i.e.,* Gomati Power Project). The Hon'ble Prime Minister of India has been laid the 750 MW Thermal Power Plant at Palatana in South Tripura District on 29th October 2005 with an estimated investment of ₹ 3900 crore.The Power Plant at Palatana will provide a major impetus to the economies of Tripura, Assam, Mizoram and Meghalaya and the entire North Eastern region as a whole.

The installed capacity was 115 MW and total power generated within the State was 666.168 MU and purchased from Central Sector Grid was 1981.413 MU in 2016-17. The total unit sold to ultimate consumers in 2015-16 was 1156.82 MU. Out of this, maximum power was sold for domestic consumption which was 439.78 MU followed by 113.26 MU for irrigation/ public water purposes, commercial consumption 74.92 MU and industrial 43.01 MU, respectively in 2015-16.

Kutir Jyoti

It is a centrally sponsored scheme to give assistance to the rural people living below poverty line (BPL). Under the scheme houses of people living below poverty line are electrified free of cost. After closure of Kutir Jyoti Scheme, similar assistance funded by the State Department of Power and Tripura State Electricity Co-orporation Ltd. (TSECL) has been continued for electrification to the household of BPL families.

Deendayal Upadhayaya Gram Jyoti Yojana (DDUGJY)

Government of India has approved DDUGJY Schemes for Tripura for a total project value of ₹ 74.12 Crores for 8 Districts. As per scheme guidelines Project Management Agency appointed and Tripartite Agreement was already signed on 28-10-2016. Preparatory works for tendering is in progress.

Major Projects in Power Sector

Tripura's power scenario is expected to get a major boost with the setting up of three gas-based thermal plants that are expected to turn around the state's economy. Three major thermal power projects totalling about 1,041 MW are now in the pipeline. Once power generation commences from these plants, Tripura will not only be self-sufficient, but could supply surplus power to other states.

The major project is the 750 MW gas-based thermal power project at Palatana in south Tripura expected to be commissioned by 2009. The Oil and Natural Gas Corporation (ONGC) has been assigned for the ₹ 40 billion-Palatana project. After commissioning of the 750 MW project, there would be provision to increase the generation capacity to 1,100 MW. There are two more power projects in the pipeline—a 280 MW thermal power project by the public sector North Eastern Electrical Power Corporation (NEEPCO) at Monarchak in west Tripura and a 21 MW gas-based unit at Baramura in west Tripura.

ADMINISTRATION

Administratively Tripura is divided into eight districts. The Assembly is unicameral with 60 Members of the Legislative Assembly, or MLAs. Tripura sends 2 representatives to the Lok Sabha and 1 representative to the Rajya Sabha. Tripura also has an autonomous tribal council, the Tripura Tribal Areas Autonomous District Council which has its head-quarters in Khumulwng. The 3-tier panchyati raj system is prevailing in the state. There are 8-Zilla Parisads, 35-Panchyat Samities and 591 elected Gram Panchyats functioning in outside Autonomous District Council areas of the state.

Name of the Districts of Tripura

1. South Tripura
2. West Tripura
3. North Tripura
4. Dhalai
5. Shepahijala
6. Khowai
7. Gomati
8. Unokati

Tripura Public Service Commission

Tripura Public Service Commission was established on 30th October, 1972, under the provisions of Article 315 of the Constitution of India. Sri G.P. Bagchi was the first Chairman and Sri I.K. Roy was the first Member of the Tripura Public Service Commission. The Commission is, at present, located at the old Assembly House of Tripura, at Akhaura Road, Agartala.

HEALTH

The state has comparatively performed better in the field of health & medical facilities despite its economic backwardness and in absence of modern healthcare facilities. In the state general medical services are free for all including indoor patients admitted in the hospital and primary health centers.

In 2005-06, a State Government Medical College has been started from August 2006, which is the first medical college in the state, and named as Agartala Government Medical College (AGMC). Setting up of Government Medical College at Agartala is a significant milestone for the health sector of the state.

Moreover, a private run Medical College has also been set-up at Hapania named as B R Ambedkar Medical College (BRAM) in October-2006.

The birth rate and death rate in the state are well below the nation rate. It can be evident from the fact that the birth rate and death rate were 13.7 and 5.5 in the state in 2016 against the all India rates of 20.4 and 6.4 in 2016, respectively. The infant mortality rate in the state was 24 against the same for 34 at all India level in 2016 which stands well below the national standard.

In 2016-17, there were 23 Hospitals, 20 Rural Hospitals & CHC, 94 PHCs, 1142 Sub-centres, 10 Blood Banks and 8 Blood Stored centers in allopathic branch through the State Government has been providing basic facility to all section of the society. There is one State Homeopathic Hospital and one State Ayurvedic Hospital in Tripura.

TOURISM

Endowed with rich variety of tourist attractions, Tripura offers vast potential for growth tourism. With an area of 10492 sq. km Tripura is one of the smallest states in the country. But the legendary state with its natural beauty of lustrous green valleys, the hill ranges with its flora and fauna, the fascinating blend of culture, glorious history and traditional unique craftsmanship is in a highly advantageous position for development of tourism.

For convenience of tourist the state has been divided into two tourist circuits. One is west-south Tripura circuit covering the tourist destination of west and south Tripura Districts and the other tourist circuits is west-north Tripura circuits covering the tourist destination of north Tripura and Dhalai District. The entire state is having huge potentiality in tourism specially eco-tourism, religious, heritage tourism, hill tourism, rural tourism, etc. The tourist locations as indicated above are given below:

West-South Tripura Circuit

Agartala, the capital of the state, having Ujjayanta Palace – a palace of old Maharaja, many temples including Buddhist temple and international boarders. Chatturdas Devata temple is a very old temple established by the Maharaja of Tripura. Sipahijala is a wild life sanctuary with distinctive flora and fauna. Kamalasagar is a tourist location on the Border with Bangladesh. It has an old Hindu temple with other facilities for the tourists. Neermahal is the only water place in the Northeast. The palace was build by Maharaja Bir Bikram Manikya Kishore Bahadur as his summer resorts. Light and sound programme has been installed there for the tourists.

Udaipur is the headquarter of South Tripura District. It has an old Kali temple build by Maharaja Dhanya Manikya 500 years ago. This is one of the 51 pithas of Hindu pilgrimage. Pilak is 100 km away from Agartala. Pilak is a place of attraction for its archaeological remains of eight / ninth centuries. Number of terracotta plaques, sealing with stupa and stone images of Avolokiteswara including image of Narasimhan have been found there which date backs of Buddhist period. The place has close association with Myanamoti and Paharpur in Bangladesh. Recently further excavation has been taken up archaeological survey of India.

West-North Tripura Circuit

The most important tourism location in this circuit is Unnakuti. It is a Shiva Pilgrim dates back to seven / ninth centuries. There are numerous rock-cut images available in the area and because of this it is a good heritage location for the tourists. Dumboor lake has an water area of 41 sq. km. Migratory birds visit the lake in winter. As a result of this Dumboor is a very good tourist location for the nature lovers/tourist.

Jampui Hills

It is the permanent seat of eternal spring situated at an altitude of 3000 ft. above mean the sea level. Jampui Hill is famous for its charming landscape and enjoyable climate.

COMMUNITIES OF TRIPURA

Tripuri Community : Tripuris constitute the weightiest section of the entire tribal community, representing more than 50% of the total tribal population of the State. The Tripuris live on the slopes of hills in a group of five to fifty families. Their houses in these areas are built of bamboo and raised five to six feet height to save themselves from the dangers of the wild animals. Nowadays a considerable section of this community are living in the plains and erecting houses like the plains' people adopting their methods of cultivation and following them in other aspects of life, such as dress, manners and cosmetics. Tripuri women rear a scarp, called

Pachra, which reaches down just below the knee. They weave in their loin-loom a small piece of cloth, which they call 'Risha', and they use this small piece of cloth as their breast garment.

Reang Community : Reangs constitute the second biggest group among the tribal population. It is generally believed that this particular community migrated to Tripura from somewhere in the Chittagong hill Tracts in the middle part of the fifteenth century. The Reangs are very disciplined community. The head of the community enjoys the title 'Rai', word is supreme in all matters of internal disputes and hence to be obeyed by all belonging to the said community. They generally avoid normal court for justice. The Reangs are very backward both educationally and economically and, therefore they are still considered to be the primitive group.

Chakma Community : People of Chakma Community in Tripura are found normally in the Sub-Divisions of Kailashahar, Amarpur, Sabroom, Udaipur, Belonia and Kanchanpur. They are followers of Buddhism. Although the Chakmas are divided into several groups and sub-sections, no major difference is noticed in the manner and customs indifferent groups. The Chakma chiefs are generally called 'Dewans' and they exercise great authority and influence within the community in all internal matters. The Chakma Women, like all other tribal women are experts in weaving. The Chakmas are very neat and clean in their domestic life.

Halam (Malsum) Community : Malsum is one of the 12 groups belonging to the Halam community of Tripura. Halam, again, originally hailed from one of the branches of Kukis. It is said that Kukis had lived in Tripura even before the Tripuris came in, to conquer the land. Those of the Kukis who had submitted to the Tripura 'Raja' came to be known as Halams. Originally the tribal was divided into 12 sub-groups of 'Dafas' but in course of time these sub-groups have split into sections and new as many as sixteen clans are found to be making up for the whole Halam community. Malsum belongs to one of these 12 groups. The Halams are followers of the 'Saka' cult, but the influence of 'Vaishnavism' is quite marked, particularly, in two sections of the community. They believe in the existence of spirit too. Their worship is solemnized with offerings and sacrifices so that nothing calamitous befalls the community in the form of crop failure or epidemic or any other natural disaster. During the festival, they sit together to settle all internal disputes, try cases or crime and inflict punishment on the offenders which make the Puja a useful social gathering in keeping peace and harmony within the community.

Garo Community : The people of Garo community live in the South and Dhalai districts of Tripura. Originally they use to live in Tong Ghar made of bamboo to save themselves from wild animals like the other tribals of Tripura. But now they prefer houses made of mud wall with 'Chan' grass as roof. They are believed to have migrated to Tripura from Garo Hills. The life style of the Garo living in Tripura is almost like the other tribal. The Heads of the community is known as Sangnakma and the priest of the community is known as Kama.

Lusai Community : The Lusai were originally inhabitant of the hills lying with east and north-east of Tripura and also to the adjoining hilly areas. They have settled down on Jampui Hills situated on the North-East boundary of the state under Kanchanpur Sub-Division in North Tripura district. Their number is very insignificant to the total population of the state. The principal means of livelihood of the Lusai still remain to be Jhum cultivation. Of course, this can be considered chiefly to the dearth of plain land in the hills. They prefer living in high altitude of the hills.

Darlong Community : The Darlongs are the sub-caste of the Lusai community. They live mostly in Kailashahar Sub-Division in North Tripura District. Their main livelihood is cultivation of pineapple, orange and cotton.

FOLK DANCES

The main folk dances are Hozagiri dance of Reang community, Garia, Jhum, Maimita, Masak Sumani and Lebang boomani dances of Tripuri community, Bizu dance of Chakma community, Cheraw and Welcome dances of Lusai community, Hai-Hak dance of Malsum community, Wangala dance of Garo Community, Sangraiaka, Chimithang, Padisha and Abhangma dances of Mog community, Garia dances of Kalai and Jamatia communities, Gajan, Dhamail, Sari and Rabindra dances of Bengali community and Basanta Rash and Pung chalam dances of Manipuri community. Each community has its own traditional musical instruments. The important musical instruments are' Khamb (Drum)', Bamboo flute, 'Lebang', 'Sarinda', 'Do-Tara', and 'Khengrong', etc. Long and intimate association of Poet Rabindranath Tagore with Tripura has added luster to the rich cultural heritage of the state. The state has produced the famous musicians Sachin Dev Barman and Rahul Dev Barman.

FAIRS AND FESTIVALS

Hojagiri Fair—The Hojagiri festival is held every year in the month of November. It is organised by the Reang community with some support from the Government. The place of the mela keeps on changing and is normally held at Karbook, Laxmichara and Kanchanpur, of which Karbook and Laxmichara are in South Tripura District and Kanchanpur is in North Tripura district.

Poush Sankranti Fair—Poush Sankranti fair, commonly known as Tirthamukh mela is one of the most important fairs in Tripura where a large number of people participate, including many tribal groups from the neighbouring states. The mela is organised every year on January 13-14 (Poush Sankranti) as per Bengali calendar year at Tirthamukh on the bank of Gomati.

Sanghati Fair—Sanghati mela is held every year on 6th & 7th December at Chandrapur under Dimatali Gaon Panchayat in Rajnagar Block.

Garia Festival—The Garia festival starts on the last day of the Bengali month Chaitra of every year and continues for seven days. The festival provides a good opportunity to see and understand the social customs, culture and rituals of the Jamatia community.

Buisu Festival—Buisu festival is held every year on the occasion of Chaitra Sankranti. It is a festival for welcoming the new Bengali year and it is also the festival for preparation of land for Jhum cultivation. Though the festival is of the Tripuri community, it is also celebrated by other Boro groups. During Buisu festival, the Tripuri community people decorate their houses by arches and flowers, take care of their livestock by decorating them with ornaments, distribute "Awam" (house made cake), wear new clothes, offer special drinks and food to their neighbours and participate in the Garia dance.

Mahamuni Festival—This festival is held near the lord Buddha temple at Bankul. It is one of the important fairs of Mog community though other communities also take active part. During the festival, the local people decorate their houses by arches and flowers, distribute Awam, wear new cloths and worship lord Buddha.

Kharchi Festival—Kharchi festival is celebrated with great joy and devotion. No other festival in Tripura is celebrated with so much of enthusiasm. It is also called 'Chaturdash' or 'Chaudda Devata Puja'. The word Kharchi is said to be a corrupt form of Khya which means earth. Kharchi Puja is, therefore, the worship of the earth—the earth that sustains mankind with all her resources. Sacrifice of goats and pigeons at the alter of gods is a usual feature of the festival.

Mamita—Mamita, the principal agricultural festival is celebrated in winter at the time of harvest of paddy.

Ker Festival—Ker festival is celebrated just after a fortnight of Kharchi Puja. The worship for 'Ker' is held only on the first Tuesday or Saturday after fourteen days of Kharchi Puja. It seems that the worship of Ker has a direct link with the worship of Kharchi, because the Ker is also worshipped by 'Chantai' the chief of the priests of old Agartala. The main feature of this festival is the worship of a long invoked bamboo which is locally known as Nagri Pura.

TRIPURA AT A GLANCE

- Area (in sq. km.) : 10,486 (0.32% of the total geographical area of India)
- Latitude : 22°56'N to 24°32' N
- Longitude : 90°09' E to 92°10'E
- Forest Area (in sq. km.) : 7,726 (73.68% of state's area)
- No. of Districts : 8
- Name of the Districts : South Tripura, West Tripura, North Tripura, Dhalai, Khowai, Gomati, Shepahijala, Unokati
- Lok Sabha Constituencies : 2
- Rajya Sabha Seat : 1
- Vidhan Sabha Constituencies : 60
- Nature of Legislature : Unicameral
- Capital : Agartala
- Languages : Bengali and Kakborak
- Total Population (as per 2011 census) : 36,73,917 (0.30% population of India)
- Male : 18,74,376
- Female : 17,99,541
- Decadal Growth (2001-2011) : 14.84%
- Literacy Rate : 87.2%
- Male Literacy Rate : 91.5%
- Female Literacy Rate : 82.7%
- Density (per sq. km.) : 350
- Sex Ratio (per 1000 males) : 960
- No. of Universities : 2
  1. Tripura University
  2. ICFAI University
- No. of National Parks : None

- State Animal : Phayre's Langur
- State Bird : Dukul (the green Imperial pigeon)
- State Flower : Nageshwar (Mesua ferrea)
- State Tree : Agar
- Important Tribes : Tripura, Reang, Jamatia, Chakma, Halam, Mag, Munda, Any Kuki Tribe, and Garo
- Major Festivals : Buisu, Mahamuni, Kharchi, Mamita, Ker
- Name of National Highways : NH-44, NH-44A

OBJECTIVE QUESTIONS

1. What is the area of Tripura?
A. 10,486 sq. km. B. 5,450 sq. km.
C. 9,892 sq. km. D. None of these

2. What is the latitude of Tripura?
A. 22°56′N to 24°32′N B. 24°50′N to 26°44′N
C. 23°51′N to 24°32′N D. None of these

3. Tripura is situated on the longitude between
A. 90°09′E and 92°10′E B. 89°01′E and 91°05′E
C. 87°05′E and 90°02′E D. None of these

4. The total area under forests in Tripura is
A. 7,726 sq. km. B. 5,425 sq. km.
C. 7,892 sq. km. D. None of these

5. How many districts there are in Tripura?
A. 8 B. 5
C. 6 D. None of these

6. Number of Lok Sabha constituencies in Tripura is
A. 2 B. 3
C. 4 D. None of these

7. Tripura Vidhan Sabha consists of
A. 60 members B. 40 members
C. 30 members D. None of these

8. What is the name of the capital of Tripura?
A. Agartala B. Itanagar
C. Kohima D. None of these

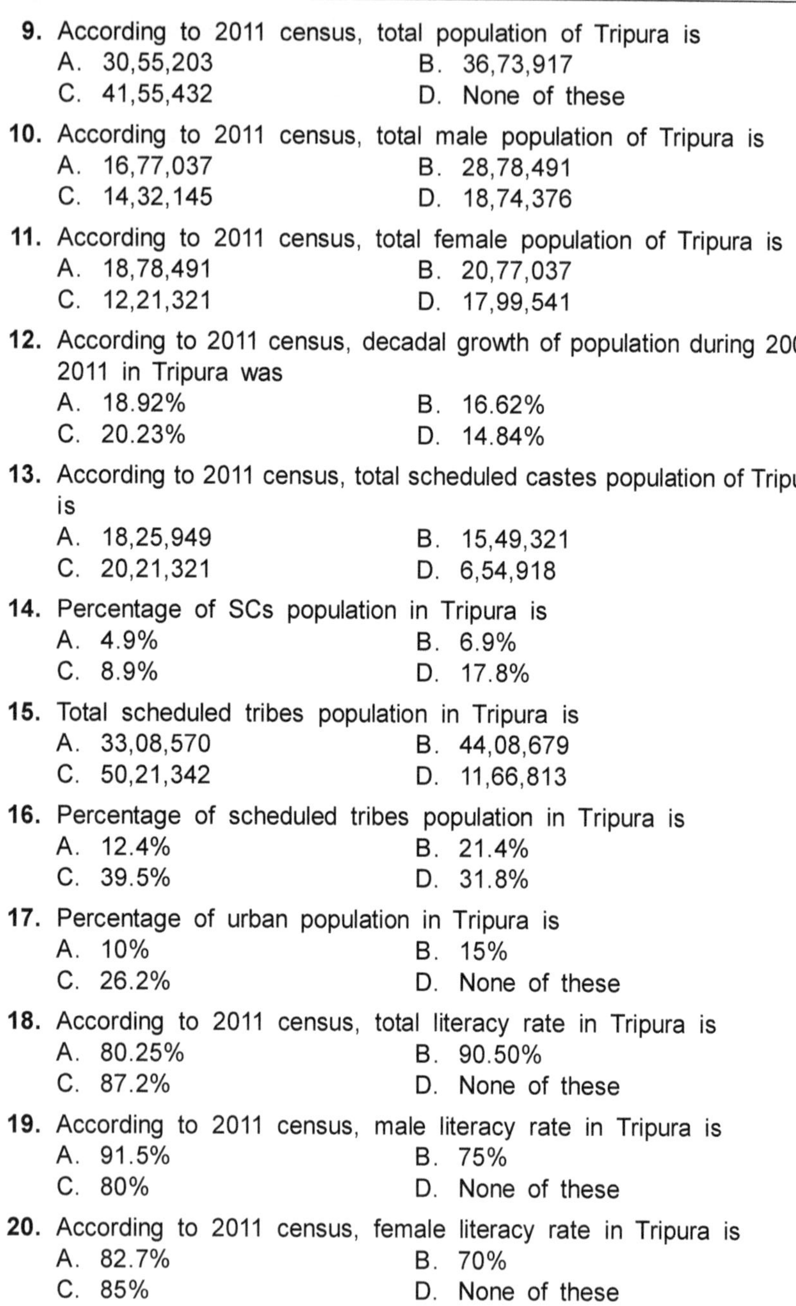

9. According to 2011 census, total population of Tripura is
A. 30,55,203 B. 36,73,917
C. 41,55,432 D. None of these

10. According to 2011 census, total male population of Tripura is
A. 16,77,037 B. 28,78,491
C. 14,32,145 D. 18,74,376

11. According to 2011 census, total female population of Tripura is
A. 18,78,491 B. 20,77,037
C. 12,21,321 D. 17,99,541

12. According to 2011 census, decadal growth of population during 2001-2011 in Tripura was
A. 18.92% B. 16.62%
C. 20.23% D. 14.84%

13. According to 2011 census, total scheduled castes population of Tripura is
A. 18,25,949 B. 15,49,321
C. 20,21,321 D. 6,54,918

14. Percentage of SCs population in Tripura is
A. 4.9% B. 6.9%
C. 8.9% D. 17.8%

15. Total scheduled tribes population in Tripura is
A. 33,08,570 B. 44,08,679
C. 50,21,342 D. 11,66,813

16. Percentage of scheduled tribes population in Tripura is
A. 12.4% B. 21.4%
C. 39.5% D. 31.8%

17. Percentage of urban population in Tripura is
A. 10% B. 15%
C. 26.2% D. None of these

18. According to 2011 census, total literacy rate in Tripura is
A. 80.25% B. 90.50%
C. 87.2% D. None of these

19. According to 2011 census, male literacy rate in Tripura is
A. 91.5% B. 75%
C. 80% D. None of these

20. According to 2011 census, female literacy rate in Tripura is
A. 82.7% B. 70%
C. 85% D. None of these

21. Density of population in Tripura is
A. 375 per sq. km. B. 400 per sq. km.
C. 450 per sq. km. D. 350 per sq. km.

22. Sex ratio of population in Tripura is
A. 960 B. 950
C. 990 D. None of these

23. State animal of Tripura is
A. Phayre's Langur B. Elephant
C. Sangal D. None of these

24. What is the name of the state bird of Tripura?
A. Dukul B. Asian Koel
C. Peacock D. None of these

25. What is the name of the state flower of Tripura?
A. Lotus B. Palash
C. Nageshwar D. None of these

26. What is the name of the state tree of Tripura?
A. Agar B. Peepal
C. Deodar D. None of these

27. Orange basket of Tripura is
A. Jampui Hills B. Sakhan Hills
C. Bara Mura Hills D. None of these

28. Highest peak of the Tripura state is
A. Betling Shiv B. Tawitlang
C. Zopuitlang D. None of these

29. The largest river of Tripura is
A. Gomati B. Muhuri
C. Manu D. None of these

30. Total forest area in Tripura is
A. 7,726 sq. km. B. 5,432 sq. km.
C. 3,432 sq. km. D. None of these

31. Second Rubber capital of India is
A. Kerala B. Tripura
C. Mizoram D. None of these

32. District with maximum population is
A. West Tripura B. North Tripura
C. South Tripura D. None of these

33. District with minimum population is
A. Unokati B. South Tripura
C. North Tripura D. None of these

34. Longest National Highway of Tripura is
A. NH-44 B. NH-45
C. NH-65 D. None of these

35. Hozagiri dance is associated with
A. Reang community
B. Tripuri community
C. Chakma community
D. None of these

36. Bizu dance is associated with
A. Chakma community B. Garo community
C. Mog community D. None of these

37. According to area, the largest district of Tripura is
A. West Tripura B. Dhalai
C. South Tripura D. None of these

38. Important soils of Tripura is
A. Reddish yellow brown sandy soils
B. Red loam and sandy loam soils
C. Older alluvial soils
D. None of these

39. Hai-Hak dance is associated with
A. Malsum community B. Garo community
C. Reang community D. None of these

40. Cheraw dance is associated with
A. Lusai community B. Malsum community
C. Mog community D. None of these

ANSWERS

1	2	3	4	5	6	7	8	9	10
A	A	A	A	A	A	A	A	B	D
11	**12**	**13**	**14**	**15**	**16**	**17**	**18**	**19**	**20**
D	D	D	D	D	D	C	C	A	A
21	**22**	**23**	**24**	**25**	**26**	**27**	**28**	**29**	**30**
D	A	A	A	C	A	A	A	A	A
31	**32**	**33**	**34**	**35**	**36**	**37**	**38**	**39**	**40**
B	A	A	A	A	A	B	B	A	A

●●●●●●

YOUR SPACE

YOUR SPACE

www.ingramcontent.com/pod-product-compliance
Ingram Content Group UK Ltd.
Pitfield, Milton Keynes, MK11 3LW, UK
UKHW021707190726
13853UKWH00001B/453